A HEAPIN' HELPING OF TRUE GRIZZARD

A HEAPIN' HELPING OF TRUE GRIZZARD

DOWN HOME AGAIN WITH

LEWIS GRIZZARD

ELVIS IS DEAD AND I DON'T FEEL SO GOOD MYSELF

SHOOT LOW, BOYS-- THEY'RE RIDIN' SHETLAND PONIES

Galahad Books
New York

Published in 1991 by

Galahad Books
A division of LDAP, Inc.
386 Park Avenue South
Suite 1913
New York, NY 10016

Galahad Books is a registered trademark of LDAP, Inc.

Published by arrangement with Peachtree Publishers, Ltd.

Library of Congress Catalog Card Number: 91-73470

ISBN: 0-88365-779-1

Printed in the United States of America.

ACKNOWLEDGEMENTS

ARE THE GOOD TIMES REALLY OVER by Merle Haggard
(c) 1982 by Shade Tree Music, Inc.
All rights reserved   Used by permission

RAINBOW STEW by Merle Haggard
(c) 1982 and 1984 by Shade Tree Music, Inc.
All rights reserved   Used by permission

HAPPY TRAILS by Dale Evans
COPYRIGHT (c) 1951 and 1952 by PARAMOUNT-ROY
ROGERS MUSIC CO., INC.
COPYRIGHT RENEWED 1979 and 1980 and assigned to
PARAMOUNT-ROY ROGERS MUSIC CO., INC.

OLD DOGS, CHILDREN, AND WATERMELON WINE by Tom T. Hall
(c) 1972 Hallnote Music
All rights reserved   Used by permission

OKIE FROM MUSKOGEE by Merle Haggard and Roy Edward Burris
(c) 1969 Blue Book Music
All rights reserved   Used by permission

LOVE ME TENDER by Elvis Presley and Vera Matson
COPYRIGHT (c) 1956 by Elvis Presley Music, Inc.
All rights administered by Unichappell Music, Inc.
(Rightsong Music, Publisher)

WALKING THE FLOOR OVER YOU by Ernest Tubb
COPYRIGHT (c) 1941 by American Music, Inc.
COPYRIGHT renewed, assigned to Unichappell Music, Inc.
(Rightsong Music, Publisher)

I REMEMBER THE YEAR CLAYTON DELANEY DIED by Tom T. Hall
COPYRIGHT (c) 1971 by Newkeys Music, Inc.
Assigned to Unichappell Music, Inc. and Morris Music, Inc.
All rights controlled by Unichappell Music, Inc.

CONTENTS

Elvis Is Dead
And I Don't Feel
So Good Myself

Dedication

To Danny Thompson, Bobby Entrekin, Mike Murphy, Dudley Stamps, Charles Moore, Clyde Elrod, Worm Elrod, and Anthony Yeager — the boys from Moreland, who I hope and pray didn't grow up to be as confused as I am.

And to the memory of Eddie Estes, a great centerfielder.

A Last
Toast
To The
King

WE WERE SITTING on the beach in Hilton Head, South Carolina, me and Price and Franklin. We were mired in those squatty folding chairs, the kind the old people take down to the surf and sit in while the salt water splashes over them. We were drinking cold beer and acting our age.

You can always tell the approximate age of people by watching what they do when they go to the beach. Babies, of course, dabble in the sand and splash around in the shallow water.

When a kid is about ten or twelve, he goes out farther and rides the waves and balks at his mother's motions that it's time to leave.

"Come on, Timmy. It's time to go back to the motel."

"Can't we stay just a little bit longer?"

"No. Your daddy is ready to leave."

"But I want to swim some more."

"I said come here, young man."

"Let me ride just one more wave. Please?"

1

"Don't make me call your daddy."

"I'll ride just one more and then I'll be ready to go."

"Okay, but just one more."

Parents never win at the beach, at least in these permissive times they don't. A kid can always just-one-more his parents into another thirty minutes of wave riding.

When children become teen-agers, the girls stop going into the water because they're afraid they will get their hair wet. What they do instead is put on tiny little swimsuits and lie on towels getting tanned. Teen-aged boys throw frisbees.

There should be a law against throwing frisbees on beaches. In the first place, throwing a frisbee is a mindless exercise that can't be any fun whatsoever. After you've seen one frisbee float through the air, you've seen them all. They might as well try catching horseflies.

Also, on crowded beaches there isn't room for teen-aged boys to throw frisbees. Frisbees are difficult to control and difficult to catch, so they're always landing on people who are trying to relax in the sun. Sometimes, frisbees even knock over somebody's beer.

A kid knocked over my beer with a frisbee at the beach once. I threatened him with a lawsuit and then put this curse on him: "May your voice never change and your zits win prizes at county fairs." I hate it when somebody knocks over my beer at the beach.

When kids are college age, the girls still lie on towels getting tanned and worrying about getting their hair wet. The boys, meanwhile, have given up throwing frisbees and have joined the girls, lying next to them on their own towels.

They play loud rock music, and when the girls ask them to rub suntan oil on their backs, they enthusiastically oblige ... especially if the girl has unsnapped the back of her tiny top

2

and the boy knows that her breasts are unleashed, for all practical purposes. The beach habits of people this age are basically preliminary sexual exercises, but rarely do they lead to anything more advanced later in the day. As numerous studies have shown, it is quite uncomfortable to attempt to have sex after an afternoon of lying in the sun because of the unpleasant feeling that individuals get when they rub their sunburned skin against that of someone whose epidermis is in the same painful condition.

At about age thirty, most people have the good sense to stop frying their skin in the sun for hours. They know by then that having sex is more fun than having a sunburn; they have heeded all the reports about how lying in the sun causes skin cancer; and they are usually working on their first nervous breakdown by age thirty, and all they want to do at the beach is sit there and relax while drinking cold beer.

The three of us that day at Hilton Head had already tiptoed into our thirties and the beer was going down exceptionally well. I have no idea what women talk about when they're sitting on a beach together without any men around, but when no women are present, men talk about the physical attributes of everything that happens to walk past them — or is lying close to them on a towel — wearing a bikini.

Me and Price and Franklin were doing just that:

"Good God."

"Where?"

"Left."

"Good God."

"How old do you think she is?"

"Eighteen."

"No way. Sixteen."

"Did they look like that when we were sixteen?"

"They couldn't have."

"Why not?"

"If they had, I wouldn't have lived this long. Some daddy would have shot me."

"Yeah, and they got the pill today, too."

"I wonder if the boys their age know how lucky they are."

"They don't have any idea."

"Wonder how old they are when they start these days?"

"Rodney Dangerfield said the kids are doing it so young these days that his daughter bought a box of Cracker Jacks and the prize was a diaphragm."

"Great line."

"Look coming here."

"It's a land whale."

"Damn, she's fat."

"If somebody told her to haul ass, she'd have to make two trips."

"That's awful."

"Hey, we're out of beer."

I remember distinctly that it was Franklin who went back to the condo to get more beer. I also remember distinctly that the month was August and the year was 1977. We had the radio playing. It was a country station.

Franklin was gone thirty minutes. When he came back, he had another twelve-pack. He also had a troubled look on his face.

"What took you so long?" Price asked him. "You didn't call Sweet Thing back home, did you?"

"You're not going to believe what I just heard on television," he answered.

I had just taken the first pull on my fresh beer when I

4

heard him utter three incredible words.

"Elvis is dead," he said.

Elvis is dead. The words didn't fit somehow. The queen of England is dead. There has been a revolution in South America and the dictator is dead. Some rock singer has been found in his hotel room with a needle in his arm and he is dead. All that made sense, but not *Elvis is dead.*

"They figure he had a heart attack," said the bad news bearer.

A heart attack? Elvis Presley couldn't have a heart attack. He was too young to have a heart attack. He was too young to have anything like that. Elvis Presley was my idol when I was a kid. Elvis changed my life. Elvis turned on my entire generation. I saw *Love Me Tender* three times. He died in *Love Me Tender,* but that was just a movie.

I figured this was some sort of joke. Right, Elvis Presley had a heart attack. And where did they find his body? In Heartbreak Hotel, of course.

The music had stopped on the radio. A man was talking.

"Elvis Presley is dead," said the voice. "He was forty-two."

Forty-two? That had to be wrong, too. How could he be that old? Elvis had to be younger than that. He was one of us, wasn't he? If he was forty-two, maybe he could have had a heart attack. If he was over forty, that meant he probably had wrinkles and maybe his hair had already fallen out and he had been wearing a wig.

But if Elvis Presley was forty-two and old enough to die, what did that say about me and the generation he had captured? He had been what separated us from our parents. He had been our liberator. He played the background music while we grew up.

Elvis is dead. Suddenly, I didn't feel so good myself.

"Damn," said Price, "if Elvis is dead, that means we're getting old, too."

"Damn if it don't," said Franklin.

I asked for another beer.

The announcer on the radio had stopped talking, and the three of us fell silent as an eerie sound came forth. It was Elvis's voice. It was a dead man's voice. Elvis was singing "Don't Be Cruel." It was spooky.

"'Don't Be Cruel'," said Price. "That was his best ever."

"'One Night With You' was my favorite," Franklin said. "I remember dancing with Doris Ann Plummer and singing along with Elvis in her ear. 'Ooooooooone ni-ite with yuuuuu is all I'm way-ayting fooor.' Doris Ann said I sounded just like Elvis, and soon as I got her in the car after the dance, it was all over."

"Everything he did was great," I said.

Elvis went on singing. I sat, still stupefied from the news, and listened. My friends went on talking.

"My old man hated Elvis."

"So did mine."

"He was always screaming at me, 'Get that garbage off the radio!'"

"Mine was a religious nut. He said the devil had sent Elvis, and anybody who listened to his music was going to hell."

"I wish my old man was alive today to see who the kids are idolizing now."

"Yeah, Elvis wouldn't look so bad compared to some of those weirdos they got today."

"He probably wouldn't even be noticed."

"You really scored with a girl because she thought you sounded like Elvis?"

"Doris Ann Plummer, right in the back seat out behind

6

the National Guard Armory."

"I always used Johnny Mathis."

"Well, Doris Ann wasn't exactly a great conquest. I found out later she'd do it if you sang like Lassie."

"Everybody had somebody like that in their school."

"Yeah, but just one."

"Imagine if it had been like it is now back then."

"I'd have never graduated from high school."

"I guess we were pretty naive back then compared to the kids now."

"Maybe we're better off."

"Maybe. I wonder if we'd have taken drugs if we'd had 'em back then."

"Hell, I thought drinking a beer was the wildest thing I could do."

"I went to a fraternity party at Auburn when I was a senior in high school. I drank gin and 7-Up and danced with college girls. I didn't think there was anything you could do any better or wilder than that."

"We didn't have it so bad growing up."

"At least we had Elvis."

"He was the greatest ever."

"The King."

"I don't think there will ever be anything like him again."

"Hard to believe he's dead."

"Think he was on drugs?"

"Probably."

"Ready for another beer?"

"Let's drink one to Elvis."

"To Elvis."

"To Elvis."

I joined in. "To Elvis."

The King was still singing on the radio:

"Love me tender,
Love me true,
Make all my dreams fulfilled.
For my darling, I love you.
And I always will."

* * *

I have never forgotten that day at the beach. It was like the day John Kennedy was killed. Like the day Martin Luther King was killed. Like the day Robert Kennedy was killed. Like the day Nixon resigned.

You never forget days like that, and you're never quite the same after them. There have been so many days like that, it seems, for my generation — the Baby Boomers who were minding to our business of growing up when all hell broke loose in the early sixties.

A few weeks after Elvis's death, I heard another piece of startling news. I heard they found Elvis dead in his bathroom. I heard he died straining for a bowel movement.

The King, we had called him, but he had gotten fat and at the age of forty-two he had died straining for a bowel movement. Or so was the rumor. I have spent much of the past seven years hoping against hope that it wasn't true.

When Life Was Black And White

I AM THIRTY-EIGHT years old — it's approximately half-time of the promised three score and ten — and I don't have any idea what is taking place around me anymore.

Lord knows, I have tried to understand. I have dutifully watched "Donahue" in an attempt to broaden myself into a creature adjusted to the eighties, but it has been a fruitless and frustrating endeavor.

How did Phil Donahue do it? He's even older than I am, with the gray hair to show for it, but he seems to understand what people mean when they talk about the new way to live. Me, I feel like an alien in my own country. These new lifestyles seem to be in direct contrast to the way they taught living when I was a child. Back then, *gay* meant, "1. Happy and carefree; merry. 2. Brightly colorful and ornamental. 3. Jaunty; sporty. 4. Full of or given to lighthearted pleasure. 5. Rakish; libertine." (That's straight from my high school dictionary.) Pot was something you cooked in, and back then nobody ate mushrooms. Where did I miss a turn?

The first hint that the world was taking leave of me came after Elvis died. The women who mourned him were *older* and had beehive hairdos and children of their own. Their teeny-bopper, socks-rolled-down days were far behind them. They were my age and they were weeping not only for Elvis, I think now, but for the realization that an era and a time — their time — was passing to another generation. To know that Elvis had gotten old and sick and fat enough to die was to know that their own youth had faded as well.

Elvis, forty-two. Elvis, dead. The voice that sang for the children of the late forties and early fifties stilled, and in its place a cacophony of raucous melodies from scruffy characters playing to the screams of young earthlings of the modern generation, to whom happiness and normalcy was a computerized hamburger at McDonald's and mandatory attendance at earsplitting concerts given by people dressed as dragons or barely dressed at all. Elvis may have shaken his pelvis, but he never by-God showed it to anybody on stage.

Why this gap between me and the younger generation? Why, in my thirties, do I have more in common with people twenty years older than with people five or ten years younger? Where is my tolerance for change and modernization? Why would I enjoy hitting Boy George in the mouth? Where did the years go and where did the insanity of the eighties come from? And why did I ever leave home in the first place?

Home. That's probably it. I don't seem to fit in today because it was so different yesterday.

Home. I think of it and the way it was every time I see or hear something modern that challenges tradition as I came to know it.

10

Home. I was born in 1946, the son of a soldier who lived through seven years of combat and then drank his way right out of the service, but who still stood and sang the national anthem to the top of his forceful voice at the several hundred ball games we watched together.

Home. It was a broken home. That came when I was six and my mother ran for her parents and took me with her. The four of us lived in my grandparents' home. We warmed ourselves by kerosene, we ate from a bountiful garden, and our pattern of living was based on two books — the Bible and the Sears Roebuck catalog.

Everything came in black and white.

* * *

Moreland, Georgia, had perhaps three hundred inhabitants when I moved there in 1952. The population is about the same today, and Moreland still doesn't have a red light.

Some other things have changed, however. There are two tennis courts in Moreland. Back then, we played baseball and dammed creeks, and that was enough. Cureton and Cole's store, where the old men sat around the stove and spit and imparted wisdom, is boarded shut. I don't know where the old men in Moreland spit and impart wisdom nowadays.

Perhaps spitting and wisdom-imparting around a stove have gone the way of ice cream cups with pictures of movie stars on the bottom side of the lids. I purchased hundreds of ice cream cups at Cureton and Cole's, licking the faces of everybody from Andy Devine to Yvonne DeCarlo. I haven't seen ice cream cups like that in years, but even if they were still around, I wouldn't buy one; I'd be afraid I might lick away the vanilla on the bottom of my lid only to find John

11

Travolta smiling at me. What a horrid thought.

Those were good and honest people who raised me and taught me. They farmed, they worked in the hosiery mill that sat on the town square, and some went to the county seat six miles away where they welded and trimmed aluminum and sweated hourly-wage sweat — the kind that makes people hard and reserved and resolved there is a better world awaiting in the next life.

We had barbecues and street square dances in Moreland. We had two truckstops that were also beer joints, and the truckers played the pinball machines and the jukeboxes. The local beer drinkers parked their cars out back, presumably out of sight.

The religion in town was either Baptist or Methodist, and it was hardshell and certainly not tolerant of drinking. The church ladies were always gossiping about whose cars had been spotted behind the truckstops.

There was one fellow, however, who didn't care whether they saw his car or not. Pop Towns worked part-time at the post office, but the highlight of his day took place at the railroad yard. The train didn't stop in Moreland, so the outgoing mail had to be attached to a hook next to the tracks to be picked off when the train sped past. It was Pop's job to hang the mail.

Every morning at ten, when the northbound came through, and every evening at six, when the southbound passed, Pop would push his wheelbarrow filled with a sack of mail from the post office down to the tracks. There he would hang the mail, and we'd all stand around and watch as the train roared by. Then Pop would get in his car, drive over to one of the truckstops, park contemptuously out front, and have himself several beers.

One day the ladies of the church came to Pop's house in an effort to save him from the demon malt. I wasn't there when it happened, of course, but the word got around that when Pop answered the door for the ladies, he came with a beer in his hand.

Hilda Landon began reciting various scriptures regarding drunkenness. Pop countered by sicking his dog, Norman, on the ladies, and they scattered in various directions.

Pop, they said, laughed at the sight of his dog chasing off the ladies of the church, and once back inside his house, he had himself another beer, secure in the fact that he and Norman would never be bothered by another tolerance committee.

They found Pop dead one morning after he failed to make his appointment with the mail train, and the ladies of the church all said the Lord was getting even with Pop for all his sinful ways.

I sort of doubted that. Pop always had a good joke to tell and always was kind to his dog, and although I was no expert on the scriptures, I was of the belief that a good heart would get you a just reward in the afterlife as quick as anything else.

We also had a town drunk, Curtis "Fruit Jar" Hainey, but the ladies of the church figured he was too far gone to waste their efforts on. Curtis walked funny, like his knees were made of rubber. Somebody said it was because he once drank some rubbing alcohol when the local bootlegger left town for two weeks and Curtis came up dry and desperate. I figured the Lord could have had a little something to do with this one.

Although Moreland was a small town, not unlike so many others across the country in the early 1950s, we still had

13

plenty of scandal, intrigue, and entertainment.

It was whispered, for example, that Runelle Sheets, a high school girl who suddenly went to live with her cousin in Atlanta, actually was pregnant and had gone off to one of *those* homes.

Nobody ever verified the rumor about Runelle, but they said her daddy refused to speak her name in his house anymore and had threatened to kill a boy who lived over near Raymond. That was enough for a summer's full of satisfying speculation.

For further entertainment, we had a town idiot, Crazy Melvin, who allegedly was shell-shocked in Korea. Well, sort of. The story went that when Crazy Melvin heard the first shot fired, he began to run and when next seen had taken off his uniform, save his helmet and boots, and was perched in his nakedness in a small tree, refusing to climb down until frostbite threatened his privates.

They sent Crazy Melvin home after that, and following some months in the hospital, the Army decided that Melvin wasn't about to stop squatting naked in trees, so they released him in the custody of his parents.

Once back in Moreland, however, Crazy Melvin continued to do odd things, such as take off all his clothes, save his brogans and his straw hat. They finally sent Melvin to Atlanta to see a psychiatrist. When he came back, the psychiatrist had cured him of squatting naked in trees. Unfortunately, Melvin had ridden a trolley while in Atlanta and returned home thinking he was one. Every time you were walking to the store or to church and crossed paths with Crazy Melvin, you had to give him a nickel.

"Please step to the rear of the trolley," he would say, and then he'd make sounds like a trolley bell. The church later

14

got up enough money to buy Melvin one of those coin-holders bus drivers wear, so it was easier for him to make change when you didn't have a nickel.

* * *

Those were the days, when young boys roamed carefree and confidently around the streets of Moreland — Every-town, USA.

We were Baby Boomers all, born of patriots, honed by the traditional work ethic. That meant you worked your tail off and never quit until the job was done, and you saved every penny you could and never spent money on anything that didn't have at least some practical value. You kept the Word, never questioned authority, loved your country, did your duty, never forgot where you came from, bathed daily when there was plenty of water in the well, helped your neighbors, and were kind to little children, old people, and dogs. You never bought a car that was any color like red or yellow, stayed at home unless it was absolutely necessary to leave (such as going to church Sunday and for Wednesday night prayer meeting), kept your hair short and your face cleanshaven. You were suspicious of rich people, lawyers, yankee tourists, Catholics and Jehovah's Witnesses who tried to sell subscriptions to "The Watchtower" door-to-door, anybody who had a job where he had to wear a tie to work, and Republicans.

We were isolated in rural self-sufficiency for the most part. Television was only a rumor. We kept to ourselves unless we went to the county seat of Newnan to see a movie or to get a haircut or to see the little alligator they kept in a drink box at Mr. Lancaster's service station.

I never did find out how the little alligator got into a drink box at a service station in Newnan, Georgia, but rumor had it that Mr. Lancaster had brought it back from Florida to keep people from breaking into his station after he closed at night. In fact, Mr. Lancaster had a handwritten sign in front of his station that read, "This service station is guarded by my alligator three nights a week. Guess which three nights."

In such a closed, tightly-knit society, it was impossible not to feel a strong sense of belonging. Even for a newcomer.

When I first moved to Moreland at age seven, I was instantly befriended by the local boys. In those idyllic days, we molded friendships that would last for lifetimes.

There was Danny Thompson, who lived just across the cornfield from me, next door to Little Eddie Estes. Down the road from Danny was where Mike Murphy lived. Clyde and Worm Elrod lived near the Methodist Church. Bobby Entrekin and Dudley Stamps resided in Bexton, which was no town at all but simply a scattering of houses along a blacktop road a mile or so out of Moreland. There was Anthony Yeager, who lived over near Mr. Ralph Evans's store, and Charles Moore was just down the road from him.

Clyde Elrod was a couple of years older than his brother Worm, who was my age. Clyde had one ambition in his life, and that was to follow his father's footsteps into the Navy. Clyde often wore his father's old Navy clothes and regaled us with his father's Navy stories. Clyde's father apparently single-handedly won the battle for U.S. naval supremacy in World War II.

16

Worm got his name at Boy Scout camp one summer. There is only one thing worse than biting into an apple and finding a worm, and that's biting into an apple and finding half a worm, which is what happened to Worm Elrod and is how he got his nickname. Clyde and Worm did not get along that well, due to a heated sibling rivalry. Their father often had to separate them from various entanglements, and Worm invariably got the worst of it. Only when Clyde graduated from high school and left to join the Navy was it certain that Worm would live to see adulthood.

Anthony Yeager joined the gang later. He was the first of us to obtain his driver's license, and his popularity increased immediately. As teen-agers, we roamed in Yeager's Ford and slipped off for beer and to smoke. Once we went all the way to Fayetteville to the Highway 85 Drive-In and saw our first movie in which women appeared naked from the waist up.

Funny, what the memory recalls. The movie was *Bachelor Tom Peeping,* and it was billed as a documentary filmed at a nudist camp. At one point, Bachelor Tom was confronted by a huge-breasted woman who was covered only by a large inner tube that appeared to have come from the innards of a large tractor tire. As she lowered the tube, we watched in utter disbelief.

"Nice tubes you have, my dear," said Bachelor Tom.

Yeager was the first total devotee to country music I ever met, and he is at least partially responsible for my late-blooming interest in that sort of music. Yeager owned an old guitar that he couldn't play, but he tried anyway, and common were the nights we would find a quiet place in the woods, park his car, and serenade the surrounding critters.

Yeager's heroes were Hank Williams and Ernest Tubb. His favorite songs were Hank's "I'm So Lonesome I Could Cry" — later butchered by B.J. Thomas — and Ernest's classic, "I'm Walking the Floor Over You."

Hank was dead and long gone by then, but one day Yeager heard that Ernest Tubb, accompanied by picker-supreme Billy Byrd, was to perform at the high school auditorium in nearby Griffin. Me and Yeager and Dudley Stamps and Danny Thompson went. It was our first concert. Ernest slayed us, especially Yeager.

"I'm walkin' the floor over you.
I can't sleep a wink, that is true.
I'm hopin' and I'm prayin'
That my heart won't break in two.
I'm walkin' the floor over you."

Whenever Ernest Tubb would call in Billy Byrd for a guitar interlude, he would say, "Awwwwwww, Billy Byrd," which Yeager thought was a nice touch. For months, Yeager would say "Awwwwwww, Billy Byrd" for no reason whatsoever. Later he began saying, "Put a feather in your butt and pick it out, Billy Byrd," again for no reason except that it seemed to give him great joy to say it.

Like I said, it's funny what details the memory recalls.

Dudley Stamps. He was the crazy one. He once drove his father's truck into White Oak Creek to see if trucks will float. They won't. There was not a water tower or a forest ranger tower in three counties he hadn't climbed. When he was old enough to get a driver's license, his parents bought him a used 1958 Thunderbird with a factory under the hood.

I was riding one night with Dudley when the State Patrol stopped him. His T-bird had been clocked at 110 MPH, according to the patrolman. Dudley was incensed and launched into an argument with the officer. He insisted he was doing at least 125.

Mike Murphy. He had a brother and sister and his father was called "Mr. Red." Mr. Red Murphy was the postmaster and helped with the Boy Scouts. With the possible exception of the Methodist and Baptist preachers, he was the most respected man in town. Mike had to work more than the rest of us. Mr. Red kept all his children busy tending the family acreage.

"You don't see Red Murphy's children out gallivantin' all over town," the old men around the stove used to say down at Cureton and Cole's. "Red keeps 'em in the fields where there ain't no trouble."

This was the late 1950s, when "gallivanting" meant doing just about anything that had no practical end to it, such as riding bicycles, roller-skating on the square, and hanging out at the store eating Zagnut candy bars and drinking NuGrapes or what was commonly referred to as "Big Orange bellywashers." Gallivanting, like most things modern, seems to have grown somewhat sterile and electronic. Today, I suppose when children gallivant it means they hang around in shopping malls, playing video games and eating frozen yogurt.

The day Mr. Red died was an awful day. It was the practice at the Moreland Methodist Church to return to the sanctuary after Sunday School for a quick hymn or two and for

19

announcements by Sunday School Superintendent Fox Covin. Fox would also call on those having birthdays, and the celebrants would stand as we cheered them in song.

That Sunday morning, Fox Covin announced it was Mr. Red's birthday and asked his daughter to stand for him as we sang. As everyone in church knew, Mr. Red had been hospitalized the day before for what was alleged to be a minor problem.

Soon after we sang to Mr. Red, another member of the family came into the church and whisked the Murphy children away. Something was whispered to Fox Covin, and after the children were safely out of earshot, he told the congregation that Red Murphy was dead.

We cried and then we prayed. Mike was no more than twelve or thirteen at the time. He had to take on a great deal of the responsibility of the farm after that, so his opportunity to gallivant with the rest of us was shortened even further.

"Mike Murphy will grow up to be a fine man," my mother used to say.

Bobby Entrekin. I loved his father. I had secretly wished there was some way my mother could have married Mr. Bob Entrekin, but there was his wife, Miss Willie, with whom to contend, and a quiet, soft, loving woman she was. I decided to remain content with spending my weekends at the Entrekin home.

Mr. Bob worked nights. Miss Willie worked days at one of the grocery stores in the county seat. The Entrekins, I noticed, ate better than the rest of us. While my family's diet consisted mostly of what we grew from our garden or raised in our chicken coops, the Entrekins always had such delights as store-bought sandwich meat and boxed dough-nuts, the sort with the sweet, white powder around them.

The standing contention was that because Miss Willie was employed at the grocery store, she was given discounts on such elaborate foodstuffs others in the community would have found terribly wasteful to purchase.

Whatever, as much as I enjoyed the company of my friend Bobby Entrekin, it may have been the lure of the delights of his family refrigerator and his father that were the most binding seal on our friendship.

Bobby's father was unlike any man I had ever met before. He had a deep, forceful voice. His knowledge of sport was unparalleled in the community. He had once been an out-standing amateur baseball player, and on autumn Satur-days, Bobby and I would join him at radioside to listen to Southeastern Conference college football games — as com-forting and delicious an exercise as I have ever known. My own father, having split for parts unknown, had shared Mr. Bob's affinity for sports and other such manly interests, and Mr. Bob stood in for him nicely.

Mr. Bob also had more dimension to him than any other man I had known. He had educated himself. He had trav-eled a bit. He sent off for classical records, and when I spent the weekends with Bobby, his father would awaken us on Sunday mornings for church with those foreign sounds.

As Beethoven roared through the little Entrekin house out on Bexton Road, he would say to us, "Boys, that is what you call good music." How uncharacteristic of the time and place from which I sprung, but how pleasant the memory.

Bobby was a con man from his earliest days. He slicked classmates out of their lunch desserts, and by schoolday's

21

end, he usually had increased his marble holdings considerably.

Only once did he put an unpleasant shuck on me. Mr. Bob had driven us into Newnan, where the nearest picture show was located. The Alamo Theatre sat on Newnan's court square, across the street from the side entrance to the county courthouse. Admission to the movie was a dime. There were soft drinks for a nickel and small bags of popcorn for the same price.

As we walked toward the Alamo, we came upon a bus parked on the court square.

"Boys," said a man sitting outside the bus, "come on inside and see the world's fattest woman."

"How fat is she?" Bobby asked.

"Find out for yourself for only fifteen cents, kid," said the man.

Bobby started inside while I did some quick arithmetic. I had twenty cents. That was a dime for admission to the picture show and a dime for a soft drink and popcorn. If I paid fifteen cents to see the fat lady, I couldn't get in to see the movie.

I mentioned this bit of financial difficulty to Bobby.

"Don't worry," he said. "I'll loan you enough to get into the show."

We each dropped fifteen cents into the man's cigar box of coins and stepped inside the bus.

The smell got us first. A hog would have buried its snout in the mud to have escaped it. Then we saw the fat lady. She was enormous. She dripped fat. She was laid out on a divan, attempting to fan away the heat and the stench. We both ran out of the bus toward the movie house.

When we arrived at the ticket window, I reminded Bobby

22

of his offer to stake me to a ticket.

"I was only kidding," he said, as he pranced into the theater. I sat on the curb and cried. Later, when I told his father what Bobby had done, Mr. Bob played a symphony upon his son's rear and allowed me to watch. I took shameful pleasure in the sweet revenge.

Charles Moore. His mother called him "Cholly," and he eventually achieved some renown in high school when The Beatles hit in 1964 because Charles, even with his short hair, was a dead-ringer for a seventeen-year-old Paul McCartney. Charles was never able to make any money off this resemblance — that was before the imitation craze, e.g., the Elvis impersonators after his death and the three or four thousand young black kids currently doing Michael Jackson — but he obviously took a great deal of pleasure from standing in the middle of a group of giggling girls who were saying things like, "Oh, Charles, you look just like Paul."

What I remember Charles for most, however, is the fight we had in the seventh grade over a baseball score. I was a fierce and loyal Dodger fan. Charles held the same allegiance to the Milwaukee Braves.

I arrived at school one morning with a score from the evening before, Dodgers over the Braves. I had heard it on the radio.

"The Dodgers beat the Braves last night," I boasted to Charles.

"No they didn't," he said.

"I heard it on the radio," I continued.

"I don't care what you heard," he said. "The Braves won."

The principal had to pull us apart.

When I went home that afternoon, I called Mr. Bob Entrekin, who subscribed to the afternoon paper with the complete scores, and asked him to verify the fact that the Dodgers had, indeed, defeated the Braves so I could call Charles Moore and instruct him to kiss my tail.

The Braves had won, said Mr. Bob. I feigned a sore throat and didn't go to school the next two days.

Danny Thompson. We were best friends before high school. Danny was the best athlete in our class. At the countywide field day competition, he ran fourth in the potato race. A potato race works — or worked, since I doubt potato racing has lingered with everybody throwing those silly frisbees today — this way:

There were four cans (the kind that large quantities of mustard and canned peaches came in) spaced at intervals of ten yards. The boy running first can dashed the first ten yards, picked the potato out of the can, and raced back and handed it to the boy running second can.

He then dropped the potato into the team can at the starting line and hurried to the second can twenty yards away. The team that got all four potatoes in its can first won the medals.

Danny ran fourth can because he was the fastest boy in our class. We probably would have won the county potato race, had I not stumbled and dropped my potato as I tried to depart from the second can.

Danny was also rather possessive about his belongings. He received a new football for Christmas one year. It was a Sammy Baugh model, and it had white stripes around each end. We were perhaps ten when Danny got the football.

We gathered for a game of touch a few days after Christmas, but Danny didn't bring his new football.

"I'm saving it," he explained.

When I would visit Danny, he would pull his new football out of his closet and allow me to hold it. He would never take it outside, however.

"I'm saving it," he would say again. That was nearly thirty years ago. We never did get to play with Danny's football.

One morning in the fifth grade, I looked over at Danny and his face was in his hands. He was crying. I had never seen Danny cry before. The teacher whispered something to him and then took him out of the room.

Word travels fast in a small town. Danny's mother and his father had separated. He and I were even closer in our friendship after that. We shared a loss of parent uncommon to children then, but we rolled quite well with our punch, I suppose. We spent hours together deep down in the woods behind his house. He talked of his mother. I talked of my father.

Danny wanted us to become blood brothers. He had seen two Indians on television cut their fingers and then allow their blood to mix. I wanted to be Danny's blood brother, but I was afraid to cut my finger. I suggested that we swap comic books instead.

* * *

It was a simple childhood, one that I didn't fully cherish until I had long grown out of it. Only then did I appreciate the fact that I was allowed to grow into manhood having never once spent a day at the country club pool, or playing baseball where they put the ball on a tee like they do for

25

children today, or growing my hair down over my shoulders, or wearing T-shirts advertising punk rock bands, or smoking anything stronger than a rabbit tobacco cigarette wrapped in paper torn from a brown bag and, later, an occasional Marlboro Dudley Stamps would bring on camping trips from his father's store.

It was a most happy childhood, because the only real fear we had was that we might somehow find ourselves at odds with Frankie Garfield. Frankie was the town bully who often made life miserable for all of us, especially any new child who moved into Moreland. There was the new kid with the harelip, for instance.

The afternoon of his first day in school, the new kid rode his bicycle to Cureton and Cole's, where Frankie was involved in beating up a couple of fifth graders for their NuGrapes and Zagnut candy bars.

The new kid parked his bicycle, and as he walked to the entrance of the store, he reached down to pick up a shiny nail off the ground. Frankie spotted him.

"Hey, Harelip," he called, "that's my nail."

Nobody had bothered to inform the new kid about Frankie Garfield. The rest of us knew that if Frankie said the nail was his, the best move was to drop the nail immediately, apologize profusely, and then offer to buy Frankie anything inside the store he desired.

The new kid, however, made a serious, nearly fatal, mistake. He indicated, in no uncertain terms, that Frankie was filled with a rather unpleasant substance common to barnyards. Then he put the nail in his pocket and began to walk inside the store.

He didn't make it past the first step before Frankie began to beat him unmercifully. At first, I think Frankie was sim-

26

ply amusing himself, as a dog amuses himself by catching a turtle in his mouth and slinging it around in the air.

Then the new kid made another mistake. He tried to fight back against Frankie. Now Frankie was mad. When he finally tired of beating his victim, Frankie left him there in a crumpled heap and rode off on the new kid's bicycle.

I suppose Frankie did have some degree of heart about him. He let the new kid keep the nail.

We were involved in some occasional juvenile delinquency, but nothing more flagrant than stealing a few watermelons, or shooting out windows in abandoned houses, or pilfering a few peaches over at Cates's fruit stand.

We went to church, didn't talk back to our elders, studied history in which America never lost a war, and were basically what our parents wanted us to be. Except when it came to Elvis.

* * *

Whatever else we were, we were the first children of television, and it was television that brought us Elvis. He would prove to be the first break between our parents and ourselves. That disagreement seems so mild today after the generational war that broke out in the late sixties, but those were more timid times when naiveté was still in flower.

Elvis was a Pied Piper wearing ducktails. He sang and he moaned and wiggled, and we followed him ... taking our first frightening steps of independence.

Guilt
Trip
In A
Cadillac

RADIO PERHAPS WOULD have made Elvis popular, but
television made him The King. We could *see* him, and
there never had been anything like him before.

The only music I knew prior to Elvis was the hymns from
the Methodist Cokesbury hymnal; "My Bucket's Got a Hole
in It" and "Good Night, Irene" from my mother's singing
while she ironed; and "Peace in the Valley," which I had
learned watching "The Red Foley Show" on Saturday nights
after my aunt bought the first television in the family.

But Elvis. Ducktails. His guitar. Uh-uh, Baby, don't you
step on my blue suede shoes, and don't be cruel to a heart
that's true.

Elvis thrust a rebellious mood upon us. I was ten or eleven
when I decided to grow my own ducktails and refused to get
my little-boy flattop renewed. As my hair grew out, I pushed
back the sides by greasing them down, and then I brought
my hair together at the back of my head, giving it the
appearance of the north end of a southbound duck. I

wouldn't wash my hair, either, for fear it might lose what I considered to be a perfect set.

"If you don't wash your hair, young man," my mother would warn me, "you're going to get head lice."

I didn't believe her. Nothing, not even head lice, could live in that much greasy gook.

I also pushed my pants down low like Elvis wore his.

"Pull your pants up before they fall off," my mother would say.

"This is how Elvis wears his pants," would be my inevitable reply.

"I don't know what you children see in him," she would counter.

I wrote her off as completely without musical taste and suggested that Red Foley was an incompetent old geezer who couldn't carry Elvis's pick.

"I don't know what's wrong with young'uns these days," was my mother's subsequent lament.

My stepfather eventually entered the ducktail disagreement and dragged me to the barber to reinstate my shorn looks. I cried and pouted and refused to come to the dinner table. Why were these people so insistent that I maintain the status quo when there was something new out there to behold?

We fought the Elvis battle in my house daily. Sample warfare:

"How can you stand that singing?"

"Elvis is a great singer."

"Sounds like a lot of hollering and screaming to me."

"It's rock 'n' roll."

"It's garbage."

"It's Elvis."

"It's garbage."

"It is not."

"Don't you talk back to me, young man!"

"I wasn't talking back."

"You're talking back now."

"I am not."

"Turn off that music right now and go to bed. This Elvis is ruining all our children."

I suppose if it hadn't been Elvis who ruined us, it would have been something, or somebody, else. But it *was* Elvis, and it was his music that set us off on a course different from that of our parents.

"That Elvis," the old men around the stove at Cureton and Cole's would say, "ain't nothin' but a white nigger."

"Don't sing nothin' but nigger music."

"That little ol' gal of mine got to watchin' him on the teevee and he started all that movin' around like he does — look like a damn dog tryin' to hump on the back of a bitch in heat — and I made her shet him off. Ought not allow such as that on the teevee."

"Preacher preached on him last week. Said he was trash and his music was trash."

"He's ruinin' the young'uns."

The teachers at Moreland School caught one of the Turnipseed boys, I think it was Bobby Gene, shaking and humping like Elvis to the delight of a group of fifth-grade girls on the playground one morning during recess.

They took him to the principal, who paddled him and sent a note home to his parents, explaining his lewd behavior. Bobby Gene's daddy whipped him again.

"Do your Elvis for us, Bobby Gene," we said when he came back to school.

"Can't," he replied. "I'm too sore."

Bobby Gene Turnipseed may have done the best Elvis impersonation in Moreland, but each of Elvis's male followers had his own version. After my stepfather forced me to have my ducktails sheared back into a flattop, my Elvis lost a little something, but I still prided myself on the ability to lift the right side of my lip, à la Elvis's half-smile, half-snarl that sent the girls into fits of screaming and hand-clutching.

There was a girl in my Sunday School class who was a desirable young thing, and as our Sunday School teacher read our lesson one morning, I decided to do my Elvis half-smile, half-snarl for the latest object of my ardor.

Recall that we were children of church-minded people, and I was quite aware of the wages of sin. I once snitched a grape at Cureton and Cole's, and my cousin saw me and told me I was going to hell for thievery. I was so disturbed that I went back to the store and confessed my crime to Mr. J.W. Thompson, one of the owners. He was so moved by my admission of guilt that he gave me an entire sack of grapes free and assured me I'd have to steal a car or somebody's dog to qualify for eternal damnation. When my cousin asked me to share my grapes with her, I told her to go to.... Well, I ate all the grapes myself and spit the seeds at her.

Stealing grapes was one thing, but thinking unspeakable thoughts about girls while in church and curling my lip at my prepubescent Cleopatra while the lesson was being read probably would bring harsh punishment from above. I couldn't remember which thou-shalt-not such activity fell under — I wasn't certain what *covet* meant, but I figured it had something to do with wanting another boy's bicycle — so I decided to take a chance and do my Elvis lip trick at the

31

girl anyway.

I curled up the right side of my lip perfectly as Cleo looked over at me. I didn't know what to expect. Would she absolutely *melt?* Would she want to meet me after church and go over to what was left of the abandoned cotton gin and give me kisses and squeezes?

She didn't do either. What she did was tell the Sunday School teacher I was making weird faces at her while the lesson was being read. The teacher told my mother about it, and my punishment was to read the entire book of Deuteronomy and present a report on it to the class the next Sunday. I learned a valuable lesson from all that: When you're in church, keep your mind on baseball or what you're going to have for lunch, not on something sweet and soft and perfumed wearing a sundress. Church and Evening in Paris simply don't mix.

Never one to be selfish, I attempted to share my ability to mime Elvis's facial expressions with others, especially with Little Eddie Estes. Little Eddie was a couple of years younger than me and I served as his self-appointed mentor. I taught him how to bunt, where to look in the Sears Roebuck catalog for the most scintillating pictures of women in their underpants, how to tell if a watermelon is ripe (you cut out a plug and if what you see inside is red, it's ripe), and I also attempted to instruct him in mimicking Elvis.

"What you do is this," I said to Little Eddie. "You curl your lip to the right a little bit, like the dog just did something smelly. If you want to add Elvis's movements to this, you bring one leg around like a wasp has crawled inside your pants leg, and then you move the other and groan like when your mother insists you eat boiled cabbage."

32

Little Eddie made a gallant attempt. He got the lip fine and he groaned perfectly, but he couldn't get the legs to shake in the correct manner.

"I couldn't shake my legs, either, when I first started doing Elvis," I told him. "What you need to do is practice in front of a mirror."

Several days later, Little Eddie's father found his son curling his lip and groaning and shaking his legs in front of a mirror in his bedroom and thought he was having some sort of seizure. His mother gave him a dose of Castor Oil and put him to bed.

* * *

I don't suppose that any generation has really under-stood the next, and every generation has steadfastly insisted that the younger adapt its particular values and views.

My parents' generation, true to form, sought to bring up its young in its mold, but it also had a firm resolve to do something more for us.

It was much later in my life, perhaps at a time I was feeling terribly sorry for myself and looking for a way out of that constant dilemma, that I decided my parents' generation may have endured more hardship and offered more sacri-fices than any other previous generation of Americans.

So they never had to cross the Rockies in covered wagons and worry about being scalped. But my parents, both of whom were born in 1912, would live through and be directly affected by two World Wars, one Great Depression, and whatever you call Korea. And when they had been through all that, they were ushered into the Cold War and had to decide whether or not to build a fallout shelter.

33

It is no wonder that the men and women who came from those harried times were patriots, were traditionalists, were believers in the idea that he who worked and practiced thrift prospered, and he who allowed the sun to catch him sleeping and was wasteful perished.

These were hard people, who had lived through hard times. But they endured and the country endured, and they came away from their experiences with a deep belief in a system that had been tested but had emerged with glorious victory.

Looking back on my relationship with my own parents and with others from their generation, I think they also felt a sense of duty to their children to make certain that, at whatever cost, their children would be spared the adversity they had seen.

Have we, the Baby Boomers, not heard our parents say a thousand times, "We want you to have it better than we did"?

They wanted to protect us. They wanted to educate us. They wanted us to be doctors and lawyers and stockbrokers, not farmers and mill hands. They hounded us to study and to strive and avoid winding up in a job that paid an hourly wage. They may have mistrusted individuals their own age who had educations and who went to work wearing ties, but that's exactly what they wanted for us. And they made us feel terribly guilty if we did not share their desires.

"Have you done your homework?" my mother would ask.

"I'll do it later."

"You will do it now, young man. I don't want you winding up on the third shift at Flagg-Utica."

Flagg-Utica was a local textile plant.

"I haven't bought anything new to wear in years so I could save for your education," my mother would continue on her guilt trip, "and you don't have the gratitude to do your homework."

Somehow, I never could figure how failing to read three chapters in my geography book about the various sorts of vegetation to be found in a tropical rain forest had anything to do with facing a life as a mill hand. But with enough guilt as a catalyst, you can read anything, even geography books and Deuteronomy.

I suppose our parents also were trying to protect us when they voiced their displeasure with Elvis. They knew he was something different, too, and they were afraid of where he might lead — thinking evil thoughts about girls in Sunday School, for example.

We want you to have it better than we did, they said, and that covered just about everything. They wanted us to have money and comforts; they wanted us to have knowledge and vision; they wanted a better world for us, one free from war and bitter sacrifice.

They are old now, my parents' generation, and I suppose they think they got what they wanted. I did my homework and I got the education my mother saved for, and I live in an air-conditioned house with a microwave oven, an automatic ice-maker, and a Jenn-Air grill on the stove. I also have two color television sets with remote control, a pair of Gucci loafers, and a tennis racquet that cost more than the 1947 Chevrolet my mother once bought. I eat steak whenever I want it, I've been to Europe a couple of times and nobody shot at me, and I have a nice car.

The car. It's a perfect manifestation of having achieved the success my parents wanted for me, but such success can be bittersweet. While we're having it better than our parents did, they now may feel, in some instances, that we've actually gone further than they intended. They may suspect, as the phrase went, that we've forgotten "where we came from."

Allow me to explain.

After I got my first job out of college, I bought myself a Pontiac. Later, I bought another Pontiac, bigger and with more features than the previous one. Then I lost my head and bought one of those British roadsters that was approximately the size of a bumper car at the amusement park but not built nearly as solidly.

After the sports car had driven me sufficiently nuts, I decided to go back to a full-sized sedan, something fitting a person who was having it better than his parents did.

I got myself a Cadillac.

Nobody in my family had ever owned a Cadillac, so I figured if I had one, there could be no question that I had fulfilled my mother's wishes by making something of myself.

I had a former schoolmate who sold Cadillacs, so I went to see him and priced a couple. I couldn't have paid for the back seat, much less an entire Cadillac.

"Have you thought about leasing?" my friend asked me.

As a matter of fact, I hadn't. As a matter of fact, I never had even heard of leasing an automobile.

"It's the latest thing," said my friend, who explained that I wouldn't have to fork over any huge down payment, and for a modest (by Arab oil sheik standards) monthly installment, I could be driving around in a brand-new Cadillac.

I bit.

"You want power steering and power brakes, of course," said my friend.

"Of course."

"And do you want leather upholstery?"

"Of course."

"And how about wire wheelcovers and a sun roof?"

"Of course."

"And eight-track stereo?"

"Of course."

"Let me see if I have this straight," my friend summarized. "You want the kind of Cadillac that if you drove it home to Moreland and parked it in your mother's yard, half the town would want to come by and see it. Right?"

"But, of course," I said.

I drove my new Cadillac with the power steering and the power brakes and the leather upholstery and the wire wheelcovers and the eight-track stereo off the lot and directly home to Moreland.

"It must have been expensive," said my mother.

"Not really," I explained. "I leased it."

"Couldn't you have done just as well with a Chevrolet? I always had good luck with Chevrolets."

"I just thought it was time I got myself a Cadillac," I explained. "I've worked hard."

"I know that, son," said my mother, "but I don't want you just throwing your money away on fancy cars."

Suddenly, I felt guilty for driving up in my mother's yard in a Cadillac. I was feeling guilty because I didn't think a Chevrolet was good enough for me anymore. I could hear the old men sitting around the stove:

"Got yourself a Cadillac, huh? Boy, ain't you big-time?"

"Hey, look who got hisself a Cadillac, ol' college-boy here. Boy, where'd you learn high-falootin' things like drivin' a Cadillac? Didn't learn that from your mama, I know that. She never drove nothing but Chevrolets."

The only person who came by to see my car while I was

visiting my mother was Crazy Melvin.

"What kind of car is it?" he asked me.

"Chevrolet," I said.

"Thought so," said Crazy Melvin as he walked away.

Guilt was a very big part of my generation's adult life. If you didn't do well enough, you were guilty because you'd let your parents down. But if you did too well, and came home driving a Cadillac and wearing sunglasses, you felt guilty because you obviously had forgotten your roots and had turned into a big-city high-roller that you had no business turning into.

The old men at the store: "You drivin' that Cadillac is like puttin' a ten dollar saddle on a thousand dollar horse."

Despite the Cadillac, which now has more than 100,000 miles on it and is five years old (I figure if I drive it long enough, my mother will appreciate the sound common sense I used in not trading for a new car until my old one was completely worn out), despite the education, despite all the gadgetry I own, despite the fact that I didn't wind up on the third shift at Flagg-Utica, I'm not so certain that I *am* having it better than my parents' generation did.

Let me clarify this point: I wouldn't have wanted to go through World Wars and the Great Depression, and I like my creature comforts and the cruise control on my car, but did my parents ever have to eat a plastic breakfast at McDonald's while some guy mopped under their table spreading the aroma of ammonia?

Did they ever have to fight five o'clock traffic on a freeway when they were my age? Did they ever have to worry about getting herpes? Couldn't they eat bacon and all those other foods that are supposed to give me everything from St. Vitus Dance to cancer without worrying?

Did they ever have to put up with calling somebody and getting a recorded message? Did they ever have to make their own salads in restaurants or pump their own gasoline at exorbitant prices in gasoline stations? Didn't they get free glasses when they bought gas, and didn't the attendant always wash their windshield and check their oil without being asked?

Did my parents' generation go to movies and not understand them at all? Did they ever have to deal with women's liberation, gay rights, the Moral Majority, the anti-nuke movement, a dozen kinds of racism, palimony, sex discrimination suits, and Phil Donahue making you wonder if you really have any business on this planet anymore?

Did they have to endure Valley Girls, punk rock, rock videos, the "moonwalk," break dancing, ghetto blasters, and "The Catlins"?

So their kids worshipped Elvis. My generation's children follow Michael Jackson, who wears one glove and his sunglasses at night, and sings songs with names like "Beat It." It also is rumored that he takes female hormones to nullify his voice change. I cannot verify this, but there are rumors he recently was seen hanging his panty hose on a shower rod. My generation's children also follow something called "Culture Club," which features something called Boy George, who dresses like Zasu Pitts.

My parents' generation had Roosevelt for a president. We had Nixon.

They won their war. We lost ours.

They knew exactly what their roles in family and society were. Most of us don't have any idea what ours are anymore.

They had corns on their toes. We have identity crises.

They got married first and then lived together. We do it

just the opposite today.

They fell in love. We fall, or try to, into meaningful relationships.

Did Lou Gehrig use cocaine? Did Jack Benny freebase? Did Barbara Stanwyck get naked on the silver screen? Did they have to put up with Jane Fonda?

I obviously can't speak for all of us, but here is one Baby Boomer who liked it better when it was simpler. My parents sent me out into this world to make for myself a better life than they had and maybe I achieved that in some way. But the everlasting dilemma facing me is that although I live in a new world, I was reared to live in the old one.

I remain the patriot they taught me to be. I like music you can whistle to. If ever I marry again, it will have to be to a woman who will cook. She can be a lawyer or work construction in the daytime, and she can have her own bank account and wear a coat and tie for all I care, but I want a home-cooked meal occasionally where absolutely nothing has passed through a microwave.

I don't understand the gay movement. I don't care if you make love to Nash Ramblers, as long as you're discreet about it.

I don't use drugs, and I don't understand why anybody else does as long as there's cold beer around.

I think computers are dangerous, men who wear earrings are weird, the last thing that was any good on television was "The Andy Griffith Show," and I never thought Phyllis George had any business talking about football with Brent Musberger on television.

In his classic song, "Are the Good Times Really Over for Good?", Merle Haggard says it best:

"Wish Coke was still cola,
A joint, a bad place to be ...
It was back before Nixon lied to us all on TV ...
Before microwave ovens, when a girl could still cook and still
would ...
Is the best of the free life behind us now,
Are the good times really over for good?"

My sentiments exactly. If I could have the good times back, I would bring back 1962. At least, most of it. I was sixteen then. I had my driver's license, a blonde girlfriend, and my mother awakened me in the mornings and fed me at night.

Elvis was still singing, Kennedy was still president, Sandy Koufax was still pitching, John Wayne was still acting, Arnold Palmer was still winning golf tournaments, you could still get hand-cut french fries in restaurants, there was no such thing as acid rain or Three Mile Island, men got their hair cut in barber shops and women got theirs cut at beauty parlors, there was no such person as Calvin Klein, nobody used the word *psychedelic,* nobody had ever heard of Vietnam, and when nobody bombed anybody during the Cuban Missile Crisis, I was convinced that the world was probably safe from nuclear annihilation ... an idea I do not hold to with much force anymore.

1962. It was a beauty.

So what happened to the simple life the boys from Moreland knew? And when did all the change begin?

I think I can answer the second question. It was one morning in November, 1963, and I was changing classes in high school.

4 Camelot In Bloody Ruin

*L*ET THE WORD *go forth from this time and place... that the torch has been passed to a new generation of Americans...."*
John F. Kennedy, January 20, 1961

There was one family of Catholics in Moreland in 1960. They had to drive ten miles to the county seat to go to church. I didn't think there was anything particularly different about them except that on Fridays, when the rest of us were attempting to force down what they said was meatloaf but tasted like Alpo looks, the kids from the Catholic family were eating what appeared to be a tasty serving of fried fish. Had it not been for the fact that it would have put the good Methodists and Baptists in my family into shock and running fits, I might have become a Catholic, too, just to avoid the Friday meatloaf.

The adults in town didn't trust Catholics. One of the old men down at the store said he heard they stole babies. Somebody else said Catholics drank a lot, and half the time

42

they didn't even speak English when they were holding church services.

John Kennedy frightened the local voting bloc, perhaps a hundred-or-so strong. He was Catholic and his daddy was rich, and despite the fact we're talking lifelong Democrats here, they were having a difficult time accepting the idea that a person with religious beliefs so foreign to their own might actually occupy the White House.

The old men around the stove:

"I ain't sure we ought to elect no Cathlic."

"I ain't votin' for him. He'd take all his orders from the Vaddican."

"The what?"

"The Vaddican."

"Where's that?"

"Itly."

"Reckon that's so?"

"'Course it's so. Them Cathlics stick together like buttermilk sticks to your chin."

"You ever know'd any Cathlics?"

"Naw, but I think one come in the truckstop a week or so ago."

"How'd you know it was a Cathlic?"

"He's wearing a white shirt. Who else 'round here wears white shirts?"

If Elvis was the first break between the Baby Boomers and their parents, then John Kennedy — at least in rural Georgia, which was my only horizon at the time — was a second. Kennedy never started the youthful explosion that Elvis had, but there was something about the man that appealed to us. It was later described as "vigah." Although I was too young to vote in the 1960 presidential election, I did my part to elect Kennedy by running down Richard Nixon.

I was born under Truman and then came Ike. The General was okay, but I didn't like the way Nixon, his vice president for eight years, looked even then. He already had those jowls, and when he talked, it seemed like his mouth was full of spit and he needed to swallow.

I also was never able to understand how Nixon fathered any children, because I was convinced he slept in his suit. I suspect Richard Nixon was born wearing a tiny little suit and tie, and his aunts and uncles probably stood around his crib and looked at his beady little eyes and at his jowls — I'm sure he was born with them, too — and said things like, "Well, let's hope and pray he grows out of it."

He didn't, of course. The older he got, the shiftier he looked, and that's why Kennedy beat him in 1960. When they debated, Nixon looked like a 1952 Ford with a busted tailpipe and foam rubber dice hanging off his rear-view mirror; Kennedy was a Rolls Royce in comparison.

All the girls at school liked Kennedy, too. "He's sooo cute," was their usual adept analysis of his platform.

Historians who have looked back on the brief thousand days that John Kennedy was our president have failed to note that Kennedy did, in fact, accomplish an important feat with his looks. Remember his hair? John Kennedy's hair was sort of fluffy. Nixon probably greased his down with whatever it was I used to slick down my ducktails.

In the early 1960s, most men were still using Vitalis and Wildroot Creme Oil on their hair. But I don't think John Kennedy used anything like that on his. In fact, Kennedy may have been the first American male to show off "The Dry Look." It was only a few years after Kennedy became president that we celebrated the death of "The Wethead,"

44

and American men poured their hair tonic down the drain and spent millions on blow-dryers and hairspray.

Looks are important to a president, and Kennedy was the most handsome American president since Andrew Jackson — who wasn't any Tom Selleck, but at least he didn't have one of those cherub-looking faces like John Quincy Adams, and he didn't wear a powdered wig.

Look at the appearances of our presidents over the years. The pictures of George Washington that were in our history books made the father of our country look like somebody's sweet little grandmother. Abraham Lincoln was no day at the beach, either, and Rutherford B. Hayes had that long scraggly beard, and William Taft was fat. FDR was fairly handsome, but he used that long cigarette holder that made him appear a bit stuffy, I thought. Truman wore funny hats and bow ties, and Eisenhower was militarily rigid and grandfatherly.

John Kennedy, however, *was* the torchbearer for the new generation. If the times were Camelot, then he was certainly Arthur. He seemed more of an admired, understanding big brother to us than an awesome patriarch ruling from some distant perch.

The youth of the early sixties knew little of the system, other than what we had learned in Civics class, but here was a man with whom we were able to relate — if not to his substance, then most certainly to his style.

The Cuban Missile Crisis brought us even closer to him. He told the Russians where he wanted them to stick their missiles and in the meantime created several marvelously exciting days at my high school. I didn't pay a great deal of attention to the crisis at first. Basketball practice had started, and that had me too occupied to consider the end of the world as we knew it.

I was in Jacobs's Drug Store in Newnan eating a banana split the night the president went on television in October of 1962 and told the nation that we were about this far from having to sink a few Russian ships and maybe start World War III. I hesitated and watched and listened for a few moments, but then I went back to the banana split.

The next day at school, however, our principal, Mr. O.P. Evans, called the student body together and began to prepare us for the nuclear attack he seemed certain would come before the noon lunch bell.

Mr. Evans was a tall, forceful man with a deep, booming voice that was a fearful and commanding thing. He ran the school with a Bible in one hand and a paddle in the other. The school was his passion, and even an imminent nuclear attack would not deter him from making certain that we would be a model of order until the last one of us had been melted into a nuclear ash.

We were told that when (I don't think he ever mentioned an "if" anywhere) the call came to Mr. Evans's office (probably directly from Washington) to inform him that the bombs and missiles were on the way, we would be hastened back to assembly for further instructions. At that point, a decision would be made on whether or not to close school and send us home. In the event we could not safely evacuate, we would remain at school and be given subsequent assignments as to where we would bed down for the night.

That idea caused a great stirring of interest among the boys. Would we get to sleep near the girls? Could we slip around and perhaps catch them in nothing but their underpants? Bring on the bombs and missiles. Mr. Evans quickly dashed our hopes, however, by stating that the boys would be herded to the gymnasium, while the girls would sleep at the other end of the school in the cafeteria and the student activities room, where the Coke and candy machines were also located, damn the luck.

He instructed us to bring canned goods to store in our lockers the following day, presuming there was one, in case the school ran out of food and we had to spend the winter inside the building waiting for the fallout to subside. Students also were to bring blankets and soap, an extra toothbrush, and a change of clothes and underwear. The sacks of clothes and underwear were stored on the stage in the assembly room. Having been shut out of actually getting to see our female classmates down to their skivvies, a group of us went for the next best thing and sneaked into the assembly room during the post-lunch rest period and went through the sacks trying to match girls with panties and bras.

The possibility of an attack did lose some of its glamour, however, when Mr. Evans further announced that as long as a single teacher survived, classes would continue and gum chewing would remain a capital offense.

The attack never came, of course, but we did find out that Gayle Spangler, who always was going off to Atlanta on weekends and was allegedly keeping company with college boys and going to wild fraternity parties, had a pair of panties with the 1962 Georgia Tech football schedule printed on the crotch.

John Kennedy was hailed as a conqueror after backing down the Russians and their missiles, but the triumphant mood of the country was short-lived. One moment Camelot was there, and the next it lay in bloody ruin.

It was the autumn of my senior year. November, 1963. I

47

was changing morning classes. I had just finished Spanish, which I hated. I particularly hated those silly records they played to us in Spanish class.

"El burro es un animal de Mexico, Espana, y Norte Americana, tambien. Repeata, por favor."

Thirty students with heavy Southern accents would repeat: "El boorow ez uhn anymahl de Mexeecoh, Espainya, why Gnawertee Amuricainya, tambiann."

I was strolling down the hallway toward geometry class. Something was happening. The teachers had come out into the hall and were herding students into classrooms.

"Don't go to your next class. Come into my room. Quickly," said a teacher to me.

The halls were cleared. There was an eerie silence. Is the place on fire? Have the Russians decided to attack after all? Has somebody been caught chewing gum? I noticed the teacher sitting in the desk in front of me. She was holding back tears.

The voice. I had heard that powerful voice so many times, but now it seemed to crack and strain.

"Your attention, please," said Mr. Evans over the intercom. "We have just received word that President John Kennedy has been shot in Dallas. We have no other word at this time. May we all bow our heads in prayer."

I can't remember Mr. Evans's prayer word-for-word. It's been more than twenty years. But I think I can still manage its essence:

"Gawd, Our Father. We beseech Thee. A brilliant young leader has been shot. He is a man we love. He is a man

we trust. He is our president. Our Father, we beseech
Thee now to rest Your gentle hand upon this man and to
spare him, O Gawd. Spare him, so that he can continue to
lead us, to guide us, to keep us safe from our enemies,
to show us how to make our country even greater, to bring
justice to all our people, to make for these students,
who soon will go out into the world alone, a safe and
shining place to live and work and grow fruitful. Spare
John Kennedy, O Gawd. Spare our beloved president.
Amen."

We raised our heads. No one spoke. Some of the girls cried.

"Maybe it's not true," somebody finally said.

"It's true," said someone else, "or Mr. Evans wouldn't have stopped classes for it."

All doubt then faded. It *was* true.

We waited. I don't know how long we waited. Maybe it was seconds. Maybe it was minutes. Finally, the voice came back again.

"Students and faculty of Newnan High School," Mr. Evans began, "President John Fitzgerald Kennedy is dead."

The class idiot was Harley Doakes, whose father hated Kennedy because he had wanted to desegregate the schools. When Mr. Evans announced that the president was dead, Harley Doakes cheered. Somebody in the back of the room threw a book at him and called him a stupid son of a bitch.

* * *

Nothing was the same after that. Ever again. I trace my world going completely bananas back to that single moment when the shots first cracked in Dallas.

What, if anything, has made any sense since? John Kennedy was dead and we were left with Lyndon Johnson, who was low enough to pick up a dog by its ears. He proceeds to get us involved up to *our* ears in Vietnam, and when he finally decides he's had enough, here comes Nixon again. Why wouldn't this man just go away?

I had all sorts of trouble trying to decide who I wanted to be president in 1972. Picking between Richard Nixon and George McGovern was like picking between sores in your mouth or a bad case of hemorrhoids. I wanted Nixon out, but I didn't want McGovern in.

McGovern was the hippie candidate. I had been raised a patriot. I reluctantly voted for Nixon. I admit he did a few things. He opened China, although I'm still not sure what good it did. If you've seen one Chinese urn, you've seen them all; I still don't know how to use chopsticks; and I never did like sweet and sour pork.

It was under Nixon that Vietnam finally came to a merciful end, of course, and there was that marvelous, moving moment when the POW's came home, but it was impossible for me to put heroic garb on Richard Nixon. There always was the nagging feeling each time I saw him or listened to him that he was somehow putting a Bobby Entrekin shuck on me.

Watergate was all I needed. There I had been a decade earlier — a high school senior with a crew cut and even clearer-cut ideals and values. Then the president is shot, and next comes Vietnam, and then somebody shoots Robert Kennedy, and Martin Luther King is gunned down, and another assassin puts George Wallace in a wheelchair for life. And on top of that, we find out the current president is, indeed, a crook (not to mention a liar with a filthy mouth) and he's run out of office practically on a rail.

I no longer had any idea what to believe or whom to trust. I was nearing thirty, and practically every sacred cow I had known had been butchered in one way or another.

Nothing was the same anymore. I had seen students burning campus buildings and students being gunned down on campuses by National Guardsmen.

I had been divorced once by then and was working on a second. Half the country was smoking dope. Gasoline was four times what it had cost before. Men were growing their hair over their ears and wearing double-knit trousers.

And they weren't singing the old songs anymore, either. In fact, it was soon after the death of John Kennedy that the music headed somewhere I didn't want to go.

If Elvis was a break between me and my parents and my roots, then it was The Beatles who forced me back toward them.

Where Rock 'n' Roll Went Wrong

A S MOST MUSIC historians know, soon after Elvis became the undisputed King, Colonel Tom Parker hid him out for nearly the next two decades. The only time we were able to see him was at a rare concert or in one of those idiotic movies he began making, such as *Viva Las Vegas*, which featured Elvis singing and mouthing ridiculous dialogue while several dozen scantily-clad starlets cooed and wiggled. Today, Elvis movies normally are shown very late at night after the adults have gone to bed, so they won't be embarrassed in front of their children.

However, the rock 'n' roll storm that Elvis started did not subside after he took leave of the public. As a matter of fact, the music flourished and reached new heights, and when it got its own television show, our parents' battle to save us from what some had considered a heathen sound was over. They had lost.

Dick Clark was apparently a very mature nine-year-old when he first appeared on "American Bandstand," because that has been nearly thirty years ago and he still doesn't look like he has darkened the doors to forty.

Bandstand. I wouldn't miss it for free Scrambler rides and cotton candy at the county fair. The music they were playing was *our* music, and the dances they were dancing were *our* dances. It was live on television, and Philadelphia, from whence Bandstand came, was the new center of our universe. (Previously, it had been Atlanta, where our parents occasionally took us to see the building where they kept all the things you could order from the Sears Roebuck catalog, and to wrestling matches and gospel singings.)

Danny Thompson and I always watched Bandstand together in the afternoons. Danny was not nearly the geographical wizard I was (I had been born seventy-five miles from Moreland in Ft. Benning, Georgia, and had traveled as far away as Arkansas as the quintessential Army brat before my parents had divorced) so anything that had to do with where some place was, Danny asked me.

"Where is Philadelphia, anyway?" he queried one afternoon as we watched the kids on Bandstand do the Hop to Danny and the Juniors's "At the Hop."

"Pennsylvania," I told him.

"How far is that?"

"Thousands of miles."

"Wish I could go."

"To see Bandstand?"

"See it up close."

"Wish we lived in Philadelphia."

"We'd go on Bandstand every day, wouldn't we?"

Besides the music, Danny and I enjoyed watching Bandstand in order to select objects of lust from the group of Philadelphia girls who were regulars. I picked out a blonde with large breasts. Her name was Annette something-or-other. Danny picked out a raven-haired beauty named Shirley, who chewed gum; we could never tell exactly how she voted when she rated a record because in the first place she talked funny, being from Philadelphia, and secondly it's difficult to discern what someone is saying when they're saying it through three sticks of Juicy Fruit gum.

We spent hours discussing whether or not, at their advanced ages of probably sixteen, they were engaging in any sort of sexual activity off camera.

"Wonder if Annette and Shirley do it?"

"I bet Annette does."

"Why?"

"She's got blonde hair. Blondes do it more than other girls."

"How do you know that?"

"My cousin told me. He said you see a girl who's blonde, and she'll do it."

"I'd like to do it with Annette."

"I'd like to do it with Shirley."

"Shirley's got black hair."

"I'd still like to do it with her."

"I'd give a hundred dollars to do it with Annette."

"I'd give two hundred to do it with Shirley."

"You don't have two hundred dollars."

"I could get it."

"How?"

"Sell my bicycle."

"You'd sell your bicycle to do it with Shirley?"

"You wouldn't sell yours to do it with Annette?"

"Maybe I would."

Of course, I would have. The desire to do it strikes young

in boys, and the delicious idea of doing it with a Bandstand regular was my first real sexual fantasy (which must be accepted as proof of our parents' fears that interest in rock 'n' roll did, indeed, prompt the sexual juices to flow).

* * *

The music was good back then. There were The Drifters, and The Penguins, and Paul and Paula, and Barbara Lewis, and Mary Wells, and Clyde McPhatter; and Sam Cook sang about the men workin' on the "chain ga-e-yang." We had Bobby Helms doing "Special Angel," and there was Jerry Butler talking about his days getting shorter and his nights getting longer. There were great songs like "A Little Bit of Soap" and "Duke of Earl" and Ernie Kado singing about his mother-in-law.

We danced and held each other close and took two steps forward and one back to "In the Still of the Night," and later we shagged to beach music — The Tams, The Showmen — and we twisted with Chubby Checker and did the Monkey with Major Lance. We had the soul sounds of James Brown — "Mr. Dynamite, Mr. Please Please Me Himself, the Hardest Workin' Man in Show Business" — and Jackie Wilson sang "Lonely Teardrops," and Marvin Gaye did "Stubborn Kind of Fellow," and Maurice Williams and the Zodiacs did "Stay." And I don't want to leave out Fats (Antoine) Domino and Chuck Berry and Joe Tex and Bobby Blue Bland and Soloman Burke and Jimmy Reed moaning over radio station WLAC, Gallatin, Tennessee, brought to you by John R., the Jivin' Hoss Man, and Ernie's Record Mart and White Rose Petroleum Jelly, with "a thousand-and-one different uses, and you know what that one is for, girl."

There were a thousand singers for a thousand songs. It was truly an enchanted time. But then ever-so-slowly yet ever-so-suddenly, it changed. It seemed that one day Buddy Holly died, and the next day The Beatles were in Shea Stadium.

I'm not certain what it was that caused me to reject The Beatles from the start, but I suspect that even then I saw them as a portent of ill changes that soon would arise — not only in music, but in practically everything else I held dear.

The Beatles got off to a bad start with me because the first thing I heard them sing in 1964 was "I Wanna Hold Your Hand," and it was basically impossible to do any of the dances I knew — the Shag, the Mashed Potato, the Monkey, the Pony, the Gator, the Fish, the Hitchhike, the Twist, or the Virginia Reel— to that first song. About all you could do to "I Wanna Hold Your Hand" was jump and stomp and scream, which, of course, is what every female teeny-bopper at the time was doing whenever The Beatles struck guitar and drum and opened their mouths.

Also, patriot that I was, I stood four-square against the importation of foreign music, just as I have since stood steadfastly against the importation of Japanese cars and Yugoslavian placekickers. The only materials we really need to import from foreign countries, in my way of thinking, are porno movies. It doesn't matter that you can't understand what anybody is saying in those movies anyway, and I like the imagination of, say, the French when it comes to doing interesting things while naked.

But the British? I still have problems with them, especially with the current royal family. I'm sick and tired of Lady Di getting pregnant, I don't care if Prince Andrew is dating Marilyn Chambers, and every time the Queen comes to the U.S., she is always getting offended by something a well-meaning colonist has done to her. I wish she would stay in Buckingham Palace and give the Cisco Kid his hat back.

Even then, I didn't like the way The Beatles looked. I thought their hair was too long, I didn't like those silly-looking suits with the skinny ties they wore, and Ringo reminded me of the ugliest boy in my school, Grady "The Beak" Calhoun, whose nose was so big that when he tried to look sideways he couldn't see out of but one eye. Grady was a terrible hitter on the baseball team because his nose blocked half of his vision.

Soon after The Beatles arrived in the U.S., I started college. At the fraternity house, we were able to hold on to our music for a time. The jukebox was filled with the old songs, and when we hired a band, we had black bands whose music you could dance to and spill beer out of your Humdinger milkshake cup on your date. The Four Tops and The Temptations, The Isley Brothers and Doug Clark and the Hot Nuts, and Percy Sledge (which always sounded to me like something that might clog your drain) were still in demand at college campuses — at least all over the South. A few white bands were still in vogue as well, the most notable of which was The Swinging Medallions. They sang "Double Shot of My Baby's Love," and even now when I hear that song, it makes me want to go stand outside in the hot sun with a milkshake cup full of beer in one hand and a slightly-drenched nineteen-year-old coed in the other.

But the music, our music, didn't last. At least, it didn't remain dominant. Elvis's music was switched to country stations, and every wormy-looking kid with a guitar in England turned up in the United States, and rock 'n' roll meant something entirely different to us all of a sudden.

I didn't like the new sounds or the new people who were making them. I found The Rolling Stones disgusting and The Dave Clark Five about a handful short.

Suddenly came the dissent associated with the Vietnam escalation, and with that came hippies and flower children. And one day I found myself (just as my own parents had done when Elvis peaked) condemning modern music as the hedonistic, un-American, ill-tempered, God-awful, indecent warblings of scrungy, tatooed, long-haired, uncouth, drugged-out, so-called musicians.

I didn't know Jimi Hendrix was alive until he overdosed and died, and I thought Janis Joplin was Missouri's entry in the Miss America pageant.

All the new groups had such odd names. There was Bread, and Cream, for instance. And there was Jefferson Airplane and Iron Butterfly and Grand Funk Railroad and a group named Traffic. I wondered why so many groups were named after various modes of transportation. I theorized that it was because those performers had all been deprived of electric trains as children.

I expected the members of musical groups to wear the same clothing when they performed — like white suits with white tails — and to do little steps together like "The Temptation Walk."

These new groups, however, apparently wore whatever they found in the dirty clothes hamper each morning before a performance. T-shirts and filthy jeans seemed to be the most popular garb. Some, of course, performed without shirts. I found this to be particularly disturbing, since I have no use whatsoever for any music made by a person who looks as if he has just come in the house from mowing the grass on an August afternoon and his wife won't let him sit

58

down on the good furniture because he'll sweat all over it and probably cause mildew.

I didn't like drug songs and anti-war songs, and I didn't like songs that were often downright explicit. Even The Beatles just wanted to hold somebody's hand. The new groups, however, wanted to take off all their clothes, get in the bed, smoke a bunch of dope, and do all sorts of French things that have no business being watched, discussed, or sung about outside a porno flick on the sleazy side of town.

The only piece of raw rock 'n' roll we ever knew about before The Beatles came along was a song by The Kingsmen called "Louie, Louie," and we really weren't certain that what they were saying about "Louie, Louie" wasn't just a rumor.

It was basically impossible to understand the words, except the part which went, "Louie, Lou-eye, Ohhhhh, baby, we gotta go." After that, it sounded like, "Evahni ettin, Ah fackon nin."

The smart money had it, however, that if you slowed the record down from 45 RPM to 33 RPM, you could make out some of the words and that the song was really about doing something quite filthy. Naturally, we all rushed home to slow down the record. I still couldn't make out any of the words. It simply sounded like I was hearing the bass portion of "Evahni ettin, Ah fackon nin."

I made myself a vow never to spend money on any of this new music. But as naive as I was concerning what was taking place in my once placid, sensible world, I was bound to break my vow. I did so by attending an Elton John concert ... completely by mistake.

I was dating a girl who was several years younger than me. I was in my late twenties at the time, but she could still

59

remember where everybody sat in her high school algebra class.

"What do you want to do Friday night?" I vividly recall asking this young woman.

"Elton John is in town," she said.

"He's somebody you went to school with?" I asked, in all honesty.

"You've never heard of Elton John?" she said, an unmistakable tinge of amazement in her voice.

"Well, I've been working pretty hard and...."

"Elton John is a wonderful entertainer. You would love him."

She was a lovely child and had big blue eyes, so I managed to purchase excellent tickets for the Elton John concert — third row from the stage.

I had never been to a concert by anybody even remotely connected with modern rock music. As a matter of fact, the only concert I had been to in years was one that Jerry Lee Lewis gave. "The Killer" came out and did all his hits, and everybody drank beer and had a great time. I didn't see more than a dozen fights break out the entire night.

What I didn't know about attending an Elton John concert was that Elton didn't come on stage until his warm-up group had finished its act. I don't remember the name of the group that opened the show, but I do remember that they were louder than a train wreck.

When I was able to catch a word here and there in one of their songs, it sounded like the singer was screaming (as in pain) in an English accent. One man beat on a drum; another, who wasn't wearing a shirt, played guitar. They were very pale-looking individuals.

"What's the name of this group?" I tried to ask my date

over the commotion. I heard her say, "Stark Naked and the Car Thieves." I thought that was a strange name, even for an English rock group, so between numbers I asked her again. Turned out I had misunderstood her; their real name was "Clark Dead Boy and the Bereaved."

"So what was the name of that song?" I pursued.

"'Kick Me Out of My Rut'," she answered. I was having trouble hearing, however; my eardrums had gone into my abdomen to get away from the noise. I thought she said, "Kick Me Out on My Butt."

After the next number, I asked her to name that tune, too.

"It's called 'I Can Smell Your Love on Your Breath'."

That's what she said, but what I heard was, "Your Breath Smells Like a Dog Died in Your Mouth," which sounded a great deal like "Kick Me Out on My Butt."

Finally, Elton John came out. He wore an Uncle Sam suit and large sunglasses.

"Is this man homosexual?" I asked my date.

"Bisexual," she answered.

That must come in handy when he has to go to the bathroom, I thought to myself. If there's a line in one, he can simply walk across to the other.

I had no idea what Elton John was singing about, but at least he didn't sing it as loudly as did Stark Naked and the Car Thieves.

As the concert wore on, I began to smell a strange aroma.

"I think somebody's jeans are on fire," I said. "Do you smell that?"

"It's marijuana," said my date. "Everybody has a hit when they come to an Elton John concert."

I looked around me. My fellow concert-goers, some of

whom weren't as old as my socks, were staring bleary-eyed at the stage. Down each row, handmade cigarettes were passed back and forth. Even when the cigarettes became very short, the people continued to drag on them.

Suddenly, down my row came one of the funny cigarettes. My date took it in hand, took a deep puff, held in the smoke, then passed it to me.

"No thanks," I said. "I think I'll go to the concession stand and get a beer."

"Go ahead," said my date. "It'll loosen you up."

This was my moment of decision. I had never tried marijuana before. I had never even seen any up close, but now here I sat holding some, listening to a bisexual Englishman wearing an Uncle Sam suit sing songs I didn't understand. I was completely lost in this maze and wanted to bolt from the concert hall and go immediately to where there was a jukebox, buy myself a longneck beer, and play a truck-driving son by Dave Dudley — something I could understand.

I looked at the marijuana cigarette again. Would I have an irresistible urge to rape and pillage if I took a drag?

It was very short. "You need a roach clip," said my date.

"There're bugs in this stuff?" I asked.

"When a joint is short like that, it's called a roach," she explained, pulling a bobby pin from her purse. "Hold it with this."

I took the pin in one hand and clipped it on the cigarette I was holding in the other.

"Take a good deep drag and hold it in," said my date.

"Suck it or send it down," said somebody at the end of my row.

I continued to look at the roach. The smoke got into my

eyes and they began to burn. Suddenly, to my horror, I noticed the fire at the end of the roach was missing. It had become dislodged from the clip and had rolled down between my legs. I quickly reached between my rear and the seat cushion to find it, lest I set the entire arena aflame.

"Hey, man," yelled the insistent one down the row, "where's that joint?"

"It's down here," I said, stooping over like a fool with my hand between my legs, searching for what was left of the marijuana.

"Groovy, man," he said. "I never thought of sticking it there."

Mercifully, Elton John finally completed his concert and I was free to leave.

"Well," said my date when we were in the car, "wasn't he great?"

"Save the fact that I burned a hole in the seat of my pants, burned my eyes from all the smoke, and lost partial hearing in both ears from attempting to listen to a nuclear explosion from the third row back, I suppose it wasn't all that bad."

"Good," she answered. "Let's go hear Reggae next. What do you think of Reggae?"

"I think he's the most overpaid outfielder in baseball," I answered.

That was our last date.

* * *

I honestly didn't think that the music and the people who made it could get worse than it was during the seventies, but again my naiveté was showing. What currently is regarded as "rock" is totally beyond me, especially when I'm switching around on my cable TV and come across one of those music video things.

In the first place, I don't understand what anybody is singing about. I heard a song on a video channel that was, appropriately enough, entitled "Radio."

The lyrics went like this:

"Radio. Radio. Radio.
Radio. Radio. Radio.
Radio. Radio. Radio."

An eleven-year-old child with a stuttering problem, I'm convinced, wrote that song.

Secondly, I do not understand what these people are doing when they're singing their songs on videos. I see people dressed like chickens, people singing while standing on their heads, and people — perhaps I'm using that term too loosely — diving into swimming pools filled with green Jell-O while they're still singing those songs. Every video I've ever seen has reminded me of the nightmares I have after eating too much Mexican food. It's music to throw-up by, I suppose.

I thought the names of the groups and the names of the songs were strange in the seventies, but the eighties have brought total insanity to popular music.

There are groups now like ZZ Top, The Cars, The Dead Kennedys, the B-52's, Run D.M.C., Duke Jupiter, Blond Ambition, Wall of Voodoo, The Cramps, The Razors, The Swimming Pool Q's, Modern Mannequins, Future Reference, The Divorcees, The Pigs, The Fabulous Knobs, Outa Hand, Late Bronze Age, Go Van Go, Riff-Raff, St. Vitus Dance, Kodac Harrison and Contraband, Subterraneans,

Corn, and Wee-Wee Pole.

Wee-Wee Pole? Now, somebody had to think of that name, and my imagination runs in all sorts of directions considering what prompted such a title for an alleged musical group. What comes to my mind first is this scene: There are a few guys snorting airplane glue or something in the back of their van, and one of 'em says, "Hey, why don't we start a band?", sort of a modern-day version of Mickey Rooney's Andy Hardy saying to Judy Garland and the gang, "Hey, why don't we give a show?"

Two other guys think this is a terrific idea, despite the fact that none of them has any musical talent whatsoever, which is no longer important if you want to start a band. The first order of business is to figure out what to call yourselves.

Before they can decide on a name, one of the guys indicates he needs to go to the bathroom, which reminds the others they need to do the same. So the entire group goes outside the van and begins to wee-wee on the first thing they see, which happens to be a telephone pole. The rest is history.

I seem to notice a pattern in names for rock groups today. The names usually either have to do with some sort of animal (The Pigs), something that doesn't make any sense whatsoever (Run D.M.C.) or something totally distasteful or vulgar (The Dead Kennedys and The Cramps).

If this is such a hot item, I would like to get into the business of naming rock groups myself. I likely could make a lot of money doing it, perhaps even start some sort of service. You send me twenty bucks, and I'll come up with a name for your rock group that will embarrass your parents to the point that they'll wish they'd come along when birth control was more widely accepted.

For groups that wanted animal names, I'd have Hog Wild and the Pork Bellies, Rabid Raccoon, Dead Dog and the Bloated Five, and Squid.

For names of rock groups that didn't make any sense whatsoever, the selection would include Oshkosh Ice Cream, Polished Cement, Snarknavel, and MDC Gravel.

In the totally disgusting and vulgar category, you could select from Umbilical Dan and the Chords, Potato Poothead, Battery Acid, Rat Poison, Willie and the Warts, and The Dingleberry Five.

You don't think things could ever get that weird with modern music? Of course, they can. Of course, they will. We've already got Michael Jackson, who sings a lot higher than Mahalia and probably lost his other glove doing something strange with Brooke Shields. (I once opined in another forum that if they ever made a remake of *Gone With the Wind*, Michael Jackson would make a perfect Butterfly McQueen's "Prissy.")

And then there's Boy George and Culture Club, of course. I've seen more culture on buttermilk.

Recently I heard a great curse: "May the next skirt you chase be worn by Boy George." What I want to know is, Does he shave his legs and have a period?

I have a theory about where all these people who make today's rock music came from. Remember when you were in high school and there were always a bunch of kids who were really thin and wormy, back when "punk" meant somebody who had a lot of zits and hung around playing pinball machines and never got asked to parties and never had dates and never played sports?

Well, they all grew up to be rock stars. That's what happened to them. It's the revenge of the nerds.

As much as I despise today's rock music, I must admit that it is even more popular with today's youth than Elvis's music was with my generation. I base this statement on the fact that I could go fifteen minutes to eat or to take a bath or to walk to school or to ride a bus without listening to my music. Kids today can't do that, so they have given the term portable radio an entirely new meaning. I'm talking about, of course, the Sony Walkman and the Ghetto Blaster Age that we are presently living through.

The Sony Walkman, I can take. Some adults even use these machines (which mercifully include earphones so nobody else will be disturbed) to listen to educational tapes and soft music that will put them to sleep in airplanes. I cannot resist the urge, however, when I see somebody tuned out of the regular world and tuned in to a taped version to ask, "What's the score?"

But ghetto blasters — which generally are about the size of a five-hundred-watt radio station — are something else entirely. Young people should be allowed to listen to any sort of music they like, but I shouldn't have to listen to it with them.

When I hear indecipherable music played two decibels above the sound the 4:15 flight to Cleveland makes when it takes off, it makes me nervous, unable to concentrate. And it eventually makes me angry enough to take the ghetto blaster from which the noise is emanating and stomp on it, even if doing so might mean having to defend my life against the owner, who suddenly has been deprived of something to get down on the street and dance on his head to.

Young people play their ghetto blasters on city streets where people with jobs are trying to have nervous breakdowns in peace. They play them on various forms of public transportation. They play them in fast-food restaurants or any time there is somebody else around to offend and render deaf.

There are laws against cursing in public, against spitting in public, against wee-weeing on telephone poles in public, and there should be laws against playing ghetto blasters in public.

* * *

This calamitous change in music, that began in the late sixties and has continued to the point of today's strange lyrics and stranger people, left me with a choice: Either I could totally change my tastes and my way of thinking and follow this metamorphosis, or I could look elsewhere and hope to find musical solace for the soul in another area.

I was lucky, in retrospect, to have had that second choice. The rock 'n' roll I knew was gone; I had absolutely no taste for music sung by fat ladies with high voices in a language I didn't understand; I have never liked any music where any part of it was made by an oboe or flute; I didn't mind a little Big Band now and then, and I could enjoy Sinatra on occasion, but that was my parents' music. Were it not for yet another choice, I might easily have become a musical orphan.

The war in Vietnam and the war against it at home were raging, and Americans had to pick a side. There were doves and flower children on one side and hawks and the guys at the VFW on the other. One kind of music raged against the war, while another kind was saying, "Love it or leave it."

It was Merle Haggard who gave me my new musical

direction. They used to say of Merle Haggard that he did all the things Johnny Cash was supposed to have done, such as serve time in prison.

It really didn't matter. Merle sang it sweet and from the heart, not to mention through the nose. He sang, "When you're runnin' down my country, Hoss, you're walkin' on the fightin' side of me." And he sang, "We don't smoke marijuana in Muscogee," and what I heard, I was drawn to. Now, pop open a longneck and let me tell you the rest of the story ... the best of the story.

They Call It Blue-Eyed Soul

I AM QUITE proud of the fact that I heard of Willie Nelson before most other Americans. This is sort of like being a style-setter and being one of the first people to know when white socks went out.

I'm not certain of the exact date when I first heard Willie sing and attached voice and song to name, but it was sometime during the late sixties after I had made the decision to abandon rock 'n' roll and place my musical interests elsewhere.

What eventually led me to country — before country was cool, if you'll allow me to steal a line from Barbara Mandrell — was, first, an Atlanta radio station changing its format. The station, WPLO-AM, had been a rock 'n' roll station during my youth, but when rock changed, so did WPLO. It went country.

It wasn't just that WPLO began playing country music, was the way they played it that caught my ear. They avoided the cornball, which had been SOP for all country stations.

Remember the old country disc-jockeys back before country started washing its feet more than once a week?

"Hello there, friends and neighbors, this is your old Cuzzin Cholly, brangin' you some good ol' pickin' and fiddlin'. Yessiree, Bob, we gone have us a good time this here afternoon, and jist remember this here is all brought to you by Lon and Randy's Feed Store on the Pickett Road, yore hog pellet headquarters, and by them good folks over at the Piggly-Wiggly — my ol' Uncle Peahead calls that the Hoggly-Woggly — featuring bargains this week on neck bones, Cardui tablets, and septic tank aroma bars. Now, let's jist sit back and enjoy some good ol' country music. Here's a new'un by Nubbin Straker entitled 'I'm a Floatin' Corncob in the Slopjar of Love.'"

Such was offensive even to a ruralite like myself, who was quite familiar, indeed, with slopjars, the forerunner to the automatic garbage disposal.

I had occasionally drifted across WSM, clear-channel, Nashville, Tennessee, on Saturday nights and listened to the Grand Ole Opry, but even the commercials bothered me there. Somebody was always singing about Black Draught, which I seem to recall was a laxative, and about Goo-Goo Cluster candy bars.

What WPLO did was to put a disc-jockey on the air introducing country music who didn't sound like he just crawled out from under a slopjar, and nobody sang commercials about laxatives and candy, and I could understand the words to the music, and the singers sounded as though they didn't look like something that would crawl under the refrigerator when the lights went on in the kitchen.

Actually, my pilgrimage to country was a pretty short trip.

Despite my early affair with Elvis, nobody could grow up in a small rural town like Moreland, Georgia, in the 1950s and not have at least some appreciation for the way country music sounds when a jukebox is blaring it out from the inside of a truckstop on a hot, thick, summer's night, when the neon is bright and the bugs are bad.

My favorite of the two truckstops in Moreland was Steve's, where the waitress paid off on the pinball machines at the rate of ten cents an extra game; where the cheeseburgers were thick and greasy; where if you were tall enough to reach the counter, you were old enough to drink beer; and where they had an all-country jukebox that played twenty-four hours a day for what must have been fifteen years.

Once I learned in which directions the magnet pulled, I could easily turn fifty cents into a dollar-and-a-half at the pinball machines, and I spent many hours of my youth at that practice alongside the jukebox that was full of coins and country.

There was Hank Williams, still barely cold in his grave, and Faron Young, Little Jimmy Dickens, Eddy Arnold, Hawkshaw Hawkins, Cowboy Copas, Patsy Cline, Loretta Lynn, Hank Locklin, Roy Acuff, Ernest Tubb, Miss Kitty Wells, Gentleman Jim Reeves, the Wilburn Brothers, Lefty Frizell, Lonzo and Oscar, and Webb Pierce singing, among other great hits, "In the Jailhouse Now" and "There Stands the Glass."

In the late sixties, another generation of country stars began to blossom. Johnny Cash put on his black outfit and sang "Ring of Fire," and people talked about the time he had spent in prison, which apparently gave him credentials to wail about life's miseries.

Misery. That's what a lot of early country music was really

all about.

At the same time, former rockers like Conway Twitty and Jerry Lee Lewis were joining the fold, and they brought fans with them. Finally there was music that people like me, who thought Led Zeppelin had something to do with the octane level of gasoline, could listen to without getting a splitting headache.

Back in those days, Willie Nelson was just another short-haired Nashville songwriter. But once I heard him do a song called "Bloody Mary Morning" — she left last night and this is morning, and I might as well start drinking early so I can hurry up and pass out and forget her — I was hooked. He almost *talked* that song in a clear and piercing, if not somewhat nasal, tone. I hummed it for days.

Later, I heard him do "I Gotta Get Drunk and I Sure Do Hate It" and his own "Crazy" and "Ain't It Funny How Time Slips Away," and I became a devotee. I told other people about him, but they sort of looked at me sideways, the way a dog does when he's trying to figure out what on earth you're talking about. Pretty soon I got used to that look.

Despite the growing popularity of country music, there were still those holdouts who felt that all country wore a straw hat with the price tag hanging off (sorry, Miss Minnie). I picked up a date one evening, and when I started my car, the radio began playing George Jones doing the classic "Ol' King Kong Was Just a Little Monkey Compared to My Love for You."

My date immediately reached for the selector buttons on my radio and punched until she found some whiny Simon and Garfunkel song.

"What are you doing?" I asked in genuine horror.

"Somebody put your radio on a country station," said my

73

date, in the same voice she would have used to tell me a large dog had committed a horrid indiscretion in the front seat while I was out of my car.

This was not the same young woman who later dragged me to the Elton John concert, but they probably were second cousins now that I think back on it.

"*I* put my car radio on a country station," I said proudly.

The girl made a horrible face. Maybe a dog did commit an indiscretion on the front seat while I was out of my car. But no, it was worse. My date was turning up her nose at country music.

"You actually listen to that crap?" she asked.

"Crap?" I said. "You're calling country music crap?"

"That's exactly what it is. Crap."

"And what is that you're listening to?"

"Simon and Garfunkel."

"Hippie music."

"No, it isn't."

"Yes, it is. That kind of music is exactly what's wrong with this country."

"Are you some kind of Bircher or religious nut?" she asked.

"No," I said, "but I like country music and I don't like anybody who doesn't, and I will thank you to keep your communist, unpatriotic, ungracious fingers off my radio."

The girl asked to be put off at the next bus stop, which I was more than happy to do. I left her standing there, and as I drove off, I punched my country station back on and disappeared down the street — alone for the evening, but proud that I would not allow even the stirrings of lustful passion to come between me and George Jones.

This probably is how the Good Ol' Boy fraternity — a

fairly recently identified sociological group — got its start. Smart-aleck women, hippies, and other non-desirables began to make fun of us for enjoying country music, and we sort of banded together in retaliation. The offshoot was that we also went in directions opposite to those who scoffed at us, such as preferring cold beer in longneck bottles to white wine, pickup trucks to Volvos, and, in many instances, our dogs to women who would dare move our radio dials off a country music station.

Before long, country music was appealing to individuals who previously thought they were incapable of enjoying it. This phenomenon was called "crossover," which meant that even yankees had begun listening to country music without remarking about how corny it sounded. The first time I saw this conversion was in Chicago, where I was once held prisoner for three winters.

Powerful Chicago radio station WMAQ had recently changed its format to country and was running away with the ratings. The station even went as far as to sponsor a country concert at the Ivanhoe Theatre on the fashionable, trendy, north side. Billy "Crash" Craddock and Don Williams were the entertainers.

There wasn't an empty seat in the house, which was the first thing that surprised me. I didn't think that more than a handful of Chicagoans had ever heard of either artist. Crash Craddock came out in a red outfit with sparkling rhinestones, and instantly I thought I was back home in the National Guard Armory with Ernest Tubb on stage and every country girl within six counties down in front of the stage taking Ernest's picture while he sang, "It's a long ways from Nashville to Berlin, Honey, so keep them cards and letters comin' in."

Crash did all his big numbers, including the moving ballad "If I Could Write a Song," while midwestern ladies who had the night off from the bowling leagues snapped pictures of him and his funky Santa suit.

It was Don Williams, however, singing soft and low, who stole the show. He came out wearing a floppy hat — the kind Gabby Hayes used to wear — and proceeded to sing non-stop for two hours. When he was done, three thousand frostbitten yankees stood as one and cheered his marvelous, mellow performance.

He had done "Amanda," of course, and "You're My Best Friend" and "She Never Knew Me." And during his encore, I felt I was at some sort of evangelical celebration where the entire audience suddenly had seen the light and had come forward en masse for the altar call.

The entire evening had, in fact, been a wonderful religious experience, and I do not make a spiritual allusion here without basis.

Remember Tom T. Hall's "I Remember the Year Clayton Delaney Died"? Clayton Delaney, so the song went, had been an extraordinary guitar-picker (that's different from "guitarist"), and he also drank a bit and was a rounder. But as he lay dying, the story went on, Clayton Delaney got religion. Tom T. finished the ballad with the suggestion that Clayton's deathbed conversion, and the fact that he could flat pick, probably led him to his just reward. Sang Tom T. in the last verse:

> "*I know there's a lot of good preachers,*
> *Who know a lot more than I do.*
> *But it could be the Good Lord*
> *Likes a little pickin', too.*"

76

* * *

The pure state of country music — once called "blue-eyed soul" — was bound to go the route of all else once good and simple, of course. I don't know who or what is to blame for the fact that country has forsaken its roots. Today flutists are playing background (and probably oboists, too, although I don't think I would recognize the sound of an oboe if I heard it), country stars are making movies, New York has its own country music night club and radio station, the rhinestones have been replaced by tight jeans and occasionally even tuxedos, nobody remembers Faron Young or Webb Pierce anymore, and half of what you hear that's supposed to be country today isn't country at all, but rather some sort of unholy mix better left for Wee-Wee Pole and the other musical fruits.

We have to start somewhere in tracing what caused country to go cosmopolitan, however, so I think we should start with Dolly Parton's breasts.

It's not Dolly Parton's fault that she has big breasts, and I dare say she still would be a rare talent without her chesty appearance. However, when Dolly Parton became a big country star, people started noticing her breasts more than her singing. Suddenly everybody else wanted to get into the act, and sex subsequently found its way on country stations where once Miss Kitty Wells, in ankle-length skirt and cowgirl boots, had trod.

Pretty soon the Mandrell sisters were wiggling a lot, and the girls on "Hee Haw" were half-naked for each performance, and Conway Twitty was singing, "Pardner, there's a tiger in those tight-fittin' jeans."

77

Has anyone noticed the sexual overtones that have found their way into modern country music? Conway ought to have his mouth washed out. He sang another song about "Even with your hair up in curlers, I'd still love to lay you down." And there was the one where he sang about the girl "who had never been this far before, bum-bum-bum," and he even had the audacity to remake a Pointer Sisters hit, where he suggests, "You want a lover who will spend some time; not come and go with a heated rush."

Country singers today think nothing of crooning about "the first time we went all the way," and "When we were down to nothing, nothing sure looked good on you," and "If I don't feel like a man, feel again." All of this likely would leave an old pioneer purist like Roy Acuff with his yo-yo in a knot.

I also blame Willie Nelson for a lot of this country-gone-chic. I could overlook the beard and the headband and the ponytails, but then he went one step over the line.

I was at a Willie concert, all ready to cry in my beer and stomp my feet. Then I noticed that the crowd was changing a bit. There was the cowboy-hatted contingent and the GOB's, but there were also people apparently leftover from that Elton John concert, and those weren't Marlboros they were smoking.

Willie put on his usual grand show. He opened, as always, with "Whiskey River," and then he did a medley of his older material. He knocked us over with "The Red-Headed Stranger," which has an ending line that always brings a cheer from the male contingent in the audience: "You can't hang a man for killing a woman who was trying to steal his horse."

It was somewhere in "The Red-Headed Stranger (From

Blue Rock, Montana)," as a matter of fact, that I noticed something strange about Willie Nelson.

He was wearing an earring. Or, at least, he appeared to be wearing an earring. I asked a companion sitting next to me to verify my observation.

"Damn if he ain't," was his reply.

It took me a week or so to figure out how I felt about such a thing. To begin with, I naturally had some doubts about a man wearing an earring, the same sort of doubts I would have had about a man wearing undershorts with pictures of flowers on them. I don't even think Elton John wore an earring, and I'm certain you could have threatened to bash Ernest Tubb's guitar and he still would have refused to wear an earring.

I doubt seriously if there's anything in the Bible that warns against men wearing earrings, but there should be. "Woe be unto ye if ye stick an earring in thy ear and aren't named Rachel or Ruby Ann," is what it should say.

I was pleased at first that country music had become so universally accepted, but did that mean country music eventually was going to lose all its purity? The way Willie Nelson sang, I supposed I could overlook the earring, too, but where would all this eventually lead?

Crossover not only meant their coming to us, I determined, but it also could mean our going over to them. Would we have bisexual country stars and country stars who dressed as bats and stuck out their tongues at the audience? Would country music no longer embrace its classic subjects — cheatin' and fightin' and truckin' and drinkin' and cryin' — but begin to embrace drugs and anarchy? Would the time come when I could no longer differentiate between country music and rock music, because all music would have

79

blended into a form without identity?

These were troubling thoughts. If country music lost its identity, if it were swallowed up into a giant, black hole where electronic gadgets screamed and screeched, where drums pounded out ancient rhythms, who would be left to sing for those of us who fed it during its hungry years?

Willie Nelson wearing an earring. He had told us in "I'd Have to Be Crazy" that he had grown a beard "just to see what the rednecks would do," but did he have to give us this rigid a test?

I never quite forgave Willie Nelson for the earring, but I continued to listen to his music, giving him the benefit of the doubt. I figured he was on the road so much that he didn't get a balanced diet, which caused him to be constipated a lot, which is a direct cause of strange behavior. A person who is constipated all the time suffers great fits of anxiety that go along with it, and maybe Willie had been so anxious that it had affected his ability to think clearly. So one day he said to himself, "I think I'll buy an earring and stick it in my ear, and maybe that'll take my mind off being constipated."

How I wish Willie had consulted me before he did that. A few swigs of Milk of Magnesia probably would have had the same effect and wouldn't have been nearly as unsettling to his fans.

* * *

Here's what I wish would happen to country music: I wish they would give it back to the loyalists and the traditionalists.

I wish somebody would start a new brand of music called "Neo-Country" or "Randy Rural," and anybody who wanted to sing with flutes and oboes and loud guitars, and sing lyrics you would be embarrassed for your mother to hear, could go off and listen to that. The rest of us, including Willie and his pal Waylon, could go on back to Luckenbach, Texas, and get back to the basics of country music.

I want the kind of country music George Jones sings. George sings like a steel guitar sounds. I want to hear more of George singing "If drinkin' don't kill me, then her memory will."

I want Willie to take out the earring and sing more songs like "Faded Love," that he did with Ray Price, and "Railroad Lady," that he did in memory of Lefty Frizell. In recent times, Willie has sung with Spaniard Julio Iglesias, and he's making an album with Frank Sinatra. Where will it end — Willie and Pavarotti singing opera together?

I want more Moe Bandy rodeo songs. I want more pure sounds like Larry Gatlin, more lyrical quality like Tom T. Hall brings to his music. I want Gene Watson and Rex Allen, Jr., and a few Chet Atkins instrumentals and less Eddie Rabbitt. Said my boyhood friend and idol, Weyman C. Wannamaker, Jr., a great American, who is also a country music fan, "If that mess Eddie Rabbitt sings is country, my dog's a P-H-damn-D."

I want Kenny Rogers to take a few months off and never sing another song like "Coward of the County." I want George Strait to make more songs like "Amarillo by Morning," with those mournful fiddles in the background. I never want to hear John Anderson sing "Swingin" again.

I don't want Alabama to do anymore truck-driving songs like "18-Wheeler." Dave Dudley and Red Sovine should do truck-driving songs; Alabama should do "Old Flame" and "She's a Lady, Down on Love."

I want more Joe Stampley and more country songs like "You're a Hard Dog to Keep Under the Porch" and "Don't Come Home a-Drinkin' with Lovin' on Your Mind" and less like "If I Said You Had a Beautiful Body, Would You Hold It Against Me?"

I want country songs with twin-fiddle intros, and I want Charley Pride to do what he does best — sing the old songs Hank used to sing — and I want Hank, Jr., to forget the hard country and try singing the sweet songs that make you want to cry and call your ex-wife and ask for forgiveness, like Don Williams sings.

I want Conway Twitty to clean up his act, but I don't want Merle Haggard to change a thing.

Country music is too much fun to allow it to be spoiled. No other sort of music offers such classic lines:

— "If fingerprints showed up on skin, wonder whose I'd find on you?"

— "My wife just ran off with my best friend, and I miss him."

— "You're the reason our children are ugly."

— "If you're gonna cheat on me, don't cheat in our home town."

— "I've got the all-overs for you all over me."

— "It's not love, but it's not bad."

— And the immortal: "I gave her a ring and she gave me a finger."

I also believe that all country music should fall under one of the following categories:

— CHEATIN' SONGS: She ran off.

— LOVIN' AND FORGIVIN' SONGS: She came back.

— HURTIN' SONGS: The hussy ran off again.

— DRINKIN' SONGS: Nobody here to cook me anything

to eat, so I might as well get drunk.
— TRUCKIN' SONGS: She run off on a train. I think I'll derail that sucker.
— PRISON SONGS: They take derailing trains serious in Mississippi.
— RODEO SONGS: Soon as she got out of the hospital after the train wreck, she took up with a bullrider.
— NEVER-GIVE-UP-HOPE SONGS: I wonder if her sister still lives in Tupelo.

* * *

I've taken a lot of abuse in my lifetime for being a country music fan, but it's all been worth it. Quite frankly, country music has helped me through many tough times. Whatever the problem, there's always meaning in country music, something to lean on.

Want to know what's really important in life? Country music has the answer to that in Tom T. Hall's "Old Dogs, Children, and Watermelon Wine":

> *"Old dogs care about you,*
> *Even when you make mistakes.*
> *And God bless little children,*
> *While they're still too young to hate.*
> *I tried it all when I was young,*
> *And in my natural prime.*
> *Now, it's old dogs and children,*
> *And watermelon wine."*

Freedom. There are times I have paid dearly to get it or to regain it. Perhaps I should have listened to Kris Kristofferson:

> *"Freedom's just another word*
> *For nothin' left to lose...."*

There is something about country music that should appeal to every writer, to everyone who has something in his heart and wants others to feel what he feels.

I've written lots of country songs, myself. Unfortunately, nobody has ever bothered to record one, but that still doesn't stop me from having a few beers occasionally and knocking out a few country lyrics — which is the way most country songs come to be written. People who write rock songs, on the other hand, apparently do so while being stoned (in the Biblical sense).

I've written some very poignant country songs, as a matter of fact. After a six-pack one night, I came up with this one:

> *"Singles bars ain't no place,*
> *Ain't no place for a lady.*
> *It's dark, talk is cheap,*
> *And the men are all shady.*
> *But where does she go,*
> *And is it so wrong,*
> *When a lady's been single too long?"*

Impressed? That's nothing. I also wrote:

> *"You say she gave you her number, friend*
> *Well ain't that just fine.*
> *I know it's Heartbreak six, fourteen-ten,*

'Cause that number used to be mine."

I even wrote a train song once, and it went something like this:

"Sweet, sweet Jesus,
I never gave you thanks
That once as a youth,
Through the middle of Georgia,
I rode the Nancy Hanks."

Sometimes when the lyrics won't come, when the beer won't go down easy, I write titles instead. I have some wonderful new titles just waiting for words.

How about, "I'd Marry Your Dog Just to Be a Part of Your Family"?

Or, "Who's Gonna Cut My Toenails After You're Gone?"

I like this one, too: "You Threw Up On the Carpet of My Love;" or, "You'll Never Get Away From Me Darling, Because Even When You're Taking a Shower with Somebody Else, I'll Be the Soap on Your Rag."

The words to that one will probably go something like this:

"I know I whine a lot
And occasionally I nag,
But you'll never get away from me, darling,
'Cause even when you're taking a shower
With somebody else,
I'll be the soap on your rag."

I admit it needs a little work, but at least you get the idea.

Perhaps the real point here is that when Elvis and rock 'n' roll came along and caught me as a boy, I followed them off despite my parents' rages against them. But when they led too far, country music called me back, and I forevermore will be grateful. Without it, who knows? I might have wound up one day with hair down to my shoulders, sandals on my feet, a ghetto blaster over my shoulder, and smelling like The Goat Man.

The Goat Man? He may have been the original hippie.

A Hairy Ode To The Goat Man

TAKE IT ALL down to the lowest common denominator, shake off all the dust and heave out all the bull, and most of the problems we had with each other in the late sixties and early seventies really were about hair.

Think about it. Let's suppose that student protesters who were burning buildings and marching and demonstrating against the war in Vietnam had shown up at the rallies wearing khaki pants, nice button-down, blue Oxford-cloth shirts, Weejuns, and short hair. I contend we wouldn't have had near the commotion that we did.

Older people would have looked at them and instead of saying, "You godless, bed-wetting, pinko, Commie, nasty, long-haired hippies," they might have said, "Gee, those youngsters certainly are vocal against the war, but isn't it wonderful to see boys and girls that age taking an active interest in government."

I'm not certain why, but most rebellions, however small, usually start with somebody doing something funky with their hair. Remember that at the Boston Tea Party, American revolutionaries grew their hair long, put it up in ponytails, donned feathers, and went out and started a war. Almost two hundred years later, a bunch of actors started a rebellion on Broadway with a musical called *Hair.* Some things never change.

The history of my own hair is one of coming and going.

When I was a baby, so my mother says, I had blond curls. She cut them off and still has them in a box somewhere. She can keep them.

When I was old enough to have my first haircut, my father, the soldier, took me to a barber shop and had them cut all my hair off. I doubt that he asked the barber to sweep my chopped locks off the floor so he could keep them in a small box, because like most military men, my father had no use for hair whatsoever. I never would have attempted to grow Elvis ducktails, had I lived with my father at the time, for fear he would have called me "Louise" instead of the name they gave me.

After I got over the ducktails thing, I went back to a crew cut because that's what all the other boys wore. I allowed the crew cut to grow out before I started college, but I remained a relative skinhead through college and into my early adult years. I didn't want anybody to think I was having anything to do with the hippie and anti-war movements.

Actually, I never saw a live hippie until after I was out of college. Come to think of it, I didn't see any dead ones, either. The University of Georgia was not exactly a hotbed of activism when I was in school there between 1964 and 1968. We were too busy enjoying the school's recent upsurge in football success after a long Dark Age. The only drugs I knew about were those pills you took to stay up all night and study because you'd been drinking beer and partying all weekend, celebrating Georgia's victory over Auburn.

I distinctly remember the first hippie-in-the-flesh I ever saw. The year was 1968. I had just taken a job in Atlanta. One day I was driving along Peachtree Street and entered the 10th Street area, once known for a country music juke joint called Al's Corral. Often had I been to Al's, where the beer was cold and the music made you want to cry.

But by 1968, the 10th Street area had changed. It had become the Deep South's answer to Haight-Asbury.

Hippies were everywhere — tall hippies, short hippies, boy hippies, and girl hippiettes. Gaggles of hippies sat on the sidewalks; one played guitar, while the others sang along or sat quietly listening to the music or picking their feet.

I must admit that I have done, and still do, my own share of foot-picking, but I consider it an exercise that should take place only in private and only occasionally. A person who picks his feet more than twice a month probably has some serious mental disorder, possibly dating back to his youth when he went around barefooted in the front yard and suffered stubbed toes or came down with planter's warts from stepping on places where frogs went to the bathroom. (It is common knowledge that one thing that causes warts is frog pee-pee. You probably could look it up in a medical book somewhere.)

Foot-picking, I also admit, can be an enjoyable experience. When I pick my feet, maybe once every three or four months, I first dig under my toenails and remove any foreign matter such as sock lint. Then I rub my fingers between my toes, which also removes weird stuff that hides in there. Rubbing between your toes makes you tingly all over.

89

Next, I pick at any callouses on the bottom of my feet. Since I rarely go barefoot anymore, especially outdoors where I might step into some frog pee-pee, I don't have to worry about warts.

I conclude my foot-picking by washing my hands thoroughly.

As I sat at a traffic light on Peachtree Street in the 10th Street area that day back in 1968, I watched one hippie in particular who apparently thought nothing of picking his feet in front of five o'clock traffic on the busiest street in town.

He had taken off his sandals and parked them next to him on the curb. I never could have been a hippie, if for no other reason than because I refuse to wear sandals, the official shoe of hippiedom. Sandals look awful, especially if you wear long, dark socks with them.

As a boy, I had noticed tourists from up north who were driving through Moreland on their way to Florida and had stopped at Bohannon's Service Station for gasoline. Yankee men tourists inevitably wore Bermuda shorts and sandals and long, black socks they pulled up almost to their armpits. Occasionally, however, a yankee tourist would come through and go to the other extreme. He would roll his socks down all the way to his ankles, which made him and his sandals look even sillier. I vowed never to wear sandals, even if it meant walking through a frog latrine barefooted.

I continued to watch the hippie pick at his feet. He dug under a nail with concentration and resolve. Since he wore no socks at all, I knew it wasn't sock lint he was removing. Perhaps it was road tar or some sort of animal leavings. The man looked as if he'd been sleeping with goats.

After completing his nail work, the hippie turned his

90

attention to between his toes. I don't know what causes strange substances to get between your toes, especially if you're in an urban setting and far from the nearest chicken yard. But I do know from personal experience that if you don't wash your feet often and your feet sweat a lot, you will have a gooey material between your toes. This substance normally is referred to as toe jelly or toe cheese. Since hippies seldom washed their feet, I figured he had a blue-ribbon supply of toe jelly between his toes.

At any rate, the light finally changed, and I drove away convinced that besides the political differences between me and hippies, there was one other major difference: I don't pick my feet in public.

That was just one of the reasons I never considered becoming a hippie, of course. Another was that they reminded me too much of The Goat Man, who is another story.

* * *

Once or twice a year, when I was growing up, The Goat Man would come through Moreland and park his goats and the wagon they pulled in front of the Masonic Hall, where he would camp for a couple of days.

The Goat Man had a long beard and wore tattered clothing and a pair of high-top tennis shoes, which he probably slept in. When, and if, The Goat Man ever got around to picking his feet, he probably found all sorts of things between his toes — even small animals that had gone there to hibernate for the winter.

The Goat Man was a fairly nice person, if you could stand the smell. Herds of goats give out a distinctive aroma, reminiscent of chitterlings while they're being cooked. People who live with herds of goats and sleep in their tennis shoes in the back of wagons take on the smell of their goats, which mixes with their own noxious odor, thereby creating a blend that would shock the olfactory nerves of a buzzard.

The Goat Man always carried around chewing gum for the children who came to see him and his goats, and we normally could hold our breath just long enough to get a couple of sticks of Juicy Fruit from him before we had to run for fresh air.

The Goat Man told great stories, though.

"Been all the way to Alaska and back since I was here last," he would say. "Got so cold, I had to sleep between my goats to keep warm."

Somebody would ask how long it took him to get to Alaska and back.

"These old goats here," he would answer, pointing to his herd, "were just babies when I left. They were great-grandparents by the time we got back."

The more I think about it, perhaps The Goat Man *was* the original hippie. He spurned the establishment life and indicated that he would rather share his being with goats than with other people.

I'm not certain if The Goat Man is still alive, or if he even lived long enough to see the hippie movement. I sort of hope he did, and I hope he took credit for starting it. A man who has spent his life huddling against the cold between goats needs to know he has left some sort of legacy, no matter how much it might smell.

* * *

There were certain beliefs, whether real or imagined, concerning hippies that were strongly held by those of us outside the movement.

There was the hair thing, of course. It was The Beatles who first hid their ears under their locks, but the hippies took it further and grew their hair over their shoulders and down even to their rears. And they grew long beards. That is, the male hippies grew long beards. Girl hippiettes, most of whom couldn't grow beards, allowed the hair under their arms and on their legs to grow.

In some cultures, men find female underarm hair to be quite desirable. Not so with American men — not even hippies, I would wager. That makes me somewhat suspect of one of those beliefs we had about hippies, that their "Make love, not war" ideas meant they were spending a lot of time having sex with one another.

I really doubt that now. Sleeping with goats is one thing, but making love to a hairy-legged girl with hairy underarms is an even more disgusting notion. I suspect that when we thought hippies were having all that sex, they probably weren't doing anything more intimate than picking one another's feet.

We firmly believed that hippies didn't wash their hair often and probably had cootie bugs roaming around on their scalps.

I'm not exactly certain what a cootie bug is, but there was a boy in my school whose head was allegedly infested with them. He was always scratching at his scalp, and he soon absorbed the nickname (or should I say nickmane?) of "Coot." The teacher finally called the health department and they came and got "Coot" and gave him some sort of treatment. He never scratched his head much after he was de-cootied, which was one of the first miracles of modern medical techniques I ever saw.

It was the fact that hippies wore their hair long and probably had cootie bugs that caused me to begin shampooing every day. Previously, I had not shampooed more than once or twice a week, because when I did my hair would become quite dry and stick up all over my head. A date once remarked that it looked like I was wearing a cocker spaniel on my head. I decided, however, that it would be easier to get another date than to get rid of cootie bugs.

It was the order of that day to make fun of hippies' long hair. The most popular game was to question the gender of a male hippie whose hair flowed down his back like Trigger's tail.

"See that?" somebody would ask, pointing to a nearby hippie.

"I see it, but I don't know what it is," would come the reply.

"Is it male or female?"

"Can't tell."

"It's wearing a man's clothes."

"But it's got hair like a girl."

"Maybe it's one of them she-men. They got those operations now, you know."

"Naw, it's just one of them nasty-headed hippies."

"Yeah, see it doin' that peace sign? All them hippies give that peace sign."

"Yeah, well give the son of a bitch half of it back."

The truth is, those of us in the straight world didn't like hippies and didn't trust them and wanted them to go away so our world could go back to being normal.

We wanted to win the war in Vietnam and bring the boys home victorious and have ticker tape parades for generals and show the evil communistic world that you don't mess with the United States of by-God America. Hippies wanted peace, even a dishonorable one. The cowards.

Hippies smoked dope and took LSD and God knows what else. We wondered why they couldn't be satisfied with beer like the rest of us.

Hippies liked flowers. We liked football.

Hippies listened to musical groups with names like Led Zeppelin and Cream and Jefferson Airplane and Blind Faith and The Grateful Dead and The Moody Blues. We still liked Merle Haggard and "Okie From Muscogee."

> *"Leather boots are still in style if a man needs foot-wear.*
> *Beads and Roman sandals won't be seen.*
> *And football's still the roughest thing on the campus.*
> *And the kids here still respect the college dean."*

Hippies looked filthy. We smelled like Aqua-Velva men.

Hippies didn't work. We busted our tails for promotions.

Hippies wore sandals and patched jeans. We wore wing tips and three-piece suits.

Hippies joined communes. We joined the Rotary Club.

Hippies danced nude in the mud. We worked on our golf games.

There were, of course, many people in my age group who broke away and went off to become hippies. I knew of only one, however. He was Stinky Drake, who was from Moreland and was a couple of years older than me.

As I look back, I can see now that even as a child Stinky showed evidence that one day he might grow up to be a hippie. He never played baseball with the rest of us. He spent his time making belts and Indian moccasins from a kit he had ordered from an ad in the *Grit* newspaper. He did other strange things, too, like the time we went on a Boy Scout trip and we caught a large number of catfish and tied them on a stringer. When nobody was looking, Stinky took the fish off the stringer and set them free.

"What if you were a fish?" Stinky asked his irate campmates. "Would you want to be stuck on a stringer, or to be free to go back to your family in the river?"

We realized there was no point in arguing with anybody who worried about fish being taken from their families, so we tied Stinky to a tree and went back to breaking up fish families for our evening meal. Stinky wouldn't eat that night because he said it would make him feel guilty eating somebody's father or mother.

It wasn't long afterwards that Stinky became the first vegetarian I ever met. At school they served him a special plate; nobody would eat with him and Stinky soon became known as "Bean Breath."

In high school, Stinky joined the Drama Club and wrote a poem for the school paper entitled "An Ode to Vegetables." I remember the closing lines:

> *"Just because I don't eat meat*
> *Doesn't mean that I'm not neat."*

I suppose we were cruel to Stinky, which caused him to rebel against the norm even more. After he graduated from high school, we heard he went off in the mountains somewhere and ate a lot of roots and berries and lived on what he could earn selling the belts and Indian moccasins he still made.

Next, we heard that he had broken his parents' hearts by

growing his hair long and taking up dope-smoking and running off to Canada to avoid the draft. He also was living in sin with a woman who didn't wear shoes or shave under her arms. He had met her at a rock concert.

I don't have any idea what ever happened to Stinky, but I suppose he's still out there in the hills somewhere, dressed like Cochise and munching on sunflower seeds.

* * *

It is odd — and beneficial, too — how time changes ideas and mends feelings. After the war in Vietnam ended, most of the hippies bathed themselves, cut their hair, quit wearing sandals, and quit picking their feet. Today most of them are stockbrokers or fertilizer salesmen.

But they left their mark, and again it was the hair. Do you know who wears their hair long today? Good ol' boys, that's who. You can see it coming out from under their International Harvester and Red Man caps. Know who wears their hair neat and short? Gays and those men you see in clothing ads in the Sunday *New York Times Magazine* (although that may be a redundancy).

As for my own hair, here's the rest of the shaggy story:

After the war, longer hair became the accepted fashion for men, and I followed suit. Sideburns even made a comeback. I had long hair and sideburns, and all of a sudden it wasn't possible to go to a regular barber shop anymore. Men had to go to stylists, and where they once had paid three bucks for a haircut, it was now costing them $12.50 and they had to make an appointment.

The first time I went to a hair stylist — it was around 1974 — I made an appointment with the renowned Mr. Phyllis.

"What on earth have you been shampooing with, my dear boy?" asked Mr. Phyllis.

"Soap," I said.

"Oh, God, no," Mr. Phyllis recoiled in horror. "Soap dries the hair and splits the ends."

I started to say my end had been split my entire life, but I decided it would not be wise to talk about such while I was alone in the room with Mr. Phyllis.

He immediately took charge of my hair. He shampooed it with an odd-smelling substance, put conditioner on it, and then "sculptured" it. Finally he put the blow dryer to me, and when it was over, I paid him the $12.50.

I felt a little cheated. At the barber shop, not only had I been charged a mere three bucks, but the barber usually told me a joke, too.

"Fellow had these two sows he wanted to get mated," went my barber's favorite joke. "He didn't have a boar, but he knew a fellow who did. So he called him up and asked if he could bring his two sows up to his farm and let that ol' boar have a go at 'em.

"The fellow said to bring 'em on up, so he put the two sows in the back of his pickup and drove 'em to his neighbor's farm.

"That ol' boar got real interested in his job and really did some work on the two sows. There was all sorts of gruntin' and oinkin' goin' on, 'cause when you got three thousand pounds of pork in the heat of passion, you got something wild.

"Anyway, when the ol' boar was finished, the man asked his neighbor how he would know if the job had took. His neighbor said to look out at his hogs the next morning, and if they were layin' up in the sunshine, everything was okay.

98

But if they were still wallowin' in the mud, he'd have to bring 'em back.

"Next morning, he looked out his window and his hogs were wallowin' in the mud, so he put 'em back in his truck and drove 'em back to see the boar again.

"Same thing happened. His neighbor's wife broke out in a sweat watchin' them hogs, and the dogs got to barkin' loud and they had to throw cold water on 'em.

"Next mornin', though, it was the same thing. Them two hogs was still wallowin' in the mud. Man took his hogs up there a third time. Next mornin', he couldn't bear to look out at his hog pen, so he said to his wife, 'Honey, look out there and tell me if my hogs are sittin' in the sunshine or wallowin' in the mud.'

"She looked out the window and said, 'Neither one.'

"The man said, 'Well, where are they?'

"The fellow's wife said, 'One of 'em's in the truck ridin' shotgun, and the other one's blowin' the horn.'"

Mr. Phyllis didn't know any jokes, or at least not any like that. He was always too busy talking about his cat or watering the plants in his salon to tell jokes.

After I had gone to the trouble of having my hair styled, I thought it would be wise to take care of what my $12.50 had bought me, so I vowed never to wash my hair with soap again and went out to buy some shampoo.

"Do you have any shampoo for men?" I asked a saleslady in the cosmetics department.

"I think you will like this," she answered, handing me a bottle of shampoo. "It has the faint aroma of apricot."

Apricot?

"If you don't care for apricot," the woman continued, "perhaps you would like something with an herbal essence."

What I really wanted, I said, was something that smelled like soap. I didn't want to go around with my head smelling like a fruit salad.

I also purchased an electric hair dryer, of course. Previously, I had allowed my hair to dry naturally. When I was in a hurry, I would simply shake my head back and forth like a dog does when he's wet. With longer hair, however, I was told that this was impossible, even though I knew I'd seen a collie dry itself off with just two or three good shakes.

After purchasing the hair dryer, I also had to buy hairspray. When I bought it, I said a silent prayer that my father wasn't somewhere looking down upon his only son buying gook that sprayed out of a can to keep my hair in its original, upright and locked position after it had been blown dry and styled each morning.

But it had been so much simpler for my father. He hadn't needed shampoo or hair dryers or hairspray, because nobody else used anything like that when he was a young man about town. Men were men in his day. He would have hit Mr. Phyllis square in the mouth if that dandy had tried to sculpt his hair.

The hair situation is even more confusing today. Mine is shorter than it was when I first allowed it to grow in the seventies, but it still covers my ears. I got rid of the sideburns, but now I've got a beard and a mustache. I'm not certain what my father would think of that.

"Ain't but two kinds of people who wear beards and mustaches," he likely would have said. "That's queers and movie stars, and I ain't seen none of your movies lately."

But if he's concerned about my hirsute appearance, I wonder what he thinks about punk rockers who have their hair styled to look like the back of a horned frog. And I

100

wonder what he thinks of people these days who dye their hair all sorts of colors, including orange and pink. My only hope is that heaven has mellowed him.

But what of me? I'm still here trying to deal with all this craziness. Hair and music have been a problem, but I have managed to cope with them after some degree of agony. But there have been so many other changes and dilemmas in the modern world. For instance, whose idea was it that men all of a sudden were supposed to be sensitive and enjoy fooling around with flowers and were even supposed to cry in front of women if they felt like it?

Each time I thought I knew all the answers to modern-day questions, somebody would up and change the questions.

And just when I thought there was nothing left to go haywire, I lost complete touch with the reality that was once men's clothing.

Excuse me for a moment, while I change into my leisure suit.

The Great Double-Knit Dilemma

WHEN WE'RE YOUNG, we naturally attempt to dress as our peers do, lest we be ostracized and laughed at. My wardrobe in college, for instance, consisted of the traditional khaki pants and button-down Gant shirts, a couple of V-neck sweaters, a London Fog raincoat, and a pair of Weejuns.

I also had a couple of pairs of socks, but I wore them only to funerals, weddings, or when I had to visit the dean. It was considered quite the fashion not to wear socks with Weejuns. I didn't know this when I arrived on campus at the University of Georgia, but soon after pledging a fraternity, one of my brothers in the bonds, Wally Walrus we called him, took me aside and explained the business about the socks.

The way we dressed on Deep South campuses in the sixties was, of course, quite different from the way students dressed at those schools where there was much dissent about all that was traditional. I'm happy the movement did not hit at Georgia until I was out of school; otherwise, I might have had to find a second-hand store to buy myself some blue jeans with patches and an old Army jacket, like the kids were wearing while they were taking over the administration building at Hofstra or some such place as that.

The way we dressed back then, and the way I continued to dress for several years out of school, is now called the "preppie look." This style of dress is yet the target of much derision from those who still don't understand that it does make a difference what sort of animal emblem appears on one's shirt. Some things, I would say to them, are simply the result of good breeding and cannot be explained to anyone who wears Hush Puppies.

I *would* say that, but I won't, because I admit there was a time when I became totally confused about what to wear, and there was a time when I also allowed myself to stray from tradition as far as my clothing was concerned.

I blame all this on Richard Nixon, too. How could one not go off course a bit with all the disillusionment that came with Watergate? It was about the time they caught Nixon up to his ears in justice obstructing that I went out and did something entirely crazy. I bought a new shirt that didn't have any buttons on the collar.

This particular shirt was a dress shirt, and it was sort of a light brown, as I recall. Men not only had started wearing their hair longer, but they also were wearing colorful dress shirts with no buttons on the collars. Since my peers at that point were mostly a bunch of guys who hung around local taverns and belched a lot, I was without any sort of guidance as to what currently was regarded as proper attire for a young man nearing his thirties.

It was about the same time, unfortunately, that the double-knit polyester craze hit full force. I'm not certain who invented double-knit fabrics, but rumor says it was first manufactured in a clothing plant in Fort Deposit, Alabama. This cannot be verified, however, because some years ago a mysterious fire erupted in the warehouse and 26,000 knit leisure suits were destroyed.

The owner, Delbert Gumbatz, was last seen catching the bus to Montgomery. He was wearing a Big Orange leisure suit — a favorite among Tennessee football fans. The last person to see him was the insurance man who signed the check for the fire, which, incidentally, smoldered for nearly six months.

Most everybody was wearing some sort of polyester or double-knit in those days, especially at bowling alleys and Moose Club dances. Such material was so popular, in fact, that several people were severely injured when they were trampled by a mob of shoppers in Good Sam, Ohio, who had just been informed, "Attention, K-Mart shoppers. On aisle seven tonight we have a special on men's leisure suits — all you can haul out of here for $29.95."

After I bought my brown dress shirt with no buttons on the collar, I lost complete control and bought myself a double-knit shirt. It didn't have any buttons on the collar, either, and it featured pictures of exotic-looking birds. To accent this outfit, I also purchased a pair of double-knit trousers. I looked like Marlin Perkins taking the afternoon off from hunting baboons in the wilds of Africa for Mutual of Omaha.

It could have been worse, of course. I could have bought myself a Nehru jacket and one of those medallions on a chain that people who wore Nehru jackets wore around their necks. What stopped me was an experience I had with a friend on the way to lunch one day. He was resplendent in his white Nehru jacket, a pair of white pants, and white patent-leather shoes. His medallion had a picture of Art Garfunkel on it. I was thinking how sharp he looked when three kids stopped him on the street and wanted to buy Eskimo Pies from him. Then two teen-agers thought he was the leader of some religious cult and offered their week's supply of marijuana and asked him to bless their headbands.

I chilled on the Nehru suit.

Later, I considered buying myself a leisure suit, maybe a baby blue one to wear with my Marlin Perkins jungle shirt. I went as far as going into a men's store and asking to see their selection.

"I would like to see a leisure suit," I said to the clerk, who was chewing gum and wearing enough polyester to start his own bingo parlor.

"And what color did we have in mind?" he asked me between chomps on his Juicy Fruit.

"Blue," I said.

"Navy, midnight, morning sky, or baby?" he asked.

"Baby," I said.

He brought out something from the newly-created Tennessee Ernie Ford line, perfect for a night of dining and dancing in the Billy Budd Room at the local Holiday Inn.

"It's you," said the clerk.

"No, it's not," I said. "It's a conventioneer from Nebraska sipping a pina colada and trying to get up the courage to ask a fat girl with a beehive hairdo to dance." I left the store and never considered buying a leisure suit again.

Soon, however, I was once again faced with a dilemma

concerning men's fashions: Would I, or would I not, buy myself a neck chain?

Neck chains were big in singles bars in those days. I suppose that was because women were changing, too, and they had shamelessly indicated that the sight of men's chest hairs made them tingle in places they used to deny they even had, until their husbands pressed them on their wedding nights. So men quit wearing undershirts and started leaving their shirts unbuttoned to their navels, and I suppose neck chains and medallions were a way for men not to feel their chests were totally naked.

I happen to be blessed with a great deal of chest hair, and I readily imagined myself at singles bars covered with young women who wanted to run their fingers through it. So I put on my jungle shirt, buttoned only the bottom button, and went out amongst the night.

Not a single young woman expressed a desire to run her fingers through my chest hair, but I did scare off a dog in the parking lot when he saw my shirt.

I decided a neck chain was what I was missing, so I went the next day to a jewelry store.

"Do you have chains for men?" I asked the clerk.

"You kinky devil," he said.

"I beg your pardon," I replied.

"Didn't mean to insult you," the clerk went on. "I like a little S and M myself occasionally."

"S and M?" I said, completely puzzled.

"Don't kid with me," the clerk said. "We don't have any chains here, but I know where you can get a great deal on whips and leather underwear."

I decided that perhaps I wasn't ready for neck chains just yet. Luckily, however, a friend of mine had just returned

106

from California and had the answer — a string of beads. At first, I was a bit wary of them.

"What's that around your neck?" I asked him.

"Beads," he said. "Everybody in California is wearing beads."

"Isn't that a little, well, sissy?" I asked.

"Get off my back with your macho trip," said my friend. "This is 1974."

Macho. What was this *macho*? Some sort of Mexican dish he had eaten in California? My friend explained.

"What *macho* means," he began, "is a man trying to be like John Wayne all the time — aggressive, insensitive, a slave to old traditions and old hang-ups. If a man wants to make a statement about himself, if he wants to wear a string of beads to say he is caring and sensitive and secure within himself, then he can today without fear of being stereotyped. These beads are my way of saying that I am *laid back,* man."

The entire conversation was far over my head. "Laid back?" I asked.

"Where have you been?" asked my friend. "For years, men have been taught that it's not okay for them to cry, it's not okay for them to enjoy flowers or to dress colorfully or to wear ornamental jewelry. Men who did that were — what was your term? — sissies. Well, we don't have to be like that anymore. Now, we can do our own things. Women really go for guys who can feel, who can share their thoughts, who like poetry and art and antiques and don't mind admitting it. It's even okay for a man to have a cat now."

I was taken aback by all this. True, I had been taught that a man was supposed to be strong and aggressive, and I had always despised cats.

I vowed to change my ways. I borrowed my friend's beads, bought a copy of Kahlil Gibran's *The Prophet,* and took a girl out on a date to the art museum and later to an antique store, where we browsed and looked at brass beds and old pictures of somebody else's grandparents. I thought that was very sensitive of me.

When we reached her house at the end of our date, she said, "I find you so comfortable to be with. You're so sensitive and you don't mind sharing your thoughts. You're so, well, *laid back.*"

I thought I spotted an opening and asked if I could spend the night with her.

"Silly boy," she said. "My cat would be so jealous."

These were trying times for me. With apologies to George Gobel, the world around me seemed to be a tuxedo and I was still a pair of brown shoes.

Leisure suits. Neck chains. Kinky. Macho. Laid back. Men crying and keeping company with cats. Everywhere I looked, there was upheaval and change. And more was on the way.

Women's stated interest in men's chest hairs, which led to the unbuttoned shirts and neck chains and beads, was followed by another shocking admission — they also enjoyed looking at our butts and seeing us in our underpants.

Let's begin with the underpants. The basic rules for men's underpants always had gone something like this:

After a boy-child passes the diaper stage, he moves into what is known as "grippers," or "jockey shorts." These shorts fit very tightly, since small boys have not yet reached the point where tight underwear can cause discomfort and migraine headaches. Before a boy's voice changes, it is perfectly okay for his jockey shorts to have pictures on them, as long as they're pictures of Army tanks or cowboys. Birds and flowers are totally unacceptable.

Once a boy reaches his teens and begins undressing in locker rooms in front of his friends, he still can wear jockey shorts, but forget the pictures of Army tanks and cowboys. Boys at this stage wear plain, white jockey shorts, but they have to be more careful about shorts that fit too snugly because of the aforementioned headaches.

Upon graduation, a young man is fully expected to change into boxer shorts. These shorts are white and they hit just above the knees. A young man should wear this type of undershorts for the remainder of his life, even if he eventually winds up with a truss underneath his clothing, too.

That's the way it used to be, back in a simpler time. Then came Jim Palmer.

Jim Palmer is a famous baseball pitcher who is quite handsome. Some advertising genius got the bright idea to take a picture of Jim Palmer in a pair of bikini-type underwear for men and put it in a lot of magazines. Men, or should I say those men who do not make a habit of looking at pictures of other men in their underpants, ignored these pictures of Jim Palmer, but women didn't.

They began to say to their mates such things as "Why don't you get some sexy underwear like Jim Palmer wears?"

A lot of men went out and did that, but it posed a real problem for others. What good did it do to wear Jim Palmer underwear if you happened to look like Yogi Berra?

I didn't know what to do. I had a couple of dozen pairs of normal, white boxer shorts, and even walking past a display of Jim Palmer bikini-type underpants made me feel quite silly. My wife at the time insisted, however, that I try out a pair, so I dutifully went into the men's underwear section of a large department store.

Why do they allow women to sell men's underwear?

"Can I help you with something?" asked the girl in the underwear department. I wondered if her father knew she had this job.

"Yes," I mumbled, "I would like to buy some underwear."

"And what type would you like, sir?" she went on.

"Well," I said, "I'm not really certain. Do you have any of those like what's-his-name, the baseball player, wears?"

"Oh, you mean the Jim Palmer jockey brief. Yes, we have all colors in four sizes — Small, Medium, Large, and XLC."

"XLC?"

"Extra Large Crotch," said the salesgirl.

I thought of running out the door. I would never see the salesgirl again, and I could tell my wife that when I got to the department store, there were a lot of fruity-looking characters buying Jim Palmer's underwear and I didn't want to be a part of it.

Before I could make my move, however, the salesgirl was standing in front of me with several pairs of Jim Palmer jockey briefs.

"I can see you're a little unsure, sir," she said. "Why don't you step into our dressing room and try on a pair and see how you like them?"

"Incidentally," I said, "what size are these?"

"Well," said the salesgirl, "it's only a guess, but I picked Small."

When nobody was looking, I slipped out of the dressing room and left my Jim Palmer jockey briefs there. I would explain to my wife that they were all out of my size, and she would understand. She would realize that they probably

110

didn't make many XLC's for guys, well, guys like me.

"All out of Small, huh?" replied my wife.

Jim Palmer was recently released by the Baltimore Orioles and his baseball career is likely over, so I hope he'll put his pants back on and leave the rest of us alone for awhile.

The second part of the problem, as you remember, was that women enjoyed looking at men's butts. They even had calendars with pictures of naked men showing off their buns. This feminine interest in men's hindparts led to another problem regarding the wardrobe, but first some background:

Previous to the revelation that women enjoyed the aesthetic qualities of the male hindpart, men spent little time considering the shape of their hips, much less the presentation of same. They selected a pair of trousers on the basis of comfort alone. Consequently, most men walked around in baggy pants, which offered the ultimate in comfort and free movement, but which also totally veiled the male rear and suggested on some occasions that a family of gypsies had moved out of the seat.

Women's liberation came along, however, and the baggy pants industry went bust, but a boom followed in the blue jean game.

Before, only cowboys and young men under the age of seventeen had worn blue jeans. There was an obvious reason for cowboys' wearing this attire. You can get all sorts of substances on a pair of jeans, like what cows leave all over the dusty trail, and still not have to wash them for weeks at a time ... especially if all the other cowboys' jeans are smelly, too.

Most little boys wanted to be just like the cowboys back then, so their mothers dressed them in jeans. I not only

111

wanted to be a cowboy when I was a child, I was convinced I *was* one. As a matter of fact, I was convinced I was Roy Rogers, who was my favorite western star.

Before we moved to tiny Moreland, we lived in a large apartment complex in Virginia while my father soldiered. I got lost one day. I began to cry. (Cowboys never cry unless they're five and hopelessly lost and hungry and want their mothers.) A kind lady attempted to find out where I lived so she could take me home.

"What's your name, little boy?" she asked.

"Roy Rogers," I said.

She called the resident manager's office and asked where the Rogers family lived. There was no family by that name in the apartment complex.

"Are you certain your name is Roy Rogers?" she asked me again.

"Does Trigger have a long tail?" I asked her back.

Finally, the lady began calling all the apartments asking if anybody had a retarded child who thought he was Roy Rogers. Thankfully, my mother claimed me when the lady reached her.

After high school, a male was expected to step out of his blue jeans and into a pair of baggy pants. It was in this style of dress that he then would leave home for the serious effort of educating himself further, learning a trade, or joining the armed forces, which strenuously objected to any form of tight-fitting trousers since they would deter swift movement on the battlefield.

That has all changed, however. Today, men normally have a closetful of blue jeans, because nothing shows off the hips better than a pair of tight-fitting blue jeans, and they're considered appropriate attire for practically every occasion

112

except state funerals.

Most men, raised under the old rules of loose-fitting pants, had to learn a number of new rules about buying jeans:

1. They had to remember to buy their jeans at least two inches smaller in the waist than the jeans and trousers they bought before Women's Liberation. Some jeans advertised a "skosh" more room in the seat, but I don't think they sold very well. That one little "skosh" just might be enough to cause you to go unnoticed by a gaggle of gimlet-eyed legal secretaries hip-watching during a Friday afternoon happy hour.

2. They had to remember that if they decided to bend over for any reason while wearing tight-fitting jeans, they should take a deep breath first to avoid passing out. Rule 2-A is, if you bend over and hear a ripping sound, place both hands over your backside and run backwards towards the nearest restroom. At an outdoor function, cover and run backwards towards the nearest heavy growth of kudzu.

3. It was important to note that tight-fitting jeans could be the devil to remove from your body. Men had to remember always to carry a pocketknife with them when they were wearing their tight jeans, just in case it became necessary to cut them away from their bodies in an extreme emergency ... such as if they were sick and tired of sleeping in them.

4. Men had to accept the fact that while they were wearing tight jeans, they absolutely had to hold their stomachs in at all times, even though doing so would cause their faces to turn red and their eyes to bug out (not to mention the possibility of swollen ankles).

It was in the late seventies that I finally relented and went out and bought my first pair of adult blue jeans. I was

113

surprised at the varieties available. Even the noted snooty designers Bill Blass and Calvin Klein had jeans lines, which suddenly cost what a man used to pay for a Sunday suit.

I bought myself a pair of tight-fitting Kleins and wore them out of the store and headed to the nearest singles bar. I ordered a drink and made certain I kept my backside pointed toward the tables of legal secretaries sipping pina coladas, figuring the sight of my new jeans hugging closely to my hips would knock the umbrellas right out of their glasses.

Unfortunately, no action was forthcoming. A man standing next to me in a pair of tight-fitting Bill Blass jeans finally turned to me and said, "How long you been here?"

"Couple of beers," I answered.

"Me, too," he replied. "I don't think I've gotten one glance."

There was something terribly wrong here. We had both spent half a week's salary on a pair of designer jeans that we had stuffed ourselves into, and all the women who were supposed to go wild at the sight of men's hips hadn't shown the slightest interest.

"I guess it's like my old grandpa used to say," said Bill Blass. "'It don't matter what kind of rifle you have if you ain't got any ammunition to load it with.'"

I finished my beer, went home, and cut myself out of my Calvin Klein jeans. I spent the remainder of the evening attempting to learn to breathe normally again.

* * *

I have never ceased to be amazed by the lengths men will go to satisfy a feminine whim. Take aftershave lotion. God

114

gave men Old Spice aftershave lotion, and that should have been enough. But, no. Women decided that Old Spice, which is what everybody's daddy wore, wasn't nearly the sexy aroma they wanted, and so men had another problem — What sort of aftershave should I use to set my woman's blood to boiling?

There was English Leather. You know what the sexy lady on television says about that — "My men wear English Leather ... or they wear nothing at all."

I can just see it now. I go over to have dinner with her and her parents, and I show up naked as a jaybird.

"Are you crazy?" she screams at me.

"Well," I attempt to explain, "I was all out of English Leather and the stores were closed, so like you say, either I wear English Leather or I wear...."

Somebody later figured out that what a woman really wanted to smell on a man was his natural odor with a little perfume thrown in. The upshoot of that revelation was something called "musk." I could never bring myself to splash anything called "musk" all over my face. It sounded too much like the way it smelled in the kitchen after I hadn't taken the garbage out for a week.

Pete Rose tried to get us back on track and away from all those exotic perfumed potions when he claimed "a man wants to smell like a man" and urged us all to buy Aqua Velva, first cousin to Old Spice. Of course, with Pete Rose's money, he could splash tobacco juice on his face and still make out.

The big question facing men today is, if I use Paco Rabanne cologne, will I score as much as the guys in their advertisements obviously do?

I never have actually smelled Paco Rabanne, but their

115

ads, which also appear in a number of women's magazines because women are the ones who buy most of the cosmetics for men in the first place, are something else.

Get the picture: This muscular fellow is in bed and covers are all askew. It's obvious that the only thing between him and butt-naked is the sheet he has pulled up just enough to avoid embarrassing his parents, in case they happened to stumble across the ad.

He's on the telephone, talking to the woman who spent the night with him but who had to get up early for an appointment with the board of directors. She is a totally New Woman, who doesn't want children until she has been made a partner in the firm. She also is very open about her sexuality, which means she always carries an extra tooth-brush in her handbag just in case.

In a Paco Rabanne ad, you read the dialogue between the man naked in the bed and the woman on the other end of the telephone. It goes something like this:

WOMAN: "You animal."

MAN: "I was just thinking about you."

WOMAN: "You beast."

MAN: "So it was good for you. I was embarrassed to ask."

WOMAN: "My toes are still tingling."

MAN: "Down, girl."

WOMAN: "What are you doing right now?"

MAN: "I'm naked under the sheets."

WOMAN: "You devil."

MAN: "Are you coming back over tonight?"

WOMAN: "Can Burl Ives sell tea?"

MAN: "I'll splash on a lot of Paco Rabanne."

WOMAN: "Forget my career. Forget my partnership in the firm. I'll be right over."

MAN: "Sure you don't mind?"

WOMAN: "My mind might not be sure, you hunk, but the rest of me is."

Paco Rabanne for men. What is remembered is up to you.

How are men supposed to stick to something simple like Old Spice when they can pop for a little Paco Rabanne and maybe stay naked under the sheets for weeks at a time?

Sex. It's everywhere. It's in the music, it determines what clothes we wear, and even what we splash on our faces after we shave.

Do we really have it better than our parents? Sex was simple for them. All they had to do was memorize one position and remember to turn the light off.

But sex has been a whole new ball game for my generation. I'm still not certain if a *ménage à trois* is some sort of French cooking with lots of sauce or something you do naked under the sheets with a girls' volleyball team. And with my luck, about the time I find out, I'll have ulcers and will be too old for it to really matter.

One Table Daintz To Go

SEX TODAY IS just as scrambled as everything else. You can't even talk about it without getting confused. As evidence, I present a glossary of modern sexual terms:

— LOVER: Somebody you aren't married to, but you're sleeping with them anyway.

— COHABITATION: When your lover moves into your apartment and brings all of his or her clothes and starts getting his or her mail at your address. You still aren't married but you're telling your parents that any day now you will be.

— PALIMONY: What you have to pay your ex-lover monthly, even though you never did get around to marrying her.

— GAY: Formerly "queer," "fruit," or "fag." Means you and your lover can go into the same bathroom together when you stop at service stations during long trips.

— AIDS: You and your lover can share the same hospital room together, too.

— PLATO'S RETREAT: Club in New York City where anything goes, including having sex with any number of total strangers.

— HERPES: A little something to remember your last night at Plato's Retreat by.

— RELATIONSHIP: What you tell your friends you're having with your boss because "affair" sounds so tacky.

— G-SPOT: When you touch a woman there, she makes very loud noises. The next morning the kids want to know if there was a panther in your bedroom last night.

— HUNK: What women call exceptionally attractive men.

— RICHARD GERE: Hollywood hunk who has never appeared with his shirt on for more than two minutes at a time in any of his movies.

— BATTERY STOCKS: Really have nothing to do with sex, but have you noticed how much they've gone up since modern women discovered vibrators may be used for more than soothing the tired feet they used to get from standing at the ironing board?

— *PENTHOUSE* MAGAZINE FORUM: Where readers write in to tell of their unusual sexual experiences. Many of these experiences are totally sick and perverted, and the magazine is nothing more than a blight on public decency. Nice people would never be caught reading such trash.

— *PENTHOUSE* MAGAZINE CIRCULATION: It's somewhere in the millions.

— X-RATED: Movie industry rating for film that includes explicit sex scenes.

— R-RATED: Movie industry rating for film that includes explicit sex scenes, but there is some semblance of a plot.

— PG-RATED: Movie industry rating for film where the

119

sex scenes are not quite as steamy, the plot may actually make sense, and your parents won't be totally embarrassed to watch it.

— *PLAYBOY* CHANNEL: Cable television channel that features X-rated films in your very own home and usually shows the most explicit sex scenes after your parents are asleep. The sound tracks on these films are optional, so there's no need to turn up the volume and risk awakening your parents.

— THE POPE: Powerful religious figure who recently said sex is sinful unless it's being performed for the strict purpose of procreation.

— JERRY FALWELL: Another powerful religious figure who would like to see sex done away with altogether, but he hasn't been able to come up with a viable alternative.

— JOGGING, RACQUETBALL, PLAYING *TRIVIAL PURSUIT,* AND BACKGAMMON: A few activities that have failed miserably as alternatives to sex, but people keep trying them anyway.

— S AND M: Odd sexual activity, involving whips and black leather outfits, which may be traced back to former cowboy star Lash Larue.

— KINKY: Sexual behavior involving the use of duck feathers.

— PERVERTED: You use the whole duck.

See what I mean? That's why so many sex manuals make it to the bestseller list and why the argument for sex education classes in our schools is such a good one. Perhaps if we teach our children all about sex in the schools, then they will be able to explain it to their parents.

We really didn't need sex education classes when I was in

school, because there wasn't that much to learn. You could get about all the sexual knowledge that was known at the time from an older classmate in a very short period of time ... say, just as long as it took for an older classmate to explain that all you'll ever find in a cabbage patch is cabbage and maybe a rat snake or two.

I'm not certain when sex became so confusing, but I think it was when women decided to take part in it. Frankly, I don't blame them for that, because sex — with the afore-mentioned exception of when you're sunburned and also when you're very sleepy or there's a ball game on you want to watch — can be quite a rewarding experience.

But previously, only men had sex. Women were there when all this was taking place, but theirs was basically the role of a waitress who puts the food on the table and says, "I hope you enjoy it," and then goes back to the kitchen to have a smoke.

I suspect that it was a man who got women involved in sex. It probably was the first man who made love to a woman and then wondered if it had been as pleasant for her as it had been for him, so he asked that infamous question: "Was it good for you?"

Men had never wondered that before. You didn't ask your bird dog how he enjoyed the hunting trip or your fishing worm how the water was.

I suppose our previous attitude came from the puritanical belief that sex was basically a rotten thing to do, and if a woman took some pleasure from the experience, she obviously was not the delicate flower she was supposed to be and should be tied to the dunking stool. It took women three hundred years to get over the fear that if they uttered one little sound of pleasure during sex or actually moved, they would be severely punished. I'm not certain, however, if what they feared most was the embarrassment of being dunked in public or the horror of getting their hair wet.

So when the first man asked the question, "Was it good for you?", he created a real dilemma for the woman.

If it *hadn't* been good for her and she admitted it, women's sexual liberation would have been set back another three hundred years, because her sexual partner would have gone out and told all his friends, "Aha! It's just as we expected. They really don't have any fun when they have sex."

But if she *had* enjoyed it and she said so, that same creep would have gone out and told all his friends that she was some sort of brazen hussy who actually enjoyed sex. By the time the gossip got around, the rumor would be that she had said she not only enjoyed sex but often spent ten or fifteen minutes a day thinking about it, and that kind of rumor could get you kicked out of the Junior League.

I admire that first woman who admitted she had, in fact, thoroughly enjoyed the experience of sex. It might have gone something like this:

"Sweetheart?"

"Yes, my dear?"

"May I ask you a question?"

"You want me to run to the store to get you a pack of cigarettes?"

"No, not at all. I just want to ask you a question."

"I really don't mind going to the store. I don't have to start dinner for another half hour."

"That's not it at all, sweetheart. There's just something that has been on my mind."

"You're wondering whether or not I would mind if you went bowling Friday night and then stayed out and had a few beers with the boys and came in all sloppy drunk and passed out in the floor of the living room. Of course, I don't mind, dear. I know you need some time of your own."

"That's not it at all, Sugar Love. See, some of the guys down at the plant and me were talking and this one guy wanted to know, well...."

"If I would bring my delicious brownies to the union hall for next week's meeting?"

"No, he wanted to know, uh, he just wondered if women enjoyed sex, too."

"Marvin!"

"No, Lovey, I mean it's something guys think about a lot. I mean, was what we just did, I mean, you know ... was it good for you?"

"It was great."

"It was?"

"I loved it."

"You're kidding me."

"No, I'm not. It was absolutely wonderful and let's do it again right now."

"I can't right now, Honey. I've got to run down to the plant and tell the other guys."

You can see the trouble this started. Marvin told the other guys, and then they asked their wives, and their wives said they enjoyed sex, too, and soon the word got out all over. Suddenly women all over the world were no longer ashamed to admit their interest in lovemaking, and that's how the sexual revolution began.

The sexual revolution may have liberated women sexually, but it put a great deal of heretofore unfelt pressure on men. Sometime after the first publication of *Playgirl* magazine, where handsome men posed nude for the now-

123

accepted prurient interests of women, women not only were admitting to men that they enjoyed sex, but they were answering the was-it-good-for-you question honestly. Men never have been the same sexually since.

"Sweetheart?"

"Yes, Marvin."

"Was it good for you?"

"Want to know the truth?"

"Of course, my sweet."

"No."

"Do what?"

"It wasn't good for me at all. In a recent article in *Cosmopolitan*, eight out of every ten women polled said their sexual partners did not engage in enough foreplay, were not sensitive enough to the female's needs, and insisted the lights be turned off."

"How would you have voted in that poll, my pet?"

"Turn on the lights, Speedy Gonzales, and I'll show you my ballot."

After this, of course, men had to take special care to please their sexual partners, and this was not an easy thing for them to do because of their backgrounds, and because very few of them read *Cosmo*.

This pressure also resulted in some men suffering from impotence and in the eventual creation of ESPN, the twenty-four-hour all-sports cable television network, which gives men something to do at night after their sexual partners have begun holding up rating cards like judges at diving meets. This, of course, eventually causes them to be too nervous to do anything but watch rodeos and college hockey games on the tube until three in the morning.

The sexual revolution and the revelation that women

actually enjoyed being part of the sexual experience also sent sex into a fad stage, where it remains to this day.

Having simple sex isn't enough anymore. The various sex manuals have revealed there are many kinky positions in which to have sex, such as with your favorite shortstop in the dirt part of the infield so you won't get all scratched up on the artificial turf, and there are all sorts of extracurricular activities that may be interwoven with the sex act.

Today's trendy magazines are filled with examples and instructions regarding such matters. Read the *Penthouse* Forum, for example, and you will wonder if you're the only person left alive on earth who hasn't had sex while riding in a Ferris wheel or standing on your head at a Tupperware party.

It seems that something new and confusing comes out everyday with regard to sex.

And for somebody like me, who was reared in the sexual naiveté of the fifties and who always had a great deal of trouble understanding and getting along with women in the first place, the entire sexual scene has become totally baffling and frustrating.

I'm not certain how I should act around women anymore in order to attract their attention or to arouse any sort of physical interest in me.

I've tried to be sensitive at times by pouring my beer into a glass before I drink it, but all this usually gets me is a long discussion about how her ex-husband used to make love with his socks on.

I've also tried to be like Clint Eastwood and stare at her with my cold yet lusty eyes and not say very much, but all this usually leads to is my being terribly uncomfortable. I mean, sooner or later a man needs to go to the bathroom, but you never saw Clint Eastwood putting the move on a beautiful woman and suddenly announcing that he had to go to the bathroom. He's much too cool for that. Of course, the reason he's always clenching his teeth and has that stern look about him is that he hasn't been to the bathroom in a week, and it's killing him.

I never know what to say to girls in bars anymore, either. Bogart and those guys used to walk over to a woman, light her cigarette, and say, "Sweetheart, where have you been all my life?" and that was it. My generation countered with, "What's your sign?" and "I hate to see anybody drink alone," but then women wised up to those. Now, I think the only men who ever meet women in bars and something actually comes of it are those weirdos who write to *Penthouse* Forum:

"I'm twenty-three and quite a handsome guy, if I do say so myself, and let me tell you what happened to me one recent night when I was on a business trip to Toledo.

"I walked into a bar and there was this gorgeous blonde, wearing a tight-fitting pink sweater and black leather pants and roller skates, standing alone nursing a pina colada.

"I took a spot next to her at the bar and ordered myself a gin and Pepsi. She took off her Sony Walkman and skated closer to me. I could feel her hot breath with the faint scent of coconut against my flushed face.

"We finished our drinks, and without saying a word, this voluptuous creature and I walked (she skated) out of the bar and went back to my hotel room.

"I have never spent such a night of ecstasy. She took off all my clothes and tied me to the bed with a rope she carried in her handbag, and then she skated up and down on me until I was driven out of my mind with passion.

126

"The next morning, my back looked like they had run the Indy 500 time trials on it, but I will never forget the gorgeous blonde at the bar, and now every time I see Roller Derby on television, I'm aroused. I would be interested to know if any of your other readers have ever had such an experience."

Not me, although a girl did nearly run me down on her Harley one afternoon outside a bowling alley in Houston.

Women are simply too sexually aware today for anybody to sweep them off their feet, especially in a bar where they dress seductively and go to see how many men they can reduce to sniveling idiots. It has been my experience that such women especially enjoy making vulnerable, recently-divorced men feel as though they need to go back immediately and crawl under the rock from which they obviously sprang. This story requires a little background:

I got one of my divorces when I was living in Chicago. I distinctly remember the conversation with my wife when I first learned that she was terribly unhappy being married to me. I called home one evening from work.

"Hi, sweetheart," I began. "What's for dinner?"

"What did you do for dinner before you got married?"

"What kind of question is that?"

"A perfectly good question. What did you do for dinner before you got married?"

"Ate a lot of fish sticks. Why?"

"Here's a hint: Frozen fish sticks are on sale at the Jewell Store. I'd advise you to stop there on your way home."

That was just her funny way of saying she was splitting.

Years later, I figured the whole thing out. Being a house-wife had caused her to lose her identity, and what she needed was to find her own space and establish a relationship with someone who didn't mind preparing fish sticks for *her* once in a while.

At the time, however, I was yet languishing in the idea that it should be enough for a woman that I worked hard and provided for her and didn't talk ugly about her kinfolks. That belief I had picked up from role models during my youth. The old people at home would talk about marriage and the duties of the partners in such conversations as this:

"Heard Clovis Niles is gettin' married."

"Who to?"

"Grover Turnipseed."

"He's a fine boy."

"Don't drink much."

"Works hard, too."

"Don't lay out in beer joints all night."

"Owns his own double-wide trailer."

"He'll make a good provider."

"She's a good cook."

"Sews, too."

"And cans."

In the seventies, of course, women began to want a lot more than a man who owned his own double-wide, but somehow I missed that announcement. So there I was, stuck in Chicago, the snows of winter just around the end-of-October corner, my wife gone, and fish sticks up to my ears.

I had very little luck getting dates in Chicago after my wife left. The biggest problem was that when I went into singles bars on Division Street, I usually was confronted by a lot of people wearing huge furry coats and hats and gloves — they were still trying to thaw out from the cold on the sidewalks outside. (Chicago is the coldest place on earth where polar bears don't roam free.)

The drawback to all that cold-weather gear was that it was often difficult to determine male from female. Everybody looks basically alike when they're dressed like Nanook of the North. That's why Eskimos spend a lot of time cutting holes in the ice and fishing — it's safer than making the wrong move in the igloo and winding up putting the make on the guy with whom you share your kayak.

My next problem, once I had distinguished the men from the women, was my previously admitted inability to think of anything clever to say to a total stranger in a bar. This problem was amplified by the fact that Chicago women — know affectionately as "Michigan Avenue Marauders" — were anything but gentle to poor souls like myself, who were simply looking for someone with whom to huddle against the cold.

Imagine this scene: I'm lonely and far from home. My wife has split and I'm crawling all over thirty, and whatever speed I once had on my singles bar fastball is now only a memory. But a man has to try. A man simply has to try.

She's sitting there on a stool at the bar at Butch McGuire's, and for some girl who's probably from Indiana and works for an advertising firm, she's not bad at all. (She could have been from North Dakota and pumped gas, for all I cared at the time.)

"Gee, it's cold outside," I used as an ice-breaker, if you will.

"What was your first clue, Dick Tracy?"

"That's cute. Could I buy you a drink?"

"Suit yourself."

"What will you have?"

"Cutty rocks."

"Cutty rocks, bartender. I like these Irish bars, don't you?"

"They're okay. Except you have to talk to a lot of weirdos."

"Speaking of Irishmen, hear the one about the two Irish gays?"

"No, but I get the feeling I'm going to."

"Yeah, there was Michael Fitzpatrick and Patrick Fitzmichael. Get it?"

"Thanks for the drink, Tex. I gotta catch the train to Skokie."

There was one night in Butch's when I thought I finally had scored. She was a lovely thing, standing over at the corner of the bar. Just to be sure, I looked down at her feet. She was wearing pink galoshes. Normally, the men in Chicago, even the strange ones, don't wear pink galoshes.

She was staring at me. I was certain of it. I continued to glance over at her. Each time our eyes met, she smiled. This was it! All I had to do was walk over, introduce myself, hit her with a few quick stories, and I would be in.

I didn't want to rush it, however. I ordered myself another drink, casually lit a cigarette, blew out a couple of perfectly-formed smoke rings, and tried to look slightly bored, so that when I said to her, "I really hate these kinds of places; they're nothing but meat markets," she would not doubt my sincerity.

When I thought the time was right, I strolled toward her. Her eyes were still staring directly into mine, her lips curved in a knowing smile.

"I really hate these kinds of places; they're nothing but meat markets," I began.

"I hope you don't mind if I tell you something," the lady said.

130

"I know you don't usually come on to men like this," I replied, trying to make her feel at ease with her obvious advances. "But don't feel bad about it. It's okay for a woman to do things like that today. We aren't living in the Stone Age anymore, you know."

That would do it, of course. She would recognize me as a very aware person — sensitive, caring, with a beast inside me somewhere, just waiting for the right woman to come along and awaken it.

"I don't want to embarrass you," the woman said, "but your fly is open."

I went back to my apartment, crawled under the bed, assumed the fetal position, and had a nervous breakdown.

* * *

One of the things militant feminists say about men is that we feel threatened by the new feminine aggressiveness and assertiveness. They're right, especially when they say things like that about men who remember women the way they used to be.

We're terribly confused about what women want us to do, when they want us to do it, and for how long. And we aren't certain that one day they aren't going to ditch us altogether, when somebody invents a computer that can do about three or four things at once with the proper mixture of tenderness and boldness, and after women are finished using it, it won't roll over and snore and keep them awake all night.

Do you know what's making a comeback in this country on the sex front? Strip joints, that's what. Strip joints are making a comeback because men can go in there an ogle and whistle and make all those remarks they learned in the

Navy, and the women won't get angry and call their sisters-in-arms and cause the men all sorts of embarrassment and bodily pain.

I wandered into a place one night in Memphis called The Yellow Pussycat. All around me were young women. They were quite naked and they were dancing. I ordered myself a drink and began to watch. Soon, I was approached by one of the young women who had been dancing.

"Wanta table daintz?" she asked. ("Daintz" is the way "dance" comes out when a naked Southern girl with a mouthful of gum says it.)

"What's a table dance?" I asked.

She rolled her eyes as if to ponder what primitive means of transportation recently had dropped me at this address.

"You pay me seven dollars," she said, "and I daintz on your table."

"A sort of private dance, huh?" I probed.

She rolled her eyes again. "Others can watch if they want to," she explained, "but they won't get to see nothin' up close like you will."

Good sport that I am, I paid the seven bucks and experienced my first table dance. The problem was that I am easily embarrassed and often feel quite self-conscious in public, and here I was — a total stranger in a place that obviously wasn't the Christian Science Reading Room, and a young woman I never had seen before in my life was dancing on my table, often moving close enough for me to see the innermost construction of her navel.

I didn't want to stare directly at her and appear like some old lecher, but on the other hand, I had paid the seven bucks and felt obliged to get my money's worth by watching every twitch and strut.

132

Had we been sipping wine alone together and Table Daintzer had suddenly been so moved by the music and the passion and the subsequent giddiness that she had climbed atop a nearby table to disrobe and move sensuously to the music, I would have thoroughly enjoyed the experience. In this setting, however, I was more than uncomfortable.

After the table dance was mercifully over, she asked me if I wanted another, and I said, "Thank you, but no." Then she said that if I would buy her a bottle of champagne (she split the cost with the house twenty-eighty, she explained, and needed the money in order to pay for her little sister's operation), she would join me at my table and we could talk.

Naturally, I wanted to help all I could with her little sister's operation, so I ordered the champagne and we sat and talked. It was the first time I had had a conversation with a woman in years that we didn't have to discuss her career.

I admit openly and without shame that I am intimidated by today's modern woman. The female role models I had as a child were my mother, who still made homemade biscuits in the morning, and my teachers, who were too busy teaching me how to long divide to tell me that when I grew up, women would be drinking and smoking and sweating in public and telling dirty jokes and would punch you in the mouth if you made a remark they deemed sexist.

Women didn't sweat, or at least I didn't think they did, until the late sixties. I went to school with little girls who wore sundresses and thought it terribly unfeminine to engage in any sort of activity that might indicate they hadn't been born with their sweat glands nailed completely shut, so they could grow up to be cheerleaders and could lift their hands to clap and not be concerned that somebody would see wet spots under their arms. There was even the axiom that "horses sweat, men perspire, and women *glow.*"

That didn't change in college, either. The girls there wore cute little outfits and were in school to find husbands. The only ones who were in school to learn anything were the ones who wore thick glasses and played horn. They all eventually grew up to become militant feminists, of course, and they're getting back at us now for all those years the rest of us were busy having parties and picking mates, while they were down at the music room blowing into a stupid trumpet or tuba. The fact that most militant feminists wear thick glasses and have pooched-out lips from too many nights of blowing into horns is proof of my contention.

It was sweat, I think, that finally led to most women's casting aside their previous role as demure little things, to be left in the kitchen while the men withdrew to the study for cigars and brandy to discuss the pros and cons of the designated hitter.

I saw it coming in 1968. The University of Georgia at that time was intent on keeping passion to a minimum on campus. The free-sex movement had started on some Northern campuses, but at Georgia, students had remained in the political and moral status quo. Once you gave a girl your fraternity pin, you might expect a little something more than a kiss goodnight — especially if Georgia had won its football game that week — but nobody ever was late for botany class because they had lost track of the time during a heated moment of noonday passion.

One of the ways the university attempted to keep the status quo was by not allowing coeds to walk around campus in their gym shorts after P.E. classes, thus tempting male students.

134

For years coeds never muttered a sound about this rule. After P.E., they simply put their raincoats around their gym outfits and went to their next class. They never complained in hot weather, of course, because since *ladies* didn't sweat and smell gamey, walking around in a raincoat didn't bother them, even if they had just completed a rousing game of volleyball and the temperature was over ninety degrees.

In the spring of 1968, however, a young coed named DeLores Perkwater, who wore thick glasses and played horn, passed out in class from heat exposure following her gym session. When they took her raincoat off, they noticed she was perspiring profusely.

Even the more demure coeds from the finest sororities subsequently decided that making them wear raincoats after gym class was cruel and unusual punishment, and the first notice I had of what was to come in the feminist movement occurred soon after. A number of slogan-chanting Georgia coeds, marching in the name of DeLores Perkwater, took over the administration building and refused to leave until the university rescinded the gym shorts rule.

Officials might have won out, but the protest took place late in spring quarter, and after the coeds had been inside the administration building (which was not air-conditioned at the time) for several days without benefit of bathing, the atmosphere became so pungent that the university decided to give in.

"Coeds Free To Sweat!" screamed the headlines in the school newspaper, and soon women all over the country began sweating in public and thinking nothing of it. This eventually led women to begin exercising, building their bodies, and applying for jobs as construction workers and goat ropers and all sorts of other jobs previously performed

135

by men only.

Once women began to do all that, there was no stopping them. And they owe it all to DeLores Perkwater, now commander of the 14th Bomber Wing of the National Organization of Women.

* * *

I'm not certain what my own future will be regarding women. I am currently single, and I don't know what sort of woman I would want to marry if ever I married again.

I still would like to have a wife who cooks a meal occasionally, even if she happens to be the governor. I still like women who don't know everything that I know, so I can tell them something occasionally and they can look at me like I'm quite intelligent. In other words, I want a woman who I stand at least an even chance at beating in a game of *Trivial Pursuit* and who doesn't understand the infield fly ruie, so I can take her to baseball games and put my arm around her and say things like, "Well, sweetheart, it's like this...."

I do not want a woman who has hairy legs like mine. I don't want a woman who is in any shape or form involved in the martial arts, and I don't want a woman who comes to bed smelling like a can of Penzoil because her hobby is rebuilding race cars for the Junior Johnson racing team.

I don't want a woman who introduces me to all sorts of strange sexual techniques that she picked up on a recent business trip to the Orient. I don't want a woman who knees me in the belly when I forget to put the top back on the toothpaste, and I don't want a woman who gets into drinking bouts with Marine recruits and maintains a winning percentage.

136

It's the same old problem for me: I want a woman like women were in 1962, because I remember them as being soft and nice to hold and, like Merle Haggard said, they could still cook back then and still would. I don't mind if girls grow up to be president these days, and I don't think women should be given smaller wages simply because they're women, but what do I do with these old-fashioned feelings that were instilled in me? What can I do about the fact that a woman in a coat and tie carrying a briefcase doesn't do much for me in the area of physical attraction? I didn't come here to take out a loan, madam, I wanted to hug you and kiss you on your mouth.

What I'm doing here is dilly-dallying around. I know exactly what I want in a woman.

I want a woman who was raised in a rural atmosphere and whose mother taught her to bake pies and fry chicken and make gravy and iced tea.

I want her to have no ambition beyond making me very happy and comfortable, including giving me back rubs at night and not complaining when I keep the television on until two in the morning watching a ball game from the West Coast.

I want her to be good to my dog, and I want her to take her own overheads when we play tennis and to lob when I tell her to. I want her to be open and willing sexually, but I don't want her to insist on anything acrobatic that could cause me to have a back injury or get an eye put out.

I want her to like country music and at least understand the basics of college football as it is played in major conferences, and I want her to make devilled eggs to carry to the games for the pre-game brunch, and if it happens to rain, I don't want to hear, "How much longer is this thing

137

going to last?"

I want her to pop me popcorn on cold nights when we're sitting in front of the fire. I want her to make certain there always is cold beer in the ice box and that I never run out of clean underwear. I want her to talk sweetly to me on mornings after I've made a fool out of myself at a party and have a terrible hangover, and I want her to be afraid of spiders and call me to come squish them when she sees one running across the floor in the kitchen.

The sad truth is that I have known and have had such women, but for one reason or other, I have let them get away. I'm not certain there are very many like them left, and it probably would serve me right if I wound up with DeLores Perkwater.

In the midst of this dilemma, I always harken back to the words of my boyhood friend and idol, Weyman C. Wannamaker, Jr., a great American, who once surveyed the changing scene of the roles for women and said, "The whole thing boils down to the fact that the opposite sex ain't nearly as opposite as it used to be."

To further complicate the matter of sex in the 1980s, of course, we are a society attempting to deal with the gay movement. I cannot quote Weyman on his thoughts regarding the gay movement, because he is not at all tolerant in that area. Okay, maybe just one quote:

"All you hear about these days," says Weyman, "is them queers (I'm sorry, but Weyman refuses to say *gay* and it took me months to get him to tone it down to *queer*) and how they have all come out of the closet. I'll tell you one thing — I bet it was a mess in that closet when they were all back up in there together."

Weyman's basic problem with the gay movement, and

138

mine as well, is that we have had no background whatsoever in dealing with something that seems quite unnatural, occasionally appalling, and, even in my most tolerant moments, something that I one day might be able to accept but never understand.

As far as I know, the first gay person I ever saw was a waiter in a spiffy Atlanta restaurant. I'm not certain why, but it seems there is an overabundant number of effeminate young men working in spiffy restaurants these days. Now, I understand that just because a male is effeminate, it doesn't necessarily mean that he's gay, and just because a man may come on as a rugged, macho-type, it doesn't necessarily mean that he's straight. However (and I promise this is the last time I'm going to quote Weyman on such a sensitive issue), when I see a young man sashay over to me in a spiffy restaurant, and he just sort of floats when he walks and he's what we used to call prissy, I cannot help but harken back to what Weyman says when he sees somebody like that: "Damn, but if I don't believe that ol' boy's about half-queer."

Anyway, some years ago I went into a restaurant, and a young man fitting the above description prissed over to my table and said in a delicate voice, "Hi, I'm Keith, and I'll be your waiter this evening." He sort of put a question mark on the end of "evening," ending his pronouncement with a bit of a wrist movement that you never see from the grill man at an all-night truckstop.

I didn't know exactly what to say, so I said, "Hi there, Keith, I'm Lewis and I'll be your customer."

All that straight, he began by telling me and my party about what *wasn't* on the menu. (I don't know why spiffy restaurants never put their good stuff on the menu, but they don't.)

139

"Tonight," said Keith, "we have some absolutely *sker-rump-tious* specials."

With that, he delivered an entire litany of dishes I had never heard of. When I said I'd just have the ground sirloin steak, well done, and some fries, he looked at me with a beady-eyed smirk as if to say, "How on earth did someone so uncivilized find my table?"

I think that's what I dislike most about going into an overpriced restaurant and having to deal with gay waiters: If you don't order something that sounds like it ought to have a part in a film with subtitles, gay waiters look at you like you've just broken wind. I try never to break wind in a restaurant, which is why I never order anything that might start my gastronomic network into embarrassing emissions.

There weren't any gay people in Moreland when I was growing up. We thought there was one once, and that led to months of gossip and suspense, but it turned out to be a false alarm.

There was this kid named Donnelle Spinks, who was about my age. His mother named him after his great aunt Donnelle, because he was her eighth and final child and she already had produced seven boys, all ugly and quite useless, and she had prayed for a girl. When Donnelle was born and turned out to be quite male, she figured she would simply make up for the Lord's obvious mistake.

She dressed Donnelle in girl's clothes until he started school and put ribbons in his hair and bought him dolls, and she would have taught him to sew and given him piano lessons had Mr. Spinks not eventually put his foot down. Donnelle, however, had to face terrible abuse from his classmates because of his name and the way he walked — it was aptly described as walking like he was trying to carry a corncob in his crack.

Donnelle also had a rather effeminate voice with a slight lisp, and when it was discovered during a recess baseball game that his throw back to the cut-off man in the infield was delivered with the wristy technique of a girl, he was further branded as "queer as a rooster that wouldn't set foot in the henhouse."

Donnelle took the blows and the nasty comments until one afternoon in the sixth grade, when Alvin Bates, a smart-aleck teacher's pet, began to chide him on the playground near where the second graders were swinging on the monkey bars.

"Hey, Donelle," said Alvin, "your mother still puttin' dresses on you?"

Donnelle was used to this sort of thing, of course. He continued to do what he always did when somebody started the queer business with him — he ignored Alvin.

But then Alvin got nasty. "Hey, Donnelle," he said, "you going to play dolls after school today?"

Donnelle was still ignoring Alvin, who hadn't had enough.

"Hey, Donnelle, you a boy or a girl?"

"Quit picking on him, Alvin," said Betty Ann Hillback, who had performed a duet with Donnelle in the piano class recital.

"What's he going to do about it, Betty Ann?" asked Alvin. "Why don't you go hide in a closet and improve the scenery around here?"

Suddenly, unexpectedly, Donnelle was walking towards Alvin. "You can't talk to her that way," he said.

"What're you going to do about it, queer boy?" Alvin replied.

Betty Ann, the nervous type, had begun to cry.

"Tell her you're sorry for saying that," Donnelle demanded of Alvin.

"Who's going to make me?"

"Tell her."

"Kiss my...."

It all happened so quickly. Donnelle pounced on Alvin and inflicted facial wounds by the dozens. Donnelle then dragged Alvin over to the monkey bars, doubled him over one, and began giving him a series of quick kicks to his rear. Alvin soon was more than ready to apologize to Betty Ann for his insult.

Later, Alvin told the teacher that Donnelle Spinks had beaten him up, and the teacher called Mr. Spinks in to discuss the violent behavior of his son.

They say that after Mr. Spinks found out Donnelle had severely thrashed another boy on the school playground, he and his son became much closer, and Mr. Spinks bought Mrs. Spinks a little poodle dog, so she would still have something to pet now that Donnelle had become Don and had taken up the habit of walking to church with Betty Ann Hillback and holding her hand. That's when we knew for sure that Donnelle wasn't gay.

Today, I have too much trouble dealing with my own problems in the area of sexual relations to spend a great deal of time being concerned with those of others. That's why if someone chooses to be gay — or can't help it — that's fine with me ... as long as they don't attempt to do whatever gay people do near where I'm eating, watching a movie or a ball game, or attempting to fish, because such antics can be terribly distracting.

I would suggest that if gay people — who seem to have

become more and more vocal and more prone to displays of public affection as their numbers and acceptance into the mainstream have grown — have the sudden urge to love on one another and they can't find a motel room or the backseat of a car parked off in the woods somewhere, they should go back into the closet. It won't be for long, and they can come right back out when they're done.

I also am against gay people as a political force, because it's not wise to mix sex and politics. Had our forefathers known what was going to happen to American sex, they likely would have put something in the Constitution about separation of sex and politics; then sixteen-year-old pages in the House of Representatives could have gone into the cloakroom alone without fear of being accosted by heavy-breathing lawmakers.

On the other side of the coin, had we had a Constitutional dictum against sex and politics, we might also have been spared John and Rita Jenrette, who tried their darnedest to give heterosexuality a bad name ... and with all of us following the sordid saga on television.

10 Eddie Haskell Is Still A Jerk

I MENTIONED EARLIER that Phil Donahue and his television show have been a great source of consternation for me. Five mornings a week, Donahue gets together with a crowd of women who live in Chicago and apparently have nothing better to do, and they discuss strange things.

One morning recently, for example, his guests were two homosexual women and a baby. The two homosexual women, who said they were very much in love, had decided they wanted a baby, so one of them was artificially inseminated with the sperm of the other's brother, and the baby on the program was the result.

One of the homosexual women was black and the other was white, and I think they named the baby something like "Joy" or "Mud." I only remember that the baby didn't have a regular name like we used to give children — a name like Randy or Arlene.

I frankly don't care if a black female homosexual and a white female homosexual decide to love each other, but I do

144

have some concern for the offspring. Having been conceived in such an unconventional manner and having been given a name that would embarrass a dog, I wonder if the child will have the desire or the opportunity to do the things that are important to most children — such as playing Little League baseball, eating crayons in school, or laughing at a clown.

What bothers me about this situation in particular, and about the Donahue show in general, is where all this might lead. Television today is probably the greatest single influence on the American public. A recent study showed that the average TV in this country is on six hours and fifty-five minutes a day; that's almost forty-nine hours a week. In a ten-year period, that's almost three years of watching TV! It's not surprising, therefore, that in many cases society has become what it watches.

So my question is this: Will all these televised discussions of aberrant lifestyles eventually make such behavior completely acceptable, and will people start producing babies with home chemistry sets and giving them names that will make it difficult for them to survive when they enter the Marine Corps?

Actually, my problems with television didn't begin with Donahue. After my Aunt Jessie, who lived next door, brought home the first television I could watch on a regular basis, it took me a year to figure out that Howdy Doody was a puppet. I presumed he had once suffered from some sort of crippling disease, and that was why he walked funny. He also had a strange mouth, which I attributed to not brushing regularly. When Howdy talked, the entire bottom portion of his mouth moved like he was trying to eat a large cantaloupe. Whole.

Finally I noticed the strings attached to him. It was like the day I found out there is no Santa Claus and the day somebody told me they heard Lash Larue was in a porno film. It broke my heart. You know kids, though. I couldn't wait to tell everybody I knew of my discovery.

"Howdy Doody isn't real," I told one of my classmates at school.

"Yes, he is," he replied.

"No, he isn't. He's just a puppet. Somebody pulls his strings and that's what makes him walk and talk."

The kid started crying. I didn't dare tell him that Clarabelle's big red nose was probably fake, too.

Soon I discovered "Superman." I enjoyed watching "The Man of Steel," but I had some problems with him, too. In the first place, I never thought Superman's disguise as Clark Kent was all that clever. Lois Lane had to be a bigger dummy than Howdy Doody not to see right through it.

Whenever Superman decided to become Clark Kent, all he did was put on a coat and tie and a pair of glasses. That's a disguise? Superman and Clark Kent talked exactly the same, were the same height and weight, and if Lois had been any kind of reporter at all, she probably would have noticed that they had the same mole or freckle or other telltale body markings.

In retrospect, Lois Lane had no business working for *The Daily Planet*. She should have been on the obit desk in Topeka.

Something else used to bother me about the "Superman" show. Anytime "The Man of Steel" had a social misfit cornered, the crook would pull out a gun and fire six shots at Superman's chest. Of course, bullets just bounced off, because you couldn't hurt Superman.

146

Even as a kid, I knew what I would have done after that. I would have gone quietly. But not the crooks on "Superman." After watching their bullets bounce harmlessly away, they would throw their guns at him. Anybody knows you don't further rile a man whom six bullets couldn't stop by throwing your gun at him.

* * *

There were a lot of family shows on television in those early days. There was "The Donna Reed Show," for example. Donna was always so pleasant. I wonder why she never had that-time-of-the-month problems like other women?

"Father Knows Best," another great family show, was one of my favorites. Even so, I used to wonder why Robert Young never took his tie off. When he came home from a long day at the insurance office, he would keep his tie on and replace his jacket with a sweater. He did the same thing later as Marcus Welby, and remember that you never saw him without a tie on when he wound up selling Sanka. He may have been the only man in history to wear a tie more than Richard Nixon.

"Leave It to Beaver" also was a big hit. In fact, it still is. "Leave It to Beaver" reruns are on several cable stations today, and a fellow named Irwyn Applebaum has even written a book entitled, "The World According to Beaver." The book contains examples of the sort of dialogue that was featured on the show. Here's one between Wally and his friend, the ever-obnoxious Eddie Haskell.

EDDIE: "Come on, Sam, time's a-wastin'."

WALLY: "Look, Eddie, I can't go with you guys today. I've got to work out in the yard."

EDDIE: "Work in the yard? Aw, come off it! We got ... Oh, good morning, Mr. and Mrs. Cleaver."

JUNE: "Hello, Eddie."

WARD: "Good morning, Eddie."

EDDIE: "Well, if you've got work to do, Wallace, I don't want to interfere. I was reading an article in the paper just the other day, and it said a certain amount of responsibility around the home is good character training. Well, good-bye, Mr. and Mrs. Cleaver."

WARD: *"Good-bye,* Eddie."

EDDIE (whispering): "Can I talk to you outside, Wally?"

WALLY: "Okay, Eddie, what's up?"

EDDIE: "Come on, Moe, drop the hoe. Lumpy's out in the car and we're ready to roll."

WALLY: "I told you, Eddie. I can't. I got work to do."

EDDIE: "Come on, Isabel, you gonna let your mother and father push you around? Why don't you read them the child labor law?"

WALLY: "Hey, Eddie, isn't it about the time of year you're supposed to shed your skin?"

I take a certain amount of comfort in knowing that Eddie Haskell comes off as just as big a jerk today as he did twenty years ago. There are so few elements of life that have gone unchanged in that period.

"The Adventures of Ozzie and Harriet" was another classic of those timid times. There was Ozzie and Harriet and David and Ricky, and they lived in a big house and everybody was happy and problems were easy to solve. Television of the fifties rarely dealt with anything more intricate than a husband forgetting an anniversary or a wife burning dinner for the husband's boss.

In those days, Ozzie was always around to talk over problems with David and Ricky. As a matter fact, I still don't know what Ozzie did for a living; I never recall his going to work. If they did "The Adventures of Ozzie and Harriet" today, Ozzie probably would be a dope dealer.

* * *

There are a lot of things I miss about television the way it used to be. I'll take John Cameron Swayze over Peter Jennings on a big story any day, and has there ever been a better detective than Sargeant Joe Friday on "Dragnet"?

Joe Friday didn't waste a lot of time keeping Los Angeles free of crime on his program. All he wanted was the facts. Today, television cops get involved in a lot of extracurricular activities, such as fooling around with women.

(Fact: Jack Webb, who played Joe Friday, died not long ago of a heart attack. Maybe he should have taken a few days off occasionally and gone to Pismo Beach with a girlfriend.)

"Amos 'n' Andy" was a favorite at my aunt's house. George "Kingfish" Stevens was always trying to con Andrew H. Brown, and sooner or late the Kingfish would end up in court with his lawyer, Algonquin J. Calhoun, representing him:

"Yo' Honor, it's easy for the prosecutor to talk that way about my client, George Stevens. It's easy 'cause my client is a crook, Yo' Honor!"

"Amos 'n' Andy" was classic humor, but unfortunately we can't watch it on television today. It's allegedly racist.

That's just another example of how confusing the modern world has become. I can't watch "Amos 'n' Andy" because it's racist, but it's okay to watch "Sanford and Son," which is filled with racist situations and remarks.

Remember the time Fred had to go to the dentist? He found out that the dentist was black and insisted on having a white man work on his mouth. And don't forget his classic line, "There ain't nothin' uglier than an old white woman."

There must be some big difference in the two programs, but I swear I can't see it. Maybe it's a matter of perspective.

I remember several years ago when I was working in Chicago, the nation's most segregated city, and caught a cab home one night after work. The cab driver was black, and we began to talk.

"Where you from?" he asked.

"Atlanta."

"Thought so," he said. "I'm from Mississippi."

Here it comes, I figured. A black cabbie is about to give me a lecture on how much better life is away from the racist jackals of the South.

"I'm going back one of these day," he said instead.

I was startled. "You don't like it here?"

"People ain't the same up here," he said. "In Mississippi, they always let you know where you stand. They put up signs down there that say, 'No Niggers Allowed.' Up here, they don't put up no signs. They just let you walk into a place and then tell you you can't stay. I liked it better when I knew ahead of time where I was wanted."

I guess that's how I feel about television these days. I liked it better when I knew what was okay to laugh at and what wasn't.

It is modern television, in fact, that has helped to foster the two most offensive Southern stereotypes — the racist redneck and the belligerent country sheriff. And nothing irritates me more than to see Southerners being portrayed on television by actors or actresses who can't speak the

150

language.

Take *y'all,* for instance. Southerners never say *you all,* and even if we did, we wouldn't use it in the singular sense. The proper word, used when speaking to two or more others, is a contraction, *y'all.*

On television, however, some honey from the Bronx who has landed a part as a Southern belle inevitably says to her lover, "Why don't *you all* come ovuh heah and sit down by lil' ol' me."

I doubt that "Amos 'n' Andy" was near the embarrassment to blacks that yankees trying to portray Southerners is to Southern whites.

* * *

Television actually was responsible for my first encounter with discrimination, because it brought major league baseball into my life.

For the first time, I could *see* Mantle and Musial and Williams and Snider. I became a hardcore Dodger fan — they were still in Brooklyn then — and consequently developed a keen hatred for the Yankees.

I mentioned my love for the Dodgers one day to a cousin, who happened to be a Yankee fan. "The Dodgers!" he said, almost spitting out the words. "They're a nigger team!"

Perhaps I had overheard the older folks talking, or perhaps I had read something in the newspapers about Jackie Robinson, the first black man in major league baseball, but I never considered it when pledging my allegiance to the Dodgers. So when my older cousin made what was obviously a derogatory remark, I was hurt and confused. I pressed my cousin for more information, but all he would

151

say was, "Niggers ain't got no business playing major league ball."

I decided to take the question to my mother. "Do niggers have any business playing major league ball?" I asked her.

"The word," she said in her sternest schoolteacher voice, "is *knee-grow*. I don't ever want to hear you say that other word in this house."

Fine, but that didn't answer the question. Frankly, I was more interested in baseball than in race relations at the time.

"I don't know anything about baseball, son," she said, "but your daddy played with Negroes in the service."

That settled it. If my father had played with Negroes, then there was no problem with Jackie Robinson playing with the Dodgers. Besides, all I wanted Robinson to do was help beat the Yankees, which is exactly what he did in the 1955 World Series.

I was so thankful for the Dodger victory that I said a prayer in church, reasoning that God, in all His infinite wisdom, certainly must be a Dodger fan, too.

* * *

Parents today are concerned that their children see too much sex and violence on television. There wasn't any sex to speak of on TV when I was a child, unless you count watching lady wrestlers tumble around with one another in those tight-fitting outfits they used to wear.

There was violence, but the victims usually deserved the thrashings they got.

Johnny Mack Brown walks into a saloon in the Five O'Clock Movie and says, "Gimme a milk." Heroes in those days didn't drink liquor, you recall.

152

"Milk?" laughs an ornery galoot standing next to JMB at the bar. "Here, tenderfoot," he continues, pushing a drink toward Johnny Mack, "try a little of this red-eye. It'll put some hair on your chest."

Johnny Mack Brown, after gulping down his milk, of course, would proceed to beat laughing boy to within an inch of his life, and the saloon would be totally destroyed in the meantime. I never thought about it much back then, but now I wonder who paid for the damages after all those saloons were destroyed.

I watched so many westerns as a kid that I'm still an expert on who rode what horse. Try me.

Gene Autry? That's a throwaway. He rode Champion. Hopalong Cassidy? A little tougher, but no problem for an expert. His horse was Topper.

How about the horses of the sidekicks? Tonto rode Scout. Frog Millhouse's horse was named Ringeye. Festus Hagan's mule on "Gunsmoke" was Ruth.

What our parents should have worried about our seeing on television was not sex and violence, but rather a way of life that was totally unrealistic — one that we would never be able to emulate. Just as viewers today are influenced by the whackos on "Donahue," we were given a model of the way a family was supposed to work when we watched early television.

Ward and June never argued on "Leave It to Beaver," and Jim and Margaret knew their roles in "Father Knows Best." Jim sat in the den with his stupid tie and sweater on, while Margaret made dinner. And none of the kids ever got into any kind of trouble that couldn't be handled in a calm family conference.

One of the most unrealistic examples which television

153

promoted was that of Roy Rogers and Dale Evans (who may have been the first feminist, now that I think about it. She kept her maiden name, and she never rode sidesaddle. Donahue would have loved her).

Roy went off everyday and fought cattle thieves, while Dale stayed home and watched over the ranch. When Roy returned, Dale cooked him something to eat, and then they'd sit around singing "Happy Trails" together. For years, "Happy Trails" was my favorite song:

> *"Happy trails to you,*
> *Until we meet again.*
> *Happy trails to you,*
> *Keep smiling until then.*
> *Happy traaaaails to youuuuuu,*
> *'Til we meeeeeet aaaaagain."*

Of course, it didn't turn out that way at all. "Happy Trails" turned into "Forty Miles of Bad Road."

I came home after a hard day's work one evening and said to my then-wife, "Rustle up some grub, woman, and call me when it's ready. Me and ol' Bullet will be out in the back-yard."

"Rustle your own grub, Roy," said my wife. "I'm taking Buttermilk and heading out for a few drinks with the girls."

* * *

I'm not certain when it was that I stopped watching television on a regular basis. I think it was soon after they took "Gunsmoke" and "Have Gun Will Travel" and "Peter Gunn" and "Perry Mason" off the air and replaced them with

154

programs that gave me headaches.

I still search for the old shows — the ones that are being rerun, thank goodness. Give me Andy and Barney and Aunt Bea and Opie over "Hart to Hart" any day. And every time I flip through the channels looking for an old program and run across "Family Feud," I secretly hope that herpes can be contracted by kissing game show contestants.

I never liked "All in the Family." Everybody was always screaming at everybody else, and it made me nervous. Maude was a grumpy old bat, and that program where Tex Ritter's son John lived with those two air-brained women was horrible. Ol' Tex must still be twirling in his grave.

I don't like soap operas, because it's too hard to remember who is pregnant and by whom, and I always had a sneaking suspicion that Laverne and Shirley were gay. But then again, I don't remember ever seeing them on "Donahue."

* * *

The movies. They can get a little crazy, too. I'm all for realism, but the language they use in today's movies is atrocious. Henry Fonda and Katherine Hepburn even used dirty words in *On Golden Pond*. And if they ever made *Gone With the Wind* over again, I can't even imagine how Rhett would tell Scarlett to take a hike this time — "Frankly, my dear, I don't ...."

When it comes to sex, movies are like everything else today — overloaded. I enjoyed sex in movies more when you *thought* they were going to do it, but you were never quite sure.

In those days, when it became apparent that a couple had

more on their minds than playing a few hands of canasta, the leading man and lady would embrace while doing-it music (violins and harps) played in the background. Then before they removed the first stitch of clothes, the camera faded off.

As a matter of fact, whenever you heard doing-it music in a movie, you knew it was safe to leave your seat and go buy a package of Milk Duds, because absolutely nothing was going to happen that you hadn't seen before. Today if you leave your seat for even a couple of minutes, you're liable to miss three gang rapes, two oral sex scenes, and enough skin to re-upholster an entire Greyhound bus.

It doesn't have to be that way, of course. Great movies still can be made without having a nudist colony as the setting. Take *Tender Mercies,* for example; Robert Duvall won an Academy Award for his performance and never took off more than his shirt.

What we need is more movies like *The Natural* and *Patton,* my all-time favorite movie. George C. Scott was even better than his cousin Randolph. I also enjoy action movies where the villains gets theirs in the end — movies like *Walking Tall,* where Joe Don Baker took a stick and destroyed an entire Tennessee roadhouse and everybody inside it.

Unfortunately, I doubt that movies ever will be the same as they used to be. Back then we went for diversion and relaxation and Milk Duds, not for some deep, sensitive message; not to see people butchered with chain saws; not to see things you used to see only in the magazines your older brother brought home from the Navy.

I give credit to the brilliant Chicago columnist Mike Royko for putting today's movies in their proper perspective. Royko sensed that when John Wayne died, the movie industry changed forevermore.

In his tribute to the Duke, Royko cited the way he handled Dirty Ned Pepper in *True Grit,* and he wondered how John Travolta would have dealt with Dirty Ned in the same situation.

"He probably would have asked him to dance," wrote Royko.

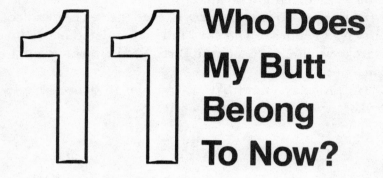

Who Does My Butt Belong To Now?

SIN, LIKE PRACTICALLY** every other element of life, isn't as simple as it used to be. And retribution, which always seemed to involve my rear end in one way or another, isn't as firm or as fast as it once was.

Of course, there are many more opportunities to sin today than there were twenty years ago. Combine that with the obvious erosion of discipline and respect for authority, and what you have is a lot of young people running around having loads of fun doing things it never occurred to the youth of twenty years ago to do.

We've already discussed sex. With the pill for safety and the *Penthouse* Forum for directions, who knows what's going on in the back seats of Toyotas these days? Whatever it is, I'm certain that the participants are much more cramped than they would have been had the 1957 Chevy lived on into the eighties.

Peeping Tomism, which was popular with my generation, also has lost its way in the modern world. We used to slip around and snoop in windows to see if we could catch girls in their underclothing. Kids today get their equivalent kicks by using computers to invade the privacy of large corporations. I suppose they see enough skin on television and in the newspaper ads for movies; they don't have to waste their time crouching outside of windows. But if I had to pick, I still would rather watch Kathy Sue Loudermilk do her famous eight-o'clock-every-Wednesday-evening striptease from the tree outside her bedroom than to gaze at the financial records of AT&T in my computer.

The sin of gluttony has even changed since I was growing up. We used to steal watermelons and then gorge ourselves. I was even known to gnaw on the rinds when I was feeling especially gluttonous. Kids today pig-out on Slurpies and Twinkies and Little Debbie Snack Cakes, and they can get pizza delivered to their doorsteps. And not long ago I was at Baskin-Robbins behind a kid who was having trouble deciding which of the thirty-one flavors he wanted, so he finally said, "I'll just have a scoop of each." When I left, he had eaten down through the Almond Toffee and was working on the Fudge Swirl and washing it all down with Tab.

Frankly, I'm glad that I'm not twenty years younger and confronted with all the temptations that the nation's youth face today. I'm glad, for example, that I never had to deal with the issue of drugs.

There certainly were no drugs in my high school, and a real druggie when I was in college was someone who took No-Doz. We knew from seeing Sal Mineo in *The Gene Krupa Story* that a thing called marijuana existed, but we had never seen any. We figured that only kids in New York City smoked it, and that was why they all looked so greasy and undernourished.

The only thing we took to alter our mental state was beer or maybe bourbon mixed with Coke. Even that was only an occasional indulgence, because beginning drinkers (as most of us were) spent a lot of time embracing the stone pony. That means we spent a lot of time throwing up into a commode, and that definitely wasn't cool.

Had drugs been available in my school days, there would have been some to try them, no doubt. Norris Brantley, for instance. He would try anything.

Norris had a big date one evening, but his parents had made him spend the afternoon painting the garage. When Norris finished, he was covered in paint and had only an hour to make himself presentable for his date. He showered and scrubbed, but he couldn't get the paint off his arms and legs.

Norris had heard that gasoline was a marvelous paint remover, so he siphoned several buckets full out of his mother's car and filled the tub. Then he sat soaking in the gasoline, waiting for it to remove the paint.

Meanwhile, Norris's mother was busy hostessing a bridge party.

"Do you smell gas fumes, Marjorie?" one of the ladies said to Mrs. Brantley.

Soon all the ladies smelled the fumes, and Mrs. Brantley began searching through the house to find the source. The closer she got to Norris's bathroom, the stronger the scent became.

She finally looked in the bathroom and found Norris sprawled out in the tub. He had passed out from breathing the gasoline fumes. Moving quickly, Mrs. Brantley pulled Norris out of the tub and, using a fireman's carry, hauled him out of the bathroom, through the den where the bridge ladies were, and out into the yard. After a few minutes, Norris revived.

Mrs. Brantley then went back inside and attempted to revive two of the bridge ladies, who had fainted at the sight of Mrs. Brantley carrying ol' naked Norris through the den.

That was the last time Norris ever tried to take a gasoline bath, but later on he tried something even more daring. He actually ate the "mystery meat" they served us in the high school cafeteria on Wednesdays, which was worse than the Friday meatloaf that had been forced upon us back at Moreland elementary.

Previously, no student had been brave enough to attempt the Wednesday mystery meat. It defied description and categorization. It was a dark, hideous-looking substance which the cooks tried to hide by covering it with gravy. Whenever a student would ask, "What is this?", the cooks would simply look at each other and smile knowingly. They would never answer the question.

Norris, who had eaten an entire package of crayons in third-grade art class on a dare, became so intrigued by the mystery meat that he actually cut a piece with his knife and fork, which required a considerable struggle, and ate it.

"What does it taste like?" somebody asked Norris.

"Sort of like a blue crayon," he answered.

We never did learn the identity of the mystery meat, but Norris later reported that he took a piece home and tried to feed it to his dog. The dog ran and hid under the bed and wouldn't come out until Norris buried the substance in the yard.

Norris would drink anything, too. We were on a camping trip when one of the kids from out in the country produced a pint of his father's white liquor, known to some as "moon-

161

shine."

"Let me have a chug of that," Norris said to the kid with the pint.

"You need to strain it first," said the kid. "It's got some leaves and dead bugs in it."

That was no problem for Norris. He took off his T-shirt and strained the pint through it. Then he took a deep pull out of the jar.

When Norris got his breath back, he said, "It ain't much to taste, but next time I got to paint the garage, I sure could use a couple of gallons."

* * *

Most of us were quite satisfied with drinking beer. The only problem was obtaining it. Unless your parents went out of town and left some in the refrigerator, or you had an older brother who would buy it for you, or you had an understanding uncle who would bring you out a case from the Moose Club, you normally had to resort to bribing curb boys.

I drank my first beer when I was six. I found a half-full can on the coffee table one morning after my parents had entertained the evening before. They were still in bed, so I picked up the can and drank what was left in it. Having never tasted cold beer, I wasn't bothered in the least that this was warm. As a matter of fact, I quite enjoyed it, and afterwards I began singing "She'll Be Coming Around the Mountain," my favorite song when I was six. Then I took myself a long nap.

I didn't try another beer until I was fourteen. Nathanial, one of the curb waiters at Steve Smith's truckstop, brought

Danny Thompson and me three tall-boy Carling Black Labels out to the back of the truckstop for the price of the beer plus a dollar for his risk and trouble.

I drank my Carling Black Labels faster than Danny did, so I threw up first. We walked home — both of us quite ill.

It was a warm night. We had no air conditioning at my house, but I was still sober enough to remember how cool the inside of a refrigerator feels on a hot summer night in Georgia. So I sat down next to the refrigerator, opened the door, and stuck my head inside on one of the racks.

Then, just as I had done eight years earlier, I took a little nap. It was in that position, sleeping with my head stuck between lettuce and banana pudding in the refrigerator, that my mother found me a couple of hours later.

"Why are you sleeping in the refrigerator?" she asked.

"I was going to get myself some leftover banana pudding," I answered, "but it was so nice and cool in here that I decided to take a nap."

I always underestimated my mother's ability to tell when I was lying.

"Let me smell your breath," she said. "I think you've been drinking."

I was dead. I let her smell my breath.

"How much did you have?" she asked.

"Two cans of beer that I remember," I answered. "I'm a little hazy on the third one."

"Did it make you sick?"

"As a dog."

"Where did you get it?"

"Curb waiter at Steve's."

My mother put me to bed, and the next morning, as I lay hovering between life and death, she brought me aspirin. I expected her to give me a long lecture about drinking, but instead all she said was, "I hope you've learned a lesson."

And I had. I learned never to drink Carling Black Label beer on a warm evening and never to stick my head in a refrigerator unless I'm wide awake.

* * *

The more I think about it, the more I'm convinced that most of us wouldn't have gotten involved with drugs even if they had been available. Our parents certainly did not condone drinking, but at least there had been beer when they were young, and most of them knew the appeal it held for adolescents.

But not drugs. They would have been outraged, and they would have cracked down hard on us. And I don't think we would have rebelled against them, either, because their disciplinary measures were fast and firm in those days.

These were not people to be trifled with. They had learned from the harsh parenting they had received, and they would stop at nothing to be sure that we understood they were in complete control.

My own dear mother had a strict rule that I was not allowed, under any circumstances, to ride on any mechanized vehicle that had less than four wheels. What she had in mind specifically was Dudley Stamps's motor scooter.

When Dudley was fourteen, his parents bought him a motor scooter. My mode of transportation at the time still required a great deal of pedaling. Dudley would ride into my yard on his scooter and invite me to go for a spin.

"You aren't going to get on any motor scooter," my mother would insist. "You could fall off and break your neck."

I knew I wasn't going to fall off and break my neck, but I couldn't convince my mother of that. When I was younger, she had been the same way about my running with a sharp stick in my hand.

"Put that stick down, young man!" she would scream at me. "You might fall and put out your eye."

For years, I have been following the papers trying to find just one instance of a child running with a sharp stick in his hand and falling and putting out an eye. I have yet to come across one, but I suppose that's the result of the constant vigil of mothers guarding against running and carrying sharp sticks simultaneously.

I rarely disobeyed my mother, but one day Dudley came by on his scooter and my mother wasn't home.

"We'll just be gone a few minutes," Dudley said. "She'll never know you went for a ride."

The thrill of riding on the scooter caused me to lose all track of time. When I returned home three hours later, my mother went into hysterics. She sentenced me to no television for a month, forbade me ever to be in the company of Dudley Stamps again until I had children of my own, and fed me liver twice a week for three months. I considered myself lucky that parents didn't have the right to give the death penalty in cases of such extreme disobedience.

I get the impression that parents of children today, in most instances, do not rule their disobedient young with the strong hand of discipline and authority that once was used.

Some parents think nothing today of allowing their four-teen-year-olds to hang out at rock concerts. Even if it weren't for all the known evils (see earlier reference to Elton John concert), attendance at such events obviously is having a detrimental effect on the hearing of today's youth. Nobody can listen to that much sound without suffering some degree of hearing impairment. Perhaps many of our children already have suffered severe hearing loss, which is why they think the music at rock concerts is appealing.

The schools aren't nearly as strict as they once were, either. If a teacher spanks a child today, she may have a lawsuit on her hands. But that's another reason I don't think many members of my generation would have gotten involved with drugs and dyed their hair orange and exhibited all the rebellious, independent behavior of seventies and eighties youth. If our parents hadn't stopped us from such, the folks at school would have had a field day with our hindparts.

Not long ago I ran into one of my former teachers.

"It was never the same after your class (Class of '64)," he said. "You were the last class that took it as we dished it out. I've missed you."

Certainly the children changed, but I wonder if the teachers didn't, too. I wonder if their growing fears of lawsuits and even their fears of some of the students didn't cause them to lose their grip.

My old high school principal, O.P. Evans, is dead now. Maybe what killed him was living long enough to see discipline erode in the public school system.

Mr. Evans always began each student assembly by reading from his worn Bible, which was held together by a few rubberbands and the grace of the book's main character. I can hear him now, booming out from the Word:

"'When I was a child, I spoke as a child ... but when I became a man, I put away childish things.'"

That was Mr. Evans's way of saying that any student

166

caught chewing gum in study hall would be beaten within an inch of his or her life. O.P. had rules and enforced them.

— No gum chewing anytime or anywhere.

— A student caught smoking faced certain suspension. This included smoking on weekends and before and after school. O.P. Evans held that when a student entered his high school, the student belonged to him until graduation.

— No fooling around between male and female students. When walking down the halls with a member of the opposite sex, for instance, a student was to maintain at least twelve inches of space between himself and herself. Those who violated this rule were taken to Mr. Harris's health class, where he lectured about pregnancy, venereal disease, and saving yourself for your life's partner.

— Any student missing time from school must bring a detailed excuse written and signed by his parents. Norris Brantley once was out of school for several days at the same time his parents were conveniently out of town. Norris attempted to write his own excuse. It said, "Please excuse Norris from class. He was real sick Oct. 29, 30, 31, and 32." As punishment, they made him eat two helpings of mystery meat for every day he was out of school.

Mr. Evans's wife, Mrs. Evans to us, was head librarian. She had rules, too:

— No reading a library book before you washed your hands. Any library book turned in with a smudge on any page would bring punishment for the smudger. I always read library books wearing the rubber gloves my mother used for washing dishes.

— No sound whatsoever in the library. This included throat-clearing, sneezing, coughing, and the sound a chair makes when it's pulled out from under a table for the purpose of sitting.

— Boys were required to remove watches and girls were required to remove any rings or bracelets while sitting at a library table, in order that the tables not be scratched.

There were no scratches on the tables in the Newnan High Library, the place was quieter than a cemetery at midnight, and there were no smudges on the books. Students took little advantage of what the library had to offer, however; it's difficult to read *Les Miserables,* for instance, when you feel like somebody is behind you holding a .45 to your head. *Go ahead, punk. Smudge that book and make my day.*

The superintendent of schools was Homer Drake. Mr. Drake wasn't a bad sort, but he had a habit of appearing unannounced in class to check on his teachers. For that reason, the teachers were terribly nervous all the time. They felt the heat of the same .45, I suppose. Consequently, very little of what went on in a Newnan High School class was frivolous. You couldn't even relax and have a few laughs in shop, lest Mr. Drake walk in and catch somebody actually enjoying themselves. The pursuit of knowledge was serious business to Homer Drake.

For added effect, Mr. Drake occasionally dropped into study hall and walked through the rows of desks pulling on boys' ears. Not only is it impossible to work out algebraic equations while the school superintendent is pulling on your ear, but it's also quite painful. One day I noticed that Mr. Drake had very large ears. I reasoned that somebody had pulled on his ears when he was a young man and this was his way of showing us that he was just one of the guys. I would have preferred that he went around goosing us in the belly instead of pulling on our ears.

My high school had traditional instructors, too. There

was Mr. Hearn, the shop teacher, for example.

"Boys," he would begin his classes every year, "the most important thing to remember while working with an electric saw is safety." With that remark, he would hold up his right hand, which was missing its two middle fingers.

We had a wonderful American history teacher named Miss McGruder. She resembled a frog. In fact, her homeroom was called "The Pond." One day she called on Harley Doakes to tell her what he had read the night before in the assignment concerning President James K. Polk.

Harley stammered for an answer.

"You don't know anything about President Polk, Harley?" she pressed.

Harley searched his mind, a brief endeavor, and finally answered, "Was he the one who invented polk and beans?"

Miss McGruder sent a note to Harley's parents, informing them of how he had answered her question.

"I'm proud of you, son," Harley's dad said to him at supper after he read the note. "I certainly didn't know where polk and beans came from."

Miss Garland taught geometry. She was very old and about half-blind. All of her students made high grades in geometry, because if a student could make a few straight lines on the blackboard with a piece of chalk, Miss Garland couldn't see well enough to know whether or not he had solved the problem correctly. She would simply squint at the board for a few seconds and say, "Oh, child, you do such grand work."

Ronnie Jenkins once drew a picture of some unidentifiable four-legged creature on the board. Miss Garland thought he had dissected an angle. She gave Ronnie an A, even though he thought an hypotenuse was a large animal he saw once at the Grant Park Zoo in Atlanta.

The teacher who ran study hall was Mrs. Carpenter, an ex-WAC sergeant. She allowed no foolishness, either. Students were to keep their eyes forward and on their books at all times ... or give her twenty-five quick push-ups.

In the stillness and silence of Mrs. Carpenter's study hall one afternoon, my eyes facing my book, I began to hum. I don't remember why; I just began to hum. The person behind me picked it up and started to hum, too. Soon, seventy-five of us were humming, our eyes still on our books and our mouths closed.

"Who's doing that humming?" shouted Mrs. Carpenter. We continued to hum.

"Stop that humming right now, or I'll send you all to Mr. Evans's office," she warned.

When we still wouldn't quit humming, she marched all seventy-five of us toward the principal's office.

"I had a good home, but I left, right, left, right....," she called out as we maneuvered down the hallway.

When Mr. Evans could not convince anyone to admit to malicious humming, he decided to punish us by administering an across-the-board, one-letter cut in citizenship grades on our next report cards. He also assigned us to memorize the Beatitudes out of the Book of Matthew. (The meek shall inherit the earth, and woe be unto the fool who hums in study hall.)

Students in future times would burn buildings, smoke dope in the hallways, pull knives on teachers, have frequent sexual encounters with one another, and listen to strange music sung by strange people with pink hair and safety pins stuck through their earlobes. We just hummed.

WHO DOES MY BUTT BELONG TO NOW?

* * *

Baby Boomers like myself went off to college in droves. Never before had a larger percentage of a generation pursued higher education. More than being what *we* wanted, it was what our parents wanted, what they had saved and scrimped for, what they had dreamed about.

We want you to have it better than we did, they said time and again, and one way we were going to have it better was to be educated. My mother, a teacher, rarely spent money on herself. She watched every penny that came in and went out of the house, and she hoarded many of them for my college.

There were few people in my hometown who had been to college. Among some of the old folks, there was even the classic resentment for and suspicion of someone who had gone, or was going, to college.

I walked into Cureton and Cole's one day, and some of the old men were seated around the stove.

"Heard you goin' off to college," said one.

"University of Georgia," I answered proudly.

"Don't you get too big for your britches and forget where you came from," I was instructed.

"I won't."

"I tell you something, when I come along, there wadn't no way you could go to college. Hell, my daddy jerked my tail out of school when I was twelve years old to help him bring in the crop. I got an education, but it wadn't from no college. I got it from behind a mule."

Somehow, I felt like a traitor. These were my people, my roots.

"I've seen a lot of 'em go off to college and get a lot of book sense, but then they still ain't got no common sense.

171

Couldn't plow a straight row if their life depended on it."

"Most of 'em go off to college in the first place 'cause they don't want to do a honest day's work."

"Hey, college boy, what you going to study for? You goan be one of them smart-ass lawyers like they got up in the city?"

I said I wasn't certain what I was going to study.

"Why don't you study to be a schoolteacher like you' mama?" somebody asked.

I said school teaching didn't appeal to me. Besides, there wasn't much money in it, I added.

"Money? That's all they think about today is money, especially them damn lawyers."

"Hey, you know the difference between a dead lawyer in the highway and a dead possum in the highway?"

"Naw."

"Dead lawyer ain't got no skid marks in front of him."

I said I'd better be leaving, but before I could go, Harvey (Dynamite) Garfield, Frankie's older brother, walked in.

"Hey, Dynamite," somebody said, "what do you think of college-boy here going off to get an education?"

"Well, it's just like I told that smart sonofabitch foreman of mine at the mill," Dynamite began. "I told him I wanted to get off the third shift and get me one of them day jobs in the office. He said I needed an education for that. I told him I didn't have no edugoddamncation, but I could whip his ass with one hand. He's goan see what he can do about my promotion."

They were still hooting as I walked out the door. I had learned a lot through the years, sitting and listening around the stove. But at that moment, I knew I would never be as welcome again. There was no place for a college boy in the

172

Order of the Stove. At that moment, I also knew my home-town never would be the same again. I was leaving it, and it would stay the same, but I would broaden.

I wondered if I would miss it. I wondered how often I would come back and, when I did, how I would be accepted — as one to be respected because he had seen the lamp of knowledge, or one to be ostracized because he felt that he wasn't good enough, that he needed to rise above his roots?

I decided two things: (1) No matter how much they had laughed and hooted, no matter what anybody thought, getting an edugoddamncation was important, especially for somebody who couldn't mug his foreman; and (2) I decided I would not go to law school.

* * *

Stories and legends abounded concerning what a young man could expect once he entered the University of Geor-gia, the nation's oldest state chartered university, which was also known — to those back in the hinterlands high schools — as The Promised Land.

I arrived on the Athens campus in September, 1964, one month before my eighteenth birthday, and was assigned a corner room in Reed Hall. My roommate, who had been selected without consulting me, was a French major who smoked Pall Mall cigarettes. In the evenings, he would sit and smoke and listen to Edith Piaff records in the haze of light coming from a blue bulb in his desk lamp.

We lasted a month together. I finally managed to get transferred to a new room and acquired a new roommate — George Cobb, Jr., from Greenville, South Carolina, whose father built golf courses. George and I got along famously.

After two or three weeks together, we decided to redecorate our room. The university had furnished our tiny cubicle with one bunk bed, two desks, and a couple of hard-back chairs. A monk would have been uncomfortable in that stark environment.

George and I rented a truck and went to a used furniture store in Athens. For fifty dollars, we purchased a used sofa, lounge chair, and ottoman. Fellow freshmen came from dorms all over the campus to view our newly refurbished room.

The University of Georgia had all sorts of rules concerning housing in 1964. Among them were:

— No alcohol inside dormitories.

— No females inside dormitories.

— No used sofas, lounge chairs, nor ottomans inside dormitories.

We had not been apprised of the third rule when we decided to redecorate, so it was somewhat of a surprise when the dean of housing paid George and me a visit one evening.

"What is all this?" the dean, a stern man, asked.

"What is all what, sir?" asked George.

"This ragged furniture," said the dean. "Where did it come from?"

"Farmer's Furniture, sir," George answered. "We think it gives the place a homey look."

"I want it out of here in the morning," the dean continued.

"Sir," said George, a business major, "this furniture represents an investment of fifty dollars on the part of my roommate and I. We also feel it is conducive to improving our study habits, because now that our room is more comfort-

174

able, we are more anxious to remain here and do our work. Could you give us some reason why we can't have furniture in our room?"

"I want it out of here by morning, or I'll kick both your butts out of school," the dean said.

Farmer's Furniture gave us only thirty dollars for the used furniture we had bought there five days earlier for fifty. We had, however, learned two new facts:

Fact one: Used furniture depreciates in value at a very fast rate.

Fact two: My butt, which once belonged to my parents and to O.P. Evans, now was under the control of the dean of housing at the University of Georgia.

But despite that unpleasant run-in with university officialdom, George and I were finding out that most of the legends we had heard concerning campus life in Athens were, indeed, true.

The beer flowed freely at Georgia. There was Allen's and Uppy's and Sarge's Place and Harry's and the Black Horse Inn, formerly the legendary Old South, located just across the street from the campus and just above the bus station. The story was still passed around about the student who spent an afternoon at Old South, then walked outside and got into his sports car that was parked in front of the bar.

As he drove to the first stoplight, his brakes failed and he drove squarely into the bus station, his car coming to rest at the ticket counter. Amidst the screams and the shattered glass, he leaned out of his car and said to the man behind the ticket counter, "Roundtrip to Savannah, please."

The best place to buy packaged beer in Athens was at Bubber's Bait Shop, which over the years had become an institution of sorts. Bubber, a gentle man, knew all his student customers by name and welcomed them with the same greeting: "Whaddahyouhave?"

"Six-pack of Blue Ribbon, Bubber."

"Bottles or cans?"

"Cans."

"Short or tall?"

"Tall."

"How 'bout a little Red Hurricane Wine to go with that?"

"I don't need any wine, Bubber."

"Ain't but ninety-seven cents a bottle."

"Next time, Bubber."

"That Red Hurricane Wine'll put hair on your chest."

"How much for the beer, Bubber?"

"Two-seventy-five with tax."

"Thanks, Bubber."

"Come again."

Bubber likely became quite wealthy selling beer at the Bait Shop, but he always was the same old Bubber. He was a very trustworthy individual, who also served as an occasional lending agency for financially-down-and-out students. Something else nice about Bubber — whenever a student was kicked out of school and stopped to say good-bye and buy a six-pack for the long ride home, Bubber often would drop a bottle of Red Hurricane wine in their sack for free.

"You going to need that," Bubber would say. "You got a lot of explaining to do."

Allen's was a legendary beer and hamburger joint where, the rumor went, a young man could drink all the draft beer he pleased at twenty-five cents a glass, regardless of whether or not he had sufficient proof that he was twenty-one, the legal drinking age in Georgia at the time.

176

My roommate George and I tested the rumor one fine autumn evening during our freshman year. Three dollars worth of draft beer each later, we were in a rather festive mood, and George began to do his impression of the sound a mule makes. It was pure genius. First, George would make a whistling sound, and then he would do a rather throaty and low "Haaaaw!" It went something like, "Hrrrrrrrt! Haaaaaw!"

I was terribly impressed.

"You try it," said George.

"Hrrt! Haaaaw!" I brayed.

"More whistle," said George.

"Hrrrrrt! Haaaaaw!" I continued.

"Perfect," said George.

After the manager of Allen's asked us to leave, George decided it would be great sport to go over in front of Farm-House, a fraternity for agricultural students, and make mule sounds.

"Hrrrrrrt! Haaaaaaw!" went George out front of Farm-House.

"Hrrrrrrt! Haaaaaaw!" I followed.

After that, we did chickens and goats and cows and ducks, and George had just broken into his rooster (not as good as his mule but still quite effective) when the smiling campus policeman got out of his car and ordered our drunken butts, as he put it, into the back seat.

He drove us to our dorm room and sent us inside, but not before taking our student I.D.'s and informing us that we would hear from the Dean of Men's office the very next morning, which we most certainly did.

Dean William Tate was a campus institution at Georgia and a gentle person until riled. We had first seen Dean Tate

177

during orientation week, when freshmen men were summoned to his annual briefing about what was considered acceptable and unacceptable behavior of students.

The dean had also told his favorite joke, the one he'd been telling freshmen students for years. It involved Robert Toombs, a Georgia student in the middle nineteenth century who later ran for governor of the state. When the Civil War broke out, Toombs joined the Confederate Army and solicited troops in front of the courthouse in Marietta, Georgia, just outside Atlanta.

"I'll tell you, men, we can whoop them yankees with cornstalks," Toombs had said to his listeners in Marietta.

After the war, Toombs came back to that same courthouse for a campaign speech. In the middle of his many promises to his audience, a man spoke up.

"Mr. Toombs," he said, "I stood right here before the war and heard you ask us to jine up with the Confederate Army. I jined and my brother jined. I got shot in the Battle of Chickamaugua and my brother got shot at Antietam. You told us then we could whoop the yankees with cornstalks. I believed you then, and I paid for it. So why should I believe you now?"

Toombs paused for a few moments and then replied, "Well, we could have whooped the yankees with cornstalks, but the sons of bitches wouldn't fight that way."

We had laughed at his story then, but we didn't crack a smile when we wound up in his office. "What in the hell did you two boys think you were doing last night?" he asked me and George.

"Just kidding around, sir," answered George.

"You boys got a strange sense of humor," said Dean Tate. "I take it you had been drinking to excess."

178

"We just had a couple of beers, sir," said George.

"Takes more than a couple of beers to make a man stand outside at two o'clock in the morning cock-a-doodle-dooing. You boys were drunk, weren't you?"

We admitted it.

"I ought to kick both your butts out of school," Dean Tate said.

There was a pause as he stared at us over his glasses. I'm certain George was thinking the same thing I was: How do you explain to your parents that you have been kicked out of school for drunken cock-a-doodle-dooing?

Finally, the dean spoke again. "But I'm going to give you boys one more chance. I'm also going to make you a promise: If I see you two roosters in here one more time, you will be only a memory around this institution. Is that clear?"

It was clear.

"We appreciate your faith in us, sir," said George.

We immediately went to Allen's to celebrate our good fortune of being able to remain in school. George lifted his first glass of beer to mine.

"To Dean Tate," he said.

"A fair man," I answered.

"To FarmHouse fraternity," said George.

"Cock-a-doodle-doo," I answered him.

"To our butts," toasted George.

"To our butts," I toasted back.

I suppose what has happened to discipline and authority these days is that most everybody has a lot more control over his or her own butt than they used to. But I'm not so certain that's all for the better.

There have been many times, even recently, when I wished somebody would take charge of mine again, if for no other reason than to render the much-needed service of pointing out to me when I was about to put it on exhibition.

12 Women Don't Wear Jocks

THE CURRENT PERIOD in which we're living is probably the worst time in history to be a man. Just my luck. We had it absolutely made for thousands of years. Cave men did a little hunting now and then, but that was about it, and they ruled their women and their roosts with clubs. If the wife, or whatever cave men called their mates in those days, got a little out of hand, a gentle tap on the head did wonders in readjusting her attitude.

Later, when men became more civilized and learned how much fun it was to fight wars, they all got together on horseback and went and sacked other countries. They raped and pillaged and generally had high times.

Throughout most of history, men stuck together and did manly things and talked about manly things. In an attempt to sustain their elite and separate status over women, they formed male-only clubs, such as the Jaycees. The Supreme Court ruled recently that the Jaycees no longer can exclude women from their membership; that's an indication of how

181

much slippage there has been in the area of male domination.

Some men today feel as though they should apologize for their fathers' attitudes toward women, and many of us have been made to feel woefully inadequate in the face of the rising force of feminism, which seems dedicated to telling men everything that is unacceptable about us.

The litany of our alleged failures is long.

Women are quick to inform us that we are lousy in bed and that we don't know how to satisfy them sexually. There is a feminist joke which says it all. A feminist asks a man, "What does a woman say when she has been totally and completely and incredibly satisfied sexually?"

The man walks into her little trap and answers politely, so he won't spoil her joke, "I don't know."

"I didn't think you would," returns the feminist, and once again the man is made to feel like a fool.

Think of all the other complaints today's women have with men: We work too hard, we're too ambitious, we drink too much, we aren't sensitive enough, and we care more about watching a stupid ball game on television than we do about spending "quality time" (a new eighties term) with them. We sexually harass women in the work environment (formerly known as the "office"), we choose which woman is to be promoted within the firm based on breast size rather than professional ability (That made sense for several hundred years. It's difficult to change overnight), and we refuse to pay women salaries equal to those men get for doing the same job — which isn't fair, of course, but it also isn't fair that men have to shave before they go to work every day, and women don't.

Not only have the Jaycees lost their ability to exclude

women, but it is almost impossible to keep women out of any location formerly reserved for men only. (Location, nothing! Women are even wearing men's underwear these days, and one smart-aleck feminist was quoted as saying, "It's only fair. Men have been trying to get in ours for years," which is a really blatant sexist remark if you think about it. I'm glad I don't have to resort to such a low grade of humor to get my points across.)

I am a former sportswriter. When I was covering sports, all press box tickets included the warning, "No women allowed in press box."

This wasn't because sportswriters didn't want women around when they were busy covering ball games; it was because the people who ran the press boxes knew that sportswriters in general are people who never let work get in the way of a good time. Were women not excluded from the press boxes, there wouldn't be room for everybody to sit down, what with all the writers and the cocktail waitresses they had met the night before.

Excluding women from the press box is against all sorts of laws these days, however, so even if a male writer did bring a cocktail waitress to the game with him, she probably would have to stand, because all the extra seats have been taken up by female sportswriters.

I must make another confession here. I'm certain there are many females eminently qualified to cover and report on sporting events, but I still would rather read a male's report, because I am not convinced, and never will be convinced, that women fully understand the subtleties and nuances of certain athletic events.

Okay, so allow women to cover tennis matches. Tennis is a very simple game. The person who hits the last winning shot wins the match. Professional tennis players like John McEnroe and Chris Evert are always complaining that the press is more interested in their private lives than in their tennis. That's because tennis, although loads of fun to play (I'm an incurable participant in the sport, myself. I have no talent for the game, but playing all afternoon certainly makes the evening beer taste better), is not that interesting to read about. I had much rather know why Chris dumped John than why she won't change her tactics and play serve-and-volley against Martina Navratilova. I already know why she won't come to the net against Martina: She's afraid that big ol' girl will knock her head off with a topspin forehand.

So it's okay with me if women cover tennis, and they can cover golf, too. If tennis is boring to read about, golf is a sleeping pill. Women can also report on other sports that encourage dozing, such as marathon races, bowling, swimming, gymnastics, ice skating, track, field, and soccer. In fact, women can even cover pro basketball and it won't bother me, because pro basketball is simple, too. The team with the biggest black man usually wins ... unless it happens to be the Boston Celtics, who have Larry Bird (the only white man in the last twenty years who doesn't suffer from the dreaded "white man's disease," which causes slowness afoot and the inability to jump very high).

What I strongly object to is women covering football and baseball, because they've never played either sport. Men are born with the innate ability to understand the blitz in football and the hit-and-run in baseball. Women may learn the basics of these sports, but I daresay few really watch anything more than how cute the football players' butts look in those tight pants, or how baseball players spend an inordinate amount of time scratching their privates and adjusting certain necessary athletic equipment that's worn under the uniform.

In fact, that may be the crux of the problem: Women cannot achieve credibility as sports reporters with men because we know they've never worn a jock strap. And if they have, I don't want to read an inside look at the problems of the Atlanta Braves' pitching staff written by some woman who obviously has problems of her own.

If women winning their way into press boxes wasn't enough (and it wasn't), women later insisted that they also be allowed to go into the locker rooms in order to hear the pearls of wisdom that players dispatch to the press following the games. I speak from authority here, because for many years it was my job to go into dressing rooms and to be the recipient of these pearls.

Players say things like: "Well, you know, I, you know, caught the, you know, ball, and then, you know, I ran, you know, just as fast, you know, as I, you know, could, and I, you know, would like to, you know, give, you know, God the credit, you know, for, you know, making me, you know, a, you know, rich superstar."

While the players are, you know, treating the press to these marvelous exhibitions of their ability to express themselves, you know, they normally are quite naked. I'm not certain what it is about ball players, but they like to sit around naked a lot, dangling their participles at whomever happens by to speak with them.

When women first attempted to enter players' locker rooms, authorities tried to block them. But a court order here and a court order there, and suddenly post-game dressing rooms, with the players sitting in front of their lockers and all sorts of women running around with note-

185

pads, looked like a Saturday afternoon flea market.

When women no longer could be kept out of dressing rooms, most players were forced to put on bathrobes. I have noticed over the past few years that athletes do not seem nearly as dedicated and don't hustle and give their all as much as they once did. This could be due to the fact that they no longer can look forward to sitting around naked after games.

"I mean, you know, before these, you know, broads started, you know, coming in here, you know, asking a lot of, you know, questions, and looking, you know, at us like we were, you know, just big hunks of, you know, meat, we could, you know, relax after the, you know, game. Man, we could, you know, sit here without no, you know, clothes on, and sort of, you know, mellow out and, you know, think about next year's, you know, contract. You know what I mean?"

I know exactly what they mean. Men enjoy and relish the companionship of other men. They simply need to be off with other men occasionally, with no women around, so they can feel comfortable expressing their thoughts and frustrations and can pass gas without having to apologize for it. (Incidentally, that's how the Jaycees originally grew to be such a large and popular organization. I think women are going to be terribly disappointed when they join the Jaycees and find out that it was nothing more than a bunch of guys getting together once a week to have some lunch and talk about raising money for charities and passing gas in peace.)

Men learn some of the most important lessons in life from hanging around with other men. Let's take baseball, for instance. Baseball is a man's game. Women get more involved with football because it's played only once a week and there's a lot of pageantry involved, but women think

186

baseball is dull.

"Why doesn't somebody *do* something?" they ask when the tension has reached the cutting edge in a baseball game. Meanwhile, the manager in the dugout is flashing signals to the third-base coach, who relays them to the batter; the catcher is trying to keep the runner on second base from stealing his signal to the pitcher; and the pitcher is signaling a pick-off attempt to the shortstop. And she asks why doesn't somebody do something.

In addition to that, the hit-and-run is completely lost on most women, and no woman on earth, even an exceptionally smart one, can comprehend the infield fly rule and why baseball simply wouldn't work very well without it.

I played baseball from the time I was five until I was eighteen, and I learned all sorts of manly things that I probably couldn't have learned anywhere else. I learned to cuss, for instance.

There are different curse words for different baseball situations. Let's say you've just led off the game at the plate and the pitcher has struck you out. When you return, bat in hand, to the dugout, the other players always inquire, "What's he got?", meaning, Is the pitcher talented?

Baseball, a *macho* sport, is very competitive by nature. No man who has just struck out to start a game is about to give the pitcher any credit, so he always answers the above question by declaring, "The sonofabitch ain't got a thing."

"Come on!" the other players then beseech the second batter, "base hit him. The sonofabitch ain't got a thing."

There are also appropriate curse words to use when the umpire has called you out and you're convinced you were safe; when you make an error and allow two unearned runs to score; when the manager did not pencil your name into

the starting lineup; and when the sonofabitch who didn't
have a thing has struck you out for the fourth straight time.
I'm making every attempt to keep this a fairly-clean book,
however, so please use your imagination to figure out which
cuss words fit which of the previously-listed situations.

I also learned a lot of clichés playing baseball — clichés
that could be used later in life as well, but clichés that women
never understand.

There was "can of corn," for example. When somebody
lofts a lazy fly ball to the outfield, the cliché everybody uses
is, "can of corn." That means it's a simple out. Later, when
another man asks you, "Think you're going to score with
Roxanne Smitherington tonight?", you can boast, "Can of
corn," meaning, turn out the lights, the party's over.

"Caught looking" is a cliché used when a batter looks at a
third strike without swinging. When a man knows his wife is
running around on him and doesn't do anything to stop the
illicit relationship (such as attempting to beat the other man
over the head with a fungo bat) and his wife eventually
ditches him for the other man, he is said to have been
"caught looking."

"It'll look like a line drive in the box score in the morning," is another great baseball cliché. It also may be adapted
to a sexual situation. In baseball, "It'll look like a line drive in
the box score in the morning" means you have reached base
safely, but you haven't hit the ball very hard. I once hit a ball
off the end of my bat. It landed on the rightfield foul line
spinning like a top.

The ball spun under the concession stand, and by the
time the right fielder retrieved it, I was on third base with a
triple. In the box score that ran in the weekly paper, however, there was a "1" by my name under the hit column. For

all anybody who wasn't at the game knew, I had knocked the cover off the ball.

Now, for the sex part. Let's say a man is out with his girl and he wants to fondle her breasts. At first, she won't allow it, but then she says she'll let him feel a little, but she won't take off her blouse.

She asks, "Is that enough for you?"

And if he has played baseball at some point in his life, he answers, "Sweetheart, it'll look like a line drive in the box score in the morning." That means, wait 'til you hear how he describes what happened to his pals when he runs into them the next morning.

* * *

Playing baseball also brings men closer together. Men who play baseball together, like men who fight wars together, always have a common bond between them.

When we were ten, Danny Thompson and I went to the county seat of Newnan to try out for Little League baseball. This was official, bonafide Little League, with new balls and bats and uniforms and smooth infields with lights and grown men to coach.

We had played the game before, but only in Danny's yard or over at the school playground, where there was always only one bat and one tattered ball, with electrical tape around it, that would get lost in the high weeds three or four times an hour, forcing the game to halt for a search.

And there were never enough gloves or players to go around. We played four-on-four or, at best, five-on-five. You left the glove you were wearing in the field when it came your time to bat, and since we never had enough players to have a rightfielder, if you hit the ball to rightfield, God forbid, you were out.

I wanted desperately to make the Little League team in Newnan. I was shaking in my Keds the afternoon Danny's father drove us for our first tryout.

The city kids from Newnan looked so much bigger than I felt, and some even wore regulation caps and baseball shoes with rubber cleats. We had heard that Newnan had a lot of rich people, but we didn't know they were *that* rich. Every kid had his own glove.

I got cut the first day, but Danny made the team. It broke my heart. I was ashamed that he had made the team and I hadn't, and I missed him those summer afternoons when he was in Newnan playing official Little League baseball and I was stuck at home swatting rocks with a broomstick out in the gravel driveway.

A summer later, however, I got a break. Of all the wonderful things that ever could have happened, the Baptist church in Moreland decided to sponsor a boys' baseball team, and it would play teams from other Baptist churches around the county.

Of course, I was a Methodist at the time, but I was fully willing to become a Baptist in order to make the team.

Before I could go through with my plan to switch denominations, however, the Baptist deacons voted to allow any boy in town who could run, hit, catch, and pitch to play on the team, thus saving me a dunking in the Baptist pool which always seemed to be covered with green scum, water bugs, and an occasional dragonfly.

We even were provided uniforms and new bats and new balls, and such was the excitement around town that several members of the team even received new gloves from their parents. I did, too, but the story isn't that simple.

My stepfather, H.B., had been a permanent member of our household for approximately a year when the Baptist church started its baseball team. He and I were not getting on together. My real father had been a pushover, but H.B. insisted on regular chores, on regular bedtimes, and on cleaning my plate, even if we were having liver.

In contrast to my father, H.B. knew little of sport. He attempted one afternoon to play catch with me, but I quickly noticed that he threw the ball with far too much wrist. "You never played baseball?" I asked him.

"Never had time," he answered. "There isn't time for anything else but work on a tobacco farm."

I wasn't impressed. With my childlike reasoning, I even lost some respect for the man. I think he sensed that.

I had a baseball glove, but it was old and the rawhide strings that held it together were falling loose all about it. I came home from the first practice with the Moreland team in tears. I had seem all my teammates sporting new gloves. I cried in my mother's arms.

"Maybe you'll get a new glove for your birthday," she suggested.

A lot of help she was. My birthday wasn't until October.

I knew what sort of glove I wanted. I had seen it at the hardware store in Newnan. It was a fielder's glove with a deep pocket, and it was autographed by Pee Wee Reese of the Dodgers. It cost thirteen dollars. I often went to sleep dreaming of that glove.

A couple of days after my tearful scene with my mother, she told me that H.B. wanted to see me in their bedroom. I presumed the worst. He had something for me to do that would involve wheelbarrows and digging around in the dirt.

I walked into the bedroom as he was putting on his tie. "Look in the sack on the bed," he said to me.

I picked up the sack and looked inside. It was a new baseball glove, but it wasn't the glove I had wanted, the glove I had dreamed about. I had never even heard of the bush-leaguer who had lent his name to it.

"That what you wanted?" H.B. said.

"I wanted a Pee Wee Reese glove," I answered.

"Who is Pee Wee Reese?" he asked.

That settled it. The man was totally without portfolio when it came to baseball. I threw the glove down and ran to my room crying.

I'm not certain when I realized that I had done something wrong. Perhaps it was in the night sometime, when I recalled the look on my stepfather's face as he watched me peer into the sack.

He had made the move. He had known that his lack of baseball expertise had disappointed and frustrated me, so he had tried to surprise me with the new glove. He had reached out to me, but I had been ungrateful.

I never got over that awful thing I did to my stepfather — it grieves me even now — but I did attempt to make amends. I told him I was sorry. I even tried the glove. It wasn't that bad a glove. The first game we played, H.B. came. I pitched and we won. After the game, he said, "You have a nice fastball."

It is amazing what bonds baseball can develop between men ... and between boys and men.

* * *

It has been nearly thirty years, but I remember the Moreland Baptist lineup as vividly as ever: Danny Thompson played first; Bobby Entrekin was at second; Wayne Moore, the coach's son, was at shortstop; Danny Boswell played third; Dudley Stamps caught; Charlie Moore was in the outfield with Mike Murphy and Eddie Estes. I pitched.

Pete Moore, "Mr. Pete" to us, was the coach. He was a short, heavy-set man of great baseball wisdom and patience. Perhaps his greatest move was to devise a plan to save our supply of new baseballs.

The problem was this: We played our home games on the Moreland School playground field. There was a wire backstop behind home plate, but it wasn't much of one. Foul balls went over and through the backstop and usually landed inside a birddog pen directly behind the field.

Given the opportunity, birddogs will chew a baseball right down to the cork in a matter of seconds.

After the birddogs had chewed up enough foul balls to threaten possible cancellation of the rest of the season, Mr. Pete decided to station team reserves in the pen to retrieve the baseballs before the dogs could get to them. We called that position, naturally enough, "birddog."

That's how Eddie Estes, who later became one of the all-time great Moreland Baptist outfielders, learned to play the game. Eddie was two years younger than the rest of us. He was also a thin child but quick as a cat. And Eddie was persistent. He came to every practice and to every game, even though he never could break into a lineup made up of older boys. That was before Mr. Pete put Eddie at "birddog."

Every game, when the rest of us would head out onto the field to take our positions, Eddie would go the other way and crawl inside the birddog pen behind the backstop. The training he got fighting birddogs for foul balls eventually

193

made him into a defensive whiz.

He made the starting lineup the next season in center-field. We were playing rival Grantville, as I recall, and I was pitching. The game reached the late innings tied.

Grantville had runners on with its slugger, one of the Massengale boys, at bat. What little curve ball I had, I hung to the Massengale boy.

The ball shot toward centerfield. Eddie turned his back toward the infield and ran. There was no fence, only a gully and a dirt road that was the centerfield boundary. A few steps before he reached the gully and the road, little Eddie jumped into the air and flung his glove skyward. When he came down, he tumbled into the gully out of sight.

He quickly emerged from the muddy pit, scratched and bleeding, but the ball was in his glove. The umpire called Massengale out. We won the game.

Mr. Pete embraced little Eddie when he returned to the bench. Mays robbing Wertz in the '54 Series hadn't been as dramatic.

"Eddie," said Mr. Pete, "that was one of the best catches I have ever seen."

"I was afraid not to catch it, Mr. Pete," Eddie responded.

Mr. Pete asked him why.

"I was afraid that if I didn't, you'd put me back at 'bird-dog.'"

* * *

There are instances now, of course, of girls actually play-ing Little League baseball. If she can go to her right and hit line drives, then I suppose it would be terribly unfair to keep her off the team. But I'm still old-fashioned enough

194

that I'd be shocked if I heard a nine-year-old girl, who had just struck out to start the game, come back to the dugout and tell her teammates, "The sonofabitch ain't got a thing."

What concerns me even more is, I'm not certain how many boys are playing baseball today. It seems to me that too many of them are playing soccer.

I dislike soccer immensely. It's a dull sport and it is not American. They play it mostly in those weird countries where the government changes hands every two or three days, supporting my suspicion that soccer is also a game that encourages political upheaval and anarchy.

All a person needs to play soccer is wind enough to run up and down a field for several hours and agility enough to bounce a ball off his head. Anybody can learn to run up and down a field for several hours, and I've watched seals in the circus bounce balls off their heads. On the other hand, I've never seen a soccer player who could dive underwater and come back with a dead fish in his mouth.

Kids are playing soccer all over America today, but are there any great soccer clichés? Of course not. People are too busy running up and down the field to think of any. As I explained before, in baseball there's all sorts of time to sit around in the dugout and think of clever things to say, like when an opposing player makes a stupid error and you say, "Nice move, Ex-Lax."

In baseball, you not only have to be able to run, but you also have to learn to bat and to catch and to throw and to slide and to spit. All baseball players spit. I doubt they ever spit in soccer, except when they fall down and get a mouthful of grass.

Once I was in London and, because there was nothing better to do, I switched on the BBC and watched the English soccer (they call it football, which is ridiculous) championship game. (After you've walked through Harrod's and been over to Buckingham Palace, London can be even more boring than soccer.)

One side would kick the ball down to the end of the field, and then the other team would kick it back. I've seen more excitement at county fair pick-up-the-duck games. The crowd, a hundred thousand or so, sang during the entire game. They apparently were just as bored as I was.

The players kicked the ball around for a couple of hours, and finally it hit a guy who wasn't looking in the back of the head and went into the goal. After much running and kicking, the guys in green finally had themselves a soccer championship by the score of 1-0.

I'm afraid that when today's young soccer players become adults, they're going to be terribly boring people and perhaps even a little fuzzy from having soccer balls bounce off their heads for so many years.

What *really* worries me, however, is the great number of today's youth who don't play baseball *or* soccer. They're in shopping malls playing those damned video games. They're all going to grow up, I fear, to have big buglike eyes from staring into too many video screens. Just listening to the infernal beeping noises those games make is enough to drive kids goofy. And trying to shoot down all those asteroids in a matter of seconds also will make a child extremely nervous and frustrated, and they may all wind up with the same bad case of the shakes overworked air controllers get.

We played indoor games when I was a kid, too, but we played educational games like rotation pool and nine-ball, which teach a youngster such important lessons as how to put reverse English on the cue ball while squinting through the smoke coming out of the cigarette he's holding in his mouth at the time.

There weren't any women allowed in pool halls, either, which offered further opportunity for male development. Girls today walk into video game arcades big as you please, and there's even a female version of "Pac-Man" — "Ms. Pac-Man," if you will.

I haven't checked to see, but if there's still a *Boy's Life* magazine, it probably carries advertisements for feminine hygiene spray these days.

* * *

One of the few remaining all-male holdouts is college fraternities. So far, women have been content to remain in their sororities. Belonging to a fraternity offers all sorts of opportunities for companionship with other men without women around. You can drink beer together and play cards together and think up nasty Homecoming floats together, and the older brothers will be available to keep you abreast of the proper way to conduct yourself as a young gentleman on campus.

I pledged Sigma Pi fraternity my freshman year at the University of Georgia. They were a great bunch of guys, the frat house was a beautiful old Southern mansion, and it was the only fraternity that offered me a bid.

Fraternity rush in my day was helpful to a young man, because it gave him the opportunity to test his fragile male ego, and it supported his theory that the more macho he acted, the better chance he had of making other young men like him.

Basically, rush worked like this: You walked into a large house filled with strangers. You had worn your best suit — your only suit, in my case — and you had doused yourself heavily with Old Spice, which your father wore. You went around shaking hands with members of the fraternity you happened to be visiting.

If your father had been a member of the fraternity and also was wealthy, you didn't have a lot to worry about. You probably could have managed a bid wearing pajamas and flip-flops. If you had no such legacy, then it was important that you did everything possible to make a good impression on the brothers.

"The most important thing," I had been told, "is to make certain you squeeze hard when you shake hands."

Nothing, of course, gives a man away like a soft handshake. Girls and wimps and nerds have handshakes that feel like you've just grasped a recently-departed grouper. Real men, the kind of men you would want in your fraternity, squeeze your hand firmly. Strength of grip was second only to size of genitalia in determining manhood. All this likely dates back to the days of the cave men, when they ran around naked and choked each other.

Each time I was extended a hand during rush, I made certain that I offered a firm shake in return. By the time I walked into my third fraternity house, my hand felt like a beer truck had run over it. I continued to squeeze firmly anyway, doing my best to ignore the pain and taking a certain amount of comfort in the fact that it was the handshake, not the aforementioned first measure of manhood, that was being checked.

There was something else I had been warned about when I went through rush. If you are included in a group that is taken on a tour of the plumbing system of the fraternity house, that particular fraternity probably doesn't want you even to be seen on its property, much less want you to be a member.

The first house I visited was SAE. From various sources, I had learned that SAE was a very prestigious fraternity and that girls from the spiffier sororities loved to date SAE's. The SAE house was nice. I especially enjoyed seeing how the water pipes in the basement were insulated so they wouldn't freeze during the wintertime.

Next, I went to Sigma Nu. They didn't show me the pipes, but they did herd me over into a corner with two exchange students and a kid with a case of terminal acne.

I didn't do any better at Phi Delta Theta, either. One of the brothers took me and two other rushees — one of whom wore thick glasses and stuttered and the other who was wearing white socks — back to the kitchen and left us with the cooks, who were peeling potatoes.

I thought I might do much better at Kappa Sig. My first cousin happened to be chapter president. When I finally was able to corner him, however, he not only disavowed our kinship, he also swore — in a very loud voice so his brothers could hear him — that he had never seen nor heard of me before. My keen deductive senses alerted me to the fact that I might as well write off any future as a Kappa Sig.

At the Kappa Alpha house, they sang "Dixie" and told stories about Robert E. Lee. The brothers there treated me like a direct descendant of William T. Sherman. I got the pipe treatment again at Sigma Chi, and at ATO they asked me to wait out on the porch until the bus came back to pick up the rushees.

I was close to giving up on any chance at becoming a

fraternity man when I walked up the stone pathway to the Sigma Pi house, an impressive antebellum structure with large white columns and rocking chairs on the front porch. To my utter surprise, the brothers never mentioned one word about the Sigma Pi plumbing system and they seemed generally interested in me and what I had to say.

They showed me the party room and the jukebox, and they took me downstairs to something called the "Boom-Boom Room," which featured a sawdust floor, booths in which to sit, and all varieties of neon beer signs. This, I determined, was where the brothers of Sigma Pi brought their dates.

"This is probably where you bring your dates," I said knowingly to the brother giving me the tour. I might have been fresh out of high school, but I wasn't a complete dummy.

"Good thinking," said my guide. "Now, let's go over here to the toilet and see if you can figure out what we do there."

I figured I was dead after that. But, to my complete surprise, I was invited back to Sigma Pi the very next night, and when the bids went out, they offered me one. I was elated but also quite concerned. If nobody else wanted me, why would Sigma Pi, and did I really want to be a member of a fraternity that would accept the likes of me? My ego was in shambles, again.

I asked a friend, who had just accepted a bid from Phi Delt, what I should do.

"Take it," he said, "before they change their minds."

I pledged Sigma Pi and was later initiated and eventually became totally content with my membership. At my fraternity, we had a rigid code regarding responsible, manly behavior. I'll just hit a few high spots.

200

— AT A PARTY: Never throw up on your date. If you feel like you must throw up, go outside and do it in the parking lot. We'll make the pledges clean it up the next morning.

Never attempt to climb onto the bandstand and sing with the band until everybody is bad drunk and won't notice you making a total fool of yourself.

If you think you have the opportunity to engage in amorous activity with your date, do not take her to any of the upstairs bedrooms. We do not want coeds to see the scummy conditions in which we live.

If you have to go to the bathroom, do not go on the shrubbery outside the fraternity house. Shrubbery is too expensive to replace. Go on the tires of somebody you don't like.

— AT FRATERNITY HOUSE DINNERS: If you do not like a certain dish, such as asparagus stalks, do not hurl it at members sitting at another table. Also, do not spit English peas at tablemates and do not drink directly from the syrup container.

— WHEN PARENTS VISIT: Hide all booze, 8mm skinflicks, condoms, love dolls, firearms and explosives, poker chips, dead animals, roach collections for Saturday night roach races, and any stolen goods.

If you have any books, spread them around your room, and if somebody's parents ask your major and you can't remember, say you're undecided between pre-med and animal husbandry.

— PROPER ATTIRE: Never wear socks with your Weejuns.

— IN CLASS: If it is absolutely necessary that you go, sit in the back of the classroom and do not ask any questions, so when you don't come back for another two weeks, perhaps the professor won't notice that you're missing.

If you thought you had a copy of the exam the night before, but then the professor hands you a test that has questions you've never even heard of, pretend to have some sort of fit and maybe they'll take you to the infirmary.

— WHEN ARRESTED: Never indicate you were part of a conspiracy involving other members of the fraternity. We are a loyal brotherhood and will make the pledges fork over enough money for your bail.

My fraternity brothers were a rather diverse lot. I had one brother who rose to the presidency of the Interfraternity Council, a rare and prestigous honor. I had another who pilfered wallets. We called him "Robin Hood."

I had fraternity brothers who majored in pre-Law and pre-Med. I had others who majored in Bubber's Bait Shop and threw up on the sawdust floor in the Boom-Boom Room. I had a fraternity brother known as "Odd-Job" because of his physical likeness to the Oriental goon who was an aide to Dr. No in the James Bond movie of the same name. I was frightened of Odd-Job, especially after I saw what he did to another fraternity brother's stereo.

It was an otherwise quiet evening on the second floor of the house where Odd-Job, for the first time in his collegiate career, actually had decided to study. This was difficult for him, however, because his roommate, who was known as "Seaweed" because his father had been a famous Marine war hero, was playing Sam the Sham and the Pharoahs's "Wooley Bully" over and over again on his stereo. Several times, Odd-Job had informed Seaweed that if he didn't quit playing the record he would tear Seaweed into small pieces and let God sort them out.

Seaweed was a stubborn person, however. Also, a stupid

one. When Odd-Job had finally had enough of Seaweed and "Wooley Bully," he walked over to the stereo, took the record off, and began biting it into tiny pieces, spitting out the pieces directly at the startled Seaweed. Odd-Job then picked up the stereo, ripped the plug out of the wall, and threw it out the second story window, rendering it a crumpled mass of electronic innards. He had Seaweed, himself, halfway out the window when cooler heads informed Odd-Job that if he murdered Seaweed, Dean Tate probably would put us on social probation and we couldn't have a party for the entire fall quarter.

"Then, you live, swine," said Odd-Job to Seaweed. He then went back to memorizing the Emily Dickinson poem he had been assigned in English Lit class.

* * *

Belonging to a college fraternity, as playing baseball had done, provided me with wonderful memories, lifelong friends, and even the opportunity to see racial harmony at its best.

As near as I can remember, a white band never set foot in the Sigma Pi house party room between the years of 1964 and 1968. White bands simply couldn't make a party come alive and turn into a raging inferno of dancing and screaming the way a black band could.

The civil rights movement was at its peak in the early sixties, but when the music was good and the beer was cold, everybody in the party room was in it together.

It was a start to the sort of feelings that eventually led Ray Charles and George Jones to record an album together; that is the very essence of racial harmony, and music was the medium.

Fortunately, this discussion can end on a further positive note. Kids today may be playing a lot of soccer when they should be playing baseball, but I hear that fraternities and the Greek system, much maligned in the seventies, are making a comeback on college campuses. I even hear that the kids are out of Army fatigues and back into Weejuns and khakis, and that many of them are now shunning drugs for beer.

These are good signs, my fellow Americans, good signs, indeed. Not all elements of modern life have gone to hell and rust.

Now, if somebody would just tell me where I could get the sort of French fries that God intended, the kind that are cut fresh in the kitchen and have never been frozen, I might even be able to see a small, twinkling of light at the end of this tunnel. "God Save the French Fry!" Won't somebody hear my plaintive cry in the wilderness of gastronomic silliness?

13 Romancing The Turnip Green

THE FRENCH FRY is a marvelous creation. I think that perhaps God, Himself, created the French fry, say on about the twelfth or thirteenth day. And it was good. French fries stayed that way for several thousand years, but then modern man started monkeying with them.

I suspect God is quite angry about it, and that may be one reason why the weather has been so loused up lately.

Here is the way the perfect French fries should be prepared:

You take an Irish potato. You wash it and then you peel it. God didn't leave the peelings on His original French fries. That may be in the Bible someplace. Probably Leviticus.

After washing and peeling the Irish potato, you cut it into slices — not too thin and not too thick. The proper size for a slice of potato soon to become a French fry is somewhere between the size of a felt-tip pen and a baby carrot.

After slicing the potato, you drop the slices into a frying pan that has been filled with cooking oil. You fry the slices

205

until they're sort of crispy on the outside but still nice and mushy on the inside. Some people drain the grease off their French fries once they're through cooking them, but in my estimation, the greasier the French fry, the better. And remember, God is on my side in this one.

My mother, a devout Methodist, could prepare wonderful French fries, and so could the cook at Steve Smith's truckstop, who served them with a hamburger steak that cost $1.25. Today that same piece of meat is called "chopped sirloin" and costs $6.95, and the French fries you get with it are awful. They also serve hard, dark rolls with it, rather than soft, white ones, and if you want a salad, you have to get up and go make it yourself at the salad bar. This borders on sacrilege.

I'm not sure who first loused up French fries, but I hope he's able to beg forgiveness on his death bed. One day we had great French fries — fresh and crispy on the outside and gushy in the middle — and then the next day they were all gone, and we were eating those French fries with crinkles that had been frozen.

Why would anybody want to put crinkles in sliced potatoes? Isn't it a lot of trouble? And why freeze something that's available fresh year-round?

French fries today are hard and have no flavor. All those fast-food places advertise that their French fries are wonderful, but the truth is they're terrible, a disgrace. I'll go down the list of fast-food French fries and tell you exactly what's wrong with them:

— McDONALD'S: Come on, the French fries they serve at McDonald's probably aren't even made out of potatoes. McDonald's probably has devised some scheme whereby they recycle those styrofoam containers the hamburgers come in back into French fries. You know how Ronald McDonald got so ugly? Eating all those styrofoam French fries, that's how.

— WENDY'S: Wendy's French fries are not as tasteless as McDonald's, but they aren't anything to write home about, either. The only thing that makes Wendy's fries halfway edible is that compared to Wendy's chili, the French fries won't make you think you're eating something that came from the mop bucket.

— BURGER CHEF AND BURGER KING: Someday, God is going to get Burger Chef and Burger King for what they've done to His French fries. I suspect they're actually crinkle-cut zucchini.

— STEAK 'N' SHAKE: What is Steak 'n' Shake trying to do — save a few bucks by cutting their French fries into tiny, thin slices? They don't think we notice that? Steak 'n' Shake could take one potato and feed half the state of Missouri. Show me a Steak 'n' Shake French fry and I'll show you what is really a potato "stick." Remember potato sticks? They were awful, but Steak 'n' Shake is trying to bring them back. They should be ashamed.

— KRYSTAL: Krystal's home office is in Chattanooga, Tennessee, so they should know better than to serve the frozen French fries they use. I love Krystal cheeseburgers; I can eat a dozen. I hate Krystal French fries. You could put them in Wendy's chili and it wouldn't improve it.

— HARDEE'S: Worst French fries on earth. I take that back.

— ARTHUR TREACHER'S FISH 'N' CHIPS: Worst French fries on earth. So bad they had to change the name to chips. I have heard it said that even the cows wouldn't claim them.

The demise of the French fry probably began when Americans decided they didn't care what they ate as long as it was prepared in a hurry. Americans do not like to wait. They would eat French fried hog snouts if they could get them without waiting.

"Hey, Martha, want some French fried hog snouts? They taste awful, but we won't have to wait for 'em to cook."

Fast food. It has become an American tradition, like getting a divorce. First, fast food did away with good French fries. Then the hamburgers went. Somebody (probably in New Jersey) started mashing out thin, flat hamburger patties, then they froze them and shipped them all over the country to fast-food hamburger places. Because they were so thin, they took only seconds to cook, and impatient Americans flocked in and bought these mass-produced burgers.

McDonald's even went a step further and started putting a "special sauce" on their hamburgers. I don't trust anything that doesn't have a name. "Special sauce" doesn't really say what's in it. It's like the "mystery meat" Norris Brantley once ate in the school cafeteria.

Why doesn't McDonald's say it's their "special pickle relish" or their "onion-based special sauce with mayonnaise"? They either don't know what's in it themselves, or they're afraid to tell us. I've eaten a McDonald's hamburger with "special sauce" only once, and that was by mistake. It tasted to me like something you'd get if you mixed Thousand Island salad dressing and Wild Russian Vanya.

The way God intended, you don't put any sort of sauce on a hamburger, special or otherwise. What you put on hamburgers is mustard and catsup, tomatoes, lettuce, onions, mayonnaise, dill pickles, or any combination thereof.

And I'll tell you what else you *do not* put on hamburgers — mushrooms. They'll put mushrooms on your hamburger if you order one in those cutsie places where there are a lot of house plants and they serve salads that cost up to $6.95.

I went into one of those places recently and ordered a simple cheeseburger. The waitress asked if I wanted it on pita bread. I didn't have any idea what pita bread was, but I knew I didn't want it covering up my cheeseburger. I asked for a regular bun like you're supposed to serve a cheeseburger on, and the waitress went off in a huff. She brought the cheeseburger back on the right bun, but she also covered it with mushrooms.

"My God!" I exclaimed. "Somebody has put toadstools on my cheeseburger."

"Those aren't toadstools," said the waitress. "They're mushrooms. We always put mushrooms on our cheeseburgers."

"Do you know, young lady," I replied, "that these are, in fact, toadstools, and do you know how toadstools got their name?"

She didn't know.

"Frogs go to the bathroom under them when it's raining," I explained to her. "Imagine how awful it would be to have warts on your tongue."

* * *

As long as we're on the subject of fast food, I must make mention of biscuits, too. All the fast-food places sell biscuits these days, and they advertise them as "just like your mother made."

I don't like for anybody to insult my mother that way. She

209

certainly didn't make biscuits like those they serve in fast-food places. She made biscuits with an old-fashioned sifter and a rolling pin, and she took each individual biscuit and patted it and shaped it with her own hands. What could McDonald's know about biscuits in the first place?

As anyone with any sense knows, the only thing you're supposed to put on biscuits is either gravy or syrup. Ask some sixteen-year-old behind a McDonald's counter to put something on your biscuit, and she likely will throw on a mess of that special sauce.

Frankly, this entire McDonald's thing bothers me. Do they really know how many billions of hamburgers they've sold? Do the managers call into some central office each night to report?

"Central, this is Topeka. We sold 406 today."

"Central, Joplin here. We did 382. We dropped three on the floor, but we washed 'em off good and sold 'em anyway."

What concerns me about McDonald's and the like is that they've brainwashed our children. Kids today have grown up with fast-food food. They don't know what a real hamburger should taste like. They enjoy going to McDonald's because they see it advertised on television, because all their friends go there, because of that silly clown, and because McDonald's serves cute little food for cute little children in those cute little boxes and containers.

The Communists don't need to bomb us to take over. All they have to do is take over the McDonald's franchises one by one, and we'll fall into their hands like a ripe plum.

I have one other complaint about McDonald's — they serve fish sandwiches. What kind of person would eat a fish sandwich? What kind of fish is it? It could be monkfish or carp, for all we know.

210

I have never eaten a fish sandwich at McDonald's or at any place else. The only person I ever saw eat a fish sandwich was an ol' boy down in south Georgia one night, when they had a fish fry at a beer joint I often frequent during trips into the region.

This ol' boy walked up to where they were frying the fish, picked up a bream, put it between two pieces of white loaf bread, and ate it, bones and all.

"That's one of them Dewberry boys," the man frying the fish said. "They're hog farmers. Hog farmers will eat anything."

* * *

There is all sorts of food that confuses me today. Take one of those fifty-three-item salad bars, for example. There's the lettuce, I know that, and there are those little red tomatoes and the onions and the cucumbers in the back. (Ever notice how they always put the good stuff at a salad bar way in the back where it's hard to reach? They really don't want you to have it, that's why. They're saving it for themselves to eat after we all leave.)

But what is all that other stuff at a salad bar? Is that yellow dish an egg or scrambled squash? What about the brown stuff? Is it the house dressing or Alpo with water added? I have even seen salad bars where there were anchovies. Now, I ask you, who would put an anchovy on a salad? Have you ever looked at those little things closely? They've got hair on them; I swear they do.

The same confusion exists in other areas. I know by now that real men don't eat quiche, but what is quiche in the first place, and why isn't it pronounced "Kwi-chie" like it's spelled?

What are bean sprouts? They look like something that washed up on the beach.

One of the new items that practically every restaurant is serving today is chicken fingers. I didn't know chickens had fingers. I knew they had toes, but I didn't know they had fingers. I guess what they're really selling is chicken toes, but how much meat can there be on one of those scrawny things?

What I secretly have always wanted to be is a restaurant critic. The mistake most restaurant critics make is assuming that we're all gourmets like they are, and that we know what they're talking about when they order *Coquille St. Jacques*. I thought he was a wide receiver at LSU.

I would aim my restaurant criticism toward people like myself, who simply want to know whether or not the food is fit to eat. I would review restaurants like this:

"I walked in and this guy in a tuxedo says to me, 'Walk this way, please,' and I said to him, 'I don't think I can walk that way,' which he didn't think was very funny.

"I had myself a beer before I ordered. It was cold, but before I could tell him to stop, the waiter had poured it into a glass. Beer tastes better out of the bottle, but I suppose they don't want any bottles around in case a fight breaks out.

"I couldn't make out a blasted thing on the menu because it was all written in a foreign language. Since I was on expense account, I told the waiter just to bring me one of all the most expensive things on the menu.

"While I was waiting on my appetizer, I noticed there was butter on the table but there weren't any crackers. I like to eat butter and crackers while I'm drinking my beer. I complained and the waiter brought some crackers, but they were the kind women put out on the coffee table when they have little get-togethers, not the kind you eat with butter or with raw oysters or crumble up in your chicken-noodle soup.

"The waiter brought out the first appetizer. It smelled like the back of the supermarket where they keep the mullet on ice. It didn't taste all that bad, but I kept thinking about those mullet that still have their eyes, and they just sort of lie there in the ice on their sides with one big eye looking up at you. I was afraid there might be a fish eye in that appetizer someplace, so I just sort of picked at it.

"Then, they brought the soup. The man said it was *vichysoisse*. I complained that it was cold. The waiter said it was supposed to be. I asked, 'Well, do you have any still in the bottle?' He looked at me funny and walked off. I crumbled up some of those crackers in my soup, but it didn't help. If I wanted to eat cold soup, I'd go down to the Mission and eat what they dish out to the winos.

"Speaking of wine, I had some. It was white. 'Would you like to smell the cork, sir?' asked the man who brought the wine. I smelled it. 'That's cork, all right,' I said. Then he poured a little in my glass, and I knew what I was supposed to do then. I tasted it.

" 'Assertive, but not offensive,' I said to the wine man. That was something I heard a guy in a movie say once. I didn't have any idea what it meant, but you're supposed to say things like that whenever there's no screw-off top on the wine bottle and you aren't drinking it out of paper cups.

"I had a salad. There wasn't anything really wrong with it, except they served those little red tomatoes on it. You ever try to eat one of those suckers? If you bite down on one, you'd better put the whole thing in your mouth. I tried biting one in half, and the juice shot all over a fat lady at the table next to me. I apologized and offered her what was left of my cold soup, but she declined.

"The main dish came out. It was chicken with some yellow sauce on it. After I scraped the sauce off to one side, it was passable. I didn't want to leave unless my plate was clean, so they wouldn't think I hadn't enjoyed whatever it was they picked out for me, so I took one of those hard rolls they served and tried to sop up the sauce. It's hard to sop sauce with a hard roll, I found out, so I put what was left of the sauce into my cold soup. I didn't taste it, but it looked like egg custard after I did that.

"As far as dessert was concerned, it was cheesecake and it stuck to the roof of my mouth. The whole meal cost $112.17, and I put on a big tip for everybody and said good-bye to the fat lady.

"I wouldn't go back there again if I had to spend my own money."

I could understand a restaurant review like that, but you never see them. What has happened to me in food, as in most everything else, is that I have gone back to basics.

I still eat lunch at my mother's house in Moreland once a week. She always apologizes when I walk in.

"Son, we don't have hardly anything to eat today," she says.

So what am I going to get here? A piece of toast and a radish? Then I go to the table and there's enough food to feed the Chinese infantry: country fried steak smothered in gravy, mashed potatoes with no lumps in them, all sorts of fresh vegetables from the garden, and hot cornbread and

214

maybe even some coconut pie.

People who live in towns where there isn't a McDonald's (Moreland is one of the five remaining towns on the face of the earth where there is no McDonald's. The other four are in Afghanistan) do not realize how good they have it. The dogs that eat the scraps at home eat better than I do in the city.

I don't like fancy food anymore. If the truth be known, I never did, but when I was younger I pretended that I liked it so nobody would think I was a misfit. I don't care what anybody thinks anymore.

I ate at Maxim's in Paris once. It took four guys to hand out the dessert — strawberries and cream. One guy held the bucket of strawberries, another held the dish of cream, and a third dipped the strawberries and the cream onto my plate. The fourth guy played the violin. You could buy a late-model used car, fully equipped, for what that meal cost, and yet it wouldn't touch what I can get at my mother's house for free.

This book was not designed to be a culinary guide, but because I consider myself an expert on eating (I took it up as a very young child), I'm going to offer you the benefit of my years of experience. I would ask you to clip these guidelines and attach them to your refrigerator door, but with the price of books today, maybe you should just turn down the ear of the page so whenever you're hungry or need advice about eating, you can turn to this spot readily.

GRIZZARD'S GUIDE FOR EATERS

1. Never eat barbecue in a place that also sells Dover Sole. Neither dish will be any good.

2. Never eat any place where they mark the restroom

doors in any fashion but "Men" and "Women" or "Ladies" and "Gentlemen." Especially do not eat in a restaurant that specializes in seafood and marks its restroom doors "Buoys" and "Gulls," because they have been too busy thinking up cutsie names for the restroom doors to really pay attention to the food.

3. Never eat in a restaurant where nobody speaks or understands English. You might get boiled horse or roasted dog if you're not careful.

4. As per our recent discussion, avoid any place that offers French fries and then serves you those with crinkles in them. Any place that doesn't have the decency to serve its customers hand-cut French fries doesn't really give a damn if the rest of its food is fresh and tasty, either.

5. Never eat anything that resembles a house plant, like asparagus, broccoli, or Brussels sprouts.

6. Never eat soup with chunks moving around in the bowl when you aren't stirring it.

7. Avoid "broasted" chicken. Chicken is supposed to be fried to a heavy crisp on the outside, and anybody who tries to cook it any other way is again toying with God's Master Plan.

8. Don't go into French restaurants. They charge you extra for drowning the food in all sorts of sauces. If the food was good to begin with, why would they need to put sauce on it?

9. If the waitresses are skinny, go somewhere else. If they won't eat the food, why should you?

10. Never eat in a restaurant where the maitre d' is a cop.

No. 10 deserves some further embellishment. I checked into a hotel late one Sunday evening. The hotel restaurant had been closed for hours, so I asked the lady behind the counter where I might get something to eat.

"How hungry are you?" she asked.

"I could eat the bellman's hat," I answered.

"In that case, you could walk across the street to The Cave."

"Is the food good?" I inquired.

"Let me put it this way," the woman answered. "Stephen King is thinking of basing his next novel on their menu, but you said you were hungry."

The Cave was located in the basement of an apartment building. I opened the door and the first person I saw was a policeman.

"How many?" he asked.

"One," I said.

"Are you a member?" continued the policeman.

"Of what, Officer?" I asked.

"This is a private club," I was told.

I knew all about private clubs. Private clubs are an ingenious way to get around a lot of sticky rules about selling booze after hours. The policeman explained that I could join The Cave for a dollar and have all the rights and privileges of other club members, such as being able to drink until four in the morning.

Such a deal. I paid my dollar and the policeman handed me a membership card. Then he took me to my table in a cozy little corner near the bandstand. As I was being seated, the thought occurred to me, Why is there a policeman here?

"I hope you won't take this the wrong way," I said to the policeman, "but are you expecting trouble here?"

"About twice a week," he answered, "somebody tries to cut the cook."

I considered going back to the hotel and munching on some of the plants in the lobby, but the waitress had already arrived and handed me the menu. It was printed on an air-sickness bag.

There is another rule to follow when you're eating in a place where the food is obviously of questionable quality: Order as simply as possible. As a matter of fact, that's probably a good rule to follow anytime you're eating out. I never order anything I can't pronounce.

"I'll have a steak," I said to the waitress, figuring that it's difficult for anybody to louse up a steak.

I waited for the waitress, who probably hadn't been nearly as ugly ten years and fifty pounds ago, to ask me how I wanted my steak cooked, but she didn't, so I said, "... and I would like it cooked medium well."

"Folks in hell would like some ice water, too, honey," she answered.

"I can't get my steak cooked medium well?"

"Depends on how sober the cook is," she said.

As I waited for my meal and silently prayed for at least some semblance of sobriety in the cook, I surveyed the scene around me. There were all sorts of individuals at the bar, including a very fat woman dressed in an extremely tight pair of red pants that had the words "Roll Tide," the University of Alabama war cry, written down each leg. I made a mental note to speak to the club officers about a stricter dress code for the members.

There also were several couples shuffling around the dance floor as the band blasted away. Bands that play in such places are always loud, because they follow an old musical adage: If you're going to sound terrible, do so as loudly as possible. Bands in such places always play the same songs, too, and they're songs that I hate. These include "Proud Mary," "Jeremiah Was a Bullfrog," "Tie a Yellow Ribbon," and "Feelings."

The band was butchering "Proud Mary" when the waitress returned with my steak. It may have been a good steak at some point in its existence, but when it reached me it resembled a shingle. I reached for my knife. Out of the corner of my eye, I noticed the policeman move his hand toward his gun.

"I'm just going to try to cut my steak," I said. I honestly had no desire to tangle with the cook. Anybody who would do what he had done to my steak obviously was not the sort of person you'd want to face with a knife.

I had a difficult time cutting the steak. In fact, I couldn't. Finally, I asked the waitress for a couple of packages of crackers and attempted to fill up on them.

As I left, the fat girl in the tight pants winked at me.

"Roll Tide," I said, trying to be nice to a fellow member. I said the wrong thing. The band had just cranked up on "Feelings."

"How 'bout a slow dance, Sweetie?" said the fat girl as she moved toward me. I hid behind the policeman, who convinced her not to drag me to the dance floor as she obviously intended to do.

I thanked the policeman, gave him my membership card back, and made myself a promise never again to go out of town when I'm hungry. If the food don't get you, a fat girl might.

* * *

It's odd how time and circumstances change the taste

buds. I travel a great deal these days. Therefore, I eat a lot of airline food and hotel food (which we eventually will get around to passing laws against). But all the while, I find myself craving the food my mother reared me on. I find myself even craving turnip greens, which is a fairly complicated story with a happy ending.

I hated turnip greens when I was a child, but they were a staple for the family. My grandfather grew them in his garden and used to make me help pick them, which was like making the guest of honor at a hanging help build the gallows.

In the first place, turnip greens emit a foul aroma when they're cooking. And they do not look appetizing. As a matter of fact, they look like something that grows on top of a pond. And the very words *turnip* and *greens* are a turn-off to the appetite as well. *Turnip* sounds like something they would find growing on your pancreas.

"Am I going to make it, doctor?"

"Removing a pancreatic turnip is a serious matter, but we'll do everything we can."

Greens. That sounds like something to do with loose bowels.

"Sarah just hasn't been herself lately."

"What's her problem?"

"Got a bad case of the greens. She's been afraid to leave the house for three days."

Now that I'm older and forced to eat modern foods, however, I enjoy the occasional turnip greens that I get. My Aunt Jessie makes them for me when I visit her. Recently, Aunt Jessie had a sort of family reunion at her house, and she cooked a huge pot of turnip greens. As I was saying how tasty they were, Aunt Jessie's daughter, cousin Glenda,

220

spoke up and said turnip greens are sort of how she came to meet her new husband. I enjoy a good love story, so I asked her to explain.

"Well," she said, "I was working at a Hardee's and Owen was working at a gas station next door. One day, I stopped to fill up my tank and he came out to wait on me.

"While the gas was pumping, we started talking and I casually asked him how he was getting along. He said everything was fine, except that somebody had given him a mess of turnip greens and he didn't have a pot to cook them in.

"I said, 'Well, I've got a pot if you've got the greens,' and next thing you know, we got married."

You'll never find that moving a love story in *True Romance*. And isn't there a country music song in all this somewhere? We could call it, "You're the Greens in My Pot of Love."

* * *

Just one more note about food (which should lead me nicely into the next chapter). One of the worst things that has happened to food in the past ten years is the microwave oven. I have one in my kitchen, but it came with the house.

I worry about food that has been prepared in a microwave oven. What is a "microwave" in the first place? Does it have to do with radiation? Whenever I eat something that has been cooked in a microwave, I feel like I should be wearing a lead vest instead of a napkin at the neck.

And why do restaurants that use microwave ovens put a sign on the door that says, "Warning: Microwave Oven in Use"? Somebody told me that if you have a pacemaker in your heart and you stand around a microwave oven, the rays or waves or whatever is inside one of those ovens can throw your pacemaker out of kilter. If a microwave oven can do something like that, what else can it do? My car occasionally won't start in the morning, usually after I've cooked some bacon in my microwave oven. You figure it out.

And you've heard that rumor about the woman who gave her cat a bath and then put him in her microwave to dry him, haven't you? Besides, if God really intended for us to have microwave ovens, why did He give us Ol' Diz charcoal?

Questions like that are always popping up these days. It's the price we pay for living in a world of modern technology. And just to be on the safe side, if I was a cat, I'd stay the hell out of the kitchen. Now, if everyone will kindly climb aboard the turnip truck to the next chapter, we will continue this discussion of modernity.

14 Somebody Pull The Plug On Modernity

I WAS VISITING the folks at home, and my stepfather walked outside to hang the week's wash on the clothesline. I went along for some fresh air.

The winds of early March flapped the sheets and pillowcases and the freshly-washed underwear. Both the sight and the sound were comforting, even reassuring. One of the things that's wrong with our society today, I thought as I watched my stepfather, is that most people are too pretentious to hang their underwear out to dry on a clothesline that any passerby can see.

Today, people prefer to dry their underwear inside their houses in a gadget called a dryer, which spins the clothes in vicious cycles, pumping electrically-heated air to them. As the clothes tumble, odd sounds come from the machine, and when they're finally dry, the machine stops automatically and gives out a signal that it desires to be unloaded.

But why would anybody want to be summoned by a machine?

Clothes dried outside by the sun and the wind and without buzzers (in Smith Barney parlance, the "old-fashioned way") have a certain feel to them. Underwear dried outside, for instance, is less likely to cause itching and, because of the natural freshness, it may not even ride up quite as readily. There's also a wonderful smell to naturally-dried clothes — the smell of the building warmth of early morning.

Maybe one reason people are more grumpy these days is that their underwear smells like coils and filters instead of like fresh sunshine. And it also rides up more aggressively, and we all know that nothing saps a person's friendliness and comfort quicker than underwear creeping into certain crevices.

Just think about a society that didn't mind hanging out its underwear for the world to see: It was a society that accepted the cards it was holding, a society that said, "My privacy is dear, but my refusal to bow to pretense is to be cherished even more." Or, put more simply, it was a society that said, "I'll hang my drawers on the line if I want to, and if mine happen to be more holey than thou's, so be it."

I wouldn't want to leave the impression that I spent an inordinate amount of my childhood staring at other folks' underwear on their clotheslines. I will admit, however, that there was occasional good sport to be had on wash day.

Miss Nellie Bascomb hung her clothes on a line in her easily accessible back yard. She wore those pink bloomers that struck just below the knee and had legs large enough for a fully-grown man to crawl through. When Miss Nellie hung out her entire compliment of bloomers, they looked like flags flapping on a mainsail.

Prissy Betty Ann Hillback, who played piano and sang solos at funerals (and who, you will remember, saved Donnelle Spinks from homosexuality), lived near Miss Nellie. One evening, a commando team of pimply-faced young men, who shall remain nameless, sneaked into Miss Nellie's back yard and took her bloomers off the line.

The raiders then slipped into Betty Ann Hillback's back yard and took her cute little step-ins, with the days of the week embroidered upon them, off the Hillbacks' clothesline and replaced them with Miss Nellie's pinks. The next morning, when Betty Ann's mother sent her out to bring in the clothes, the perpetrators of this foul deed strolled up to Betty Ann and made all sorts of hooting remarks, such as, "Hey, Betty Ann, how about loaning us a pair of your bloomers? We need a tent for a camping trip."

Betty Ann turned pinker than Miss Nellie's underpants and ran into the house. The Hillbacks, incidentally, were the first family in my hometown to buy an electric clothes dryer.

* * *

Please understand that I'm not indiscriminately opposed to modernity. Some modern inventions and conveniences, I fully condone. Here are a few:

— AIR CONDITIONING: There is absolutely no reason to sweat anymore, unless you absolutely want to, which I don't.

— AUTOMATIC TRANSMISSION: I still don't know where reverse is on a straight stick, and remember what an awful time you had with the clutch when you were stuck on a hill in traffic?

— AUTOMATIC ICE-MAKERS: Thank you, whoever invented the automatic ice-maker, for delivering me from those ice trays that froze harder than Chinese arithmetic. The lever always bent when I tried to pry open the ice.

— AUTOMATIC COFFEE-MAKERS: They would be even more automatic if somebody would think of a way to make the thing remember to go out and buy the coffee, too, but you can't have everything.

— HAAGEN-DAZS ICE CREAM: I know this doesn't exactly fit here, but I love Haagen-Dazs ice cream.

— TWENTY-FOUR-HOUR AUTOMATIC BANK TELLERS: Three times a week, I run out of cash at precisely 11:30 p.m.

— BIC PENS: You lose one, so what? For a pittance, you can buy another.

— SCREW-OFF TOPS ON BEER BOTTLES: You never have to worry about keeping a church key handy again.

— OVERSIZED TENNIS RACQUETS: You don't have to bend over as much to hit the ball anymore. Bending over is something I hate about tennis.

— ELECTRIC POPCORN POPPERS: Remember when you had to shake the pot to get the kernels to pop?

— ROACH MOTELS: They don't smell up the house like Black Flag used to and they're quite effective against roaches. I checked my Roach Motel recently and found a dozen dead roaches inside, including three in the lounge and one out by the pool.

— VIDEO CASSETTE RECORDERS: This certainly is a wonderful modern invention. You can tape television programs and watch them later, and you can rent movies and watch them in your very own home. Unfortunately, I have had a video cassette recorder for four years and I still haven't figured out how to work it. I'm waiting for a fully automatic one that you don't have to monkey with and that

226

will mail off for X-rated movies on its own.

— THE THERMOS BOTTLE: A truly amazing invention. In the summertime, I put iced tea in my thermos bottle. Thirty minutes later, I pour out the iced tea and it's still cold. In the wintertime, I put hot coffee in my thermos and thirty minutes later, I pour it out and it's still hot. In the immortal words of my boyhood friend and idol, Weyman C. Wannamaker, Jr., "How do it know?"

— REMOTE CONTROL FOR TELEVISION: This invention has changed my life. Before, when I watched television, I had to sit through all those commercials because I didn't feel like getting up and switching channels. With my remote control, I can change channels any time I want without having to leave my chair.

Do you realize what this means? I haven't had to watch a Drāno commercial — the one that shows the inside of that pipe with all the hair and various other sorts of goo inside it — in years. I also haven't had to watch any commercials advertising feminine hygiene spray or mini-pads. (Has Cathy Rigby reached menopause yet? I certainly hope so.)

And hemorrhoid commercials — I don't have to watch them anymore, either. Do they still run the one where the woman is talking about her hemorrhoids and underneath her face it says, "Roxanne Burgess, Hemorrhoid Sufferer"?

I used to wonder how they found that woman. It's not the sort of thing you hold tryouts for, I don't suppose. How would you keep each contestant's score?

Do you know what *really* would be a marvelous invention? A remote control device for life. Whenever you found yourself in an unpleasant situation, you would pull out your remote control and switch around until you found a situation you liked better.

227

Let's say you've been out half the night with your rowdy friends. You come home singing drunk, and your wife greets you at the door and begins calling you horrible names. Not to worry. You simply pull out your remote control and ZAP!, you're right back with your rowdy friends drinking beer and telling lies again.

* * *

So, you see, there are a few modern inventions that I enjoy, but there are many more that have weasled their way into our lives and have become great nuisances.

Take airplanes, for example. I realize that they date all the way back to the Wright Brothers, but airplanes didn't come into my life until after I was old enough to understand that anything going that fast and that high is inherently dangerous.

I fell in love with trains as a small boy. Somebody — it may have been what's-his-name, the guy who writes the daffy poems — once said, "After spending a day watching trains, baseball seems a silly game." (I just thought of his name: Rod McKuen, and that's the only thing he ever said worth remembering.)

Trains make sense to me. The engine moves and the cars attached behind it follow.

Trains are also romantic, especially their names. I mentioned earlier that I wrote a song about a train called the "Nancy Hanks." It ran between Atlanta and Savannah on the Central of Georgia line. Once, while riding the "Nancy Hanks" from Atlanta to Savannah, I drank fourteen beers in the club car — which was not that big a deal, but getting up and walking to the restroom twenty-six times on a train that is rocking back and forth may yet be a record for American railroads.

Another time I rode a train called the "San Francisco Zephyr" from Chicago to Frisco. (A "zephyr" is a west wind, incidentally.) Somewhere between Denver and Cheyenne, Wyoming, I met an Italian fellow in the club car. He spoke very little English; I spoke no Italian. I did, however, manage to get his name and to ask, "What do you do for a living in Italy?"

"I am painter," Oscar said.

See how romantic it is traveling by train? Have you ever had a drink with an Italian artist somewhere between Denver and Cheyenne, Wyoming, while traveling in an airplane? Neither have I.

"And what do you paint?" I asked my Italian friend. "Landscapes, still-lifes, pastels?"

"Houses," Oscar answered. "I am house painter."

Okay, so how many Italian house painters have you met on airplanes?

Eventually, my profession led me to travel a great deal. When you write books, you have to go many places in an attempt to sell those books. Also, people will invite you to make speeches in front of large groups (that frankly would rather have skipped the dinner and the speaker and kept the cocktail party going).

It soon became evident to me that either I would have to give up the rails as my primary mode of transportation or get a new profession, such as working in a liquor store.

In a more civilized time, a book publisher would say, "Could you be in Bakersfield, California, by Friday?" They would say that on the previous Saturday.

"Certainly," you would answer. "I can connect with the

229

'Super Chief' in Chicago and be there in plenty of time."

But book publishers don't say that anymore. Now they say, "Can you be in Bakersfield by five this afternoon?", and they say that at ten in the morning. And you answer, "No problem. I'll shave and shower and catch the noon flight, and with the time change, I'll be able to get a haircut at the the airport in L.A."

Anyway, the guy at the liquor store said he didn't need any help, so I had to take up flying.

The main reason I've never liked flying is that I'm terrified at the very thought of it. My friends have all attempted to make me feel better by pointing out that more people die from slipping in the bathtub than in commercial airplane crashes. If there were any way to travel by bathtub, I tell them, I certainly would do it.

If airplanes are so safe, why do they make you strap yourself in the seat? And why do they always point out, "Your seat cushions may be used for flotation"? If I had wanted to float to Bakersfield, I would have chartered a canoe.

And I still don't understand how those big suckers fly. I have a friend who is brilliant in the area of engineering and such. One day, we were riding near the airport and a large plane took off over our car.

"What makes those big suckers fly?" I asked him.

"Well, you see, there is the air foil and lift and blah, blah, blah, technical, technical...."

"I know all that," I said, "but what I really want to know is, What makes those big suckers fly?"

Faced with the option of either flying or drawing unemployment, I searched for ways to control my terror. For the benefit of others who may feel the same, here is how I cope with my own fear:

— I drink a lot before getting on the plane. I'm not talking about having one drink or two. I'm talking about joining all the airlines' private clubs, where the booze is free, and drinking six or eight double screwdrivers and then calling for one of those buggies they carry handicapped people in to take me to my gate.

— I drink a lot while I'm in the air, and I ask the stewardesses to allow me to mix my own drinks, so they'll be very strong. The only problem with drinking this much is that sometimes when the airplane lands, I get off and cannot remember what city I was traveling to. So I ask and somebody tells me, but then I can't remember what I was supposed to do when I got there, so I go back to Delta's Crown Room or Eastern's Ionosphere Lounge and have another drink.

— When I have a choice, I prefer to fly with the airline that has had the latest crash. I figure my odds are better on an airline that isn't due.

— I never fly on the national airlines of Communist countries, or countries where they think cows are sacred and allow them to wander around in the streets.

— I never fly on commuter airlines. If the pilots are so good, why are they stuck flying for Air Chance ("We'll take a chance, if you will")? Besides, you know what they serve you to eat on airlines like that? The stewardess passes around an apple and a pocket knife.

— No matter what, I never go to the toilet in an airplane to do anything I can't do standing up. This eventually may lead to a very embarrassing situation for me, but I don't want them to pick through the charred remains of a crash and find me with my pants down sitting on a toilet.

— I call the pilot the night before takeoff to make certain that he isn't drinking and that he is in bed early.

— I am able to relax a bit after the seat belt sign goes off and the pilot comes on the intercom. If they've turned off the warning light and the pilot doesn't have anything to do but talk on the intercom, I figure all is well in the cockpit. On some flights, the pilot never comes on the intercom. I order another drink when that happens.

— I pray a lot. There are no atheists in a foxhole, and I doubt there are any in a 727 that is passing through heavy turbulence after takeoff from Philadelphia at night. I try never to have any dirty thoughts on an airplane, so God will like me and listen to my prayers.

Even if airplanes weren't frightening, they still would be a large pain. The food, of course, is awful; all airports are crowded; and there's usually a baby crying on every airplane (must be some sort of FAA regulation).

Planes are also frequently late, they can't take off or land in heavy fog, and sometimes too many planes are waiting to land or take off. Waiting to take off isn't that unsettling, but circling around waiting to land, knowing that a frustrated and overworked air controller is the only thing between you and a mid-air collision, is not a happy thought.

Keeping up with airline fares these days is also a big headache. I always feel guilty when I fly because I might not have gotten the best fare. You have to be careful trying to get too good a deal, however. I saw advertised recently a flight between Atlanta and New York for $26. I called the airline to inquire. The hitch was that you had to ride in a crate in the cargo hold.

Think how much better the world would be today if the

airplane had never been invented. There wouldn't be any
threat of nuclear war. How are the Russians going to drop a
bomb on us without an airplane? They sure couldn't throw
it out the back of a panel truck.

And if flying had never been invented, we wouldn't have
spent all that money on the Space Program, in which we sent
a bunch of people to the moon to find out that it looks a lot
like Nevada.

If we didn't have airplanes and still took trains, we would
know a lot more about our country. You would be surprised
how much of the country you can see from a train window.
Did you know, for instance, that there are more piles of junk
in Newark, New Jersey, than anywhere else in America?

If there were no airplanes, we wouldn't have to put up
with Frank Borman, and no matter what a terrorist threatened to do, there is no way he could hijack a train to Cuba.
And did you ever lose your bags on a train trip? Of course
not. I took a flight between Atlanta and Charlotte once, but
the airline sent my bags to Caracas.

Planes cause people to be in a rush. They cause them to go
a lot of places they probably wouldn't go to if they thought
about it long enough — places like Nassau and New York
City and Cannes, France, where I flew to once. After about
an hour, watching barebreasted women gets boring; then
you have to go back to the hotel, where every Algerian and
his brother-in-law is in the lobby having a loud argument.

And finally, if we hadn't been smart enough to invent
airplanes, we likely wouldn't have been smart enough to
invent computers, either; and I definitely could do without
computers. In fact, I may be one of the last holdouts against
computers, and I can prove it by explaining that I am typing
these very words on a 1959 manual Royal typewriter for

which I paid ninety bucks and wouldn't sell for five times that, because I don't know if I would be able to find another one.

People in the swing of modern ways often say to me, "Why don't you get yourself one of those word processors? It would make writing a lot easier for you."

No, it wouldn't. First, I would have to sit for hours at a time staring at a television screen with words on it. It would be like watching one of those cable television stations where they play music in the background and words appear on the screen, giving you the news and baseball linescores.

If I watch one of those stations for longer than ten minutes, I get sick to my stomach. It's the same feeling I get when I try to read in a car.

Also, I don't know where the words go in one of those word processors. You type a lot of words onto the screen, which will hold just so many, and then they disappear. What if they accidentally went into somebody else's word processor? Not that anybody else would want my words, but some things I write never appear in print and would tend to embarrass me if somebody else were to look at them.

All of journalism has gone to computers these days. In fact, nobody types on paper anymore. When I was an editor, we had paper all over the place, especially on the floor. It gave the office a homey look. Now, there is no paper and there is carpet on the floor. I walk into a newspaper office today and I feel like opening a checking account.

When I write, I like to hear some noise. I enjoy hearing the tap-tap-tap of the keys on my Royal manual. When I hear that sound, especially if I hear it without interruption, I know I'm getting something accomplished. As with any machine, however, minor problems occasionally occur with my typewriter. For instance, I once wrote an entire book without the letter "e" available to me, because the "e" character had broken on its key.

When I handed in my manuscript, the editor said, "What are all these blank spaces on your manuscript?"

"Wherever you see a blank space," I said, "that's where an 'e' goes."

There's also the small matter of maintaining a fresh ribbon in a manual typewriter, and sometimes the keys get stuck together and you get ink all over your hands trying to pry them apart. I'm constantly getting the "g," "j," and "f" keys stuck together, because I have bricks for hands. But at least my manual typewriter can't be knocked out by lightning and won't go on the fritz if I happen to spill coffee on it.

Frankly, I don't dislike computers as much as I dislike people who spend a lot of time operating them. They speak to one another in a language I don't understand, and I'm convinced they think they're a lot smarter than people who don't know anything about computers. I have a feeling that these are the same people who carried around slide rules when I was in high school and college and thought spending an afternoon discussing logarithms was keen fun.

Computers also have become an excuse. For example, "Pardon me, but is flight 108 to Cleveland on time?"

"Sorry, sir, but our computer is down."

I think what they really mean is that they have lost flight 108 to Cleveland but won't admit it. That's something else I never had to deal with when I rode trains.

"Is ol' 98 running on time?"

"She was about two minutes late into Steamboat Junction, but she's highballin' now."

Once, a large company owed me some money. It never

came. I called and inquired about my check.

"Our computers have been down," I was told.

"Isn't there a company officer somewhere who can simply write a check and then you could mail it to me?"

"All our checks and mailing are done by computer."

I know what they were doing. They were using my money to pay for the repairs on their stupid computers.

I'm afraid we are ruining an entire generation of Americans by getting our children involved in computers at a very young age. In some elementary schools today, kids bring their own computers to class. All I needed in elementary school was a box of crayons and milk money.

You give a kid a computer and strange things can happen. One of the little boogers eventually will figure out how to launch a Pershing missile, and try explaining to what's left of the Kremlin that little Johnny Manderson of Fort Worth, Texas, was just kidding around on his computer. I say put a twenty-one-year-old age limit on computers and send the kids outside to play ball or go drag racing. Should a kid really know his user I.D. before he knows how many fingers to hold up for his age?

My first experience with computers came when I entered college. They handed me computer cards as I enrolled in different classes. Each computer card had written on it, "Do not fold, bend, staple, or mutilate." I wondered what would happen if I should fold, bend, staple, or mutilate one of the cards.

My curiosity finally got to me, so I bent and folded and stapled and mutilated and even poured catsup on my computer card. There were no serious injuries or substantial penalties forthcoming, but it took me two quarters to get my standing as a home economics major changed.

All sorts of things puzzle me about computers:

— Computer shopping: Do we really want to shop by computer? The instant you see a TV commercial, you press a button on your computer and a conveyor belt delivers Ginsu knives to your kitchen and deducts $14.95 from your account. Could you really tell if a pair of loafers would fit by looking at them on a video monitor?

— Easy-to-use computers: That's easy for somebody else to say. I can barely operate a bottle of aspirin.

— Talking computers: Now there are even cars that talk to you. "You need gas, you need gas," says your car. Talking cars give me gas.

— Understanding computers: Where do all those cables on computers go to? Is there a little Oriental guy in a room somewhere with an abacus going a mile a minute? What's the difference between "software" and "hardware"? Is one part wool and itches a lot? Is a "semiconductor" a person who works for the railroad part-time?

— Computer dating: What if the computer doesn't mind girls who don't shave their legs and gets me a date with one? I'm the one who has to kiss her goodnight, not the computer.

— Personal computers: I don't want to get personal with a computer. I wasn't compatible with three wives. How am I supposed to be compatible with IBM?

You know something else about computers? There's nothing funny about them. In doing research for this chapter, I looked in several computer magazines. There was not a single joke section or cartoon in any of them.

The big question we must all ask is, Where is this computer business going to end? How much of our lives are they going to take over? The first computer filled a warehouse.

Now, a computer the size of your fingernail can do the same amount of computing. Will they eventually be like contact lenses, only worse? You see somebody down on their hands and knees and you say, "Lose something?"

"Yeah," comes the answer. "I dropped my computer. I know it's here in the grass somewhere."

Computers can even talk to each other now, so what's to keep them from plotting against us? And here is something else to worry about: What if all the computers on earth went down at one time? Life as we know it would come to a standstill all over the planet. The only people who would know how to carry on would be natives who live in the African bush who never have heard of computers, and me, who has steadfastly refused to learn to operate one.

Frankly, I'm sort of looking forward to that day. I could dress up in a loin cloth with my friends from the bush, and we could dance up and down and I could laugh and say, "I told you so," and poke all those uppity computer-types in their butts with my spear.

I want to get even with computers and the people who build them and the people who run them. That desire peaked recently at the airport in Jacksonville, Florida.

I was awaiting a flight. I went into the airport lounge to have my normal six or eight pre-flight double screwdrivers. There was nothing that looked unusual about the bar — just a couple of barmaids serving a weary traveler here and there.

"Can I help you?" one of the barmaids asked me.

"Double screwdriver, please," I said, "and a little heavier on the screw than the driver, if you will. The weather's bad out and I have to fly."

The barmaid didn't understand my little joke.

238

"What I'm trying to say," I explained, "is could you give me a little extra vodka and a little less orange juice in my drink. I'm nervous when I fly, and the more I drink, the more comfortable is my flight."

"All I can give you," replied the barmaid, "is what the computer shoots out."

"I beg your pardon?" I asked, somewhat in shock.

"The cash register has got this computer in it, and it's hooked up to the little hoses that we pour the liquor out of. All I do is mash the button, and the computer squirts out a shot, and it all gets rung up on the cash register."

"Let me see if I have this straight," I said. "You have no power whatsoever over how the drinks are poured? A computer measures the amount of booze I get in my drink, and there's no way you can change that?"

"Right," said the barmaid.

"In that case," I said, "bring me the coldest beer you have."

"Ain't got no cold beer," said the barmaid. "The cooler's busted."

The flight was delayed two hours because of the bad weather. I caught a cab to the nearest convenience store, bought two quart bottles of beer, and drank them out of a paper sack, eating peanuts and Slim Jims and watching the rain fall. Computerized drinking is the final straw, I thought to myself, and I prayed silently for the day that somebody, or something, would pull the plug on all this madness.

* * *

My incompatibility with modernity does not cease with

airplanes and computers. Here are some other modern conveniences that aren't.

— Telephones: Do you really think we've made a lot of progress in telephones? We haven't. Telephones, when I was a kid, were very simple to operate. You didn't even have to dial the blasted things. You just picked up the receiver, and when somebody else came on the line, you said, "Hilda, get me the courthouse."

Gossip was a lot easier to keep up with then, too, if you were on a party line. And telephone operators would make long distance calls for you, and if the line was busy, they would say, "Would you like for me to keep trying and call you back?" That was service.

I'm very confused about telephones today. I am not certain who's in charge of the telephones anymore, and there are all sorts of things you have to decide when you have a telephone installed.

Telephones used to be black. That was it. They were sort of short and squatty and black. Today, you can have a telephone in the shape of a pretzel if you so desire. A pink pretzel. "Watson, come here, you *savage*."

Telephone numbers used to be fun, too. You dialed PLaza 7-3622, or WEird 9-6238 (if you were calling somebody in California). There weren't any area codes, either, and there were no such things as credit card numbers.

I have a friend who has one those new Sprint calling services. First, he has to dial a local number to get himself a dial tone (or should that be *punch* tone?) in order to make a long distance call. Then he has to punch in something called an "access code." Then he has to dial the number he's trying to reach.

"First," he was explaining to me, "I punch in the local

240

number, 355-0044, which is seven digits. Then I punch in my access code, which is 525-833-611, nine more digits. Then I punch in the number I'm calling, say, 1-817-423-5578. That's another eleven digits, and that's a total of twenty-seven digits. And just about the time I'm punching the last of them, my finger always slips and I have to start over."

I hate recording devices that answer telephones, too, because they entice people to create cute recorded messages.

"Hi, this is Bob. Well, actually it's not. This is Bob's machine. Bob got it from his mom for his last birthday. Mom said she was going to get Bob a puppy, but she was afraid it would just mess all over the carpet and Mom is very clean-conscious, so she got him this machine. Bob is out right now, but he will be back later, so at the sound of the tone, please leave your name and number and any message, and when Bob comes home he will call you back ... Beeeeeeeeeep!"

I can't help it. Whenever I call a number and get one of those recordings, I always leave a message designed to frighten whoever owns the contraption:

"Bob, this is Davenport at the IRS, and we urgently need to see you. Do not make any plans that can't be broken for the next seven years."

Whoever invented call-waiting for telephones should be taken out and shot. Nothing infuriates me more than to be talking to somebody on the telephone when that little click goes off, and they say, "Would you mind holding for just a second?"

Damn right, I mind holding. You called me; I didn't call you.

People who have these devices on their telephones have

large egos. So what if somebody calls and gets a busy signal because the person is on the phone talking to me? Who could be calling that is *that* important? I suspect that they really don't work. People simply have clicking noises put in their phones so that when I'm talking to them, I'll think they're very important and popular because a lot of other people are trying to reach them.

— Showers with complicated knobs: These are found mostly in hotels. Remember how simple showers used to be to operate? There was a knob with an "H" on it and one with a "C" on it. You turned the "H" knob for hot water and the "C" knob for cold water, and you could get your shower just right.

I go into hotels now where it would take a degree from MIT to figure out which way to turn the handle to get hot and cold water. I'm surprised that scalding hasn't reached epidemic proportions in this country.

— Self-service gas stations: You go to one pump if you have a credit card, another if you have the correct cash, or another if it's Tuesday and you're wearing green slacks. I have closed deals on houses in less time than it takes to figure out how to pump ten gallons of gasoline into my automobile.

— Beepers: You can run these days, but you can't hide.

— Eyeglasses that are supposed to turn dark when you walk outside and then clear up when you go back inside: They never clear up enough when you go back inside. I had some glasses like that. Every time I walked inside a building, somebody tried to buy pencils from me.

— Talking soft drink machines: I like to put my coins in the machine and get a soft drink. If I wanted conversation, I'd talk to my car.

242

— The designated hitter in baseball: This has nothing to do with gadgetry, but it's another ridiculous modern idea. It keeps too many old, slow, fat people in the game.

— Electric shoe shiners: They don't work. When I have my shoes shined, I want to hear a rag pop.

— Beer with lower alcohol content: This allows too many sissies into good beer joints and taverns.

— Automatic pinsetters in bowling alleys: They put a lot of good pin boys out of work, and how do those things operate in the first place?

— Commodes in public places that flush automatically: I think it is my right as an American to be able to flush any commode I might be using when I'm good and ready.

* * *

There rests in most of us, I suppose, a longing for the simpler past. I'm convinced that simplicity breeds contentment, but how can one be content when constantly befuddled by a thousand different electronic gizmos that we really don't need, and by a constant stream of new ideas that don't give a national damn for tradition?

As I grow older, I become more and more comfortable ignoring these changes and trends. I don't have to do things any more just because everybody else is doing them. Who knows? Maybe by the time I'm forty, I will be able to tell somebody who wants me to be in Bakersfield by five o'clock to go stick their head in their Jacuzzi; I'm taking the train.

The thought is a delicious one.

15 You Can't Trust A Psychiatrist With Cats

I HAVE A theory about time: The longer you live, the faster it passes. When I was fifteen and wanted my driver's license more than anything in the world, it took me exactly seventeen years to reach age sixteen. After I finally became sixteen, I wanted to be twenty-one so I could go into a bar and order a beer without fearing the Gestapo would show up at my table and take me off somewhere and beat me with rubber hoses. They could have rerun the Thousand Years War during the period it took me to go from sixteen to twenty-one.

Then things began to speed up. It took about six months for me to become twenty-five; twenty-six through twenty-nine went in about a week; and the next afternoon, I turned thirty.

Turning thirty does have some benefits. For one, it means you can smoke cigars. I have never smoked cigars, but I don't think it's appropriate for anyone to smoke them until after they've turned thirty; there's nothing more obnoxious

244

than some juvenile puffing on a big cigar and pontificating about world affairs — which inhaling cigar smoke apparently makes people do. After thirty, however, a person is finally old enough to light up a Cuesta Rey, lean back in his chair, and say the president is an idiot. Even if he is completely misinformed, people will listen to what he has to say and nod in agreement.

Another good thing about turning thirty is that you're finally old enough to realize the truth about life: It isn't fair. All young people think that Moses brought down an extra tablet from the mountain, and written on it by the hand of God was, "Life is Fair."

When my cousin got more banana pudding than I did after supper because she had eaten all her turnip greens and I had just picked at mine, I would complain to my mother, "That isn't fair."

When I was twenty-five and had cornered a beautiful young woman at a singles bar and was regaling her with my interesting tidbits of knowledge, but she wound up leaving with some guy who had large muscles and a Porsche, I turned to the bartender and said, "That isn't fair."

By the time I turned thirty, however, I had learned that what actually was written on that other tablet was, "If life had been meant to be fair, there never would have been such a thing as a proctoscopic examination."

There are some negative aspects to being thirty, of course. For example, young girls start calling you "Mister" and asking you if there was such a thing as television when you were growing up. Your parents and friends stop forgiving you for doing stupid things because you were too young and didn't know any better.

When you're thirty, you finally realize there is no chance

you're still going to be discovered by a major league scout while playing recreation league, slow-pitch softball and wind up in the big leagues and on the cover of *Sports Illustrated.*

When you're thirty, in case it hasn't happened already, you know the time is coming when you will be unable to perform sexually one evening, because your older friends have already started talking about it. The simple knowledge that it *could* happen to you will eat away at your mind, and soon that evening will come and it will go something like this:

"What's the matter?"

"I don't know."

"Is it me?"

"Of course, it's not you."

"It must be me."

"I don't know what's the matter."

"Has it happened before?"

"Of course, it hasn't happened before."

By this time, a cold sweat has covered your body and what you really want to do is hide under the bed in the dark until she leaves, and then have a nervous breakdown in private.

"Why don't we wait until morning," you say.

"I have to be up early for work."

"You don't hate me, do you?"

"Of course, I don't hate you."

"It's just that I've got a lot on my mind."

"I understand. I really do."

She doesn't really understand, of course, and she really hates you and thinks you're a wimp, and what if she goes around telling everybody? This is the stuff suicides are made of.

I had flirted a bit with adulthood before I hit my thirties. I got married for the first time when I was only nineteen. An insurance man followed me around for a month and made me feel guilty until I finally took out a policy that would make certain my bride would be kept financially secure should I die.

Should I die? The thought that I might actually die one day had never occurred to me until I took out that insurance policy. Realizing mortality is a giant step toward adulthood.

I got my first divorce when I was twenty-three. Something like that will wear off a little of your tread, too. I got married again when I was twenty-six and got divorced again when I was twenty-nine. Then something quite adult happened to me: I stopped for a few moments and had a long talk with myself to determine what it was about me that had led to two marriages and two divorces before I turned thirty.

Self-analysis is a very adult maneuver, although in my case, self-analysis did me little good. I couldn't come to any conclusions because I always was arguing with myself.

"Maybe it's because my parents divorced when I was six, and I really haven't had a role model to teach me how to fashion a happy marriage," said my ego.

"Quit making excuses. The truth is, you're a selfish, insensitive person, and nobody can live with you more than three years," said my alter ego.

"But I really tried to make a go of it."

"Tried nothing. You never tried until it was too late and you were afraid of being alone."

"I wasn't afraid of being alone."

"Yes, you were. You realized all of a sudden that if you were alone, there wouldn't be anybody around to keep your underwear clean."

247

"I can take care of my own underwear, thank you."

"How? You've never washed a pair of dirty underwear in your life. Your mother washed it for you and your wives washed it for you. When you weren't married and your underwear got dirty, you simply went out and bought new."

"So look what I did for the underwear industry. I'm basically a good person."

That sort of thing went on for months without resolution, so I did something that all modern adults eventually do. I went to see a psychiatrist.

I didn't tell anybody about this plan, however, because I was reared to believe than anybody who went to see a psychiatrist was admitting that he or she was some sort of screwball, soon to be admitted to a home where they would be kept very still and quiet. Milledgeville, a pleasant little village in central Georgia, was where the state sent its loonies when I was a kid. Anybody who went to Milledgeville for observation or admittance automatically was deemed completely out of focus.

The old men at the store:

"Heard about Tyrone Gault?"

"What happened to him?"

"They done took him to Milledgeville."

"When did he go crazy?"

"Said it come on him real sudden. He come in the house from the barn one day and told his wife one of his cows had just told him to go to town and buy a new tractor, and he thought it was the Almighty that was talking to him. He was back in a hour on a new John Deere."

"I heard about a fellow could make animals talk."

"You ain't never heard of no such thing. You ain't crazy like Tyrone Gault, are you?"

"Naw, it's a true story. There was this Injun and he was sittin' out by his tepee and this fellow walked up and said, 'Can your horse talk?'

"The Injun said of course his horse couldn't talk, so the fellow turned to the horse and said, 'Horse, is this Injun good to you? Does he ever put you up wet? Does he feed you plenty of oats?'

"Well, the horse spoke right up and said, 'Yeah, I can't complain one bit. He's pretty good to me.'

"The Injun couldn't believe his ears. Then, the fellow asked the Injun, 'Can your dog talk?' The Injun said of course his dog couldn't talk.

"So the fellow turns to the dog and says, 'Dog, does your master treat you all right? Does he give you plenty to eat and does he scratch your ears?'

"The dog said, 'He treats me just fine. Ain't a thing in the world wrong with the life I got.'

"The ol' Injun was amazed. The fellow asked him then, said, 'Can your sheep talk?', and the Injun said, 'Yes, sheep talk, but lie like hell.'"

"Get away from here with your foolishness."

"It's a shame 'bout Tyrone Gault, though."

"I feel sorry for his wife and children. Don't reckon he'll ever get out of Milledgeville. They say once you're down there, you don't ever get back right."

"I heard tell the same thing. I wonder what his wife would take for that new tractor?"

Even from a background of complete misunderstanding about mental health, I figured I had no choice but to seek psychiatric help. I decided, however, to pay cash for my treatments and not give my real name, in case the psychiatrist wanted to have me committed.

249

I was living in Chicago at the time, which added to the possibility that I might be crazy. I looked in the yellow pages, found a psychiatrist's office near my apartment, phoned him, and made an appointment.

I should have expected something was wrong the moment I stepped into the psychiatrist's office, which wasn't an office at all but the man's apartment. There were two cats sitting on the couch. A cat never has done anything all that terrible to me personally, but I don't like cats because they're sneaky and snooty, especially if you're a man. Women and cats seem to be able to get along together, to understand each other. Most men don't understand either one.

I sat down on the man's couch between the cats and immediately got cat hairs all over my slacks and the back of my shirt.

"Irene, you and Sparkle leave the room, please," the psychiatrist said to his cats. Not only did the man keep cats in his apartment, where they could get cat hair all over everything, but he had named them "Irene" and "Sparkle."

The psychiatrist looked a bit feline-like himself; he was thin and had beady eyes. We began by talking about my childhood. I told him about my parents' divorce and the fact that I was having problems staying married.

"Did your mother give you a lot of attention as a child?" he asked.

Yes, I answered.

"How about affection?"

I said yes to that, too. Once my mother came to school to pick me up in the third grade and she kissed me, and my friends saw her do it and made fun of me the next day at school. I didn't tell the psychiatrist that, however. He looked as if he had been a big sissy when he was a kid, so I didn't want to offend him by telling him how much I tried to avoid being connected to that description in any manner.

"Did your mother read you stories when you were a child?" he asked.

Sure, I said. "The Little Engine That Could," "Billy Goat Gruff," and "Little Black Sambo," because it wasn't considered racist and you could even name a restaurant chain after it in those days.

"Did she put her arm around you when she read you those stories?" he continued.

I honestly didn't remember.

"Don't you think that would have been a warm, pleasant memory if she had?" asked the psychiatrist.

He was getting fairly personal. I asked him his point.

"Perhaps," he began, "you have been looking for someone to share an intimate relationship with, and because your mother never put her arm around you when she read you stories, you never felt an intimate relationship with her. So now you aren't able to construct one with anyone else."

How could I overcome this obstacle, I asked the doctor?

"Perhaps we could start now," he said. "How would you like for me to read you a story?"

Whoa, Jack, I thought to myself.

The psychiatrist reached into his bookshelf and pulled out a book. "May I come sit on the couch with you and read you a story?" he inquired.

Okay, so I was a little nervous about the way my first psychiatric session was coming along, but I figured I might as well get my money's worth. The doctor sat down on the couch with me and got cat hair all over his slacks and the back of his shirt, too.

Then he began reading me a story. It was a story about a couple of rabbits — I remember that. It might even have been quite a good story, but I was having a difficult time concentrating. Sitting on a couch covered with cat hairs, listening to another grown man read me a story about rabbits was a unique and somewhat unsettling experience.

About halfway through the book, the psychiatrist asked, "Do you want me to put my arm around you while I read you the story?"

He had dialed the wrong number this time.

"I think that's about all the therapy I can take today," I said as politely as possible as I stood up from the couch.

"But we still have fifteen minutes left," he said.

"If it's all the same to you," I replied, "I think I'll be leaving."

"But you haven't heard the rest of the story," he insisted.

"Heard all I want to hear."

"When will we see each other again?" he asked.

I was halfway to the door by then. I threw a couple of twenties and a ten on a table and tried to figure out what was happening. The man wanted to put his arm around me and read me a story. I wondered if somebody had tried to do that sort of thing to Tyrone Gault in Milledgeville. He might have talked to cows, but I was willing to bet that Tyrone was sane enough to avoid this sort of thing.

"Probably never," I answered belatedly.

As I opened the door to leave, Irene and Sparkle appeared in the hallway. I made barking sounds and growled at them, and they ran away. If I didn't get anything else for my fifty bucks, at least I got that.

I never went back to another psychiatrist. What would the next guy want to do? Put a pair of diapers on me and make

252

me suck on a pacifier?

* * *

I suppose I was thirty-one, nearly thirty-two, when I left my apprenticeship and became a full-fledged adult. That's how old I was the day Elvis died. After Elvis — whose music had launched my generation into another direction from our parents' — got fat and died, I realized that adulthood was squarely on me, whether I liked it or not. I was growing old and the world was driving me toward the grave. I was convinced it would be a short trip.

Although my childhood was filled with nothing more than the usual maladies — chicken pox, mumps, measles, etc. — I became a hypochondriac at a very young age. For example, since I was eleven years old and found a wart on the side of my wrist, I've been certain that I have cancer. It was a big, ugly wart, and when I heard that a change in a wart or a mole was one of the danger signals of cancer, I never took my eyes off it.

When I was fourteen, the wart suddenly went away, but then I worried about a mole on my back. I made the mistake of mentioning my fears to my mother. She suggested that when my uncle, a doctor, came to visit, we should have him burn it off.

Burn off my mole? You mean, set fire to it? This is modern medicine? I had seen witch doctors perform the same procedure on television. Cancer or no cancer, I wasn't about to go through anything like that. When my uncle came to visit, I hid in the pump house. Later, somebody told me that the way to get rid of warts and moles was to rub them with a dishrag and then bury the rag.

I followed those directions to the letter. The mole still hasn't disappeared, but you have to give these things time.

Most hypochondriacs enjoy going to the doctor. It gives credibility to their belief that they're seriously ill. But I'm a weird sort of hypochondriac. Although at various points in my life I have had (or thought I had) tuberculosis, leukemia, malaria, and several strokes, I always have avoided going to a doctor. I simply have chosen to sit in a dark room somewhere brooding over the possibility that I might be seriously ill.

Doctors and doctors' offices spook me. I hate sitting in a waiting room — not only frightened out of my wits that I'll soon find out I have only weeks to live, but also nervous about catching whatever the other people in the waiting room have.

That's another of the health problems I've had. Whenever anybody else has a disease, I automatically presume that, with my luck, I soon will have it, too.

A guy at work came down with kidney stones.

"He was fine one minute," somebody said, "and then he was in terrible pain."

I began to feel gnawing pains in my back and stomach and stayed out of work three days drinking beer (for medicinal purposes only) to flush out my kidney stone. I'm not certain if I got rid of the stone, but for three days, I felt absolutely no pain, save a severe headache that disappeared somewhere in the middle of my second beer of the day.

I knew another man who was having trouble with his prostrate gland. He said it hurt when he went to relieve himself, and that the biggest problem was he couldn't always finish, which resulted in a terribly embarrassing circumstance each time he wore khaki pants. "All men begin to have problems with their prostate after they get older," said my acquaintance.

All men? Older? When I was thirty-two, I had managed to avoid doctors for years. But maybe the odds finally had caught up with me. Maybe I had it, too. I decided it was time to get a professional opinion, so I looked up another doctor in the yellow pages and made myself an appointment.

I was quite proud. I had made my own doctor's appointment without anybody forcing me to do it, and I would walk in there and face whatever medicine the doctor dished out. I thought of cancelling the appointment no more than two or three hundred times, the last of which was when the nurse stuck her head into the waiting room and said, "We're ready for you now."

I could bolt away from here, I thought to myself. It's not against the law to run out of a doctor's office and refuse to take an examination. This was something I had to pay for.

The nurse sensed my hesitancy. "Be a big boy and come on in," she said.

Women do that sort of thing to you. They question your manhood in tight situations. If I had walked out of the doctor's office, it would have been a sign of weakness, so in I went.

Did you ever notice that the doctor is never ready to examine you when the nurse says he's ready to examine you? After you get out of the waiting room, there's another wait in a tiny cubicle they call the "holding room."

It's always very quiet in there, and everything is made out of cold metal, and the chair you have to sit and wait in is very uncomfortable, and I always have the feeling that I'm being watched.

"Watch him through the two-way mirror, nurse," I imagine the doctor saying, "and see if he does anything weird."

That idea, of course, makes you even more nervous, and if you have to scratch your privates, say, you're afraid the nurse might be watching you. So you just sit there in that quiet room, in that uncomfortable chair, nervous and frightened with itchy privates.

The doctor finally came in. He checked everything, including my prostate gland.

"Bend over," said the doctor.

I bent over.

Oh, God.

"Do you feel pain or pressure?" the doctor asked me.

"Both!" I screamed.

"Is it more pain or more pressure?" the doctor asked again.

"Pain! It's pain!" I shrieked.

"Are you certain?" asked the doctor.

I was certain by now. It most certainly was pain, the worst I had ever felt.

"You can straighten up now," said the doctor.

"That's easy for you to say, doctor," I replied. "You haven't just had an intimate experience with the Jolly Green Giant's first finger."

After finally conquering my fear and going to the doctor, I decided I ought to try to do something about my problem with dentists, too. I gathered all the courage I could muster and went to have my teeth checked and cleaned.

"When was the last time you went to a dentist?" he asked me.

"I was fifteen. Why do you ask?"

"No reason," replied the dentist. "It's just that I'm going to have to use an acetylene torch to get down to where I can clean these things."

The dentist asked if I wanted gas.

"I woke up with it," I answered. "I always get gas when I'm nervous."

"I mean nitrous," the dentist explained. "It'll help relax you."

I didn't know what nitrous was, but if it would ease my terror, I would take it.

"How much do you want?" was the dentist's next question.

I said two shoulder tanks should do nicely.

When I came out of my trance, the dentist said he was through cleaning and checking my teeth and that I needed seven fillings, two caps, four extractions, and a root canal.

"Soon as my prostate clears up," I said, "I'll be back."

* * *

I remember that as a child I would read things that said, "By the year 1980....", and the "1980" would look so strange to me.

"How old will we be when it's 1980?" my friend Danny Thompson, not exactly a mathematical whiz, would ask when we were boys together.

"Thirty-four," I would answer him.

"Think we'll ever really be that old?" he would ask.

"Not before 1980," I would say.

I had a feeling even back then — and the feeling grew with each passing year — that the 1980s might be somewhat traumatic for me. The sixties were turbulent, the seventies disillusioning, and what on earth would the eighties bring?

I got married again in 1980 ... for the third time.

In 1981, I went to Europe for the first time. The trip cost

me a lot of money, and I saw a lot of cathedrals and concierges with their hands held out.

I also turned thirty-five in 1981. I awakened in a motel room in Birmingham, Alabama, on my thirty-fifth birthday. I was alone. I called practically everybody I knew and mentioned I was alone in Birmingham — that's why they hadn't been able to reach me to wish me a happy thirty-fifth birthday.

"Please don't go overboard on my gift," I cautioned them all. They didn't.

Turning thirty-five also had its ill effects on me. It depressed me a bit to know that I was only five years away from forty, but I was uplifted by the thought that I was now the age my father had been when I was born, and I could easily recall his vitality during my days on his knee. I figured I still had a ways to go before it was time to put on a baseball cap and go to the park and feed pigeons and wet my pants (an indiscretion society allows to old men with worn out prostates).

In 1982, when I was thirty-six, I made another of my infrequent trips to the doctor, and this time he did find something wrong with me. My hypochondria had been vindicated; I'd been telling people for years that I wasn't well. I soon had heart surgery to repair a damaged valve.

I was convinced I was going to die, but I didn't. So what if I don't like Boy George, hair dryers, and airplanes? I'm impressed with medical science, and if there was any sort of computer involved in helping me live through my operation and making me fit again, then I vote that's one we spare when we get around to destroying the others.

I got another divorce in 1983, and that sort of brings my confused life up to date. I'm single again. I live alone in a large house with my dog. My mother is still concerned that I can't stay married and haven't produced any grandchildren.

Aging in any type of world has its negative effects — the hair grays, the eyes and legs go bad, the back hurts, the hangovers linger, and the mind starts to drift. But aging in this modern world is even worse, I think, because the older people get, the more they tend to worry, and we have everything from the killer bees heading north from Mexico to getting wiped out by nuclear war to worry about.

Next to worry, guilt is the most obnoxious part of aging.

I have a friend named Billy. He is forty-two and feels guilty and gets depressed a lot, like I do. Sometimes, we visit each other and feel guilty and depressed together. This usually is after we've gone out the night before and done something to feel guilty and be depressed about that was a lot of fun while we were doing it.

Billy and I are both divorced; we feel guilty and get depressed about that sometimes. We feel guilty because quite often being single is a wonderful state in which to live, but it was instilled in us in a simpler time that we weren't supposed to wind up in our middle ages still acting like we were nineteen. We get depressed because we tried to do what our parents taught us to do but failed, and damned if we know what to do about it now.

We feel guilty because we really don't have all that much ambition anymore. We both have concluded that the best way to live is not to have a lot of things you worry about losing, but our parents wanted us to have it better than they did, and if we just hauled off and went and lived on a boat somewhere, we would be letting them down. We get depressed because we don't know how to deal with those feelings, either.

Depression, says Billy, often takes the form of a tall man with a hat pulled down over his eyes and wearing a raincoat. Billy calls him "Mr. D."

He starts on you in your thirties, according to Billy. "He's the voice you hear in the morning after you've been out having a great time the night before. You never hear that voice when you're younger. Your conscience is basically still clear then.

"But after you get a little older, he starts on you. You remember that Christmas song you used to sing when you were a kid — 'He's making a list and checking it twice, gonna find out who's naughty and nice'? Well, it isn't Santa Claus making the list anymore. It's Mr. D."

I've had my own bouts with "Mr. D." He gets me when I awaken in hotel rooms far away from home in the morning. He's always peering around the corner at me when I'm doing something my mother and the old men at the store wouldn't approve of. He's there when I get involved in the Sunday Morning Academy Award Theater movie and don't make church. He's there after I drink too much, and he's there when I eat animal fat, reminding me that it causes cancer.

He's there whenever there is a dilemma in my life, whenever I don't know whether to go or stay, whether to join or not to get involved, whether to use my heart or my head.

Dilemmas. Has any other generation ever had to face as many as mine has? Sometimes, in recent years, I have felt that modern life is like a giant ice cream parlor with innumerable flavors. Do I stick with vanilla or go for something more exotic? And if I eat tutti-frutti, will it make me gay?

My mother could have read me rabbit stories and hugged

260

me until I turned blue in the face, but I don't think it would
have helped.

16 Maybe Someday, Rainbow Stew

FOR MOST OF my adult life, the only thing that has been perfectly clear to me has been the booze I've used to steady my nerves. You name it and it has confused me, because usually I was right in the middle of the issue, leaning towards both sides.

We could start with Vietnam. I was born a patriot of patriots, and I don't give a rat's tail for the Commies, but I also didn't want to be sent off to get shot in some rice paddy, and I didn't want anybody else to, either.

And drugs. There I was, standing off on the fringes, clinging to the cold beer in my hand while others sat in a circle and passed around a marijuana cigarette and appeared to be having a wonderful time. All I could do was seek refuge with my own kind in some beer joint, playing country music and the Bowl-A-Matic machine.

We've been all over the music. I took off after Elvis, but had I known where he and his music eventually would lead — there's a rock singer today who bites the heads off bats as part of his performance — I likely would have stayed with Red Foley.

And free sex. It has its good points, but what if I get herpes?

Constant dilemma, the legacy for my generation — the In-Betweeners — is a wearisome thing, and I don't mind admitting that I'm weary of it.

God knows, I have tried my best to fit into modern life. I bought a new house a year or so ago, and it has a Jacuzzi in the bathroom. One simply has not arrived today unless one has a Jacuzzi (which sounds like the Italian word for getting bubbles up your butt).

I've been in my Jacuzzi twice. Once, I had hurt my back playing tennis, and the doctor had said that if I had a Jacuzzi, it would be a good idea to get in it and soak my back in the hot, bubbling water.

The problem came when I tried to get out of the Jacuzzi. My back hurt so much I couldn't lift myself out. I was rescued several hours later by sheetrock workers who had come to repair a hole in the wall of my bathroom — which was the result of the first time I got into my Jacuzzi and felt those bubbles in my rear. I thought there was something strange in the tub that wanted to make friends, and in my haste to get out, I fell and knocked a hole in the wall.

So if I really am that tired of the dilemmas of modern life, what can I do about it?

First, I have to come to grips with the fact that I soon will be forty, and it's time I stopped trying to understand all that is strange and new to me. By the time a person is forty, it's much too late to comprehend anything young people are doing or thinking, and we look silly when we try.

The best thing to do is what our parents did — write off

the younger generation as totally gone to hell. If you need evidence, cite the children out in Texas who put dead bats in their mouths in an effort to emulate that nut rock singer I mentioned earlier. These children had to take rabies shots for biting bats, and our parents thought we were strange because we listened to Elvis. (I hope most parents of In-Betweeners now realize that Elvis wasn't that bad after all, compared to what is happening today. If they have, then rest well, Elvis, wherever you are; all is forgiven.)

But if kids today want to eat bats, there's nothing I can do about it, so I might as well relax and worry about something I can control. Nothing that I have control over comes to mind right off, but at least that's something else I can worry about.

After I have accepted the fact that I'm out of step with modernity, I must then look for a niche in which to crawl and rest contentedly with the idea of retirement; I'm too far gone to run in the fast lane.

I don't know if I'll ever take what seems to be a drastic step for someone who has been an urban creature for more than half his life, but I do occasionally dream of going home. Back to my roots. Back to Moreland.

Somebody once said to me, "We spend the first half of our lives trying to get away from home. We spend the second half trying to get back."

Growing up in Moreland is the primary reason I am what I am — a premature curmudgeon, longing for the simple life — and I wonder if moving back would fulfill that longing.

The boys from Moreland. Some of us got away, others didn't. Dudley Stamps is still living there. He built himself a house on the land where he was reared, and he works on cars. He steadfastly refused to budge from where he was when the changes came.

He built a stereo system in his new house that piped music into all the rooms, and he issued a dictum to his wife that never, under any circumstances, would there be anything but country music on his stereo system. He caught her disobeying his order one day — she was playing a rock 'n' roll station on the radio — and that may have been one of the things that led to their divorce. At least the man had his priorities in order.

Danny Thompson and Anthony Yeager stayed around home, too, and Clyde Elrod came back. He did just what he said he was going to do; he spent twenty years in the Navy, retired, and now drives the butane truck in Moreland. I was home for a visit not long ago, and he came by to fill my parents' tank. He told me that he used to go out on a ship for days and sit there and look out on the Indian Ocean, and all he could think about was getting back to Moreland one day.

"We didn't know how good we had it growing up," he said.

I enthusiastically concurred.

The other boys from Moreland, like me, still haven't given in to the urge to return. Bobby Entrekin has a wife and a daughter and he travels, too, so I rarely see him. I've lost track of Charlie Moore. Mike Murphy has three kids and his own business, and Worm Elrod is a hairdresser.

I suppose I also should mention Little Eddie Estes. Soon after he made that marvelous catch in centerfield to save the game against Grantville, he died in an automobile accident. He was only fourteen. His mother and daddy buried him in the Moreland Methodist cemetery, about three long fly balls from the exact spot where he made the catch.

* * *

While the rest of the world went bananas, Moreland changed very little at heart. Today, Cureton and Cole's store is boarded shut, and they're trying to refurbish the old hosiery mill and turn it into some kind of museum that reflects life in the village a hundred years ago. Moreland still respects its past, and I like that.

Steve Smith's truckstop is gone, but the interstate took most of the truck traffic anyway, and that makes Moreland even quieter. There is still no traffic light and no police department, and they still have dinner-on-the-grounds at the Methodist and Baptist churches. And you still have to drive to Luthersville in the next county to buy a bottle of whiskey. It would do me good to live someplace where the nearest bottle of whiskey is a county away.

They're still neighborly in Moreland. My Aunt Una and her husband, John, live just up the dirt road from my parents. John came down sick and they didn't know what they were going to do about plowing their garden.

"One day," my Aunt Una was telling me, "we heard this commotion out in the garden, and we looked out and there was one of our neighbors — a pilot who bought a farm down here — on his tractor plowing our garden for us. I don't know what we would have done without him."

They still plant gardens in Moreland, too, and if I lived there, there would be no reason to set foot in a McDonald's again. My Aunt Jessie, who lives on the other side of my parents' house, continues to work her own garden despite her age.

I had lunch with her recently. She served fried chicken, baked chicken, baked ham, cornbread dressing, butterbeans, field peas, green beans, fried okra, sliced home-grown tomatoes, creamed corn, mashed potatoes with gravy, several varieties of cake and three pecan pies she had baked herself, and a large container of iced tea. We sat under a big tree outside and feasted upon her offerings, and there was peace in the moment.

But even if I never take the final plunge and move back home, I know that Moreland is there, mostly yet unspoiled, and that settles me when I'm caught in a traffic jam or waiting for a light to change in the city, as I stand next to a kid with a ghetto blaster on his shoulder, beating out sounds to have a nervous breakdown by. In Moreland, the music you hear is that of one of the church choirs, drifting out the open windows on a soft, still Sunday morning.

And although I remain fearful that the world eventually will go crazy enough to spin off its axis and fly into space somewhere, there are, in fact, occasional glimpses of hope that manifest themselves.

We have a popular, conservative president who once played cowboy roles in the movies. Sigma Pi, my old fraternity at Georgia, was kicked off campus in the seventies, primarily because of drug use in the chapter. It currently is making a comeback. There was even a recent letter to the editor of the Atlanta papers written by a disgruntled University of Georgia student. His complaint was that the university faculty was too liberal for the mostly conservative student body.

I read somewhere that sales on white socks are up twenty percent. Pick-up truck sales have been on the rise for years, and more and more bars are selling beer in longneck bottles. There's a joint I go to in Atlanta where they have an all-country jukebox, including a complete study in George

Jones, and, right there on Peachtree Street in trendy Buck-head, the place is packed every night.

Tobacco chewing and snuff-dipping are in style again, and ridership on America's passenger trains is at an all-time high. There was a recent month in which there were four separate passenger train accidents, including one in New York where two trains collided head-on. One person was killed and a hundred were injured, and people who prefer planes made a big deal of it. But if I'm going to be in an accident while traveling, I still would prefer it to be on a train. Let two jets run together and see how many walk away.

Traditional clothing is in again. In fact, you're called a "preppie" if you wear button-down collars today. But I still contend there would be less crime and craziness in this country if everybody dressed nicely. You never hear of anybody robbing a liquor store dressed in a Polo shirt and a pair of khakis and Weejuns with no socks. Check police records if you don't believe me.

Some changes, like air conditioning, have been good for us all. Even people who live in the most rural areas of the country have air conditioning now. I have an acquaintance in a small town who sells air conditioning. He told me about getting a telephone call at his office from a lady who lived so far back in the country that the sun went down between her house and the road.

"She wanted to know what kind of air conditioners I had and what they cost. I was telling her about one air conditioner with this many BTU's and another air conditioner with that many BTU's. When I finished, she said, 'All I want is an air conditioner that will cool a b-u-t-t as big as a t-u-b.'"

Still, if we don't someday cut back on radical change and unchecked progress, we may all get our b-u-t-t's blown away or replaced by robots. Or else we might end up taking off all our clothes and squatting naked in trees, like Crazy Melvin, from worrying about it.

Maybe it will be us, the In-Betweeners, who finally make some sense out of the world again. We're still young enough to have the energy to do it, and, as we get older, perhaps we will have the wisdom, too. We've seen the old way of life that we were reared in, and we've seen the new one that has given us ulcers; maybe we can pick the best of each and produce a world where everybody has a fair chance and an air conditioner. But salad bars will be unlawful.

And if we're able to do that — if we're able to lead the way out of the wilderness of frightening modernity and back into the land of simplicity and contentment that we knew as children — then having lived with the dilemmas will have been worth it. Somebody has to do something before the Democrats nominate Phil Donahue for president and he up and picks Billie Jean King as his running mate.

But until that day comes, play me the old songs, bring around my old friends, keep the beer cold, and constantly remind me to cling to the immortal words of the man who sings now in the void left by Elvis, Merle Haggard:

> *"One of these days,*
> *When the air clears up*
> *And the sun comes shinin' through,*
> *We'll all be drinkin' that free Bubble-Up*
> *And eatin' that Rainbow Stew."*

SHOOT LOW, BOYS— THEY'RE RIDIN' SHETLAND PONIES

LEWIS GRIZZARD
In Search Of True Grit

To Chuck Perry, the editor's editor.

— 1 —

Walk a Mile
In the Duke's Boots

HERO. IT WAS a word I heard often in my youth. Even before I knew what it meant, what it stood for, I liked the way it sounded. HEro, as in strong and masculine. You almost grit your teeth as it rushes from the back of the mouth.

I think the first time I heard it used was in reference to my father. He was recently back from Korea, where he had been wounded and captured before escaping and being sent home. All the men who fought that war were heroes, but my father's Purple Heart certified his status.

I remember sitting in his lap with my arm around his neck and feeling the back of his head. "What are these lumps, Daddy?" I asked.

"Shrapnel," he said.

"What's that?"

He tried to explain. It all sounded so exciting, so heroic,

to a five-year-old boy. He never complained about the pain, but my mother said he used to get awful headaches. Maybe the booze helped to ease that pain. And when it beat him down and left him in ruin, they called him "hero" again as a sort of explanation. It was years before I knew what they meant.

The next hero I encountered was Roy Rogers. At age six I saw my first Roy Rogers movie, and afterwards I rode with him and Trigger and Bullet and Dale and Buttermilk on a thousand vicarious adventures through the woods near my house and once even into my mother's flower garden.

"Get out of that flower garden!" my mother screamed.

"Quiet, Mom," I whispered back. "They're about to rob the stage."

My grandfather (who was quite heroic to me, too, since all the neighborhood dogs followed him around) was also a big Roy Rogers fan. Once when we were watching Roy on TV, a collection of range riffraff kidnapped Dale and took her to the line shack. I never knew exactly what a line shack was, but there was always one in every western, and nothing good ever happened there.

As the villains tied up Dale, my grandfather yelled to the television screen, "Don't worry, Dale! Roy'll get those sons of bitches!" Which he most certainly did.

Years later I had the opportunity to interview Dale Evans, and I asked her whatever became of Trigger and Bullet. "Roy had them stuffed and put into his museum when they died," she said.

For Dale's sake, I hope Roy goes before she does.

Norris Cole was another of my early heroes. He was a year older than me and one of the greatest climbers of all time. After observing that squirrels had unusually long claws which enabled them to climb trees with ease, Norris grew his fingernails and toenails extremely long. He soon became known as Norris "Claws" Cole.

"Claws is a real good climber," his little brother Fred used to say, "but he's awful to sleep with." About twice a month Fred would have to go to the doctor for stitches after Claws had rolled over during the night and snared him. Fred eventually took to sleeping with the dogs.

Claws didn't care how tall a thing was or how much danger was involved; if it was there, he climbed it. Trees were his specialty, but he also climbed the town water tank, Confederate war memorials, forest ranger towers, the Methodist church steeple and every telephone pole in town.

All of his climbing wasn't recreational, however; he also did public service climbing. Mrs. Loot Starkins's husband, Jake, used to get very drunk, and when Mrs. Loot started screaming at him, Jake would climb to the top of the tree in their front yard to get away from her. One day Mrs. Loot screamed so much that Jake, perched safely in his tree, swore he was never coming down again. Somebody called for Claws, and he climbed up and talked Jake down out of the tree.

"How'd you do it?" one of the neighbor ladies asked.

"Told him if he didn't come down, I was going to teach Mrs. Loot how to come up," said Claws.

I heard several years ago that Claws died in a climbing accident, although more than likely it was the falling that got him.

"Reckon Claws went to heaven?" one of the locals asked when he heard about the accident.

"If they tried to keep him out," said an old man, "he'd just climb right back in."

Then, of course, there was my boyhood friend and idol, Weyman C. Wannamaker, Jr., a great American in the truest sense of the phrase. It was Weyman, for example, who taught me to shoot pool and to use the big end of the cue to hit folks over the head with in case of a disagreement.

"You had one foot off the floor when you made that shot," an unwise opponent said to Weyman one afternoon in the pool hall. Words were exchanged, and then the other fellow called Weyman a "do-do pot who doesn't love the Lord."

Weyman turned his cuestick around and raised a large lump on the head of the source of the insult. Then he pulled the victim's mouth open and inserted the five-ball. Afterwards, Weyman could have climbed onto the table and kicked balls into the pockets, and no one would have spoken on behalf of the rules of billiards. A man has to do what he has to do.

There was almost no end to Weyman's talents and his heroism. His most heroic act, however, was single-handedly removing the snake from Kathy Sue Loudermilk's dress. Of course, it was Weyman who put it there in the first place. A man has to do what he has to do.

It was just a little garden snake, but after Kathy Sue flailed around for awhile, screaming and shrieking, Weyman began to feel guilty. So he pushed everyone aside and took it upon himself to remove the snake. As the serpent worked its way south toward Kathy Sue's lovely hiney, Weyman shouted, "Don't worry, Kathy Sue. I'll stop it before it tries to make a U-turn!"

Weyman grabbed for the squirming snake, but all he came up with was a handful of Kathy Sue's shapely buttocks. The terrified snake crawled past her step-ins and headed for the apparent security of her ample bosom.

Weyman, ever vigilant in his attempt to save the lovely Kathy Sue, reached down the front of her dress in search of the snake. Five minutes later, he snatched the devil from a pit the likes of which it would never find again.

"Are you OK?" Weyman asked Kathy Sue.

"Fine," she answered, smiling at Weyman.

"Are you gonna tell your father what I did?"

"I sure am," said Kathy Sue. "I'm going to tell him you dropped a snake down my dress twice. You do have time, don't you?"

My father, of course, was a super patriot throughout his life, and one of his great pleasures was singing "The Star-Spangled Banner." He was one of the few people who could sing it without bruising the ears of those around him, and he missed no opportunity to bellow it out loud and clear.

Once at a baseball game we attended together, he sang so loudly that everyone around turned and stared. When we sat down, I said, "Daddy, it embarrasses me when you sing the national anthem that loud."

"Son," he replied, "it embarrasses me when you don't."

Years later someone came up with a term that described the sort of heroism I had come to revere. They called it True Grit, and they made a movie by the same name starring John Wayne, "The Duke," who dramatized it as well as anybody could. It was a great movie, a classic, an "outside movie."

Maybe that needs some explanation. You see, there are inside movies and outside movies. An inside movie is where most of the scenes take place inside a house, and there are a lot of women in the cast and a lot of lovey-dovey talk.

Or, worst of all, an inside movie could be an English movie. Every English movie I ever saw had all the "action" take place in a library with a group of people, dressed for dinner, jabbering nonsensically about whether Mrs. Witherington-Kent had done in Mr. Witherington-Kent with poisoned kidney pie.

Outside movies, on the other hand, always involve guns and horses or tanks and planes, and there are a minimum of women. If the hero wants a kiss, he can kiss his horse or tank.

The problem with women in outside movies is that they're always turning their ankles. Hero is trying to get out of a tight spot, and he's dragging Sweet Thing behind him, and suddenly she turns her ankle. So now he's got to pick her up and carry her.

I was watching an outside movie once with Weyman C. Wannamaker, Jr. Alan Ladd was the star, and his horse was dead, he was out of water and he was trying to get through the desert with this dancehall dolly who was tagging along behind him. Sure enough, she turned her ankle.

"What am I going to do with you now?" asked Alan Ladd.

"Leave her for the buzzards!" Weyman screamed from the audience.

Alan Ladd, gentleman that he was, picked up the girl and carried her all the way back to town. Weyman never went to see another Alan Ladd movie. *True Grit*, on the other hand, he saw forty-seven times. Now, that was the quintessential outside movie.

John Wayne played Marshall Rooster Cogburn, a one-eyed, whiskey-swilling, foul-mouthed old coot who goes riding off into Indian territory with Mattie Ross (Kim Darby) and a Texas Ranger named Le Boeuf (Glen Campbell) to find the galoot (Jeff Corey) who shot Mattie's dad and who is also a member of a gang led by the notorious Lucky Ned Pepper (Robert Duvall).

Young Mattie, an expert on human character, picks Rooster Cogburn to lead this mission because she believes he has "true grit." Or, as he is described by another member of the cast, "He's the big fella with the eye patch, and fear don't ever enter his mind."

What eventually happens is that Rooster Cogburn tracks down the varmint who killed Mattie's pa, and then he faces the entire Lucky Ned Pepper gang in a four-against-one shootout.

What a scene! What grit!

Rooster Cogburn advises Ned Pepper that he's taking him in, and Ned Pepper says that's big talk for a one-eyed fat man. So Rooster puts the reins to his horse between his teeth, cocks his rifle with his right hand and draws his pistol with his left and says, "Fill your hands, you son of a bitch!" Then Rooster charges straight ahead even though he's bad outnumbered.

Horse galloping. Hat swept back by the wind. His guns blazing, their guns blazing. Three members of the gang go down and Ned Pepper is filled with holes, but he still has the strength to fire a shot at Rooster, killing his horse.

The horse falls on one of Rooster's legs and traps him. Here comes Lucky Ned aiming to finish him off, but before he can pull the trigger, Glen Campbell picks him off and The Duke escapes another tight spot.

True Grit. John Wayne had it, all right. But so do a lot of other people of far less fame. Folks who have overcome overwhelming odds, have fought and won and fought and lost, have spit in the devil's eye, have soared with eagles despite being surrounded by turkeys, have kissed innumerable frogs in search of a prince, have been bloodied and bullied and tricked and tangled and peed on and pissed off. They're out there everywhere, these unsung heroes. None has ever wiped out an entire gang of outlaws like Rooster Cogburn did, but in their own ways they have robed themselves in The Duke's heroic garb for a moment or two.

There was the morning I drove into Tellico Plains, Tennessee, and walked into a beer joint. I asked the barmaid where I could get breakfast. She said for two dollars she would go to the grocery store and buy the fixings and cook me up something in the back.

It would have been a bargain at any price. Fried eggs. Bacon. Potatoes. I paid her the two dollars for breakfast and then handed her a two dollar tip. She smiled a toothless smile and said, "God bless you, young'un. I been savin' six months and I was just two dollars short."

"Of what?" I asked.

"Of enough to buy me some store-bought teeth," she said. "I ain't chewed nothin' in fifteen years."

I have walked the streets of Yellville, Arkansas, nodding at strangers; I have bought fresh corn from a farmwife in Lodi, Wisconsin; and I have drunk beer with a one-armed man in a beer joint in a town I can't remember somewhere in Oklahoma. I had one too many and asked him where he lost his arm. He said he couldn't remember for sure, but he was certain it would turn up any day now.

I even proposed marriage once on the road. I ate the best fried chicken on earth in the Foley Cafe and Bakery in Foley, Alabama, and I sent the waitress back to tell the woman who cooked that chicken that I would marry her on the spot.

"Doris is already married," said the waitress, "but I ain't." I wiped the grease off my hands and left Foley, Alabama, behind me as quickly as possible.

These are the people I have come to honor. Not those who bask in the spotlight, but the strong, the swift, the courageous who huddle among the masses. True grit comes in many different shapes and sizes, and it often turns up where you least expect to find it.

—— 2 ——

Profiles in True Grit

A Free Spirit On the Road

I MET AL BERGMAN completely by chance. I was driving through one of Atlanta's spiffiest neighborhoods when I noticed a police car pulled off to the side of the street, blue lights flashing. The policeman was talking to a bearded man of advancing years who appeared to have made a camp in a wooded area just off the street. I figured the policeman was running him in for vagrancy.

"I stopped to investigate a wreck and saw him," the policeman said. "I told him some of the ladies in this neighborhood might complain about him, and that he'd be better off on down the street near the park."

I walked over and introduced myself. His beard was long and full and white. He was sitting next to what appeared to be an old-fashioned wagon. His dog, a German shepherd named Jamie who was tied to a nearby tree, was finishing her supper.

Al Bergman told me he was sixty-nine and that he had retired from the real estate business in Nashville. What he was doing was walking around the United States, pulling the wagon that held his supplies.

"Been thinking about doing something like this for a long time," he said.

Got any family?

"Wife, three kids and nine grandchildren."

And what does the wife think of this odyssey?

"Let's just say it wasn't a joint decision," he answered.

Al Bergman volunteered more information about himself. Said he didn't smoke and that he had jogged for years, which was how he was able to pull his wagon. "I make fifteen miles a day on flat land and about ten when it's hilly." He said he had parachuted into Greece with the OSS during World War II, and that he had been a roadbuilder in South America and later in Vietnam.

I asked if he was afraid camping all alone.

"Jamie's a trained attack dog," he said. "And they taught us how to handle situations in the OSS. I still know how to put a piece of wire around a man's neck.

"Tell you the truth, though, I haven't had one minute's trouble. There are an awful many good people left in this country. They've offered me money and food for me and Jamie, and some of 'em want me to spend the night in their houses. But I don't want to take a thing. I want to do this all by myself."

Al said he was going south out of Atlanta and when he reached the Florida Keys, he would head back up the west coast of Florida, continue along the Gulf and on to California.

"Got to see this country one more time before I'm gone," he said. "And I want to see it the right way — from the ground at one mile an hour."

I asked Al if he were going to heed the policeman's advice and move on down the road to the park.

"No," he said. "I could make it, but I think Jamie's too tired to walk another step."

WEARING HER STORY ON HER BACK

It wasn't the sort of place I would want my mother to catch me in, but there were a few more stories to tell and we didn't want to give up the night quite yet. That's how we ended up in the strip joint.

It didn't take long to figure out the hustle. After each girl danced, she would pick out a table and join those assembled, asking to be bought a drink, which probably was nothing more than Kool-Aid but cost a cool four bucks.

"Hi, I'm Mikki," she said. "Buy me a drink?" She was blonde and young and, judging from her performance on stage, quite athletic. As she sat at our table, I noticed the tattoo on her back.

"It's a horse with wings," she said. "Me and my first husband had 'em done at the same time. He had an American flag done on his back. He was real sexy when he took his shirt off."

For four bucks I figured I might as well get the entire story, so I asked what had happened to her first husband.

"He got blowed up in a factory," she said. "Him and a lot of others. We didn't have no insurance on him, so he left me broke."

"And that's when you started stri — , I mean, dancing?"

"I got married again after that. To a soldier. But he run off."

"So then you started dancing."

"I saw an ad in the paper. I auditioned and got the job. It beats waitin' tables."

"You don't mind dancing in front of all these people without your clothes on?"

"Don't bother me. The more that watches, the more tips I get. I made $200 last weekend."

It was an orderly process: While the girls danced, the men slipped bills under garters worn at the thigh. After their routines, the dancers rewarded the tippers with a kiss.

Mikki said she wasn't going to stay in town much longer, that she was heading to Las Vegas to be a chorus girl. "I hear they make two thousand a week out there," she said.

"And you won't have to kiss anybody for tips," I added.

"Kissin' don't bother me," she said. "Kiss enough frogs and you might find a prince."

She put down her glass, winked and went back to dance and kiss again. I wondered if she would ever make it to Vegas. I wondered if she would ever find a prince. I doubted it, but tattooed strippers have a right to dream, too.

SAYING AN AGE-OLD GOODBYE

There were maybe half a hundred of us in the airport concourse waiting for the call to board. Some read. Some stared. Some stumbled through awkward goodbyes.

Jets have taken away some of the romance of saying goodbye. When you said goodbye at a train station, there were tears and long last kisses. Saying goodbye at an airport, I thought, is like leaving to go to a convenience store for a box of cereal.

Then I saw the kid and his mother. She had to be his mother. The kid was a Marine but obviously hadn't been one for long. His uniform was ill-fitting and seemed to itch. He had some hair but not much.

The kid was leaving on the plane. His mother had come to say goodbye. I let my imagination run at its own pace.

He looked nineteen, tops. She was in her late thirties or early forties, still a pretty woman. She never took her eyes off him, trying, I suspect, to memorize every detail of him so that when she missed him, which would be every day, she could recall his face and maybe ease the pain a little.

He seemed terribly uncomfortable. I guessed him to have boot camp behind him. He had been home on leave. Now he was being sent to his first assignment — adult sort of stuff. The last thing he needed was a doting mother who wouldn't take her eyes off him at the airport.

He smoked a cigarette as they talked. Or, as his mother talked. He only nodded, or grunted, or gave an occasional yes or no and then took another pull off his cigarette. He was new at cigarettes, too. He tried to flick the ashes off with a finger but flicked the fire instead. The hot ashes landed on the jacket of his uniform.

His mother quickly brushed off the fire before there was any damage to the government-issued fabric. That embarrassed the kid, too. A Marine doesn't flick the fire from his cigarette onto the jacket of his uniform, and even if he does, his mother doesn't brush it away.

I wondered about the kid's father, the mother's husband. Why hadn't he come? He was probably dead. No. He had probably split, and that's why the mother hovered about her son so and wished that he didn't have to leave her and dreaded the loneliness that surely would follow.

Their time ran out.

"When do you think you'll be back?" the mother asked.

"Christmas, I guess," the kid answered.

"It's a long time to Christmas," she said.

"Yeah," grunted the kid.

"You'll write me?"

"I'll write you."

"Be careful."

"OK."

"I love you," she said.

The kid mumbled back all that would come out. His mother kissed him. He let her, and then he disappeared down the walkway to the plane.

She wiped something from the corner of her eye and went home to wait for Christmas.

A MEMORY GOOD FOR A LIFETIME

We had only one real Christmas together, my mother, my father and I. Only one Christmas when we were actually in our own house with a tree, with coffee and cake left out for Santa, with an excited five-year-old awakening to a pair of plastic cowboy pistols, a straw cowboy hat and an auto-graphed picture of Hopalong Cassidy.

My first Christmas I was only a couple of months old; that doesn't count. Then we were traveling around for a couple of years. The Army does that to you. Then there was Korea. And then we had that one Christmas together before what-ever demons my father brought back from Korea sent him to roaming for good.

That one and only Christmas together, my father had duty until noon on Christmas eve. I waited for him at the screen door, sitting and staring until that blue Hudson, "The Blue Goose" as my father called it, pulled into the driveway. I ran out and jumped into his arms.

"Ready for Santa?" he asked.

"I've been ready since August," I shouted.

But before we could settle in for our Christmas, my father had to take care of a problem. He had found this family — the old man out of work, in need of a shave and a haircut, and his wife crying because her babies were hungry. My father, whatever else he was, was a giving man. He couldn't stand to have when others didn't.

"They're flat on their butts and it's Christmas," I remember his saying to my mother. "Nobody deserves that."

So he somehow found a barber willing to leave home on Christmas eve, and he took the old man in for a shave and a haircut. Then he bought the family groceries. Sacks and sacks of groceries. He bought toys for the kids, of which there was a house full. The poor are often fruitful.

We didn't leave them until dusk. The old man and the woman thanked us, and the kids watched us with wondering eyes. As we drove away in "The Blue Goose," my father broke down and cried. My mother cried, too. I cried because they were crying.

We all slept together that night and cried ourselves to sleep. Next morning, I had my pistols and my hat and my picture of Hopalong Cassidy.

Maybe the three of us had only one real Christmas together — my father had left by the time the next one rolled around — but it was a Christmas a man can carry around for a lifetime. Each year at Christmas, with my father long since in his grave, I thank God that one is mine to remember.

GETTING WHAT HE DESERVED

There were seven or eight of us in line, waiting to pay the cashier for our lunches. We were all in a hurry because that's the way of the American business-day lunch. At the front of the line was a woman with a small boy of about eight. He was a cute little fellow wearing jeans, sneakers and a pullover sweater. A shock of dark hair fell over his eyes.

As the woman fumbled in her purse, looking for money to pay her check, the kid noticed a display of candy bars beside the cash register and immediately wanted one.

"You can't have any candy," said his mother. "You had pie with your lunch."

"But I want some candy," said the kid. His tone was surprisingly insistent. Almost belligerent.

The mother continued her search for money in her purse, and the kid continued to whine about the candy. Then he began to stomp his foot.

The rest of us in line were beginning to get restless. We bunched a little closer together and several folks began mumbling under their breath.

"Ought to snatch him bald," said one man quietly.

The kid by now was reaching for the candy display in open opposition to his mother. She grabbed his arm and pulled it away, but not before he clutched a Snickers bar in his hand.

"Put that back!" said his mother.

"No!" shouted the child, his lips pooched out in a classic pout. It was an arrogant "No!" A why-don't-you-try-and-make-me "No!"

The line bunched even more closely together, and the man who had suggested snatching the kid bald appeared ready to do so himself. So much for the kid's shock of dark hair, I thought.

But the mother moved suddenly and with purpose. She paid the cashier, took back her change and dropped it into her purse. Then with one quick motion, she grabbed hold of the child's pullover sweater and lifted him off the floor. The moment his sneakers came back to earth, she turned his back toward her and began flailing his backside. She flailed and flailed. A look of disbelief came across the kid's face. His eyes filled with tears. He tried to break away, but that incensed his mother more, and she flailed him again.

When she had finished administering the punishment, she turned the child around and pointed a finger squarely in his sobbing face. With a voice strong and certain, she said, "The next time I tell you to do something, young man, will you do it?"

The child looked at the floor. Meekly and sincerely, he replied, "Yes, ma'am."

The mother turned to go. The child returned the Snickers bar without further hesitation and marched dutifully out behind her.

The rest of us in line broke into spontaneous applause.

A NOBLEMAN IN RAGS

Alvin was a thirty-year-old black man. He was one of the street people in our nation's capital, Washington, D.C. He had no job. No money. He slept and ate in shelters for the poor. He told horror stories about some of the folks in those shelters.

I met Alvin on a cold, fall day as we both stood in Lafayette Park across from the White House. Within sight of that great edifice and all it represents, I was a soft touch when he asked me for a handout. As I gave him a dollar, I asked how he got in the shape he was in.

"I'm from Dayton, Ohio," he answered freely. "I moved to Maryland with this woman who was in the Navy. One night I came home drunk and she started hittin' on me.

Look here at this knot on my arm. That's where she got me with a stick.

"I was drunk and I got mad and whipped her ass. The police came and got me, and I was in jail for two months. When I got out, my woman had moved off with another man. I still miss that woman. Especially at night," he said.

"I came here to look for a job, but there ain't no jobs. I had nearly 'bout a thousand dollars when I got here, but that ran out pretty fast and I started sleeping in them shelters. I called my mama in Dayton and told her a lie, and she sent me fifty dollars. She thinks I'm doin' good here, and I don't want to break her heart and tell her I been in jail."

Alvin apparently had been drinking again. When he talked about his mother, tears welled in his eyes.

"I'm gonna stay here until I get me a construction job or something like that. I ain't never gonna let my mama see me like this."

There was no way to listen to his story in the shadow of the White House and fail to see the shocking contrast between the two Americas — the one within and the one without. Across the street, Ron and Nancy and the king of Saudi Arabia, drinking champagne and eating caviar. In Lafayette Park, Alvin in his rags, begging for a handout.

I asked him if he was angry with Ronald Reagan, who is supposed to be heartless when it comes to the poor.

"He ain't the one that got drunk and beat up his woman and got throwed in jail. That was me," Alvin said. "I got myself into this mess, and I got to get myself out of it now."

I think I said something stupid like, "Well, hang in there," but forgive me. It's not every day that I'm confronted with nobility in rags.

***

Al Bergman, the sixty-nine-year-old free spirit on the road

with his dog Jamie, looking for peace and the soul of America. Mikki the stripper, a third his age but already in search of the same dream. One mother sending her Marine son off to the real world, far from her protective bosom; another trying to teach her young son discipline. And Alvin, down on his luck but not on himself or his country.

In their own ways, each of these people is an embodiment of true grit. You can hear it in their voices, see it in their eyes, feel it in their stories. It's there just as surely as it was when Marshall Rooster Cogburn took those reins between his teeth and rode out to face Lucky Ned Pepper and his gang. And yet as real as it is, it seems indefinable.

What is true grit? Where does it come from? How did it get there? These are the questions books are made of.

— 3 —

Never Go Camping With A Man Who Drinks Whiskey Sours

ONE OF THE THINGS John Wayne had going for him in *True Grit* (and in real life, for that matter) was that he looked the part. Tall, strong, ruggedly handsome and tough to the bone. The way he walked, the way he talked, the clothes he wore — all these things added to his aura.

The same was true of another of my childhood heroes, Superman. When he was dressed as Clark Kent, mild-mannered reporter for a large metropolitan newspaper — black-rimmed glasses, white shirt, striped tie, blue suit and wing-tipped shoes — nobody paid him any attention. Certainly not Lois Lane. But the minute he switched into that tight-fitting Superman costume and started leaping tall buildings in a single bound, Lois was on him like bark on a tree.

So maybe "the look" is part of the recipe for true grit. I'm not arguing that clothes make the man, but I've dated enough women hiding vast quantities of themselves under muumuus to know that diversionary tactics can work.

It's easy enough to chronicle the traditional manly characteristics which The Duke embodied. For one, he always seemed to have a couple of days worth of stubble on his chin and a little hair hanging over his collar.

I have more than a couple of days worth of stubble; I've got a beard. I decided to grow it several years ago after someone called me "fishface." I think the implication was that I have a weak chin. I found that a beard made me look more mature and even gave me an air of pseudo-sophistication. I liked it.

So I took the look one step further and started smoking cigars. They, too, I reasoned, made me look mature and urbane. One day while smoking my cigar, I accidentally knocked the fire off the end. I didn't immediately see where it fell, but I soon discovered that a burning beard gives off a terrible odor.

I gave up cigars after that frightening experience and started carrying a copy of the *Wall Street Journal* under my arm. It gave me the same aura of authority and, whereas a cigar lasts no more than an hour or so, I could carry the same *Wall Street Journal* around for a week or more before it started turning yellow and I had to buy another.

Anyway, I have the beard, and I also have the hair over the collar. In fact, I've been wearing my hair long for years. It's like a muumuu for my ears.

I never noticed that I had big ears until I was in the fourth grade and Alvin Bates pointed them out to me. "Your ears poke way out," he said. I looked in a mirror and discovered that for once in his life he wasn't lying. I also had a lot of freckles on my nose, and when I smiled I bore an amazing resemblance to Howdy Doody, the late puppet. I hoped that no one else noticed the similarity.

"How's Clarabell?" asked Alvin Bates in a loud voice the next morning when I walked into class. That was only the beginning of the abuse I took from my classmates.

"Mind putting your head down on your desk?" the girl who sat behind me asked one day during an arithmetic lesson.

I didn't have any better sense at the time than to ask her why.

"Because, Howdy," she said to the delight of the jackals sitting around her, "I can't see the blackboard for your ears."

I tried everything to make my ears grow closer to my head. At night I slept with a rubber band around my head to hold my ears in. Can you imagine how much it hurt when the rubber band broke in the middle of the night? I even tried gluing my ears to my head. Inevitably one of them would come unglued, leaving me looking like I was giving signals to a train.

My only salvation came years later when long hair, fashionably trimmed over the ears, came into style. But even that caused me some trauma.

You will remember that my father was a military man and consequently was not fond of long hair. Many times his cohorts told me the story of how he dealt with a young recruit sporting more than regulation locks:

"We had some new recruits come in to Fort Benning," the story began, "and they sent the Captain, your old man, out to look them over and get them checked out for their first day on post. He came to this little ol' skinny boy with hair down over his eyes and way down on the bottom of his neck. That wouldn't be anything today, but back then he looked real strange.

"Your daddy looked him up and down real slow and then

made a horrible face and said, 'Son, as soon as I dismiss you, I want you to go over to the hospital and check yourself in. Have the doctors give you a thorough going over.'

"The kid said to your daddy, 'Do you think there's something wrong with me, sir?'

"Your daddy said, 'Yes, indeed, soldier. I think beyond a shadow of a doubt that if the doctors look close enough, somewhere on you they will find a vagina.'"

Even after all these years, I can handle the guilt better than my uncovered ears.

***

Another thing common to men like Rooster Cogburn is that they're bad to drink or chew or do both. You can tell a lot about people by noticing what they drink. For instance, I was in a restaurant recently when a man walked in and asked the hostess, "How long before I can have a table?"

"About fifteen minutes," the hostess said.

"Good," the man answered. "That'll give me time for a whiskey sour at the bar."

I can't explain why, but a whiskey sour is a drink for a man whose mother made him practice piano a lot when he was a kid. A man who drinks whiskey sours also probably throws a baseball like a girl — limp wristed. A man who drinks whiskey sours and then eats that silly little cherry they put in the bottom probably has a cat or a poodle for a pet. In other words, I wouldn't go on a camping trip with a man who drinks whiskey sours.

Scotch drinkers are aggressive. They order like they're Charles Bronson trying to have a quick shot before returning to the subway to kill a few punks and thugs.

"What'll you have, sir?" asks the bartender.

"Cutty. Water. Rocks. Twist," growls the Scotch drinker. I think maybe Scotch drinkers wear their underwear too tight.

You have to watch people who drink vodka or gin. "Anybody who drinks see-through whiskey," an old philosopher once said, "will get crazy." Indeed. Vodka and gin drinkers are the type who leave the house to get a loaf of bread, drop by the bar for just one, and return home six weeks later. With the bread.

I wouldn't go on a camping trip with anyone who drinks vodka or gin, either. They're the types who would invite snakes, raccoons and bears over for cocktails and then wind up getting into an argument about tree frogs.

Bourbon drinkers never grow up. Eight out of ten started drinking bourbon with Coke in school and still have a pair of saddle oxfords in the closet. Bourbon drinkers don't think they've had a good time unless they get sick and pass out under a coffee table.

Then there are the white wine drinkers. Never get involved in any way with them. They either want to get married, sell you a piece of real estate or redecorate your house.

As for myself, I'm a beer drinker. We're usually honest, straightforward people. We also are usually kind and quite sentimental and will get cryin'-about-our-daddies drunk with one another. That's just before we destroy the establishment in which we're drinking because somebody made an offhand remark about Richard Petty or the memory of Patsy Cline.

Never go camping with a beer drinker, either. We're really no fun unless there's a jukebox around, and we belch a lot, which might frighten the snakes, raccoons, bears and tree frogs.

I occasionally get an urge to chew tobacco, and snuff-dipping is a part of my heritage, but I have a distinct problem with both. I'm talking about the mess they make.

There used to be two popular commercials promoting snuff, one featuring former professional football player Walt ("Just a pench between yo' cheek and gum") Garrison and another starring famous fiddle player and singer Charlie Daniels. The commercials always showed these fellows smiling as they snuffed up, but they never showed them spitting. If you dip, you spit. If you dip and don't spit, you have swallowed your snuff and soon will die a slow, agonizing death unless somebody has a stomach pump handy.

My grandmother was a snuff user. She used to send me to the store to buy her "medicine," as she called it. Then she would sit for hours with her Bible in her lap and a dip behind her lip. I knew it wasn't medicine. If it had been, no one would have kept it in their mouth that long.

One afternoon while returning from the store with my grandmother's "medicine," I decided to sample it. The convulsions began immediately. I managed to spit some of it out, but most of it went in my nose and eyes. The remaining portion I swallowed. If there had been a doctor nearby, I would have been pronounced dead on arrival at home. Month-old lettuce looked better than I did.

If there were truth in advertising, manufacturers of snuff would be required to print a warning on the side of the cans: "Dip or chew if you want, but know that you're going to have to spit every eight seconds or so and probably will get it all over your shoes."

Not only do those snuff commercials fail to show people spitting, they also never show them with spittle curling out of the corners of their mouths. "Dip or chew if you want," another warning should say, "but be prepared to look like you've been eating mud."

I have a friend who has been chewing tobacco for years. Like all other chewers, he spits a lot and juice runs out the sides of his mouth. His wife tried to get him to stop because she was offended by the little spit cups she found all over the house. There's nothing more unappealing than a cup of day-old tobacco spit.

Finally she said to him, "That's it. I've had it. Either the chewing tobacco goes or I go."

"Honey," my friend replied, "I don't have but one vice. I don't stay out drunk, I don't chase women and I'm kind to children, old people and dogs. But my daddy chewed and his daddy before him, and chewing is in my blood. Asking me to give it up is like asking a dog to stop licking his privates. I couldn't stop even if I wanted to."

His wife studied on his statement for a few moments and said, "OK, if it means that much to you, I suppose I can live with it."

Soon afterwards they were celebrating their wedding anniversary. My friend's wife gave him a leather pouch for storing his chewing tobacco and he gave her the promise that he'd go outside whenever he needed to spit.

That compromise took guts on both their parts — so much, in fact, that I was inspired to write a poem about it. It went like this:

True love.
True grit.
You need 'em both
When you've got to spit.
Ptui.

***

Another ingredient of true grit, judging from most of The Duke's movies, could be body odor. Think about it: Except for when he wrestled some galoot into the river and knocked him senseless, did you ever see that pilgrim bathe? No, sir. The Duke liked to smell like a man . . .or at least like

303

a man who had been riding the range for a month without a bath.

Back before air conditioning became one of the elements essential to life, it was perfectly all right to sweat a little and to emit an aromatic scent. Everybody did. Your mother sweated over a hot stove. Your father sweated at work and then came home and sat around in his underwear and sweated some more. At the end of a long day, nobody asked, "Where did you park your goats?" Nobody said, "Isn't it about time you looked for a reliable underarm deodorant?"

Today, sweat stains under the arms are considered only slightly less offensive than Joan Rivers. They can lead to the loss of a big account: "Sorry, Wilson, but we're going to have to find ourselves a new boy. Those perspiration stains on your shirt are a disgrace to the firm." Or to the loss of a lover: "I'll always love you, Marvin, but you've got the Okefenokee Swamp under your arms." Or even to the breakup of a family: "I'm filing for divorce, Donna. Those underarm stains on your tennis blouse are ruining the children's chances at a full and happy life."

Mandatory air conditioning not only did away with underarm sweat stains, it also led to the demise of a great tradition: the paddle fan. In the little Methodist church in my hometown, there were always Cokesbury hymnals and paddle fans along the back of each pew. The fans generally were provided by either a funeral home or an ambitious politician, with their message on one side — "Arnold's Funeral Home/Free Parking" or "Vote for Grover (Shorty) Turnipseed, County Commissioner" — and a four-color biblical scene on the other side (usually the Last Supper).

It wasn't necessary to listen to the minister's words to know whether or not he was reaching back for one of those you-had-better-change-your-evil-ways sermons. All you had to do was watch the congregation. The faster they fanned themselves, the closer to home the preacher was hitting.

The mere mention of the evils of alcohol was certain to speed the fanning strokes, and when the minister began to describe the warm climate that one who imbibed could expect at his final address, a draft no manner of air conditioner could match would roar through the sanctuary off those paper fans.

If I were a minister today, I would use a two-prong attack to challenge my backsliding flock. First, I would turn off the air conditioning some hot Sunday morning, and then I would explain the major difference between the two possible destinations that awaited them: hell for companionship, perhaps; heaven for its climate. Then I would quietly take my seat and let them sweat out their decisions without benefit of paddle fans. Now, that's the sort of situation that develops true grit.

Our preoccupation with smelling any way except natural doesn't end with air conditioning and deodorant, of course. "Is your mouthwash doing the job?" asked a commercial on television the other night. I don't know the answer to that. I brush my teeth every day whether they need it or not, and I even gargle on occasion. But how do I know if my mouth has that awful medicine smell they were talking about on TV?

I can hear my friends now: "He's a decent guy, but somebody really ought to tell him he has medicine mouth."

The same is true of shampoo. According to current commercials, if the shampoo you're using doesn't clean your hair, remove all dandruff, and leave your hair bright and shiny and full of body and smelling like a flower shop, people might not allow you in the same room with their children. You could infect the little boogers.

The new shampoos, of course, are highly scented, and one even leaves your hair smelling like apricots. Here's a hint: If you happen to be a man, never walk into a truck stop with your hair smelling like apricots. Someone likely will make fruit salad out of your head.

Come to think of it, that's probably the kind of shampoo that Lucky Ned Pepper was using, and that's why the marshall was so riled. That and the fact that just before their big shootout, Ned yelled across to Rooster Cogburn, "Hey, big guy, what's your sign?"

***

Another quality I associate with The Duke is that he was always friendly with his critters. His horse loved him. His cattle loved him. And in several movies he had a dog by his side. A man needs a good dog — one who'll fetch a stick and lick his hand. Don't forget what Bullet did for Roy Rogers and what Rin Tin Tin did for Sergeant Preston.

I'm not talking about those highfaluting purebreds who have been pampered by their owners and registered with the American Kennel Club. I don't like pampered children, and I don't like pampered dogs. I want a dog with character and personality, one who had to turn over a trash can once in a while just to keep food in his stomach. And I like a dog who knows enough about where puppies come from that he can choose his own mate and take care of business without waiting for some high-hatted human to "arrange" a canine tête-à-tête for him.

Allow me to explain the types of dogs that I like and probably the kind The Duke liked, too:

• YARD DOGS — A yard dog, usually found in the rural South, is a likable sort who hangs around the back door waiting for table scraps and who crawls under trucks to get in the shade on hot days. Yard dogs are recognizable by the oil and grease on their backs and by the humble way they walk sideways toward the individual calling them.

- HOG DOGS — These are fat little dogs who come from a union of Lord-knows-what and will eat anything that is put before them. They will lick the pan clean and beg for more. In rare cases, these dogs have been know to suck eggs. On the positive side of the ledger, such dogs make the expense of a garbage disposal unnecessary.

- LAP DOGS — These are very loving dogs who crave attention and leap onto your lap and lick your face and shed all over the sofa. They especially enjoy lying on their backs and kicking their legs back and forth while you scratch their bellies. I had a great lap dog once. My wife used to scratch the dog's belly for hours. When I asked her to do the same for me, she called her mother and told her I was perverted.

- A.J. FOYT DOGS — These dogs enjoy standing on the side of the road and racing with cars when they drive by. Every neighborhood has at least one. The problem with such dogs is that they tend to become frustrated after never being able to outrun passing cars, so they resort to gnawing the tires on your car when it's parked in the driveway. They also tend to have short life spans, because sooner or later they catch one of those cars.

- SHOE DOGS — These are dogs with a shoe fetish. Leave a pair of shoes out one night and by morning they'll have them chewed back to the raw material stage. Never take a shoe dog into a Gucci store; you could be bankrupt within minutes. Regional variations of this dog will chew eyeglasses, leather-bound books, remote control devices and Tupperware.

***

Finally, one of The Duke's most obvious characteristics, and an essential element, it seems to me, of true grit, was his self-sufficiency. He didn't need nobody for nothing.

I've always tried to emulate John Wayne in that regard. I've tried to learn to feed myself, clothe myself and fix leaky pipes. After all, you never know when your wife may leave and take your dog with her.

The first thing a breathing, self-sufficient male has to learn to do is feed himself. I'm not talking about eating out or ordering pizza. There was a time when I ordered out for pizza so many times that the delivery boy started getting phone calls and his mail at my house. But that's cheating; self-sufficiency means doing it yourself.

So, armed with determination and an unused kitchen in a new house, I set out to cook for myself. The first thing I did was buy one of those amazing food processors. "This food processor is the state of the art," said the saleslady. "You can make your own mayonnaise with it."

Why would anybody want to make their own mayonnaise, I wondered, when the Hellman's people are perfectly willing to do it for them? Self-sufficiency, I answered.

The next morning I decided to make myself a hearty omelette. I had never made one before, but I knew I needed at least eggs, onions, tomatoes, ham and cheese. First I decided to chop the onion in my new food processor. In less than ten seconds, I had a food processor full of onion juice. I have no idea what happened to the onion itself.

I immediately deleted onions from the recipe and proceeded. Next I put a piece of uncooked ham in my microwave oven and set the dial for five minutes. When I returned with the morning paper under my arm, the ham looked like Sherman had passed through Atlanta again. I mean, to a crisp.

Not to worry. Ham is high in cholesterol and unnecessary for a good omelette anyway. Remembering my experience with the onion and the food processor, I decided to slice the tomato by hand. Meanwhile, I put the cheese in the microwave to soften it.

When I had stopped the bleeding on my first two fingers, I checked the cheese in the microwave. That afternoon, it took the Roto-Rooter man only forty minutes to get the cheese unstuck from the sides of the oven.

I judiciously decided to forget about the omelette and simply have scrambled eggs with fresh orange juice. If the food processor would turn a fresh onion into onion juice, I reasoned it would do the same thing to an orange. I was correct. In seconds I had fresh orange juice. It tasted terrible, however. I later figured that maybe I should have peeled the orange.

I still had the eggs. The part that didn't stick to the bottom of the pan tasted like Silly Putty, so I threw the entire mess into my new garbage disposal which promptly clogged.

I waited until the pizza place opened and ordered a medium with everything except anchovies. It came with anchovies anyway, so I scraped them off the top of my pizza and electrocuted them in my microwave oven. I felt momentarily vindicated — after all, the microwave did what I intended it to do — but I felt far from self-sufficient.

That evening while watching television, I saw a commercial for a book that promised to save me hundreds of dollars a year in home repair and improvement bills. If I ordered one of these books, the announcer said, I would be able to fix my plumbing and even build myself a new patio.

No I wouldn't. I don't care how many of those books I read, I can't build or repair anything. A hammer is high technology to me.

When I was a kid, my mother bought me an erector set. I

read the instructions and tried to build a crane. "Oh, look," my mother exclaimed when I finished. "You've built a 1948 DeSoto with both doors missing."

I was so inept they wouldn't allow me to play with the garden hose. "Get away from that hose," my mother would say. "You know you don't know nothing about machinery."

I carried this lack of knowledge into high school, where I enrolled in shop class in an effort to improve myself. As my term project, I decided to build a chair.

"What is it?" asked the shop teacher at the end of the quarter.

"It's a chair," I said.

"Looks more like a wooden model of a 1948 DeSoto with both doors missing to me," he said.

As an adult, I've always had the same problem, particularly with automobiles. "What seems to be the problem with your car?" the auto mechanic asks me.

"It's broken," I answer.

He opens the hood and looks inside at all that infernal wiring and all those other doflatchies and what's-its that make a car run. "Here's your problem," he says. "Your lolabridgelator isn't gee-hawing with your double-low, E-flat commodgelator."

What does that mean? And how did he learn that?

Around the house I'm equally confused. When I moved into a new house and tried to take a shower, there was no hot water. I called the plumber. "Here's your problem," he said. "The letters on your shower knobs are wrong. The 'H' is on the cold knob and the 'C' is on the hot knob."

It cost me nearly $200 to have the plumber move the knobs on my pipes so I would have hot water when I turned the "H" knob.

I did think I could at least build a stand for my mailbox at the new house. I went out and bought lumber and nails and bolts. I now have the only mailbox stand in town that looks like a 1948 DeSoto with the doors missing.

Finally I did find one thing mechanical that I could fix when it broke. I can stop a commode from making that annoying sound it makes sometimes after you flush it. What you do is lift the lid off the top of the commode and fiddle with the rubber dohickey until the sound stops.

Try finding that kind of information in a stupid book.

My last attempt at self-sufficiency almost proved fatal. I had a bad case of the flu, but I resolved to lick it myself without running to the doctor to have him laugh at me. Real men stick it out.

I felt worse than a five-eyed goat in a sandstorm. I was so sick my toenails turned black. I couldn't breathe, I couldn't eat and my tongue itched. I turned to would-be friends for help and advice.

"Here's what you do," one said confidently. "You pour a glass full of bourbon and then you take a tablespoon of sugar. You eat the sugar and chase it with the glass of bourbon and then go to bed. You'll feel great the next morning."

He was partially right. I felt great while I was in the coma caused by the sugar and bourbon. When I came out of it, however, I felt just as bad as I did before.

Somebody else told me to eat lots of mustard. "It's an old custom in my family. A cup of mustard a day will cure anything."

Anything, that is, except the flu. Eating a cup of mustard without hot dogs will make your ears water.

The next advice I got was to eat honey and chase it with a heavy dose of castor oil. "Honey and castor oil will purify you and cleanse all the poison from your body," I was told.

Maybe so, but eating honey and chasing it with a heavy-duty dose of castor oil also will keep you from sitting in one place for more than five minutes for days. Captured enemy spies were threatened with the same treatment during World War II by Allied interrogators. It always worked.

Still another friend suggested that an afternoon in a sauna would be just the thing to put me back in the pink. "You get into a sauna for about an hour," said the friend, "and then you come out and drink a strong vodka tonic. Go back into the sauna for another hour and then come out and drink two vodka tonics. You return to the sauna for a third hour, then come out and finish off the bottle of vodka."

"Sounds great," I said. "A sauna should really help me."

"You kiddin'? Saunas are awful for a man in your condition, but after a bottle of vodka, who cares?"

Chicken soup was the final suggestion. "Do I put vodka or castor oil in it?" I asked sheepishly.

"No, silly. Chicken soup by itself has tremendous curative powers."

I ate so much chicken soup that I had the urge to go peck corn, but I was still too sick to get off my tail feathers and go outside.

Eventually I cured myself by doing what any real man would do in a similar situation: I pulled the covers up over my head, whined and felt sorry for myself. In a couple of days, I was fine. A victory for self-sufficiency.

***

So is it the stubbly beard, the long hair, drinking and chewing, sweating and stinking, loving dogs and being self-sufficient that gives a person true grit?

There must be more to it than that. Otherwise, how would you explain the likes of Eugene Ellis?

— 4 —

A Heaping
Helping of Grit

Setting A Shining Example

IT USED TO BE that there were a lot of people around —
on street corners, in barber shops, in train stations and
airports — who would shine your shoes for a price. But
shining shoes got to be a social stigma, a sign of subser-
vience in some people's minds, and so shoe shining has
gone the way of service at gas stations: It's there, but you
have to look for it.

When I met Eugene Ellis shining shoes in Macon, Georgia, I asked him if it bothered his self-image that he was still
shining shoes for a living. He answered my question by
looking at me like I was crazy.

Eugene Ellis is sixty-two years old. He's black. He's short,
which he says is helpful when you shine shoes because you
don't have to bend over as far. Eugene Ellis is an orphan, a
husband and a father of five. He shines shoes all day in a
barbershop, and then he shines for a good part of the

evening in a local jazz bar.

He started shining shoes on the streets of Macon when he was five. Years later at the Atlanta airport, he shined the shoes of a young senator who hoped someday to be president of the United States. John Kennedy told Eugene that when he was elected president, he would give him a job shining shoes at the White House.

"Said he'd come back and get me," recalled Eugene, "but I didn't think he would."

Eugene Ellis shined shoes at the White House for three presidents — Kennedy, Lyndon Johnson and Richard Nixon — before he decided it was time to go back home. He brought memories with him:

On Kennedy — "A good Catholic man. Real quiet. I was in the eighth car back when they shot him."

On Johnson — "If he was still president, I'd still be shining his shoes. He always took me to the ranch with him."

On Nixon — "He was a little different from the others."

Eugene shined the shoes of Hubert Humphrey, Gerald Ford, Muhammad Ali, Don McNeal and Elvis Presley. He said Elvis paid the best of the bunch.

The worst shoe to shine? "Patent leather. Can't see what you've done."

Favorite shoe to shine? "Anything in bad shape. I like to see my work when I'm finished with it."

It would be easy to try to attach some social significance to this story and say that what this country needs today is more people shining shoes like Eugene Ellis does, and wouldn't that solve some of the unemployment problem? But "let 'em shine shoes" isn't exactly my style, so I'll just let it pass with this:

Eugene Ellis, who has put three daughters through college, gets salary plus tips at a regular job. And when he pulled out his wallet to show me a card some prince gave him at the White House, it was filled with what he called his "lucky twenties." His work is inside and requires no heavy lifting, it beats scraping dead bugs off windshields, and he says that when he's got a good pair of shoes to shine and his rag is popping just right, "it's like I'm making music."

Yeah, I think that's enough said.

WISDOM IN RETROSPECT

The courtesy van showed up to take me to the airport at Salt Lake City. The driver was a woman, probably in her late thirties. They had been hard years. You can see it in a person's face sometimes.

She asked where I was headed, and I told her Atlanta.

"That's where you live?" she asked.

"Don't I sound like it?" I answered.

She just laughed. "Yeah, you do. I was married to an ol' Georgia boy once."

"Where from?"

"Albany."

There was a story there. "How in the world did someone from way out here in Utah get hooked up with someone from Albany, Georgia?"

"Met him on the bus," she said. "I was just nineteen. Was going to Boise, Idaho, to visit my grandparents. He was in the service on his way to Anchorage, Alaska. He sat down next to me when we left Salt Lake. He was a real quiet boy and shy. Didn't say a word the first hour, but then he started talking a little. I could tell he was homesick.

"He showed me some pictures he had in his wallet. When we got to Boise, he helped me get my bags off the bus and asked if he could write me some time. I said he could. Then one day he wrote and asked if I would marry him. I accepted. I was nineteen and had the moon and the stars in my eyes. We got married and drove all the way to Albany for our honeymoon," she continued.

"We had seven years together and two kids."

"You got divorced?" I pried.

"He was Baptist. I was Mormon. That was one of several things that were wrong. After I split with him I stayed single for seven more years. Then I got to figuring my kids needed a daddy, so I went out and found them one."

"How did that work out?"

"Bad. You can't make a daddy out of just anybody, I found out."

We were getting close to the airport. "You married now?" I asked, hoping for an end to the story.

"I'm living with a fellow now," said my driver. "I guess we moved in together about two years ago. My mother is shocked because we don't go ahead and get married. She says what we're doing is sinful. It might be but we're happy. I guess I'm as happy now as I've ever been. I don't want to take a chance of messing up again. Getting married don't solve any problems, it starts 'em."

As I stepped out of the van, I asked her name.

"It's Dixie."

I didn't have time to find out why. I simply said, "Stay happy, Dixie."

She smiled, nodded and drove away. Somebody in Utah has himself a good woman, I thought to myself. I just hope he knows it.

EXERCISING DISCRETION IN TENNESSEE

My friend Stephens and I were returning from a camping

trip somewhere in the hills of Tennessee when we developed an urgent thirst. He pulled into the first place with beer signs he spotted — a cement-block building with a lot of pickup trucks parked outside.

"Let's go in here," Stephens said.

The first thing I noticed inside was a pool table. Pool can be a dangerous game when played in a church basement. When played in a place like this, customers should be issued hockey helmets.

The crowd gave us the ol' they-ain't-from-around-here look as we moved quietly toward a table. I noticed a sign over the bar which said, "It is a felony to carry a weapon where alcoholic beverages are served." You didn't put a sign like that on your wall, I reasoned, unless there had been a previous incident, or incidents, to warrant it.

I usually can pick out a troublemaker, and there's one in every bar in America. In this instance, he was standing at the counter. He had long sideburns and his cigarettes rolled up in the sleeve of his shirt, a sure sign of a belligerent personality.

The tough guy picked up his beer and walked toward us. I drew a bead on the front door.

"Either of you shoot pool?" he asked.

"No," said Stephens.

"No, sir," I said.

The tough guy just grunted. "Guess I'll have to shoot by myself," he said.

Pool can be a very macho game. A man attacks a pool table, especially on the break when he makes every effort to shatter the balls.

The tough guy knew every eye was on him. He chalked his stick confidently, aimed the blue tip toward the rack of balls, closed one eye and came forward through the cue ball with an enormous grunt. But there was no ear-splitting sound of balls colliding. The tough guy had whiffed the cue ball.

The room fell silent. Nobody dared move a muscle. The tough guy, fighting to keep his cool, lined up the cue ball again as quickly as possible and this time scattered the balls around the table.

Stephens and I finished our beer, paid our tab and drove away.

"How far we been?" I asked him a little later.

"About ten miles," he said.

"Think we're safe?" I asked.

"Nothing out here but the bears and possums," he answered.

Then, and only then, did we allow ourselves the marvelous relief of howling laughter.

THE GIFT OF LOVING A CHILD

"I just want one thing," Sherry said to me. "I want people to learn of the tragedies we have been through so maybe they will understand how important it is to love their children with all their hearts and souls. To love a child is one of God's greatest gifts."

Sherry and D.A. were just kids themselves when they married nearly twenty-one years ago. Their first child was Lex, a boy. Then came another son, Allan.

"After Allan," Sherry explained, "we felt, in this day and time, that two children were enough. I was having some health problems, too, so I agreed to have my tubes tied."

They settled in the small town of Calhoun, Georgia, an hour or so north of Atlanta. Sherry taught elementary school, and D.A. became high school head football coach.

When he was four years old, Allan was diagnosed as having

318

leukemia. After several years of treatment, doctors determined that there might be hope for him if he underwent a bone marrow transplant. The family went to Seattle, Washington, for the operation. Lex was the donor for his little brother. The transplant was considered a success, and the family returned home in good spirits and resumed their lives.

"We sort of grew up with the kids ourselves, especially with Lex," said Sherry. "We always did everything together."

Several years later, Lex won a football scholarship to East Central Junior College in Mississippi. The whole family was jubilant. And when his team won a big game on the last day of September, 1983, he called his mother at three in the morning to tell her about it.

"He was so excited, and we shared that excitement," Sherry recalled. "He said he thought his team would be nationally ranked. He was on his way home for a visit before the next game."

Lex never made it home. Just a few miles outside of Calhoun, he fell asleep at the wheel and hit a truck head-on. He was killed instantly.

"On the way to the cemetery for Lex's funeral," Sherry continued, "my husband asked little Allan to look for a sign in nature that would show us that Lex was still with us. After the service at the graveside, a beautiful monarch butterfly flew between us. We believe it was a sign, and I can't think of anything more fitting than a butterfly. It is constantly on the go, just as Lex was, and it is not aggressive, and neither was our son."

When the family later redecorated their house, the wallpaper they selected was filled with butterflies.

Within a year after Lex's death, doctors discovered that Allan's leukemia has spread to his brain and spinal column.

His medication had to be discontinued to prevent further damage. The second son was dying.

"He knew he was dying, but he wasn't afraid. He knew his 'Bubba' would be waiting for him."

But Allan wasn't the only courageous member of his family. His mother and father were determined to carry on.

"We talked about the future. I even thought of seeing if I could have an operation that would allow me to have children again. But I'm too old for that," Sherry explained. "We also checked into the possibility of adopting, but there's a waiting list of several years. We have so much love to give, and we want to channel it somewhere. We know there are so many children who need it."

I asked Sherry how she and her husband had coped through their ordeal.

"We live with one thought," she said. "That God has something else planned for us. He must. He simply must."

AN OLD FOGEY WITH CLEAR VISION

My Aunt Jessie has lived in rural Georgia since 1931. She is widowed now and spends most of her time watching her "stories," which is what she calls the television soap operas. I'm not certain how old she is, and I never intend to ask, but it's a fact that she's a great-grandmother.

One of the grandchildren offered recently to take her to Atlanta to see Kenny Rogers in concert. Aunt Jessie, a lifelong devotee to country music, accepted.

Those of us who live in large urban areas learn to accept the dramatic changes which occur around us almost daily, but Aunt Jessie was shocked when she ventured from her rural security for a modern concert. It was refreshing to hear her view of it all:

"I never seen so many people in one place in my life. And when the concert finally got started, you couldn't hear a thing. Every time Kenny would start to sing, everybody would scream and holler.

"The rest of the time I couldn't see because somebody was always crawling over me to get something to eat. Looks like they would've had supper before they came to the concert, or at least brought themselves a sandwich so they wouldn't have had to leave their seats."

Aunt Jessie was amazed at the actions of some of the women at the concert. "I saw these two young girls, in britches so tight I don't know how they breathed, running all over the place, touchin' the ground just in the high places. I don't know where their mamas were. But if they had been mine, I'd have wore 'em both out for dressin' and actin' like that.

"Then there was a woman so drunk she couldn't stand up, holding a big ol' cup of beer in each hand. She could have at least stayed home if she was going to act like that.

"At the intermission I was standing in line to go to the restroom and this woman got tired of waiting, so she just pranced right into the men's room, big as you please. I thought, 'Lord, what's this world comin' to?'"

I tried to explain to Aunt Jessie that women have changed a lot since her time, and nowadays they smoke and drink in public and occasionally use profanity and generally have come a long way, baby.

"I guess I ought to be thankful for one thing," said Aunt Jessie.

"What's that?"

"That I'm still an old fogey, country woman," she said.

I'm thankful for that, too, Aunt Jessie. There aren't many of you left.

WAVING HER FLAG OF FREEDOM

We were waiting for a couple of planes. She had two, maybe three drinks. We shared a story and an opinion or two, and then she asked, "How old are you, anyway?"

"Thirty-nine," I answered.

"Same age as my husband, the sorry bastard," she said.

Ever perceptive, I asked, "You're mad at your husband?"

"Actually," she said, "he's now my ex-husband. Ran off with a girl half his age."

I made no comment. I'm old enough to know better.

"You know what's wrong with men your age?" she continued.

"Yeah," I said, "but what do you think is wrong with men my age?"

"You're all afraid of getting old, so you start chasing around after young girls." She ordered another drink. Scotch.

"How long have you been divorced?" I asked.

"Six months."

"Kids?"

"One. He's twelve. Do you know how old I am?"

When a woman asks a question like that, I always subtract five years from my best guess. "Late twenties," I answered.

"Thirty-five, and you know what's wrong with women my age?"

I had several ideas, to be sure, but the best answer at the time seemed to be shaking my head no.

"We were brought up so differently from young girls today," she began. "You take me. My mother has dominated my life. All the time I was growing up, she used to harp on me to always be a 'good girl.' And I was. I didn't dare do anything my mother wouldn't approve of. I never had a drink until I was married. I've had sex with only one man, my husband. I've been a 'good girl' all my life, and all I've got to show for it is a broken marriage and a lot of guilt."

"Yeah," I said awkwardly, "our parents sometimes leave us with a load to carry into adulthood."

"Know what I did today, though?" the woman asked. "I got dressed up in this outfit and went by my mother's house. She said, 'Oh, you look so lovely, darling. Are you going to a party?' I said, 'No, mother, I'm not going to a party. I'm going to leave here, get on an airplane and meet a man. Then I'm going to commit adultery for the first time in my life.' I thought she was going to faint. She was absolutely bewildered."

"Did she try to talk you out of it?" I wanted to know.

"I wouldn't let her. Every time she tried to preach to me, I just told her it wouldn't do any good. It's my life and I've missed so much. I've got to start being my own person, and now is as good a time as any."

She ordered one last drink. "What's so funny," she said, "is that all my mother could say to me when I left was, 'Don't do anything that will cause you to hate yourself.' If I don't do this, then I'm going to hate myself."

They called the woman's plane. She downed her drink, smiled and boarded. I hope she had a great weekend.

***

So maybe true grit has less to do with things physical and more to do with things mental. It seems to come from many sources: from religion, and sports, and living with women and dealing with living. In the words of Erskine Caldwell, "Call it experience." I've had my share.

— 5 —

Sinning and Grinning
And Knowing The
Difference

I GREW UP HEARING that good things come to those who love the Lord; the Moreland, Georgia, Methodist Church was deeply and comfortably seated in the traditional interpretation of The Word. But religion, like so many other things, isn't as simple as it used to be. Nowadays the good guys sometimes wear black and white striped hats instead of just one or the other.

Almost every day in the mail I receive a letter from some television evangelist asking me for a donation to help buy a new truck for his television equipment or to pay off the debt for the new gymnasium at New Testament University. The implication is that if I don't send them the cash, I'm on the express train for hell.

Will I end up down there with Hitler and Attila the Hun and Bonnie and Clyde just because I didn't send them five bucks for a new wrestling mat? Then again, is hell actually *down* there?

"Can you dig your way to hell?" I asked the preacher when I was a kid.

"Guess you can," he said, "but I can tell you how to get there a lot quicker."

Frankly, thinking about hell scares the you-know-where out of me. I'd much rather think about heaven. Just the other day my mail included a pamphlet entitled, "Heaven: Are You Eligible?" I took the test and scored "too close to call."

With that kind of rating, I pay close attention to all those groups who predict the coming of Judgment Day. If some guy says he has it on good authority that the end of the world is due on October 11, then I'm particularly careful that day not to do anything awful, like telling big lies, attending an adult movie or coveting my neighbor's new Porsche.

Otherwise, can you imagine your chances of getting aboard the glory train when the first question they ask you at judgment is, "For starters, what did you do today?"

"W-w-w-well, f-f-first I lied to my boss about having to go to the doctor and I went instead to see *Flesh Dance* at the Porn Palace. Then I went home and kicked the tires on my '73 Ford wagon because that's what I'm stuck with when Thorndike across the street has a new Porsche."

Take a seat, boy. The southbound leaves in just a few minutes.

I know in my heart that most of these forecasts are poppycock, but my old-fashioned upbringing always keeps me just a little uneasy. Remember, everybody thought Columbus was nuts when he bought a round-trip ticket. You just never know.

That's why I started early in life being careful not to get caught in mid-sin at the precise moment of His return. I remember my first beer. I tried to chug it down but succeeded only in gagging myself.

"What's your hurry?" asked my companion in evil.

"Beer is better when you drink it fast," I answered between coughs.

Truth is, I just wanted to finish that beer quickly so I could throw the can away and get rid of the evidence in case the Second Coming were to occur in the next five to ten minutes.

I guess it is possible to overreact to these predictions. Anytime I hear another Judgment Day date, I'm reminded of the story my grandfather used to tell about an Elmer Gantry-type preacher who came through town with his tent.

"The end is close at hand, my children," the preacher screamed one night. About that time, a small boy who had just been given a toy trumpet for his birthday walked past the tent and gave his new horn a mighty toot.

The congregation panicked and bolted out of the tent. The evangelist grabbed the cash box and cut down the street at full gallop. The little boy, wondering where everybody was headed, followed the preacher.

The preacher ran faster and faster, afraid to look back, but the little boy matched him step for step, still tooting on his new horn. Finally the preacher stopped, whipped out a switchblade and said, "Watch it, Gabe, or I'll cut you!"

My grandfather wouldn't have cared much for today's bigtime television preachers. In his oft-stated opinion, preachers were supposed to marry folks, preach funerals, mow the grass around the church and administer to the needs of the flock (that meant consoling the poor soul who lost his job, whose wife ran off, and whose trailer burned all in the same week). Our preacher even used to knock down the dirt dobbers' nests in the windows of the sanctuary so the inhabitants wouldn't bother the worshippers while he was trying to run the devil out of town on Sunday mornings.

Do you suppose that Oral Roberts or Jerry Falwell ever knocked down any dirt dobbers' nests?

My grandfather also didn't like it when younger preachers used note cards to deliver their sermons. "They ought to get it straight from the Lord," he said many a time. "Politicians use notes."

The preacher at Moreland Methodist when I was growing up suited my grandfather just fine. He drove an old car. He had only one suit. He did the yard work around the church, didn't use note cards and always attempted to answer the questions of a twelve-year-old boy when things didn't add up. Once he even preached a funeral for a dog because that little boy, who loved the dog very much, asked him to.

What would Pat Robertson say over a dog?

What bothers me today is that for every glamour boy of the pulpit, there are thousands out there who tackle the devil daily, one-on-one, with little or no audience, against long odds, and occasionally on an empty stomach.

God bless them. And God, please don't let my grandfather — I know he's around there somewhere — find out that we've got preachers down here today who use cue cards and hang out with politicians.

***

I had a dream about all this the other night. Maybe it was my grandfather passing along a little inside information. This is how it went:

God called in the angel who is in charge of keeping an eye on what's going on in the United States. "What's all this fussing about religion and politics? I thought I had Ben

Franklin and his friends work out the separation of church and state a couple of weeks ago," God said.

"Actually," said the angel, "it's been a couple of weeks heaven time, but to folks on earth it's been more than two hundred years. But every so often, they decide to argue it again."

"Who started it this time?"

"I suppose it was Jerry Falwell and the Moral Majority," answered the angel.

"Jerry who and the Moral what?"

"Jerry Falwell and the Moral Majority. Falwell is a television evangelist and he heads a fundamentalist organization called the Moral Majority. They support President Reagan because they think you are a Republican."

"Whatever gave them an idea like that?" asked God.

"They think you sent President Reagan, a Republican, to save the morals of the country because he believes in a lot of the same things as they do."

"For instance?"

"Well, President Reagan believes in prayer in public schools, and so does the Moral Majority."

"So what's the big deal? I get thousands of prayers a day from students in public schools. Here, look at this one that came in yesterday. Pretty creative for a tenth grader:"

> O Lord, hear my anxious plea.
> Algebra is killing me.
> I know not of 'x' or 'y,'
> And probably won't until the day I die.
> Please, Lord, help me at this hour
> As I take my case to the highest power.
> I care not for fame nor loot,
> Just help me find one square root.

Latin and Grammar are also trouble.
Guide me through this daily double.
And, Lord, please let me see
One passing mark in Chemistry.

Lord, why am I such a dope in school?
My teachers think I'm such a fool.
One said, 'Son, you're a horrid flop.
You bent the saw and failed at shop.'
My days in class are filled with remorse.
I can't even pass the easiest course.
I hunkered down and bowed my neck,
But I burnt the cake and flagged Home Ec.

In English Lit, I studied hard
And read all the words of the Bard.
But my mind is like a hateful Judas.
It couldn't recall, 'Et tu, Brutus?'

Lord, will there ever be
A tougher subject than History?
Into the past I steadfastly delve,
From Plymouth Rock to 1812.
I learn of all those patriotic folk,
From John Q. Adams to James K. Polk.
But test time comes and I fall on my tail.
Was it Patrick Henry or Nathan Hale?

Lord, must I offer an apology
For three times failing Biology?
Why is it I'm in such a fog
Concerning the innards of a frog?
I push and strive and strain and grope

To come to terms with the microscope.
Lord, please forgive my derision,
But who gives a hoot for cellular division?

Lord, I wish that I could vanish
When the teacher calls on me in Spanish.
And I promise, it's a cinch,
I'll never learn a word of French.

Down in gym I take P.E.
Calisthenics will be the death of me.
I have all the grace of a mop.
I made an 'F' in side straddle hop.

Lord, is there anything I can't flub?
Will I ever be in Beta Club?
I have never found the key to knowledge,
And my folks want me to go to college.
Oh, such a thing I constantly dread.
I'd as soon join the Marines instead.
Lord, please give me a sign
That you've been listening all this time.
If you will help, I'll give my all,
And won't even chew gum in study hall.
Please lead me out of this constant coma,
And give me a chance at my diploma.
Let others fight about church and state.
I pray only to graduate. Amen.

"Now, that's a prayer worthy of my time," said God. "But apparently that's not good enough for this Falwell fellow. Tell me more about him."

"Well, he has his own television show."

"When does he visit the sick?"

"He doesn't have time for that. If he's not preaching on the air, he's busy fund raising for his ministry or else he's on one of those news shows like, 'This Week With David Brinkley,' telling people where you stand on this and that."

"Just what I needed," said God, "another spokesman." God thought for a moment and then said to the angel, "I want you to do something for me. I want you to deliver a few messages. First, tell both sides that I don't want to be any part of their political squabble. Their forefathers had the good sense to leave me out of politics, and I don't see why they can't.

"Also, tell Reagan to forget about school prayer for awhile and instead find a way to talk to the Russians before they find a way to destroy what I've created. Then tell that Falwell fellow to stop using my name to boost his television ratings and stop trying to run the country from his pulpit. Can you handle all that?" God asked the angel.

"Yes, ma'am," the angel replied.

***

Apparently that message I dreamed hasn't been delivered quite yet, because the Moral Majority is still busy trying to convince us that they have all the answers. Me, I'm more confused than ever. It's gotten to the point that I'm not sure I know sin when I see it. Or hear it. According to the Moral Majority, music is one of the major mediums of the devil today, and nowhere is the temperature hotter than in country music.

I'll be the first to admit that some questionable lyrics have sneaked into country music in recent years, but are the dials "down there" really tuned to WSM? In an attempt to get this disturbing issue cleared up, I contacted Mrs. Debbie Sue Ann Betty Jo Jenkins of Blue Ball, Arkansas. She's the

Moral Majority's expert on the state of country music.

"May I call you Debbie Sue Ann Betty Jo?" I asked when I reached her on the phone.

"Call me anything but 'Barracuda,'" she replied. "That's what Conway Twitty called me when I tried to stop his show in Little Rock."

"You tried to stop the Conway Twitty show?"

"He was singing that trashy song about meeting a woman in a bar who was wearing tight britches," Mrs. Jenkins explained.

I know the song in question, entitled "Tight-fittin' Jeans," and I suppose it is a little suggestive. I asked Mrs. Jenkins which part of the song offended her most.

"The part where the woman tells Conway Twitty, 'Pardner, there's a tiger in these tight-fittin' jeans.'"

I quickly realized that Debbie Sue Ann Betty Jo, Mrs. Jenkins, was a bit of a tiger herself. Anybody who would try to stop Conway Twitty as he groaned to his legion of fans is not the sort of person to be taken lightly.

"What other songs offend the Moral Majority?" I asked.

"Anything by Barbara Mandrell," she said.

Barbara Mandrell a musical filth peddler? I couldn't believe it.

"Imagine such perversion as inviting a man to eat crackers in bed with you in a song," explained Mrs. Jenkins, referring of course to Ms. Mandrell's hit song, "You Can Eat Crackers in My Bed Anytime." She continued, "Decent people would never do such a thing. Beds are for sleeping and nothing else."

"What does Mr. Jenkins think about that?" I asked.

"He doesn't even like crackers," she said.

Mrs. Jenkins went on to list several other songs which the Moral Majority disapproves of:

• "My Favorite Memory" by Merle Haggard. One line recalls "sleeping all night long on the floor." "Probably ate a bunch of crackers before they dozed off," said Mrs. Jenkins.

• "Best Bedroom in Town" by Tammy Wynette. "Doesn't anybody ever get out of bed in Nashville?" asked Mrs. Jenkins.

• "If I Said You Had a Beautiful Body Would You Hold It Against Me?" by the Bellamy Brothers. "Utter trash," said Mrs. Jenkins. "I'll bet their mother, Mrs. Bellamy, hides herself in shame every time she hears that song. If Mr. Jenkins had ever said anything like that to me, I would have bashed in his little worm head."

• "My Baby Thinks He's a Train" by Rosanne Cash. "More perversion," explained Mrs. Jenkins. "Mr. Jenkins decided he was a Greyhound bus once and that he was leaving."

"What did you do?" I asked her.

"Bashed in his little worm head, of course."

Finally I asked Mrs. Jenkins to name the one song which she feels is most harmful.

"It's by Glen Campbell," she said.

"Glen Campbell?"

"Yes, I know it's hard to believe, but he sings a song called, 'I Love My Truck.' Can you imagine a nice boy from Arkansas getting involved in something like that?"

No, ma'am, I sure can't.

***

Gospel music, thank the Lord and Mrs. Jenkins, is still safe from such perversion, and I listen to it with gusto and a clean conscience. I get my interest in gospel music honestly. My late father could hunker down on a piano and make it sing a joyful noise as long as there was somebody around to listen.

My Uncle Dorsey on my mother's side rarely missed an all-night gospel sing at the old Atlanta Municipal Auditorium. He favored the bass singer, the tall fellow in the back who always let go on the "Wellawella's," as in, "Wellawella, evuhbody's gon' have a livin' in glowry...."

I grew up in my maternal grandmother's house, and each Sunday morning I awakened to her radio blaring out the "Gospel Jubilee." My grandmother preferred the inevitable short, baby-faced tenor in the quartet who could pop up there higher than a kite with a nearly operatic, "He's my Jeeeeesus!"

Recently I attended the National Gospel Quartet Convention in Nashville, Tennessee, and it was a glooorious event. The auditorium was encircled by those rolling motels that once were Greyhound buses, carrying groups from date to date. On the sides were the names of the groups — the Singing Echoes, the Kingsmen, this family and that.

The auditorium was maybe half full when I entered, but before the night was over it was bulging. In the hallways were booths where gospel fans could buy tapes and albums and autographed photos of their favorite performers. As each quartet left the stage, a spokesperson was given the opportunity to plug the group's wares:

"We're right over yonder at booth fifteen," a man shouted into the microphone, "and we got a three-album-for-fifteen-dollar sale on. Y'all drop by to see us."

There was passion in the music. It jumped and even rocked a bit, and it set toes to tapping and occasionally brought the audience to its feet, heads held toward the heavens, hands clapping.

"We ain't the stars of the show," a fellow said. "Jesus is the star. Let's all stand and give Him a hand!"

Another group walked on, and the lead singer said, "I

seen on the marquee out front that the Talking Heads are coming to this auditorium. There's gonna be dope-smokin', pill-poppin' and rock music. But you ain't gonna get none of that here tonight. All you gonna get high on is Jeeeesus!"

The crowd loved it.

The last group appeared on the stage and sang its hit song, "Call Me What You Want To, But When He Calls Me, Call Me Gone." The crowd roared following a rousing rendition.

"Sort of gives you glowry bumps listenin' to 'em, don't it?" said the woman sitting next to me.

It does at that. It sure does.

— 6 —

Are You Non-Essential, Undesirable, Unmentionable Or Just Undone?

SOMETIMES YOU DON'T have to go out of your way to find opportunities to develop true grit. They'll come to you. Just surviving the lunacy and frustrations of the modern world is evidence of some degree of character. Isn't that why our society always makes such a big deal out of golden wedding anniversaries?

In my particular situation, I travel a lot. Thirty years ago that would have meant many pleasurable train rides with good food, good drink and plenty of time to read or relax. Today, however, it means airports and airplanes and endless delays and migraine headaches. It starts before you even leave home.

"Good morning. Wingandaprayer Airlines. May I help you?"

"Yes," I said to the voice on the phone. "I'd like to make two round-trip reservations for the Sunday evening flight to

Pittsburgh, please."

"Will this be first class, tourist or Wingandaprayer's new cargo class?" she asked.

"Cargo class?"

"Certainly, sir. In an effort to attract your business in these competitive times, Wingandaprayer Airlines is offering an innovative and inexpensive way for you to travel by air. Cargo class simply means you ride in the cargo hold with the baggage at a huge savings in cost. This is available, however, only to those passengers who will fit into their own hanging bags."

"I'll just take tourist," I said.

"Oxygen or non-oxygen?"

"I don't understand."

"Another Wingandaprayer option in our effort to offer passengers a variety of ways to save money and still not have to take the bus," she explained. "If you prefer to bring your own oxygen tank, then your seat will not be equipped with an automatic oxygen mask release in case of sudden cabin depressurization. If Wingandaprayer doesn't have to provide you with oxygen, it can save money and pass those savings along to its customers in the form of reduced fares."

"But I don't have my own oxygen tank."

"In that case, sir, how long can you hold your breath?"

"I'll just take two seats with oxygen."

"Will you be traveling with your wife or another adult?"

"No, I'll be traveling with my nephew Robert, who's six."

"Does he chew Rootie-Tootie Bubble Gum?"

"Is that the kind that turns his teeth blue?" I asked.

"Exactly, sir, and Wingandaprayer now offers free tickets to children if they show eight Rootie-Tootie Bubble Gum wrappers when they go to the agent for their boarding passes. 'Get 'em while they're young and they're yours forever,' is what we always say at Wingandaprayer," she explained.

"So what is the adult fare?"

"Depends, sir. Will you be cashing in coupons on this trip?"

"Coupons?"

"Check your local newspaper for Wingandaprayer cost-cutting coupons. Bring the coupons with you to the ticket agent and trade them in for savings on your fare."

"OK. Now, will dinner be served on the evening flight to Pittsburgh?"

"Not in tourist, sir. Wingandaprayer lost millions last year, and in an effort to keep our own costs down, we've cut out all meal service except in first class, where passengers are allowed to bob for apples."

"I'll pack a sandwich for me and Robert. Now, will you please see if there is space available on the evening flight to Pittsburgh?"

"I have you confirmed on our 7:20 flight to Pittsburgh, sir. May I have your home address?"

"Why do you need my home address?" I asked.

"So Wingandaprayer can mail you your green stamps and toaster."

When we finally arrived at the airport and boarded the plane, we were immediately greeted by two delays. The first, said the captain, was due to "a minor mechanical problem. We should have it cleared up soon." If an airplane is going to develop a mechanical problem, whether major or minor, the best time to do so is when it's still on the ground. Nonetheless, it can be extremely unsettling to the passengers.

For example, what does the captain consider "minor"? It could be anything from a wing being loose to the navigator's pen being out of ink. Secondly, how can the captain or the passengers know for sure that the problem has been fixed? It's not exactly like dealing with someone's pickup truck, where the mechanic opens the hood, pulls at a few wires and hoses, and then says, "Try it now." If the truck doesn't start, the mechanic pulls at some different wires and hoses. With an airplane, you don't get a second chance.

I expressed my concern to a passing stewardess.

"Don't worry," she said, "our mechanic knows this plane from front to back."

If he knows so much, I thought to myself, why isn't he in the cockpit flying this sucker instead of underneath it pulling at wires and hoses? I looked out the window and saw a fellow who looked like a mechanic scratching his head with a big wrench. On his breast pocket I could read the name, Bobby Earl. Would you trust your life to a man named Bobby Earl?

Another concern was that we were flying on Sunday. Have you ever tried to find a mechanic to work on your car on Sunday? The only ones I've ever found had just been fired from Brake-O. Bobby Earl worked on the plane for about an hour. Then I heard him yell to the pilot, "Try it now!" Sure enough, it started. I didn't know whether to be happy or sad.

As we backed away from the terminal (Why do they have to call it that?), the chief stewardess announced another delay.

"Due to heavy traffic here at the airport, we are presently 108th in line for takeoff, which means we're going to spend approximately the four hours and ten minutes either taxiing slowly or sitting in line with a bunch of other planes waiting to take off," she explained.

"Wingandaprayer Airlines would like to apologize for

this inconvenience. We realize that some of you have con-
nections or important meetings in Pittsburgh and that this
sort of delay could cause you to lose your company's biggest
account, among other disastrous occurrences. But please
do not whine, because we can't help it if thirty-five other
airlines decided to schedule takeoffs at the same time we
did.

"We will do everything in our power to make up for this
excruciating experience. For those of you who might want
to read while we are taxiing out, ask your flight attendant to
bring you something from Wingandaprayer's in-flight
library. Available today are *War and Peace*, *The Rise and Fall of
the Third Reich*, and *The Complete Works of Victor Hugo*.

"Later in our taxi out, we will be offering at no charge our
'Movie While You Wait.' Our feature in first class will be the
original, uncut version of *Gone With the Wind*, while our
coach passengers will enjoy viewing *Rocky I*, *II* and *III*.

"If we still haven't taken off by that time, Wingandaprayer has other means of killing time for our passengers.
There will be a bridge tournament in rows twenty-five
through thirty. For those who prefer bingo, cards may be
purchased at a nominal charge. First officer Willard Smith,
who is just as bored as the rest of you, will be calling the
games in rows seven through twenty-four.

"In first class there will be Trivial Pursuit games and mud
wrestling for any passengers who are interested, as well as
a musical performance by two of our flight attendants,
Ramona Dentz and Glenda Jane Chastain, singing songs
they actually wrote, such as, 'I've Got the Air Sickness Bag
Blues.' Other pre-takeoff performances include a lecture by
Captain Allis Chalmers, who will explain how to hot-wire a
747, and a demonstration on in-flight macramé by navigator
Marco Polonski.

"Also, because of our long delay, our smoking passengers may wish to step outside to smoke. If so, please remember to walk along with the aircraft in case it moves so you don't get too far behind. Thank you for ridin — , I mean flying, Wingandaprayer Airlines, and have a pleasant flight."

***

If dealing with airlines doesn't test your mettle and cultivate a little true grit, then try buying or selling a house. Real estate agents are God's curse on mankind when locusts are out of season.

When you're trying to buy a house, there are basically three parties involved: (1) a large lending agency which employs no people, only computers, (2) a real estate agent, who is one of seventeen zillion housewives who got bored with Tuesday morning doubles and went out and got licensed to sell houses, and (3) a working stiff with a wife and two kids.

Here's how the game is played:

The stiff and his wife and two kids have outgrown their modest, 2BR, 1BA, brk. rch. w/o fpl. They are looking for something a little nicer and with more space. They contact a real estate agent, an attractive person named Delores who smokes a lot and drives a late-model Mercedes.

Delores takes the stiff and his wife and his two kids to look at houses that are for sale. The stiff is shown a house with three bedrooms, two baths and a fireplace in the den, which is exactly what he had in mind. Last year it cost $17,000. But that was last year.

"This honey of a place is one-five," says Delores. "One-five" is real estate saleslady talk for one hundred and five big ones. I'm talking thousands.

The poor stiff, meanwhile, is holding about half of the downpayment and facing an interest rate that would make

Shylock cringe.

"But, Darling," says his wife, "it's just perfect, and Marvin and Arnold (the two kids) can each have their own bedroom."

"Yeah, Dad," echo Marvin and Arnold.

This is where the real estate game gets interesting. There's no way the stiff can do what his father probably did — plunk down ten percent and make reasonable payments the rest of his life — so he has to engage in what is termed "creative financing." That's real estate saleslady talk for, "No way you can afford this house, turkey, but I haven't had a good commission in a month, so here's the way we're going to rig it."

There are all sorts of ways to finance a house creatively. Here are a few:

● LOAN ASSUMPTION — That's where you assume your brother-in-law, the doctor, will lend you the money for a downpayment, but he laughs in your face and asks if Marvin and Arnold can come over to help him clean his pool.

● WRAPAROUND MORTGAGE — That's where a bunch of fast-talking guys with cigars wrap you around their little fingers and you're in so deep you have to take a night job and Marvin and Arnold forget you exist.

● GRADUATED PAYMENTS — The first year you pay ten dollars a month. The next year you pay ten thousand dollars a month. The following year you live in a tent.

● STARVATION MORTGAGE PLAN — You can make your house payments, but you can't afford food for the first two years of the loan. Marvin and Arnold go to live with your brother-in-law.

● BLACKMAIL — You find out the owner of the house you are trying to buy had a sex-change operation in 1963.

343

"He" gives you the house for free and buys Marvin and Arnold a dog.

● ROB-A-LIQUOR-STORE PLAN — Just what the name implies. You rob liquor stores until you can afford the house. The real estate firm locates the stores and furnishes a stocking to go over your head. Marvin and Arnold watch the doors. Delores drives the getaway car.

Selling a house can be equally frustrating. First the house sits for six months without a single person coming to look at it, but Delores is still nauseatingly optimistic.

This house will sell. I guarantee it," she says, jingling the change in her pocket and rocking back and forth on her heels.

"Yeah, but during my lifetime?" asks the stiff.

"Trust me," says Delores, popping her gum. Didn't I buy a Pinto from her several years ago? Or was she the travel agent who sold me the Braniff charter to West Beirut?

Finally one afternoon the phone rings and Delores says, "Will it be OK to show the house later today?" What that really means is, "I'll be there in four minutes. These turkeys (prospective buyers) could be hot."

Delores's timing is magnificent. The United States Army Mule Team and its drivers were over for lunch and have just left, and she wants to show the house in four minutes.

"It'll just take me a week to hose the place down," you argue.

"Trust me," says Delores. The Pinto was lemon yellow and the engine sounded like it had emphysema.

The stiff immediately starts throwing things under chairs, under the sofa, into cabinets, and his wife puts something on the stove to boil. That's another tip from Delores: boil cinnamon to give the house a "homey" smell.

"What's that god-awful smell?" asks the man as soon as

he walks through the front door.

"Smells like cinnamon to me," says his wife.

"I can't stand the smell of cinnamon. Let's go back and take another look at that house that smelled like garlic. You know, I just love garlic."

Another trick Delores suggests is to have a fire burning in the fireplace. Gives the house a "cozy" feeling, she says.

Only problem is that stiff forgets to open the flue.

"Stay close to the floor and there's plenty of air," says Delores to the prospective buyers. "Now, in there is the master bedroom...."

"Let's get out of here," the man says to his wife. "I'll call the fire department at the first pay phone we see."

I once had a house that sat for nine months without selling. Without so much as thinking about selling. So I did what any self-respecting syndicated columnist would do: I wrote a column about an eccentric old bird who lived there before me and buried $200,000 in cash somewhere on the property just before he died. With my bad back, I couldn't even lift a shovel, I wrote, but . . .

In the words of Delores, "Trust me."

***

Unfortunately, those sorts of shenanigans are not limited to the real estate industry. Deception and misrepresentation are more prevalent today than Boy George. Our very language is twisted and distorted daily so that it's hard to know exactly what phrases mean anymore. Take politics, for example.

When a politician says, "We're still checking the results of our latest poll," what he really means is, "I paid a fortuneteller fifty bucks to predict my chances, and she said that if I got two thousand votes she'd eat her crystal ball."

Here are some of their other favorites:

- "A heavy turnout will help us." If all my cousins bother to vote, I might hit double figures.

- "I think bad weather on election day would definitely benefit my opponent." My support is so weak that I'll lose half my votes if there's more than a ten percent chance of rain.

- "We haven't had any attention from the media." I bought drinks for two television reporters and a newspaper columnist, and all I got in return was stuck with a fifty-dollar tab.

- "I don't know how my opponent could stoop so low as to bring up something like that." You rig just one little million-dollar construction bid and everybody wants to make a federal case out of it.

- "We've run a clean, honest campaign." I spent $25,000 on private detective fees and couldn't come up with a damn thing on my opponent.

- "No matter what the outcome of the election, we've made a lot of new friends all over the country." Especially the blonde at the bar at the Hyatt in San Francisco.

- "I have nothing to be ashamed of." I gave the blonde a ficticious name.

- "You can't run a campaign as inexpensively as you once could." Votes aren't nearly as cheap as they used to be.

- "I'm just a simple country boy." The closest I ever got to a cow was ordering Steak Diane at the country club.

- "It's too early to make any sort of definitive statement on how the election is going." My campaign manager hasn't returned with the booze yet.

- "I want to thank my wife for all her support during the campaign." She believed the story about the lipstick on my shirt after the campaign trip to San Francisco.

- "I would like to congratulate my opponent on his victory." All I want is five minutes alone with that sorry SOB.

- "Now that the campaign is over, I'm looking forward to getting my life back to normal." I'm not going to sober up for a week.
- "The people have spoken." If I'd known I had that many enemies, I'd have carried a gun.

Politicians and their aides also are forever coming up with catch words or phrases which I find terribly confusing. For example, not long ago President Reagan sent home a lot of "non-essential" government employees because he was fighting with Congress about getting a budget approved.

After his announcement, I couldn't help wondering, What do all those non-essential government employees do? I suppose they handle all the non-essential work the government has to do. But if thousands of government employees are non-essential, what about me? How do I know if I'm essential to the country or not?

To help myself and other Americans answer this crucial question, I devised a test to find out if you're non-essential or not. Just answer the following questions.

1. Is it absolutely necessary that you stay awake and in an upright position while performing your duties?

2. If you walked into the boss's office and demanded a raise, would he (a) give you the raise? (b) throw you out of his office? (c) mistake you for Killingsworth from accounting who died last year?

3. If you took a leave of absence and hiked the Appalachian Trail for six months and came back to work with a full beard, would anybody notice that you had been away, or, if you're female, remark how it's not everyday that you see a woman with a full beard?

4. Are you with the Ford Motor Company and presently designing a diesel Edsel?

5. If you called in sick, would the boss hire a temporary to fill in, or would he say, "Killingsworth from accounting can handle things until you get back"?

6. If you said, "But, sir, Killingsworth from accounting died last year," would the boss respond, "Too bad, he was a good man," or, "I know. That's why he'd be perfect for your job"?

7. Are you Woody Allen's weight coach?

8. If one day you didn't come to work but sent your dog instead, what most likely would happen? (a) Nobody would notice the difference; (b) The SPCA would cite you for unnecessarily boring a defenseless animal; (c) Your dog would be promoted because he was overqualified for your job.

Finally, if you had the time to take this test while at work, it's a good bet you're non-essential.

Another category of people frequently referred to by the Reagan Administration is "undesirables." You might recall several years ago when a former Secretary of the Interior suggested that The Beach Boys might attract "undesirables" to a Washington concert. The Beach Boys, incidentally, are still going strong; the former Secretary now is a fur trapper on the upper east side of Manhattan.

About that same time officials at the University of Texas opposed a Willie Nelson concert on campus because he might attract "undesirables." Since I am one of Willie's biggest fans and attend his concerts at every opportunity, does that make me an undesirable?

Once again, I devised a test to help me and other confused Americans to discover if we are, in fact, undesirable.

Just answer truthfully the following questions.

1. When you hear Willie Nelson sing "Up Against the Wall, You Redneck Mother," does it make you want to (a) beat up a hippie; (b) drink beer from a quart jar; (c) take off your shirt; (d) call your mom?

2. Does The Beach Boys's "Little Surfer Girl" make you want to (a) take narcotics; (b) quit your job and go live at the beach; (c) insult a policeman; (d) ice down some Pepsi and build a sand castle?

3. If you were to attend a Beach Boys concert, which of the following would you likely wear? (a) half a bikini; (b) T-shirt with an obscene message; (c) it doesn't matter because you're going to take it off as soon as you get good and drunk anyway; (d) Gray Flannel cologne.

4. The last time you saw a Willie Nelson concert, which of the following best describes your behavior? (a) loud and obnoxious; (b) nasty and mean; (c) it took a dozen cops to get you into the paddy wagon; (d) you read the latest issue of the *New Yorker* between numbers.

5. Which of the following do you think would come in most handy at your next Beach Boys concert? (a) a hand grenade; (b) your coke dealer; (c) assorted birth control devices; (d) an uncrowded restroom.

6. Which of the the following would you be most likely to do after attending a Willie Nelson concert? (a) get tattooed; (b) burn a city; (c) rape and pillage; (d) watch "Nightline."

That's it; you can relax now. If you answered (d) to all of the questions, you most certainly are not an undesirable. If you did not answer any questions with (d), you're invited to a party at my house next Saturday night. Dress is not required.

***

It seems to me that a lot of old-fashioned jobs have been declared non-essential or else those who worked them have been deemed undesirable. For example, what has happened to movie ushers?

It used to be that you bought your ticket and some popcorn and a nice young man in a uniform would lead you with his flashlight to an available seat. You think that wasn't an essential job? You walk into a dark movie theater these days and there's no telling what can happen. You might sit next to a weirdo who makes sucking noises with his teeth. Or worse, you could sit on top of somebody. I walked into a dark theater the other day and was about to comment on how soft and comfortable the seats were when I realized I was sitting on a fat woman's lap.

"Get off me, you weirdo!" she screamed. I scrambled away and landed in another seat on top of a small child, who pinched me. I finally found an empty seat and made sucking noises with my teeth so that I'd be left alone.

And whatever happened to the old-timey car washes? Who declared them non-essential? Years ago people at a carwash would attack your auto with brushes and rags, and then they'd sweep and vacuum the inside of the car. Not even the Methodist Youth Fellowship car washes do that anymore. It's important to have the inside of your car cleaned occasionally. I did so recently and found two dollars in change, a missing tennis shoe and an old friend I thought had moved to Wyoming.

In today's automatic car washes, I feel like I'm trapped inside a giant washing machine like a pair of soiled pajamas about to be rinsed to death. If the inside gets cleaned, it's only because my windows leak and the jet sprays soak the interior.

And where, pray tell, are the old door-to-door salesmen?

Nobody comes to my house selling magazines or encyclopedias or vacuum cleaners anymore.

"Hi," the young man would say. "My name is Harvey and I'm working my way through college and I'm trying to win this contest...."

I don't remember ever buying anything from those salesmen, but at least it kept them off the streets and gave the dogs a little sport that was safer than chasing cars. What could be more essential?

In place of those important old jobs, we now have people doing the most absurd jobs imaginable. Just who are those people in the bathrooms everywhere I go? Do their wives know what they're doing?

I've been able to go to the bathroom without assistance since I was five or six, but lately every time I turn around I'm confronted by a smiling, grown man bearing towels. For the use of one, I'm expected to drop something spendable into his tip dish. I admit that I'm not very mechanically inclined, but I can usually figure out a towel dispenser or even one of those electric blowers without help.

There are, of course, ways to avoid restroom attendants. You can leave quickly without washing your hands, or you can simply hand the towel back to the attendant, smile and say thank you. If he still wants a tip, tell him to plant his corn early next year.

Not washing your hands can be unsanitary, however, or even unsociable. I was standing at a urinal beside two fellows at a Georgia-Auburn football game once. The Georgia fan, dressed in red and black from head to toe, finished his business, zipped his pants and headed for the door.

"Hey, Bulldog," shouted the Auburn fan, "don't they teach you guys at Georgia to wash after using the bathroom?"

"No," said the Bulldog fan, "they teach us not to piss on our hands."

I'm a dyed-in-the-wool Bulldog, and that's why I don't need anybody in the bathroom handing me a towel.

***

Being non-essential, undesirable or even outmoded is minor compared to the shame that can result from being associated with unmentionables. I'm not referring to disreputable characters, but rather to women's lingerie. Buying it, even for your wife, can be more embarrassing than urinals that splash.

In the first place, you never know who might see you.

"Guess who I saw in Willoughby's buying lingerie," says one busybody to another.

"Who?"

"Harvey Nelson, that's who."

"Never would have figured him for the kinky type."

"I feel sorry for his poor wife and children."

You can't walk into a lingerie department with a big grin on your face and say, "I'm not buying these for myself," because everyone will assume that you certainly are; neither can you walk in announcing, "These are for my wife, you know," because everyone will assume that they certainly are not. In such situations, I recommend a disguise, such as wearing dark glasses and speaking with a foreign accent.

"May I help you, sir?" the saleslady will ask.

"*Si*," you answer. "I would like to look at your nightgown collection, *por favor*."

The saleslady will have no idea she is selling good ol' Harvey Nelson something that the Catwoman on Bourbon Street wouldn't wear.

"I'll tell you something, Mildred," she'll say to her friend at lunch. "Those French are everything they say they are."

There are a couple more "don'ts" which I would recommend to any man who finds himself in this situation:

● Don't ask the saleslady to try on lingerie "since you're about the same size as my wife."

● Don't inquire about the possibility of purchasing the especially attractive mannequin in the black nightie. This could lead to an embarrassing arrest.

● Don't buy your wife or mistress colored underpants with the days of the week or the Clemson football schedule printed on them. For some reason, most women don't like them.

***

One of the greatest personal adversities I must endure, one that develops patience and grit in me, is the frequent abuse of my last name. A man's name is his birthright, and to have it besmudged is a terrible thing.

Only recently someone sent me an advertisement from the local newspaper in which a grocery store was offering "Fresh Chicken Grizzards" at seventy-nine cents a pound. The loving folks who sent me the ad included a notation: "Know the difference between a gizzard and a grizzard? One's just part of a chicken. The other is the whole thing."

To think that riffraff like that are allowed to use the public mails.

What obviously happened in the ad was that someone made a small error. By inserting an *r* in gizzards (which aren't worth seventy-nine cents a pound, no matter how you spell 'em), they libeled my proud name. It's not the first time, I must admit. People of little breeding often pronounce my name without the *r*. In restaurants they're always blurting out, "Gizzard, party of four. The Gizzard party, please." I save a lot of money on tips when that happens.

Other people simply mispronounce the name by making it rhyme with lizard. It does not. Notice the two z's, which means that Grizzard should be pronounced GrizZARD, which is French in origin and means "wild stallion."

There have been some very famous GrizZARDS down through the years who have made the name synonymous with noble deeds and glory. There was Pierre GrizZARD, a famous French sheetrocker who is given credit for many of the aesthetic qualities of the Palace of Versailles.

Then there was Jean Paul GrizZARD, the French trapper who single-handedly introduced several different strains of venereal disease to the North American Indians in the middle of the eighteenth century.

And, of course, there was my great, great, great grandfather, Brigadier General Beauregard GrizZARD of the Confederate Army, who successfully defended Miami Beach against the yankees during the Civil War, something no one else has been able to do since.

Yes, mine is a proud name, steeped in history and tradition. To have it abused in some grocery ad is a personal affront to me and my kin. And for anyone who is thinking about writing me a letter referring to that insidious joke about Mr. BuzZARD who's in the yard, and Mr. TurTELL who's at the well, and Mr. RabBIT, etc., don't bother. Mr. GrizZARD has already heard it a million times.

***

Of all the trials and tribulations I face, one of the most difficult certainly is Sunday nights. I hate Sunday nights. I think this hatred goes back to my childhood.

Sunday mornings when I was growing up were wonderful. We got up early with the radio blaring gospel music through the house, ate a wonderful breakfast of homemade

354

biscuits and ham or bacon and then got ready for Sunday school.

I had only one white shirt and wore it every Sunday. My mother would wash it, hang it on the line to dry in the Southern sunshine and then iron it by hand. There is a special place in heaven for women who spent days of their lives ironing.

Sunday school itself was a social event. They put us kids in the basement and for an hour we sang songs like, "Do, Lord, oh do, Lord, oh do remember me, praise Jesus!" The sermon hour wasn't as easy. I watched the hands on my mother's watch crawl as I drew hills and birds on the title pages of the hymnals. I hope the Great Scorer doesn't hold that against me; I was only nine.

Then came that wonderful Sunday lunch, featuring fried chicken and rice and gravy and plump prizes from the garden. And, of course, more homemade biscuits. My mother always let me fork the first piece of white meat. I hope someday I love a child enough to let them do the same.

On Sunday afternoons my friends and I dammed creeks and watched trains or rode bikes or hit rocks with broom handles. Then as the sun got low in the sky, we'd gather on the front porch and start talking about supper. But it was never an organized meal — just leftover chicken and biscuits whenever you wanted it.

I think that's where my problem with Sunday evenings began. I was a grown man before I stopped pouting that my mother made me get my own supper on Sunday evenings. Inevitably there was no white meat left, only dark. And the only thing on television was Ed Sullivan with seals and jugglers. It was a depressing way to end what had been a wonderful day.

Sunday nights still feel the same way. They depress me. I take a lot of Sunday night meals alone these days, and many times I would be thankful for a cold piece of dark meat. There's still nothing much on TV, just an occasional "60 Minutes" piece on germ warfare that depresses me even more.

There's a distinct quiet on Sunday nights. A lonely quiet. I get sentimental. I call a few old friends, we talk, hang up and the quiet is even quieter. I try to work a lick but my mind won't have it. It's too late to call anyone else. I eat some tuna fish straight from the can.

I also pray on Sunday nights, whether I feel the need to or not. Give Monday a little shove, Lord. Do.

***

Finally, for those citizens of the world who endure it daily, who confront idiocy and walk away from it a better man or woman for having done so, I offer some questions and answers that don't necessarily match but are worthy of your consideration nonetheless.

THE QUESTIONS:
- Why is it that no matter which lane you're in on the expressway, the other one is always moving faster?
- Who ate the first oyster?
- Who said convenience stores are convenient? As compared to what?
- Why do service stations lock the bathroom door but leave the cash register unlocked?
- Is it really necessary for bowling balls to be that heavy?
- Do animals go to heaven when they die?
- Did Michael Jackson or Boy George every play any sports?
- What are chicken fingers that so many restaurants are

serving these days? I didn't know they had fingers.

- Why is it I have sixty channels on my television and still can't find anything worth watching?
- What makes popcorn pop?
- What happened to the power in modern automobiles? They're wonderful for funeral processions but no match for a strong headwind.
- Why aren't there any black hockey players?
- What are those little green things in fruitcake?

THE ANSWERS:

- Most of the things your mother told you are true. Disregard the part about eating liver to live longer; it's not worth it.
- Life isn't fair. That's what makes it so interesting.
- Money doesn't grow on trees, and if it did somebody else would own the orchard.
- If you have to shoot it, don't drink it.
- The greatest benefit of going to college is learning to get up in the morning without somebody making you.
- Going to church on Sunday morning will make you feel better no matter what you did on Saturday night.
- The best things in life aren't free. Just ask any poor person.
- Never buy anything from a man who jingles his change.
- If you can't flow, flee.

— 7 —

One Man's Hominy Is Another Man's Grit

Another War, Another Legacy

HE CAME WALKING ACROSS the lobby of the hotel. He was scraggly and his jeans were in need of a washing. He carried a paper sack.

He hit on the cashier first. She shooed him away with a flick of her wrist. A woman sat reading in a chair. He approached her. She looked up from her magazine only for a second and then went back to reading, ignoring his pitch. Then he saw me. If you panhandle long enough, I suppose it becomes easy to spot a soft touch.

"Sir," he began, "I wonder if I could speak with you for a moment?"

Most beggars are very polite. They can't afford not to be. He started to reach inside his sack.

"What are you selling?" I asked.

"I'm not selling anything. I'm just asking for a donation for this."

He handed me a lapel pin, a tiny American flag. The pin was attached to a card which read, "Show your colors and help a disabled veteran."

"You're a disabled veteran?" I asked the man.

"Got my card to prove it."

He pulled a tattered wallet out of his back pocket and drew out a small card. On the card, he or someone else had scrawled, "Charles Ienberg, Disabled Vet."

"World War II?" I continued.

"I ain't that old," he said. "Korea."

His breath smelled like stale beer. I thought of another man I knew who also fought in Korea and drank after he came back.

"Were you wounded?" I went on.

"See this fingernail?" he said, pointing the index finger on his right hand toward me. "They pulled the fingernail off and burned my hands with cigarettes."

"Who is 'they?'"

"North Koreans," he answered. "I jumped into South Korea and they got me and these three other fellows just like that. When we finally got out, they sent me to Seattle and I was in the hospital for a long time. I never have been the same since. They told me to quit drinking, but that ain't no easy thing to do."

"You're still drinking?"

"I'll be honest with you, sir," he said, "I need me a drink pretty bad right now. I ain't gonna lie to you. I'm hungry, but I need a drink a lot worse than I need something to eat."

I appreciated his honesty. "This is all you do, ask for donations for these pins?" I asked.

"Used to do some house painting, but I can't get no work no more. Guess I'm too old."

"How old are you?"

"Fifty-two."

He looked twenty years older than that. I pulled a five out of my pocket and handed it to him. He handed me a lapel pin. Then he thanked me for my donation, tucked his sack back under his arm and shuffled away to buy his pint.

I mentioned another lonely old soldier. I used to give him whiskey money, too. I buried him next to his mother.

Damn wars. Damn them all.

LIVING UP TO HIS CREED

When Chuck joined the Boy Scouts at age fourteen, the kids at school gave him a lot of grief about it. It wasn't exactly a groovy thing to do, joining the Scouts, especially at that mature age. "It was pretty rough on him," Chuck's scoutmaster told me.

I've forgotten all of the Boy Scout creed, but I remember that "kind" was in there somewhere. Chuck's scoutmaster recalled the time his troop was on a camping trip and Chuck found a dead mother squirrel with a lot of hungry babies in the nest. He took the babies home and fed them with an eyedropper until they were strong enough to tackle the forest on their own. That sort of thing gets out at school and a fellow might never live it down.

Chuck joined a scouting group called the Leadership Corps, where older kids teach intermediate Scouts special skills. Chuck's special skills were canoeing and swimming. So not long ago Second-Class Scout Chuck of the Leadership Corps took off on a trip to a nearby lake with some younger kids.

The group was joined by a couple of non-scouts, one a fifteen-year-old who turned out to be a lousy swimmer.

While everyone else was having fun, this kid was drowning in fourteen feet of water in the middle of the lake. The only person close to him was Chuck, who was forty yards away.

The scoutmaster told me the rest of the story:

"I was on the shore, and I saw the kid go under for the first time. Then I saw Chuck turn back toward the middle of the lake to go after him. I knew for sure I was about to see a double tragedy. I didn't see how Chuck could swim all the way out there and then save both of them.

"I jumped in my canoe, but I knew there was no way I'd get there in time. I just hoped we could pull them off the bottom of the lake and resuscitate them in time to save their lives.

"When Chuck got there, he was immediately pulled under by the struggling kid. A drowning swimmer has tremendous strength. Then I saw them come up again and Chuck had gotten away, but he wouldn't give up. He circled around the kid, talking to him, trying to calm him down. Then he went after him a second time. This time he managed to grab an arm and dragged the kid to shore. I don't know how, but he saved him."

Chuck was hesitant to talk about it, but I persisted until he told me what happened. "When we went under, I hit him in the stomach and he let go of me. I just couldn't let him drown."

"Chuck never had a lifesaving course," said the scoutmaster. "What he knew, he learned from reading the manual. He's dedicated to Scouting. He never thought of the danger. He never thought of his own safety."

I remember from the creed that Boy Scouts are also brave. Somebody ought to tell the kids at Chuck's school that you can't get much groovier than that.

DEARLY DEPARTED IS GLADLY DEPARTED

This is a true story. Believe me.

There was an automobile accident and a woman in her late thirties was killed. A local funeral home agreed to handle her service.

As friends and relatives were settling into their seats in the funeral home's chapel, a bearded man walked in and took a seat in the front row near the casket. He was dressed like Abe Lincoln, wearing a black suit and a tall black hat. The man, as it turned out, was the common-law husband of the deceased.

The service began and the minister decided to bring a full-length, no-holds-barred, fire-and-brimstone message to the mourners. As he bellowed forth, a man and a woman arrived in the chapel quarreling loudly. It was obvious to the funeral home personnel that they had been drinking.

"All I could do," said one employee, "was hope the preacher would quit soon and we could get out of the chapel before there was a ruckus."

Turns out the woman involved in the quarrel was the former common-law wife of Abe Lincoln, who was still sitting down front, and the man with whom she was at odds was her current husband.

The plot thickens.

The preacher had no intention of ending his service quickly. As he continued his message, the mourners became restless and several of them ventured into the hallway outside the chapel to stretch their legs or have a smoke. Meanwhile, the rowdy couple continued bickering in the back.

The preacher finally brought the service to an end and everyone adjourned to the cemetery for burial. As the preacher began his closing prayer at graveside, the funeral director thought to himself, "This thing is finally over. We're going to get out of here without an incident."

He was wrong. Suddenly, Abe Lincoln and his former wife's current husband squared off. They took off their coats and shouted at each other as calmer heads held them apart. Then Abe's former wife decided to get into the act and began to give him a piece of her mind. Before anybody could put out that brush fire, Abe decided he had had enough verbal abuse for one day and hauled off and decked his ex-wife.

"Cold-cocked her," was the description given by one witness.

Finally order was restored, the service was completed, everybody went home, the tent came down, the chairs were folded, the flowers were loaded on the truck and the deceased was buried.

A week later, however, a shooting was reported in town. When police arrived, Abe was firing shotgun blasts into a van occupied by his ex-wife's new husband. The fact that the van was borrowed didn't matter to Abe. He shot it anyway. Police finally subdued him and hauled him away.

All that's left to ponder is whether or not the dear departed will ever be able to rest in peace after all that's taken place since she left us.

DANCING THE NIGHT AWAY

You find these joints when life is a road trip. There in the Holiday Inn in Texarkana, or two blocks down to Shoney's and then hang a right in Rock Hill or Tupelo.

There's a bar and a bandstand, and they pour in off the main road when the darkness catches them tired and lonely. A man peddles industrial lubricants all day and his needs at night are simple: a drink, a dance and then you take your chance.

"Grover and the Groovers" are on the bandstand playing "Proud Mary," the anthem of the just-off-the-interstate roadhouse.

"Beer in a bottle," I shout to the waitress. Grover and the boys are waking the dead for miles around.

"All we got is draft," the waitress shouts back. She's early to middle forties. She outgrew her outfit when Ford was president. Somebody left her and there's the kids to feed and the "Z" she can't afford needs new tires. The story is always the same.

I can't believe they don't have beer in bottles.

"Don't want nobody to get knocked in the head," she explains.

I accept the draft. Grover asks for requests.

"Feelings!" yells a woman from across the room. Grover nods approval. I think, Oh no, not again.

The men are mostly married. Maybe a few clean one-owners, but mostly married. Their wives trust them. The women just came here to dance. They tell themselves that over and over.

Lots of beehives. The aroma of Spray 'n' Set is rampant.

I watch the phenomenon as Grover and the boys launch into "Feelings." The men, who have gathered securely at the bar as a covey, are flushed out toward the tables where the women are sitting, usually two by two.

The procedure is tough on women. Say nobody asks you to dance. Or say a man walks over and asks your friend ("If there was more light in here, he'd have asked me"). Or, worse, the one who asks is wearing a jacket with "Rockwell Power Tools" emblazoned across the back.

It's even tougher for men. I watch one of them — his shirt is a collector's item — give it a try. He takes a pull off his draft, hitches his pants and walks the long mile to where she is sitting. As he stands in front of her, his weight shifts from one foot to the other. She smiles, but her head and the beehive shake, "No."

Years ago I was sitting in such a bar with a friend. He tried. She said no, too.

"Toughest thing in the world is walking over and asking a woman to dance," I philosophized to him later.

"No, it isn't," he said. "It's walking back."

GUTS AT AN EARLY AGE

Larry has a little boy named Joe, who is six years old. When Larry talks about his son, the look in his eyes changes and the love shows through.

Little Joe is a man's kid. He's tough. Women often tell men that the problem with us is that we try to run through too many walls instead of just walking around, but Little Joe would run through a wall if his dad asked him to. There are just some things women don't understand.

Although he's only six, Little Joe joined a Midget League football team with some of the neighborhood kids. Larry told me what happened:

"Joe's the kind of kid most coaches hate to see coming," he said. "He doesn't have any talent yet, he's flat footed and slow as mud, and he weighs only about forty-five pounds. Other kids his age weigh fifty-five to sixty-five pounds. But he's tough."

The first week of practice, Joe had an accident on his bike and had six stitches taken in his leg. "But he never complained," said Larry. "He did all the running and drills. He never missed a practice. He enjoyed the drills that the other kids hated. But the thing he enjoyed most, and the thing he did best, was hitting."

"Hitting" is football talk for tackling, except it's more than that. It's tackling with unusual aggression.

"The coaches decided to put Joe in at middle linebacker. In the first game, although the other team ran us ragged, little Joe made ten individual tackles and assisted with five others. I told him how proud I was of him."

But after the team got trounced again and again, the coaches finally decided that part of the problem was little Joe — he was just too small — so they benched him.

"I was at practice when he came off the field. He tried to tell me what had happened through his sobs. I don't think the coaches knew how hard he had worked. They never knew about his injury, either. It broke the kid's heart, and mine, too, to see him play above his ability and stand and fight when other kids might have given up," said Larry.

"I would tell him that his heart will carry him farther than his legs, that you can't measure desire, that the fastest horse doesn't always win the race, that if he fights hard enough and long enough his reward will come...but in the form of a broken heart?"

I am not a father and by no means an expert, but what I would do is forget the poetic approach. I'd turn in his pads and helmet, tell him I love him and send him out in the back yard to play in the dirt, which is what a six-year-old, bless his little heart, should be doing with his spare time in the first place.

A GAMBLER ON A ROLL

I wandered into a local bar and sat next to a man who was

nursing a drink. There were two quarters sitting by his glass.

"Want to match for a drink?" he asked.

A perfect stranger wants to play a small game of chance. I was hesitant.

"I just want to see if I'm still hot. You see, I'm on an incredible roll. I've just gotten off a plane from the Bahamas where I was up over $20,000 playing blackjack. I want to see if my luck is still holding," he explained.

I told him I'd be glad to buy him a drink if he'd just tell me how to win twenty grand at blackjack. The only time I get lucky playing that game is when I get sleepy and have to go to bed.

"I just sat down at the table at six last Friday afternoon," he began. "I started off with $200. When I woke up Saturday morning, I was up $20,000. The only thing I did was not take a hit if the dealer had six or less showing. It was ten percent knowledge and ninety percent luck.

"On Saturday morning, I realized if I continued playing, I might lose all I had won, so I decided to buy something while I still had some money. I got a security guard from the hotel to go with me, and I went to downtown Nassau and bought a Presidential Rolex watch. Cost me six thousand," he continued.

"I started playing again at six Saturday night. In the first twenty minutes, I was up another $11,000. But by ten I had cooled off and was down to only $12,000, so I decided to take the money and run. The hotel paid for my room, gave me free meals with Dom Perignon and drove me to the airport in their limo."

Counting the $12,000 in cash and the six in a Rolex, he walked away an $18,000 winner.

"It was the most incredible thing that's ever happened to

me. Now, let's match for a drink."

What the heck. We both flipped.

"Same," he said. And they were.

"Once more?" he asked.

I agreed and we flipped again. He won again.

"One more time?"

"I'm already down two drinks," I said, "but let's just go to see how long this streak can last."

We flipped. He called same. I had heads. He had tails.

"Maybe the streak is finally over," I said.

"Maybe," he answered, and I thought I detected a sigh of relief.

REACHING OUT A HELPING HAND

I received a letter in the mail recently which deserves to be shared.

"I don't have much education," began the writer, "but I've got something inside me I want to get out. I thought maybe you could help me."

Not much background is necessary. The man works in a K-Mart. His wife is a nurse. He moved out of the city a few years ago so he could put some cows in a pasture and raise his kids, four of them, on a farm.

"Here I sit, pulling on a longneck beer. I'm not trying to get drunk, just trying to understand. Ten days ago my wife, myself and our four-year-old daughter visited Atlanta to see a doctor that had been recommended to us. The problem was that my little girl has crossing of her eyes. Our oldest daughter had the same problem when she was five or six, so we figured this one had the same thing.

"The first doctor referred us to another and then he sent us to another and after four doctors, my little girl was finally admitted to the hospital. Just to make sure, they said. Just a few tests. The next day we waited. We waited all day. The tests would come the next day, they said. Finally she was taken down for a brain scan. The machine was down so we waited some more.

"About six on the second day, one of the doctors came and told us that she had a tumor at the base of her brain stem. Because of its location, it is inoperable. The tumor affects her motor functions. Before she was a vivacious little blonde, looking forward to life. Now she drools and stumbles and slurs her speech. She's undergoing radiation therapy, but her prognosis is not good. My only hope is to make these last few months as enjoyable for her as possible.

"But this is not really what I wanted to say to you. I wanted to get across how I feel about those who have helped this family since this tragedy struck. We moved here from the city, and I didn't know the local people had accepted us. But I have never seen such an outpouring of love.

"I didn't know things like this went on anymore. I didn't know there were so many people who still care and love their neighbors. They have brought food. They have helped my wife. They have even contributed money.

"I wish I had the talent of a writer to really get across what is in my heart. I am so moved by how much love and kindness others have shown me, my wife and my little girl that I just want to share it with somebody else. I'm not asking for handouts, but if you see fit to use any of this letter, just tell your readers to look around them. They probably have friends they never knew they had before, friends just waiting for the chance to help them.

"And one other thing. Tell them to love their kids. One day they might not have them anymore. Thanks."

No. Thank you.

——— 8 ———

What's the Penalty For An Illegal Upchuck?

SPORTS HAS ALWAYS BEEN a great proving ground
of character. Kids grow up hearing clichés about the
values of sports:

- When the going gets tough, the tough get going.
- Quitters are always losers and losers are always quitters.
- It's not whether you win or lose but how you play the game.
- Show me a good loser and I'll show you a frequent loser.
- It ain't over till it's over.

One of the first sports a kid is exposed to is fishing, since
dad is always dragging a son or daughter along to carry the
tackle box. As a result of my childhood memories of fishing
from the banks of various lakes and rivers, I have always
maintained my affection for wetting a line.

Not long ago I was standing along the bank of a creek that runs through one of the golf courses of the magnificent Greenbriar Hotel in White Sulphur Springs, West Virginia. I was there because a man at the pro shop assured me I could catch a huge rainbow trout from that bank. I have never caught a rainbow trout — huge or otherwise. I have watched those television fishing shows where somebody is always landing a big trout, and I've read the magazine articles about techniques, but the closest I've ever been to landing one is in the fish department of the Kroger.

The man at the golf shop rented me a spinning rod and some sort of lure that looked like a roach dressed up for a night out at the disco. "This drives 'em crazy," said the man, who also explained that I could keep any four fish I caught and that the cooks up at the hotel would fillet them for me and serve them for my lunch.

Imagine the thrill: out in the wilds of West Virginia, casting for rainbow trout, and later I would dine on my own tasty catch. Eat your heart out, Gaddabout Gaddis.

The water was so clear that I could actually see the fish swimming around in the creek. They were beautiful and just the right size for eating. I made my first cast and got ready for the tug. Nothing. I cast again. Still nothing. As I was reeling in for my third cast, a trout almost had a head-on collision with my lure but managed to swerve out of the way at the last minute.

About that time, a small boy appeared and began fishing next to me.

"Toss it right in there, Scottie," said the kid's father.

Scottie was dressed in official trout fisherman's garb: floppy hat with flies stuck in it, fishing jacket with lots of pockets and a creel over his shoulder. A creel is what trout fishermen put their fish in. The guy at the pro shop had given me a plastic laundry bag for my catch. I didn't care for Scottie the minute I saw him.

Scottie cast where his dad had advised and almost immediately yelled, "Look, Dad! I've got one." The little brat reeled in a gorgeous rainbow. I reeled in and moved down the bank a little farther.

"Dad," I heard the kid say, "I've got another one!"

"Good going, Scottie," his dad answered.

Get out of my life, Scottie, I thought to myself.

I never did catch a rainbow trout that day. In fact, I didn't catch any fish that day. Not only that, I hung my line in an overhanging tree and lost that funny looking roach lure.

"Look, Dad," said Scottie. "That man has caught a tree." Dad and Scottie had a big laugh. I reeled in my line and started to head back for the pro shop with homicide on my mind.

"Would you like to have these fish Scottie caught?" the dad asked as I was leaving. "We still haven't eaten the ones we caught yesterday."

"No thanks. I hate fish," I said.

Of course, by the time I arrived back at the office, my catch was considerable and never had I enjoyed a finer meal than those rainbows I had pulled from the creek. That's another thing kids learn early about fishing — lying is part of the sport. Consider these standard examples:

QUESTION: So, how were they bitin'?
ANSWER: Had to stand behind a tree to bait our hooks.
TRUTH: The mosquitoes didn't even bother us.

QUESTION: Did you have a guide?
ANSWER: One of the best.
TRUTH: Luckily, the day we got hopelessly lost my five-

year-old kid remembered the way back to the dock. I found the bar on my own.

QUESTION: Anybody get sunburned?
ANSWER: Are you kidding me?
TRUTH: I was out of intensive care in no time.

QUESTION: How many did you catch?
ANSWER: Filled up two ice chests.
TRUTH: With beer. The fish fit in my shirt pocket.

QUESTION: What were you fishing for?
ANSWER: Trophy bass.
TRUTH: I'd have been happy with a small frog.

QUESTION: See any snakes?
ANSWER: Big moccasin fell off a tree limb into my boat, but I killed it with the paddle.
TRUTH: A Louisiana pink worm crawled out of the bait box. I made the kid put it back.

QUESTION: So what did you catch?
ANSWER: Largemouths, mostly.
TRUTH: One carp and a turtle.

QUESTION: What did you catch them on?
ANSWER: Top-water plugs.
TRUTH: The carp had a heart attack and floated to the top of the water. My kid caught the turtle and took it home for a pet.

QUESTION: Can't wait to get out there and get at 'em again, huh?
ANSWER: Next chance I get.
TRUTH: I traded my tackle box for two six-packs.

***

When I got older and more sophisticated, my friends urged me to join them in a sport more appropriate for that time in our lives — golf. I later figured out that the people who encouraged me to play golf disliked me very much. It has to be the most frustrating game ever invented.

Because of my history of heart problems, I try not to play more than once a year. In that length of time I usually forget how awful it was the last time and am willing to take another swing.

Golf, I'm convinced, was conceived by real estate developers so they would have an excuse for ruining perfectly good forests and pastures. After the golf courses are completed, these scoundrels further ravage the countryside by building condominiums along the fairways. Rich Republican retirees move into the condos and become even stuffier than they were before.

In fact, stuffiness is probably the no. 1 characteristic of golf. Have you ever listened to the announcers broadcasting the Masters golf tournament? They sound like they're doing the play-by-play for a state funeral. Golf would be more fun if somebody would belch occasionally.

My most recent annual swing at golf came in Myrtle Beach, South Carolina. A companion and I paid a week's salary for green fees, rental clubs, an electric cart and a half-dozen orange golf balls (I could have sworn they were white the last time I played, but maybe that was tennis).

On the first tee my playing partner and I made a small wager, another integral part of the game, and then proceeded to tee off. Unfortunately, my first drive sliced into the backyard of somebody's condominium where a Tupperware party was in progress. I got a free container suitable for serving congealed salads and a free drop off the coffee table.

My second shot, a three wood, caught a tree limb and bounced back toward the Tupperware party, coming to rest on a plate of cheese and crackers the ladies were munching with their white wine. This time I bought six cups and a casserole container to pay for the damages and pitched back into the fairway. I took a twelve on the first hole. My companion went one-up with an eleven.

We both went into the water on the second hole — the water in a swimming pool located behind somebody else's condominium where a woman sat reading a copy of *Cosmopolitan*. My companion removed his tennis shorts and waded into the pool to retrieve our errant shots. The woman went inside and fetched her husband, a very large man, who threatened to call the authorities if we weren't off his property in thirty seconds.

In our haste to leave, we drove the cart over one of the pool chairs, which wouldn't have been all that bad had it not been the one the woman was sitting in at the time. Luckily, the poor woman was unhurt, but her *Cosmo* got caught under one of the cart wheels and we scattered a series on unsightly liver spots for several hundred yards.

I finally shot a sixty-six on the front nine. My companion had a sixty-two and took me for a dollar. We intended to play the back nine, too, but my friend had decided to take his shirt off and catch a few rays. As we made the turn, the head pro requested that we leave the course immediately. We might have resisted, but he made the request while drawing back a four-iron.

Undaunted, we drove to the strip on Myrtle Beach and got in a quick eighteen holes at Jungle Jim's Carpet Golf, where they don't care if you take off your shirt just as long as you don't steal the scoring pencils.

Relieved to get away from the stuffiness of the regular

links, I got my dollar back on the last hole by sinking a long putt that rolled into the monkey's mouth, out through his tail, then under the giraffe's legs, dropping squarely into the cup.

Actually, golf would be a lot more fun if the rules were a little more flexible. For example, I have come up with my own rules guaranteed to add enjoyment to your round:

• THE MILLIGAN RULE — Most golfers know what a mulligan is. That's when you get to hit a second shot off the first tee because your first shot went into the next county. The "milligan" takes that a step further. If you don't like your first shot off any tee, hit another one. If that shot is lousy, too, then hit a "McMilligan," which is a third shot. If that shot is also poor, drive the cart out into the middle of the fairway about 250 yards and drop your ball there. That's called a "Grover McMilligan," named for a famous card cheat who died in a lynching accident.

• MOVING THE BALL IN THE ROUGH — Under my rules, you may not only move your ball in the rough, you also may ignore rough altogether and put your ball back in the fairway ten yards closer to the hole for each form of reptilia spotted while you were in the weeds looking for your ball. A snake and two turtles can make a long hole play much shorter.

• LOST BALL RULE — Let's say you hit your ball into the water and it can't be retrieved. What you do is subtract two strokes from your eventual score on the hole. You deserve it. You just paid three bucks for a brand-new golf ball, and now it sleeps with the fishes.

• SAND RULE — Whose idea was it to put sand on a golf course in the first place? When your ball goes into the sand, remove it as quickly as possible to a nice flat place on the green. That's called a "sandie" in golfing lingo.

- TREE RULE — If you were aiming at a tree and hit it, then you must play the ball as it lies. However, if you were aiming down the middle of the fairway and hit a tree, don't let it ruin your round. Move the ball fifty yards closer to the green for each variety of pine tree you can name.
- TWO-PUTT RULE — If you still aren't in the hole after two putts, pick up your ball and place it in the cup. If your opponent complains, put his head in the hole.
- BEER RULE — At the end of your round, count up the total number of beers you drank during your round and subtract that number from your score. If you had been sober, that's probably what you would have shot in the first place.

***

Golf is not the only game that could benefit from a few adjustments in the rules. Professional tennis, basketball and baseball also could be made more exciting.

In tennis, for example, one of the biggest problems today is players berating the officials. Every time they disagree with a call, they question some linesperson's parentage.

I propose arming each linesperson and the umpire with a big stick, just the kind you would take along on a walk in the woods in case you had to beat a snake. Let's say John McEnroe, one of the most frequent offenders, is playing. He serves, rushes to the net, hits a backhand volley which his opponent returns down the line. The linesperson signals that the ball is in.

"What?" screams McEnroe, turning red in the face. He stomps the ground, breaks his racquet and pulls his hair. Then he calls the linesperson a dirty, rotten so-and-so with everybody in attendance listening. At that point, the linesperson gets out of his or her chair, walks over to McEnroe and bashes him over the head with the stick. A couple of times having a tune played on his noggin will improve his behavior immensely and thereby make the game more enjoyable for the rest of us.

My friend and step-brother Ludlow Porch, a great philosopher, came up with a similar plan to bring baseball more in line with popular tastes.

"Americans love rough contact sports," Ludlow explained, "like football and boxing and hockey and pool."

Pool is a rough contact sport?

"Not the game itself," he said, "but the knife fight that breaks out every night in any decent pool hall certainly is."

So Ludlow has a plan to put more rough stuff into baseball.

"You add two new players. One plays behind the shortstop. That's your left-mugger. Another plays behind second base, and he's your right-mugger. Now, say the batter hits the ball to the third baseman. He throws it to the right-mugger. The runner is not allowed to stop on a base, so he is chased by the right-mugger, who, in order to get the runner out, must knock him to the ground and hit him square in the mouth with the ball and hold him down long enough for the umpire to count to three."

But isn't that terribly unfair to the baserunner, not to mention dangerous?

"There is one other thing," Ludlow said. "The guy who hits the ball gets to carry something with him for protection when he meets a mugger on the basepaths."

And what is that?

"His bat."

The biggest problem with basketball is that all the players have outgrown the game. Guards used to be quick little fellows who could dribble through a church picnic without getting potato salad on the ball. They shot two-handed set shots from the cheap seats and married squatty home-ec majors, and they produced more guards and squatty home-ec majors.

Today guards are so tall they don't even need a ladder to get arrested for peeping into the third floor of the girls' dorm to see if the home-ec majors really have thighs as big as their own.

The big man in basketball used to be any awkward boy over six feet tall who didn't mind being called "Stretch." Today, the big men are what former coach Al McGuire calls "aircraft carriers." You could land on them. They marry girls nobody used to want to dance with and together they produce more "aircraft carriers."

What I propose is legislation to prohibit anyone over six-five from marrying anyone over five-six. That way we won't have to ruin the game for future generations by raising the basket (or, if you're a Democrat, by lowering the floor).

A second way to improve basketball is to do away with the clock. Without a doubt, the "stall," designed to run time off the clock, is the worst thing ever introduced to basketball. It's about as exciting as watching cabbage boil. The rule should be that the first team to score one hundred points wins the game. Clean and simple. And the wives of the losing team have to provide punch and cookies following the game.

***

After my bad experiences with golf, I gave up participatory sports and became a professional spectator. I started with one of the loveliest spectacles of all — the Kentucky Derby.

I reached Louisville, Kentucky, site of "The Derby," after

sixteen hours on an Amtrak train. I could have made it faster in a wheelbarrow but probably wouldn't have had nearly as much fun. The club cars are pretty small in most wheelbarrows. Upon my arrival, my hosts informed me that we did not actually have seats at Churchill Downs. Instead, we were going to leave at six A.M. to attempt to fight off fifty thousand others for a spot in the infield to watch a five o'clock race.

"Will we be able to see any of the Derby from that vantage point?" I asked.

"If you actually wanted to see the race," my host said, "what are you doing in Louisville? You could have stayed home and watched it on television."

So I trekked out to the track at sunrise the next morning and pretended to have a good time until the preliminary races started sometime after lunch. That's when I broke away from my group to try out the new system I had devised for betting and winning on the horses.

My plan was to bet on horses with names that began with an *l* or an *m* or a *g*, which are my initials. That meant that I bet on Lollipop, Milky Way and Gone for Good.

Lollipop couldn't have won on six legs. Milky Way melted in the stretch and Gone for Good is exactly what happened to the two bucks I bet on him.

In the next race I bet on a horse named Liar's Poker. If anybody sees Liar's Poker, tell him to find another line of work. Later I heard two guys talking about a horse that was supposed to be a good mudder. Mudder starts with an *m*, so I bet two dollars on him. Unfortunately, it was a clear day at Churchill Downs and the stupid horse came in last — in the next race.

In desperation I went down next to the track and leaned on the rail, hoping to pick up some tips that way. One of the guys who rides the horses that accompany the thoroughbreds to the gate rode past.

"Hey, fellow, got any good tips today?" I asked him.

"Yeah," he said, "we just painted that rail."

Now I hate horses, too.

***

I finally decided that the best sport for me was good ol' American football. Nothing frilly, no condominiums along the sidelines, just cold beer and fried chicken on a tailgate before the game.

I started with college football and was having a great time until I became disillusioned. I discovered quite by accident that some college football teams were actually cheating. Obviously they never heard another of those childhood clichés: Cheaters never win.

What happened was that this kid in my hometown was being recruited by the University of Florida, a school which has been caught more than once with its hand in the proverbial cookie jar. He received a letter from the head coach and brought it over to Bogator Green's mechanic and body shop for us to see. Here's what the letter said:

"Dear Prospective Florida Football Recruit:

"Soon you will be deciding where you will be playing college football for the next four years. As head coach at the University of Florida, I thought you might like to know what to expect when you visit with our recruiters and when you visit here on the Florida campus.

"Our recruiters are very nice people and they are very generous. Let's say, for instance, that you really like the new Corvette that one of our recruiters drives when he visits your home. You might try asking if he would mind if you took the car for a spin. The recruiter might surprise you by saying, 'I really don't need a car like this, so why don't you borrow it?'

"This, of course, would not mean the coach was actually giving you the car, which is against NCAA regulations; it would mean he was lending it to you. Simply remember to leave the keys in the car following your final year of eligibility.

"Since NCAA regulations allow only one official visit to each campus, we want your stay on the Florida campus to be a memorable one. Make certain you do not miss the Florida School of Forestry's famous 'money tree.' On the tree you will find bills of various denominations that always seem to blossom during recruiting season. The bigger bills, incidentally, are toward the top for all you blue-chippers who excel in the vertical leap.

"You may also be asking yourself, If I sign with Florida, how many tickets will I get? We will provide enough tickets so your parents and relatives will be able to see you play. Let's say you received twenty tickets per game. You give your parents one each and your sister and her boyfriend one each. That leaves sixteen tickets. What should you do with them? Why not sell your remaining tickets to a wealthy alumnus? It is against NCAA rules to sell the tickets for more than the price marked on the ticket, but if a wealthy alumnus happens to drop a couple of hundreds out of his pocket during the transaction and you happen to find them after he walks away, is that your fault?

"Some of you might also want to earn money in the off-season. At Florida we offer a complete job placement plan for our student athletes. For example, you might be in charge of making certain the house plants in the head coach's office always have plenty of water. This will teach you how to handle responsibility, as well as earn off-season bucks. This job, incidentally, is currently paying $400 per week.

"You may also want to meet some of the top Florida alumni and boosters. We could arrange for you to meet George Steinbrenner, the wealthy owner of the New York Yankees, at his Bay Harbor Inn in Tampa. If there should be a mix-up at the reservations desk and you are not charged for your three-bedroom suite, leave quietly by the side door so as not to embarrass anyone..

"You may want to know, too, If I sign with Florida, will I be playing for winning teams? We are installing a new system at Florida that should guarantee us many wins. I can't go into details, but it was designed by a loyal Florida alumnus currently working with the CIA.

"Finally, you may be wondering if you are academically qualified for a football scholarship to Florida. Here's a test: How many teams are in the Big Ten? If your answer was ten, no sweat. If it wasn't, we'll think of something.

"See you soon, and go Gators!"

***

I also have a problem with professional football — I can't

understand the terminology that the announcers use. After many Sunday afternoons in front of the tube with dictionary and notepad at hand, I have come up with a guide to modern football lingo which I hope will help others:

• HANG TIME — What time they will be hanging this or that coach for failing to win his division. Sometimes head coaches are hung in effigy. This year they probably will be hung in Denver and New Orleans as well.

• NICKEL BACK — Fifth-round draft choice out of Arkansas State whose agent got him a $150,000-per-year, no-cut contract and he isn't worth a nickel.

• "HI, MOM!" — The most intelligent statement an NFL wide receiver can think of on the spur of the moment when the television camera catches him picking his nose after a long touchdown reception.

• ERIC HIPPLE — What gets in a player's bellybutton after he crawls around on artificial turf for a couple of hours.

• AHMAD RASHAD — Disease a player can get between his toes if he doesn't change his socks often enough.

• TWO-MINUTE WARNING — When a player is caught in a compromising position with a teammate's wife in the teammate's house and the teammate pulls into the driveway unexpectedly. The player has approximately two minutes to get dressed and sneak out the back door before his teammate catches him and breaks his face.

• ILLEGAL CHUCK — Illegally impeding the progress of a receiver named Chuck who is more than five yards down the field.

• ILLEGAL UPCHUCK — Throwing up on the playing surface. Five yard penalty if the surface is grass, fifteen if it is artificial turf.

• ATTACKING UNDER THE COVERAGE — How to

make friends with a Dallas Cowboys cheerleader.

- BUMP AND RUN — What to do in case you smash into a Rolls in the parking lot before the game in your 1973 Plymouth Fury.

- 3-4 — How many beers a Pittsburgh Steelers fan has before breakfast on the day of a big game.

- HOWARD COSELL — The end of the horse you never saw when "Mr. Ed" was still on television.

For anyone who doesn't know, the preceding terms apply to American football, not rugby which the English call football and not to that half-breed which the Canadians mistakenly call football.

Several years ago when the National Football League went on strike, American television stations broadcast several Canadian football games to try to satisfy the public's appetite, but I don't think it worked. I was standing in Sonny Bryan's barbecue joint in Dallas, a hotbed of football if ever there was one, when two ol' boys came in talking about a Canadian football game they had seen on TV.

"Frank," the first one said to his buddy, "I believe that was the worst thing I ever saw. I'd just as soon watch a soccer game from Afghanistan."

"Earl," said the other, "I don't think they play soccer in Afghanistan."

"Well, I'd just as soon watch it anyway. When I turned on my set the score in that football game was 14-1. I'm talking about *one*, Frank. How in the hell can you score just one point in a football game?"

"I think it has something to do with not being able to run a punt out of the end zone," said Frank.

"That's another thing," said Earl. "Them end zones are big enough to graze a hundred head of cattle in. And the dad-blame field is 110 yards long. Didn't they read the rule book when they started playing football in Canada?"

"Well, at least it was football," said Frank.

"Wasn't no such a thing," answered Earl. "Listen to me. I been to ever' Cowboys game since we got us a team. I seen Meredith. I seen Staubach. I seen 'em all. And I ain't interested in watching no bunch of castoffs who couldn't play for TCU run around on no oversized football field in some foreign country where all they got is snow and gooses."

"You mean snow and geese," said Frank.

"Them too," said Earl. "And I'll tell you something else. They got strange names for their teams up there. They got a team called the Argonauts. What do you reckon an Argonaut is?"

"I think it's some kind of moose," said Frank. "They got lots of mooses in Canada."

"Mooses?" asked Earl.

"Mooses," answered Frank.

"Let me ask you something, Frank," said Earl. "If gooses is geese, then how come mooses ain't meese?"

"Dang if I know," said Frank. "I don't speak a word of Canadian."

My sentiments, exactly.

9

Fill 'er Up?
Regular or Harold?

IT'S TOUGH BEING a male chauvinist these days. Talk about something that will build character and develop grit. I can't even joke about it for fear that some woman will do severe harm to my person (body would be a sexist term in that context). The only reason more men aren't being beaten up by women these days is that no matter how far they've come in other areas, most women still can't run very fast and they'll take a double-pump fake every time.

The fact of the matter is that I don't have many chauvinistic attitudes myself, but since some of my friends do, I decided to help them by starting a Male Chauvinist Hotline. Through my newspaper column, I answered questions regarding men's and women's rights. Following are a few of the more helpful selections:

QUESTION: What makes you think you're such an expert on women?

ANSWER: I have been married three times, and I was deeply involved with several other women who auditioned for the part.

QUESTION: Isn't it true that women are more easily frightened than men?
ANSWER: Just because they always go to the restroom in pairs? Of course not.

QUESTION: I work in a steel mill. My foreman says he is going to have to hire some broads. Do I have to put up with that?
ANSWER: Yes, but look on the bright side. Maybe one of your female co-workers will let you have one of her stuffed celery stalks for lunch one day.

QUESTION: My girlfriend is always telling me what great athletes women make. I don't believe that because I still haven't seen a woman who can slam dunk a basketball. How can I overcome such a sexist feeling?
ANSWER: Next time you want your dinner cooked, call Julius Erving.

QUESTION: My wife says I never do anything to make her feel younger. Her birthday is next week. What should I give her?
ANSWER: A six-pack of Oil of Olay.

QUESTION: How many women does it take to replace a lightbulb?
ANSWER: Three. That's one to call her mother for advice on the subject, one to mix the strawberry daiquiris, and one to light the candles when mother doesn't answer.

Despite my vast knowledge of feminine ways, I confess

I've had my share of problems with them, too. I was once married to a young woman who became angry at me for missing a dinner party she was giving for her parents. I missed the dinner because I was playing tennis and the match went three sets and then we had to drink a beer.

The next morning I awoke to find my wife had taken one of the Ginsu knives I had bought for her birthday and cut the strings out of my tennis rackets. I learned my lesson well: I never bought her any more sharp instruments for her birthday.

But that incident was nothing compared to what happened to some of my friends. One fellow's girlfriend discovered he was fooling around with somebody else, so she slipped into his apartment while he was working, took a jar of honey from the refrigerator and poured it all over the kitchen floor. Then she opened the kitchen door and invited in every ant within three counties.

My friend Rigsby probably got it worse than anybody. When his first wife caught him messing around, she went into his closet and cut the ends off all of his ties and one leg off of each pair of pants.

"My second wife topped that," explained Rigsby. "She took all my suits and loaded them into the trash compactor. Take my word for it, a trash compactor adds new meaning to the word wrinkle. Then my third wife scored the coup de grâce. I had a convertible that I kept parked in the garage. She got so mad at me one day that she called a concrete company and had them fill my convertible with cement."

"Well," I said, "it looks like you're doing all right. You must have gotten a sympathetic jury for your divorce case."

"Sympathetic?" said Rigsby. "They came back in after a couple of hours of deliberations and asked the judge for more instruction."

"What could they want after two hours?"

"They wanted to know if they could give the death penalty in an alimony case."

I get pretty much the same treatment from my secretary, the lovely Miss Wanda Fribish. Behind every successful man, one can usually find a pleasant, agreeable, supportive secretary. Behind a failure like myself, however, you take what you can get, which is how I came to hire Miss Fribish.

To keep her from pouring glue over the keys of my typewriter or pulling some such feminist prank, I usually buy her off each Christmas by taking her to lunch at the place of her choice. Last year she chose El Flasho's Burrito Barn, famous for its all-you-can-drink frozen margarita special.

We settled in at a table in El Flasho's and ordered our first round of margaritas. After the third round, Miss Fribish started fidgeting and I could tell she had something on her mind. On the fourth margarita, it spewed forth.

"Come here, Four Eyes," she said, wiping the salt off her mustache and grasping me in a hammerlock, a technique she learned in the Militant Feminist Karate, Kung Fu and Secretarial School, of which she is a proud graduate. "There's a few things I want to get straight with you, you little pencil-necked geek."

"Please continue," I gasped, offering myself, as usual, as the open-minded, willing-to-listen employer.

"I'm sick of working for you," she went on. "The pay's lousy, the hours are miserable, and I have to talk to your creepy friends on the phone. Besides that, I'm tired of your constant sexual harassment."

I normally wouldn't argue with a person holding me in a hammerlock, but I asked Miss Fribish what she was referring to.

"You know what I'm talking about, you lecherous leech," she patiently explained. "Every time I walk into your office, I can feel your eyes undressing me."

I assured Miss Fribish that when I stared at her, it had nothing to do with any sexual intentions or desires. I tried to explain that she often startles me with her attire, like the time she came to work wearing a pair of steel-toed combat boots and a camouflage outfit.

"You know perfectly well why I wore that," she said. "Some of the sisters and I were launching a commando raid on an all-male Rotary Club luncheon, and I didn't want to have to go home and change."

After Miss Fribish reminded me, I remembered the incident well. When the cops arrived, they found her with a Rotarian under each arm, ramming their heads together in time to "Camptown Races," which the organization's piano player was performing to open the meeting.

"One more 'doo-da,'" said the investigating officer, "and the two victims might have suffered permanent brain damage."

Recalling the plight of those two Rotarians, I decided it was an opportune time to give Miss Fribish the small raise I had been considering, and I promised never to look at her with anything but business on my mind.

Of course, Miss Fribish's commando unit finally got what they wanted a couple of years ago when the Supreme Court ruled that the Jaycees and other such groups could not exclude women from their memberships.

Shortly afterwards, I received a call from my old friend Gilbert, who had a novel idea. "Listen to this," he said excitedly. "I'm going to start a club that will be for men only."

"Listen, Gilbert," I said, "you obviously haven't been keeping up with the news. You can't exclude women from clubs anymore."

"No," he argued, "you don't understand. I'm not going to exclude them. I'm just going to start a club that they won't want to belong to. We'll do only the things they don't like. We won't say we're for men only, but as soon as any woman joins she'll be so disgusted that she'll quit. It's a great plan!"

I asked what sort of disgusting and appalling things the members of Gilbert's club would do.

"Just the usual stuff we used to do in the old days," he said. "First of all, we're not going to serve white wine in the bar. That'll cut out two-thirds of the women who might want to be members. Then we're going to drink a lot of beer and belch and fart whenever we feel like it, and we're going to smoke big cigars and blow smoke all over the room. Women hate cigar smoke. And finally, we'll tell all the sexist jokes we used to, like the one about why God created women in the first place."

I asked Gilbert what he intended to name his new club, but he didn't get to tell me.

"I don't have time to talk anymore right now. My wife is having the girls over for a Tupperware party, and if I don't have this house cleaned up by six, she'll kill me."

Admission to previously all-men's organizations was just one of many equal opportunity advancements women have made in recent years. In fact, I can't think of any place between here and outer space where they're not.

Just the other day I stopped into a service station and a woman attendant came out. She seemed quite capable of handling her job and opened with the standard dialogue, except for a small change.

"Fill him up?" she asked.

"Please," I said.

"Regular or Harold?"

"Harold? What happened to Ethyl?"

"She's running for Congress."

I was watching television and a female evangelist came on asking for donations. "This broadcast is run on faith alone," she said. "Send us what you can, we'll take a check or money order, and the Lord will bless you. She told me so Herself."

Next day I walked into a hardware store and there was a woman behind the counter.

"I'd like a garden hose," I said.

"What shade?" she asked.

"I'm not certain," I replied, somewhat taken aback.

"So what color is your lawn?" she continued.

"Green."

"Then I'd suggest something in a soft pastel," she said, "either a melon or perhaps this delightful pink."

I also asked if she knew where I could pick up a used winch.

"Try the bus station about midnight," she replied.

***

One of the few remaining places where men can still be left alone with other men is the old-fashioned barber shop. These are the places that kept their names — the Sportsman Barber Shop, or Haynie's Barber Shop — when others became "styling salons." A man can be as sexist as he wants in such a setting.

"Heard about the two young bulls that met at the fence?" asked my barber, who always has an off-color joke. "One bull says it's great where he is. Plenty of grass to graze on, lots of shade trees around and plenty of heifers to keep him company. He says it's just like heaven on his side of the fence, and he asks the other young bull what it's like on his side.

"The other bull says it's awful. There's not much grass, no trees to stand under when it gets hot and there aren't any heifers at all. He says the only company he's got is an old washed-up steer and all he wants to do is talk about his operation."

My barber also trims my mustache, which qualifies me for another story.

"I got a friend," he says, "who grew himself one of these long, handlebar mustaches. Fellow asked him, 'Don't that mustache bother the women when they kiss you?' My friend said, 'Not a bit. They don't mind going through a little briar patch to get to a picnic.'"

The barber finished my trim and slapped the back of my neck with some cologne. "You need a little of this boy-dog smell," he said.

Yeah, I reckon I do. Don't we all?

***

With the possible exception of the old-fashioned barber shop, women are gaining equality with men in all areas. But lest there be any confusion, I should point out that women themselves are not equal in all respects. As one who has traveled and researched across this great country of ours, I must confess that there are considerable inequities between Northern women and Southern women.

First, there is the matter of yankee women not shaving their legs. This, according to the famous Southern author Homer Southwell, is a custom that began in Buffalo, New York, during the Great Snow Storm of '26. Women found that by not shaving their legs they were afforded natural protection against the snow and cold, and so the entire female population of Buffalo went hairy-legged that winter.

This led, incidentally, to a dramatic fall in the birth rate in Buffalo and also led to the popular folk song, "Buffalo Girls, Won't You Come Out Tonight (And Graze by the Light of the Moon)?"

Most Southern women, of course, wouldn't be caught dead without shaved legs — even big, fat, ugly Southern women who bark at the moon and run rabbits.

Southern women also make better cooks than Northern women. There are even women left in the South who will arise early in the morning and cook their men hot biscuits. Not "whomp biscuits," where you whomp the can on the side of the table, but real biscuits as the Lord intended man to have.

Northern women make good cooks if you like to eat things that still have their heads and eyes, cooked in a big pot with carrots and asparagus and other houseplants.

Southern women aren't as mean as Northern women. Both bear watching closely, mind you, but a Southern woman usually will forgive you two or three times more than a Northern woman before she pulls a knife on you.

Most importantly, Southern women know how to scrunch better. Scrunch is nothing dirty. It's where on a cold night you scrunch up together in order to get cozy and warm. Southern women can flat scrunch. I tried once to scrunch with a yankee girl, but she hadn't shaved her legs and it was like trying to cuddle with a hundred-pound Brillo pad.

So I admit it — even though I'm pretty much an expert on women and certainly open-minded to a new order, I've had my share of trouble with them. But who hasn't? John Wayne had about as many run-ins with them in real life as he did on the silver screen. Heck, even the president of the United States has trouble with women.

I read just the other day where Ronald Reagan and a group of his advisers had a midnight session trying to come up with a plan to bridge the president's gender gap.

"Criminy," said the President, "no matter what I do or say, I can't seem to make America's women happy."

The room was quiet as the President paced. Suddenly he stopped and said, "I think I've got it! Why don't we send every woman in America a big bouquet of flowers with a nice little card attached?"

"Not a bad idea, Mr. President," said one of the advisers. "What would the card say?"

"Something very sweet and tender," said the President. "Women are pushovers for flowers and sweet, tender cards. It could say, 'Roses are red, daisies are yellow, your loving President is a really sweet fellow.'"

"I don't think it would fly," said another adviser. "Women would think you were just trying to buy them off with flowers."

"How about candy then?" asked the President. "Once Mrs. Reagan got very mad at me for talking to a visiting emissary's wife too long at a party, so the next day I bought her a big box of candy and she forgave me."

"Same problem," said the disagreeing aide. "The days when you could woo an American woman with candy and flowers are over."

"Fur stoles are even out of the question?" asked the President.

"You'd lose the conservationist vote if you did that," said another presidential confidant.

The President thought some more. "I think I have it this time," he said. "Whenever candy or flowers or a new fur doesn't work with Mrs. Reagan, I always take her out to a nice restaurant. What if I took all the American women out for dinner? We could go to a real nice place and have champagne, and they could order anything on the menu they wanted. Maybe afterwards, we could go some place romantic for a glass of cognac."

"Now you're really getting some place," another aide spoke up. "You could make it a very intimate evening. Just you and a few million American women."

"It would be very charming," said the President. "I would look into their eyes and tell them how beautiful they all were this evening, and we could have strolling violins to play 'Moonlight Becomes You' to increase the romantic effect."

The adviser who earlier had been against flowers and candy lit a cigarette, blew a puff of smoke and asked, "How long would it take to put something like this together? We're running out of time, you know."

"I don't think it would take too long," said the President. "Of course, we would have to wait long enough for all the women in America to have their hair done and maybe buy a new dress for the occasion."

"I know the maitre d' at Tiberio's," said another aide. "I could find out when he could take a party of several million."

The plan was put into place. The President would phone each woman to be invited and ask her to a quiet dinner with him, "so we can get to know each other a little better." The President would wear his best tux and dash on a little Paco Rabanne cologne, and before the evening was over, the women of America would be eating out of his hand.

Just then Mrs. Reagan came down from the presidential bedroom in her nightgown. "Isn't it time you came to bed?" she asked the President. "My feet are cold."

"Not now, honey," he said. "We're holding man talks."

***

It's been said before, but I agree that bucket seats may have done more to separate men and women than the Baptist church. Back when cars and trucks were equipped with bench seats, women cuddled up next to their men so that sometimes you couldn't tell who was driving.

My boyhood friend and idol, Weyman C. Wannamaker, Jr., a great American, once nearly totaled his 1957 red Chevrolet while out on a date with Kathy Sue Loudermilk. They were driving along a back road looking for a place to stop and discuss one of Weyman's favorite philosophical questions — Is wrestling fake? — when Kathy Sue inched her way over to him. She kept inching, as a matter of fact, until she was slap dab in his lap behind the wheel. Then she proceeded to kiss him squarely on the mouth in a most passionate fashion, which was the only way she knew how.

By the time Weyman managed to bring the '57 Chevy to a halt, he had run over two road signs, three possums and Curtis "Fruit Jar" Hainey, the town drunk. The road signs were demolished, two of the three possums passed away and "Fruit Jar" swore off drinking for an hour.

The man who invented bucket seats obviously never dated Kathy Sue.

There's an old story which says it best:

A man and his wife are riding along and his wife spots a younger couple huddled close together in another car.

"We used to do that twenty-five years ago, honey," she says to her husband. "Why did we stop?"

"Don't ask me," he replies. "I haven't moved."

That's sort of how I feel about the women's movement in general — I haven't moved.

— 10 —

Profiles In
Gray Grit

AS AN ONLY CHILD in a traditional Southern family, I
grew up around adults. Not just my parents, but
grandparents and uncles and aunts as well. It was an
extended family long before anyone decided to call it that.

While they sat on the front porch rocking and shelling
peas and telling tales, I picked beggar lice off my pants legs
and listened closely. That was probably the best education I
ever received, and as I look back on it now from the perspective of near-middle age, I realize there was more
wisdom on that porch than I ever imagined.

Listen to a few of these stories of senior citizens and you'll
see what I mean.

A PRIVATE WAR ON HUNGER

My grandmother, Willie Word, declared her own war on

hunger years before it became the international issue that it is today. "Every stray dog and cat in the county seems to wind up here," she used to say. It was easy to figure out why. Every stray dog and cat in the county had gotten the word that when all else failed, you always could get a handout at Willie Word's house.

My grandmother also made certain that birds around her yard never went hungry, and when my grandfather complained that the worms had gotten to his tomatoes, she would say, "Even worms have to have something to eat, you know."

She fed her family well, too, of course. My favorite from her table was pork chops. Biting through the flaky crust and succulent meat remains my taste buds' unanimous choice as childhood's best culinary memory. I was an admitted glutton when it came to Mama Willie's pork chops. She always cooked two each for every member of the family, but I always managed to get three.

"Want my last pork chop?" she inevitably asked me, and I inevitably accepted.

One afternoon as I was walking home from a friend's house, I spotted an old man, a tramp, I supposed, lying on the front steps of the Baptist church across the street from where we lived. When I got inside, I told Mama Willie about him.

"He's probably hungry," said my grandmother, who promptly went across the street and fetched him.

He was hungry. You could see it in his eyes as he watched Mama Willie prepare dinner, to which she had invited him. A pork chop dinner. I counted heads and pork chops as we prepared to deliver the blessing. There were five people and only eight pork chops. I was immediately concerned about my usual three.

Mama Willie passed out the pork chops. She placed two on my plate, two on my mother's plate and two on my grandfather's plate. Somebody, I reasoned, is going to miss out on a marvelous pork chop dinner if this trend continues. Then my grandmother gave the ragged old man the other two chops, denying herself any meat that night.

Where, I wondered, is my usual third chop coming from? I ate my first one in a hurry. As I started on my second, I noticed my grandmother staring at me. I looked down at the second pork chop. I looked back at Mama Willie. She motioned her head toward the tramp, who had gone through his two chops in record time and was now attacking the bones. I knew what she wanted me to do.

I had to spit out the words. "Would you like my last pork chop?"

"I'd be much obliged," he said.

I looked back at my grandmother. She was smiling at me.

I haven't sent any money to help the starving people in Ethiopia yet, but I think I will. The memory of that smile demands it.

STILL A FLAME IN THE FIREPLACE

The Atlanta Braves were playing the Toronto Blue Jays in a spring training game in West Palm Beach, Florida. Three or four thousand of us sat blissfully in the sun and watched.

There was more to watch than just the game, however. For instance, there was the girl, a young blonde thing. She wore high heels and tight white pants that came to a few inches below her knees. Had we been hit by high water, she would have been prepared. Call her "The Walker."

She sat for an inning before she started strutting about the stands. To quote William Price Fox, when she moved, the motion in her high-water britches looked like two bob-cats fighting in a croker sack.

When I wasn't watching The Walker, I was watching the old men. What better way to while away a retirement after-noon than to sit and warm yourself over a leisurely baseball game that really doesn't count anyway? If and when I become an old man, I want to come to these games and sit with others my age. I'll probably say a lot of outrageous things. Old men can get away with such as that.

The kids today idolize the current players and go for their autographs like a hound on a good scent. Their heroes still wear the uniform. We middle-agers are losing our heroes in a hurry. Pete Rose and Phil Niekro are still around, but how can I get excited about Dennis Lamp when Sandy Koufax is still fresh on my mind? The old men have their memories, too, and you can hear them in the stands still praising Williams, DiMaggio, Gehrig and even Ruth.

"Now, those were ballplayers," the old men say. "You never saw those guys sitting out a game with a hangnail or a little cold."

There were probably eight of them, the old men, sitting together near me. They sat through the last innings like crows perched on a powerline, silent and staring. When the game was over, they moved slowly out to the aisle. Two needed assistance in walking. They were held on each side by the steadier hands of their companions.

When they reached the walkway out of the stadium, they said their goodbyes. A friend next to me observed, "They seem very sincere about saying goodbye. I guess when you get to be that age, you never know how many empty seats will be on your row tomorrow."

At precisely that moment, The Walker came by. The old men looked at the curves she was throwing, and one smiled at his friend and gave him a knowing wink.

Yeah, they're all getting on, I thought to myself. But bless their hearts, with apologies to Charlie Dressen, they ain't dead yet.

NEW TRICKS FOR AN OLD DOG

My friend Milton is sixty-six. He looks sixty-six. He's been around, Milton has. He was a newspaper copy boy once. He was in the Army. He has seen the world. He has seen this country, all of it, twice — both times from the window of a Greyhound bus.

His first trip was in 1966. It cost him $99 for an unlimited travel ticket, and he used it. New York. Chicago. Seattle. Los Angeles. Back home to Atlanta.

"I mooched off relatives whenever possible," Milton told me. "Other times I'd see a town I liked, get off the bus and stay a couple of days. If it turned out I didn't like the town, I'd grab the next bus out."

Several years ago, Milton took the grand tour again. This time it cost him $159. "I did thirty states and probably one hundred cities," he said. "You get used to the bus. Last time I checked, I still had my spine."

On Milton's first trip, one of his stops was Iowa City, where he walked the campus of the University of Iowa. "I was just walking around looking, waiting for another bus. But something about that campus struck me. It was winter. I looked up at all those towers of learning. I studied all the statuary, and I got an inspiration. I even said a prayer about it. I was determined to get back into college, even at my age."

Almost two decades later, he did it. The Georgia legislature passed a bill granting free tuition to anyone over sixty-two who wanted to attend college.

"It was a dream come true," said Milton. "I really just wanted to see if I could do the work. I didn't know if my brain cells had deteriorated to the point where I couldn't retain anything. I haven't done a lot to prolong them, you know. I've done some riotous living, and I've knocked around half the world on planes and buses and trains, and I've been hit in the head a lot with baseballs. But I'm amazed at what I'm learning. I never knew I was so stupid before."

Milton, of course, isn't stupid at all. He's wise even beyond his years. Old dog Milton is learning new tricks. Don't get old, he advises, just get busy.

"I feel like Alice in Wonderland. I'm in my third childhood. Now, all I want to do is live long enough to graduate."

Any man who can survive two bus trips around this country is a good bet to live through four years of college. Give 'em hell, Milton.

A SOLDIER FOR LIFE

Major Harvey Banks of the Salvation Army retired from active duty way back in the late 1930's. His health was failing, and he was well into his sixties anyway. He tried taking it easy for awhile. Maybe for the first couple of days. But Major Harvey Banks wasn't one to sit still if somebody could use his help.

He visited jails and prisons and sang songs and played music for the inmates. He tried to convince them that his God was theirs, too. He got involved with caring for unwed mothers, and he worked tirelessly in welfare and disaster relief.

"The only difference between Major Banks when he was

retired and Major Banks when he was active," a friend of his told me, "was that after he retired, they put an *R* at the end of his name."

You see these people who work for the Salvation Army and you wonder about them. What prompts a person to spend his or her life wearing that silly uniform, standing on a street corner tooting a horn or ringing a bell? It's certainly not the money. The base pay for a married Salvation Army officer is approximately $150 a week. If you've got forty-five years in and you're married, you pull in a cool $175 or so a week. Single officers get about sixty percent of those figures.

"We do get our housing," said one member of the Army.

After his retirement, such as it was, Major Banks received a small pension, and his working daughter helped him make ends meet. An old friend said of him, "He lived on faith. The extra energy God gave him, he used in the interest of other people."

Major Banks was born in 1873 in Ontario, Canada. The Salvation Army had been started in London in 1865. It came to this country when Major Banks was six years old. Thirteen years later he joined.

In August of 1982 in an Atlanta, Georgia, nursing home, more than forty years after he had retired from "active duty" due to health reasons, Major Harvey C. Banks died. He was 109.

"He was just as lively as ever, still had a great sense of humor, still had a twinkle in his eyes, still loved to sing and listen to music," said another friend at the Salvation Army headquarters.

There was no long period of suffering for Major Banks. His illness and his subsequent death came quickly. He was the oldest living Salvation Army officer in the world, a man who first gave one life to the assistance of the lost and failing, and then turned around and gave another.

The good die young, they say. Not always, thank God. Not always.

CAMPAIGNING FOR THE LORD

The first time I met Ottis "Smokey" Bailey, he was standing on a corner of Peachtree Street in downtown Atlanta handing out Bibles. Smokey holds that everybody ought to own at least one.

"I don't care what kind of misery you got," Smokey says, "the Book can set you free."

Smokey was doubling as a janitor in an apartment house at the time. He had one room in the basement, and that's where he kept his stacks of Bibles he gave away to anybody who would take one from him. "People are always giving me Bibles to give away," he said, "but I don't never take one from nobody unless they got an extra. If you ever get without a Bible, you're lookin' at the devil right in his eyeballs."

Smokey and I eventually sort of teamed up in his handing-out-Bibles venture. He was the brains and the legs of the operation. I took over the financial and public relations parts. First I wrote a newspaper column about him, asking for spare Bibles. They came in by the truckloads. "I made sure that everybody who sent one in had an extra," I assured Smokey. He seemed relieved.

Later, the management company at the apartment house decided that Smokey was handing out Bibles when he should have been replacing screens, so they put him and his Bibles out on the street. That's when I got involved in the financial end of our business: I gave Smokey twenty dollars.

He's still handing out Bibles, and he'll preach any-time anybody will listen. And I still pass him a twenty occasionally.

"You know, things been tough on me since my mama died back in '78." Smokey doesn't need to remind me, but he always does just the same.

After a considerable absence, Smokey reappeared in my office just the other day. Outside the streets were flooded with an April Atlanta monsoon.

"You lookin' well," Smokey said.

"You, too," I answered. "How's it going with the Bibles?"

"Couldn't be better," he said, "but I'm having a little trouble at the hotel where I'm living."

"Rent trouble?"

"Yeah. I could use about thirty," he said. Inflation, I reasoned. I asked Smokey if he could come back later since I was out of cash.

"Could you just give me a check now, brother? It's doing some powerful raining out there."

Try that line the next time you visit your banker for a loan.

I wrote the check. Smokey blessed me a couple of times and headed for the door. I looked out my office window a few minutes later and saw him walking down the sidewalk, bound for the nearest bank, I suppose. At that very moment, the sun peeked out from behind the clouds for the first time in days.

SERVICE THE WAY IT OUGHT TO BE

David Poole and his brother Robert opened their little garage back in the sixties. They were tired of getting some-body else's grease under their fingernails, so they decided to give it a shot on their own. Working a mechanic's flat rate for a greedy dealer can be a going-nowhere treadmill.

For a time it was a good life and a good living for the Poole brothers. They are good, honest mechanics, and they aren't interested in ripping off their customers.

"They've been servicing my cars about as long as I've been driving," a customer told me. "If everybody operated the same way they do, this would be a better world to live in."

A couple of honest, hard-working mechanics satisfying their customers. What a nice little scenario in today's grab-what-you-can scheme of things. Only this story doesn't have a happy ending. A couple of years ago, the break-ins started.

"Had five or six in one year," David Poole said. "We figured we knew who was doing most of it, but we couldn't prove nothing. Police said we'd have to catch him with the goods. It was this little boy, about sixteen. He cleaned us out one time. I mean, he took everything we had, including an old wood step stool and even the nozzles off the air hoses."

The burglaries continued, so the Poole brothers started taking their tools home with them. "Then somebody came in one night and stole all our antifreeze," David said. "Finally we just decided we'd had enough."

After more than twenty years in business, the Poole brothers gave up, victims of urban crime, victims of a judicial system that couldn't stop a two-bit kid burglar from robbing a couple of hardworking, grown men.

"I'm sixty-one," said David Poole. "They've taken things we can't afford to replace now, and I don't feel like starting over anyway. So we just closed for good."

To show the Pooles how much they were appreciated, many of their customers got together and gave them a surprise party at the garage just before it closed. "That was really something," said David Poole, choking on the emotion.

"You know what worries me most about closing?" he asked. "It's the older ladies who have been coming in here ever since we started in business. They don't know a thing about what's wrong with their cars, or what needs to be done. I don't know where they'll go now. I just hope nobody takes advantage of them."

Me, too, David. But I wouldn't bet the nozzle off an air hose that somebody won't.

A WEAK BODY BUT A STRONG WILL

The old man was born in 1888. That's five wars ago, from the Spanish-American to Vietnam. Think of the changes in his lifetime, from horse and buggy to men walking on the moon.

He farmed nearly all his life. Even as he reached the age where he couldn't farm on a large scale anymore, he still maintained his garden.

One of his grandchildren was saying, "I can remember twenty years ago when my mother used to say, 'We've got to go visit Grandpa and Grandma. They won't be around much longer.' That was two decades ago, and they were both in their seventies then."

The grandchildren and great-grandchildren loved the old man. He handed out quarters every time they drove to the country to visit with him, and he obviously took pride in seeing his children's children frolic on the good earth.

He had white hair and wore thin, wire-rimmed glasses until he was well into his nineties. Then he had the cataracts removed and didn't need his glasses anymore. When he took the test to get his driver's license renewed a couple of years ago, his eyesight was nearly perfect.

He had been married to the same woman for more than seventy years. She doted on him. She took care of him. The kids used to wonder what would become of Grandpa if anything ever happened to Grandma.

It came on her slowly. Senility creeps in at first, but then it gains momentum and devours its victim. She started to forget little things. Then she couldn't remember what day it was, who had come to visit last week, where she had put things in the kitchen. When she reached the state where Grandpa could no longer care for her, the kids tried hiring a housekeeper, but Grandma couldn't understand why there was a strange woman in her house and once chased away the housekeeper with a broom.

Without his wife to tend his needs as she had done for most of his life, the old man's health began to deteriorate, too. Just like that. The kids decided their only recourse was to put the couple in a nursing home. In some instances, nursing homes serve a good purpose, I suppose. Neglected and lonely old people are able to get the care they need and are able to have companions.

But sometimes when old people are uprooted, it doesn't work so well. Their roots run too deeply into their home places to pull them away. I remember when my own grandfather died. My grandmother, although she was in ill health herself, couldn't be budged out of the tiny house she had shared with the man she loved.

The old man didn't take to the nursing home. His wife reached the point where she didn't know who he was anymore. The children of four generations visited when they could, but they always found the old man lonely and depressed.

"Every time one of us would go to visit him," one of the grandchildren recalled, "he would beg us to bring him a gun. He'd say, 'Let me get this thing over with now.'"

The old man stopped eating. He brooded and cried. He begged to die. Without his wife and away from his home and garden and his dog, he saw no reason to live. They found him in bed one morning not long ago. He had died in his sleep. He was ninety-five.

"He just willed himself to death," said the grandchild. "I guess it was a blessing that he was able to do that."

Medical science has developed all sorts of means to keep people alive, but maybe sometimes it is better to die than to live on beyond your time. The old man was able to make that choice on his own. Maybe that is a blessing, rest his weary soul.

HONEST, MOM, IT'S NO TROUBLE

It's the same story every year at Christmas.

"Son," says my mother, "you don't have to get me anything for Christmas this year."

And I say, "I know that, Mother, but I want to get you something for Christmas."

"Well, I just don't want to be any trouble."

"It won't be any trouble, Mother. That's part of the enjoyment of Christmas, buying gifts."

"There's just no reason to waste your money on me, son."

"Buying you a Christmas present isn't exactly wasting my money," I argue.

"But there's really nothing I need."

"There must be something you need or want."

"You gave me pajamas last year. I have plenty of pajamas."

"So how about house shoes, the fluffy kind?"

"I have a closet full of house shoes already," she says.

"How about a nice nightgown?"

"I'll never use all the nightgowns I have now. Why don't you just take the money you would have spent on me and buy yourself something nice? Do you have a warm coat?"

"Yes, Mother. Three of 'em."

"How about sweaters?"

"I could start my own line of sweaters, I have so many."

"How about a hat?"

"I don't wear hats."

"Well, how do you keep your head warm?"

"My head doesn't get cold."

"You need a hat in the winter. You might catch a cold if you don't wear a hat."

"This is ridiculous. We're supposed to be talking about what I'm going to get you for Christmas."

"What could you get me? I never go anywhere anymore."

"How about a jacuzzi?"

"A what?"

"You'd love it. A jacuzzi is a tub that you fill with hot water, and there are all these jets shooting out water. You sit in there and it's very relaxing. It would be great for your arthritis."

"I never heard of such a thing," she parries.

"What we could do is knock out a wall and extend the bathroom and put the jacuzzi there."

"I don't want a bunch of carpenters sawing and hammering and tracking mud into the house. Don't get me a bacuzzi."

"Jacuzzi."

"However you say it, I don't want it."

"I know there must be something you'd like to have for

Christmas," I persist.

"OK. What I really would like is a pantsuit to wear when I go to the doctor."

"Great. Why didn't you say that in the first place?"

"I didn't want to be a bother."

"It's no bother. What size?"

"Sixteen. Don't let 'em sell you a fourteen, because that's too small."

"What color?"

"Any color, except red."

"Why not red?"

"I'm too old to wear red."

"OK, one non-red pantsuit. Anything else?"

"That's plenty, son. I don't want to be a bother to you."

The pantsuit I bought my mother is blue. It was no bother whatsoever.

11

Ugly Goes Clear
To the Bone

AMERICA AND MOST of the civilized world has a
fascination with health and beauty. When was the last
time you saw a billboard or a television commercial featuring a fat, ugly person? For those of us not blessed with an
attractive countenance, these can be very trying times.

I've had this problem for years. In fact, when I was born
they called in a vet. My mother was caught two days later in
the nursery trying to switch my ID bracelet with that of
another child. As I was growing up, she tried the old trick of
tying a pork chop around my neck so the dogs would play
with me. The dogs preferred to dig for turnips in the garden
instead.

When my sight started failing in grammar school and I
had to get glasses, that didn't help my looks much either.
My classmates always called me "D.U." That stood for
"double ugly."

"Beauty is only skin deep," I would argue.

"Yeah," they would reply, "but ugly goes clear to the bone."

In the seventh grade we had a Halloween masquerade party at school. The scariest costumes were awarded prizes. The kid who placed first went as me.

Finally in high school my looks became an asset. I was asked to join the Future Farmers of America because they needed a scarecrow for the Spring Corn Festival.

In college everybody went to the beach during spring break, but I was afraid to be seen with my shirt off. So I joined a health spa and asked the instructor what I could do to build up my muscles.

"You want my honest opinion?" he asked.

"Give it to me straight," I said.

"You're wasting your time. It would take you six months just to get into shape to take your 'before' picture."

Not long ago I was showing a friend some of my childhood pictures. "You looked like that?" the friend said.

"That's the way I looked."

"Well, let me ask you something. Did any of your mother's children live?"

***

When the graze craze hit in the late 1960's, the favorite war cry of the health food set was, "You are what you eat." If that were so, I would have been a stick of bologna by the time I was ten. Ugly bologna.

"What's for lunch today?" I would ask my mother.

"Bologna sandwiches," she inevitably would reply.

After six years of the same dialogue, I finally stopped asking. And if I complained, my mother made it into an international incident.

"This stuff makes me want to throw up," I would argue.

418

"How can you say that with all the starving children in China?" she would counter.

"Name one and we'll send him some of this bologna."

"There's nothing wrong with bologna," she would say. "It's nutritious, it's a bargain and it sticks to your ribs."

What good are fat ribs unless you're a side of barbecue? I always wished it would stick to the roof of my mouth so I wouldn't have to swallow any more of it.

One day while eating yet another bologna sandwich, it occurred to me to ask, "Just what is bologna?"

A hush fell across the room. You would have thought I had asked for an explanation of sexual reproduction. "Well, son," stammered my mother, looking for a way out, "you're not old enough to be asking about such things. Just hush up and eat your bologna."

I don't know if my mother really ever knew what was in bologna, because I still don't know myself. I'm almost afraid to find out for fear that it's something awful. All I know for sure is that I ate a horsecart full of it in my youth. (Why did I say horsecart?)

As I look back on it now, I realize that I learned a great deal from eating all that bologna. I'm sure it has made me a better person. While other kids brought ham sandwiches to school, I ate bologna and learned humility and courage. Believe me, it takes courage to eat that stuff day after day.

But eating bologna, as distasteful as it was, didn't compare to the trauma of being forced to try liver. I knew what it was, and I didn't want any part of it.

"Just try it with a little onion and pepper," said my mother. "You'll find that it's pretty good."

I would have put Forty Mule Team Borax on it if she had let me — anything to kill the taste.

Years later I devised a plan to eradicate crime in America,

and liver formed the guts of the plan. (Why did I say guts?) My unique plan called for crime to be punishable not only by a prison term, but also by being made to eat a food befitting the crime.

For example, a person convicted of first-degree murder would be sentenced to life in prison with nothing to eat except liver three times a day. Manslaughter would get you twenty years of liver, only with onions. Armed robbery would be five to ten of macaroni and cheese, the kind they used to serve in the school cafeteria. Talk about sticking to the roof of your mouth . . . Kidnappers could look forward to ten years of Brussels sprouts, embezzlers to ten years of pork and beans straight from the can and a conviction for fraud would net a sentence of ten years of nothing but Jello — with bits of bologna inside.

Is your kid a wimp or a troublemaker? Does he hang out with punk rockers and whine about everything? Fill him up to his pierced ears with bologna and liver and you'll see an immediate improvement in his character.

It's time to get back to basics, America. Stand up and be counted.

***

Growing up eating bologna and liver may have helped my character, but it didn't do a thing to improve my looks. I still scared cats. But leaving home and not eating bologna and liver didn't seem to help either.

"Gee, I didn't know you'd been in a wreck," people used to say. I hadn't.

Part of the reason for my ongoing uglies may have been my bad eating, drinking and smoking habits. Apparently I was not alone, however, since most people who live by themselves tend to have bad eating habits, I've read. Therefore, in my endless effort to help my fellow Americans, several years ago I developed "The Grizzard Diet for Single Non-Cookers Who Are in a Hurry."

The staples of this revolutionary diet are Maalox (the family-sized bottle), cold tuna salad sandwiches from vending machines, pizza to go and large quantities of alcohol. Of course, you are offered a number of choices to avoid monotony. For example, here's a typical day on "The Grizzard Diet for SN-CWAIAH":

BREAKFAST — Order out for pizza, preferably pepperoni and scrambled eggs. If you can't find anything open at that time of day, eat the cole slaw left over from the night before's Kentucky Fried Chicken dinner.

LUNCH — Rolaids and a large Pepsi.

AFTERNOON SNACK — Maalox and a pint of chocolate milk.

DINNER — Go to a bar and drink yourself silly. Then ask the bartender for a bowl full of olives and maraschino cherries.

LATE-NIGHT SNACK — Call a married friend and ask if they had anything left over from dinner.

The advantage of this diet is that all of the meals are interchangeable. The disadvantage is that after about three months, you look like a prisoner of war; this diet will either kill you or make you tough (see earlier reference to, "When the going gets tough, the tough get going"). After six months friends assume you have anorexia nervosa and feel sorry for you. A single female friend of mine who adhered to this diet for several months was very nearly killed in an accident at a fast-food restaurant. A nearsighted cleaning woman mistook her for a mop and had done half the kitchen floor with the girl's head before she realized the mop was making gurgling sounds when it was raised out of the bucket.

I also lost too much weight on the "Single Non-Cookers Who Are in a Hurry" diet and had to visit weight-gaining expert Cordie Mae Poovey, an old acquaintance from my school days, to get help. When Cordie Mae was eleven, she was already a herd. She once hijacked the local ice cream wagon and ate nine sundaes and seventeen Eskimo Pies before releasing the driver, who was unharmed except for the black eye Cordie Mae gave him when he initially refused to tell her where he kept the chocolate syrup and whipped cream.

Cordie Mae, currently employed in the Broken Bottle Lounge as a bouncer and stand-in when the mechanical bull goes on the blink, was more than happy to share with me her can't-miss, five-day, weight-gain plan. "Indulge and bulge," she told me.

MONDAY

BREAKFAST — Pancakes with heavy syrup, a dozen eggs, a loaf of toast and a large watermelon, if in season. If not, substitute a pizza with extra cheese.

LUNCH — A pone of cornbread crumbled into a gallon of buttermilk with a six-pack of tall Pabst as a chaser.

DINNER — A barbecued goat and six Twinkies.

TUESDAY

BREAKFAST — Same as Monday, only add bananas. Enough to feed a family of gorillas for a week.

LUNCH — A school of catfish. Fried. With hush puppies, French fries and enough volume and variety of Girl Scout cookies to buy the local troop an Oldsmobile.

DINNER — A dozen biscuits, smothered in gravy, mashed potatoes with four sticks of butter, a coconut cake and two quarts of Buffalo Rock ginger ale to wash it all down.

WEDNESDAY

BREAKFAST — Grits, served in a large trough, hot with butter and cheese. If you're really hungry, mix in a mess of collards.

LUNCH — Three bowls of chili, a box of Oreos and a long nap.

DINNER — An entire pig, cooked any way you like it. Do not try to put the entire pig in your mouth at once.

THURSDAY

BREAKFAST — A chocolate milkshake, four Hershey bars, three fudgesicles and a half-dozen Reese's Peanut Butter Cups, including the wrappers.

LUNCH — Pig out at McDonald's. If the clown shows up, eat his shoes.

DINNER — Eat a large T-bone steak with all the trimmings. Then drag the bone out in the yard and howl at the moon. Be careful of ticks.

FRIDAY

BREAKFAST — An omelette the size of a Chevy pickup and a large pickle.

LUNCH — A dozen cans of Vienna sausages, a large package of soda crackers and a raw Vidalia onion twice as big as the pickle you had for breakfast.

DINNER — Go to an all-night diner and eat until the sun comes up, or until they run out of food, whichever occurs first. If you get hungry on the way home, stop and buy four dozen Moon Pies and a large jar of mayonnaise.

***

Between the "Single Non-Cookers" diet and Cordie Mae's advice, my body was more confused than I was. Neither of us would have recognized a healthy lifestyle if it had been naked at the beach. In order to save my sanity, I returned to my typewriter and devised "Grizzard's Rationalization Chart of Overeaters, Smokers and Boozers," to be used whenever you slip off the wagon but don't feel like unloading the guilt.

Here's how it works. Food, for instance, will not cause you to gain weight if:

- You eat it standing up.
- You eat it off someone else's plate.
- Your mom cooked it.
- You offer it to the dog first.
- You eat it in the dark.
- You do not chew it.
- You are eating because you're depressed about all the starving people in the world.
- It is smaller than a regulation NBA basketball.
- It's your birthday.
- It's Chester A. Arthur's birthday.

For smokers, there are some equally effective rationalizations. For example, another cigarette won't hurt you if:

- You don't smoke it all the way down to the filter.
- It's not your regular brand.
- You bummed it.

- You throw away the rest of the pack.
- You make a contribution to the American Cancer Society.

Been hitting the bottle a little too hard? One more drink won't hurt you if:
- It's a special occasion, like Happy Hour.
- Something from your past has been eating at you lately, like the death of your dog Skippy when you were four.
- You drink to a worthy cause, like finding a cure for Leon Spinks.
- You use lots of ice.
- The bottle was a gift.
- It was almost empty anyway.
- You make it last longer than the National Hockey League season, which is the only thing that lasts longer than pregnancy.
- You drink it out of a coffee cup.

***

Starting from where I did — that is, uglier than a '47 Packard on blocks — I don't suppose my bad eating, smoking and drinking habits really did all that much harm. They were just a logical extension of me, sort of like clothes.

My clothes. Now, there's another problem. I never could figure out what was in and what was out. When the hippies were wearing sandals, jeans and T-shirts in the late sixties, I was still in my penny loafers, slacks and oxford cloth shirts. By the time my outfit came back into style in the early eighties, I was wearing popsicle-colored leisure suits. In fact, the only people still wearing leisure suits then were me and Slim Whitman.

What did everybody else do with theirs? I admit I haven't been to any bowling league awards banquets or wrestling matches or Moose Club dances lately, but it seems that even that crowd has dumped the leisure suit.

So where are they? They didn't just sprout little polyester legs and walk away. In an attempt to answer this permanent press-ing question, I tried to contact designer Leon "The Needle" Tackeeinksi of Fort Deposit, Alabama, who first introduced the leisure suit to America. Unfortunately, Mr. Tackeeinski could not be located.

"One day," said a man who answered the phone at the Fort Deposit bus station, "he got on the three o'clock north-bound and we haven't heard from him since."

When I asked if Mr. Tackeeinski had closed his leisure suit factory before leaving town, the man told me about a mysterious fire the night before his departure which destroyed the entire factory.

"It was a horrible thing," he said. "Half the town was overcome by polyester fumes and couldn't resist the sudden urge to go to Sears-Roebuck and order white shoes and belts."

Perhaps that's the clue I've been looking for to explain what happened to all the leisure suits in this country. Maybe American men, in a burst of fashion consciousness, all went out in their back yards and burned their leisure suits.

"That is highly possible," said a local scientist I contacted about my theory. "As you no doubt have noticed, we have been having strange weather the past few years. One expla-nation could be that the fumes from all those leisure suits burning rose into the earth's atmosphere, creating what could be called the 'Polyester Zone.' This layer of gases could have a strange effect on our weather. During the hurricane season last year, for instance, I recall that we had one named Delbert that swept in off the Gulf coast and headed straight to the nearest K-Mart."

There is one other possibility about what happened to all the leisure suits. Maybe the Japanese recycled them and are using them to make seat covers for Isuzus. I'm considering using my leisure suits for the same purpose; I'm just not sure how my car will look with orange sherbert-colored seats.

***

The beautiful people of the world, those whose pictures appear on billboards and in television commercials, seldom have to worry about their clothes. If their faces are pretty enough, nobody looks any lower. Or if they have great bodies, nobody cares what they're wearing or even *if* they're wearing. And if they show up dressed in something terribly out of date, people just presume they're being trend-setters.

So why is it that when I show up wearing a blazer with five-inch lapels and Guccis without socks, everybody presumes I'm tacky instead of trendy? Why? Because my face gives it away. No one who looks like Alfred E. Newman can be a trend-setter.

Kathy Sue Loudermilk never had that problem. She was the first real beauty queen I ever knew. She won the coveted Miss Collard Festival Queen title seven years in a row, breaking the record of Cordie Mae Poovey who had won four consecutive titles by threatening the judges.

Kathy Sue turned her victory into a bigtime modeling career and later appeared on a billboard advertisement for Cleghorn Dairies buttermilk. "Cleghorn's Buttermilk — Buy It By the Jugs" is what the copy under Kathy Sue's picture said.

She was justifiably proud of her looks. A reporter for the local newspaper once asked Kathy Sue, "Do you consider yourself a sex symbol?"

She answered him by asking, "Does a duck have lips?"

But many of today's beauty queens can't decide if they're proud of their bodies or embarrassed by them. Half of the contest winners, who've paraded around in bathing suits that wouldn't create suntan lines, say, "I can't stand a man who wants me only for my body. I have a brain, too, and I can use it. I know the capitals of six states and I went to a museum once."

A former Miss Universe from Venezuela said her looks were secondary to her mind. "I want to be an architect and design beautiful buildings," she said. "But buildings with a purpose — for the poor." I'm sure the poor people in Venezuela appreciated that. Give them a few beautiful buildings and maybe they'll quit complaining about being cold and hungry.

Then there are the other beauty queens who are so proud of their endowments that they sometimes forget to keep their clothes on. I recently wrote a treatise on the subject, which I will read at the upcoming Coweta County Moose Club Convention, entitled, "I've Seen England, I've Seen France, I've Seen Miss America Without Her Underpants (With Apologies and Thanks to Vanessa Williams)." I wonder where this new trend will lead?

***

ATLANTIC CITY, NEW JERSEY — DECEMBER, 1999: Twenty-one-year-old Roxanne "Boom Boom" LaTouche, Miss California, was crowned Miss America for 1999 here Saturday evening, becoming the first stripper ever to win the prestigious title.

Miss LaTouche brought both the audience and the judges to their feet with a nude break dance in the talent competition. As pageant emcee Bob Guccione sang the traditional

Miss America theme song, "There She Is, Money in the Bank," Miss LaTouche bumped and grinded down the runway wearing her new crown and, again, to the delight of the all-male audience and male judges, nothing else.

"It just goes to show you," said the beaming Miss LaTouche, "that any girl in this country can become Miss America if she has the correct ideals and values and a new breast implant."

For the last three years, Miss LaTouche has been the star performer at the Yellow Pussy Cat Lounge in Encino, California, where she became famous for her widely heralded ability to strip completely nude while juggling three large cats. Asked if she would return to her position at the lounge, Miss LaTouche announced that she would be attempting instead a career in the movies.

Her agent, Marvin "The Shark" Perronowski, who is also part owner of the Yellow Pussy Cat, said his client is expected to sign a contract with Sin Flick Productions in Hollywood and will star in the full-length porno film titled, "Deep Throat Meets Bert Parks."

Miss LaTouche attended Candy Barr Memorial High School in Encino, where she was captain of the cheerleading squad and became the first cheerleader in the history of the school to have her sweater retired upon graduation.

First runner-up in the pageant was Miss Indiana, who was given temporary parole from the Indiana State Women's Prison in order to compete in the event. She was doing five to ten for armed robbery. Upon learning that she had not won the crown, Miss Indiana pulled a knife on two of the judges but was quickly whisked away by her parole officer.

Second runner-up was Miss Nevada, a stunning Las Vegas showgirl who was named Miss Congeniality by a unanimous vote after a closed-door session with the judges, two of whom — both elderly — were treated and released at a local hospital following the performance.

Third runner-up was Miss New York, daughter of former Miss America Vanessa Williams. Immediately following the contest, Miss New York announced her engagement to Miss Alaska. Former Miss America Williams, incidentally, attended the pageant and told reporters that she plans to enter politics and hopes to be the vice presidential candidate on the Ducks Unlimited ticket in the 2000 presidential election.

Miss LaTouche, meanwhile, begins a national tour next week in which she will make appearances on various talk shows, including the popular NBC "Tonight Show" with host Harry Reems.

"This is one of the best Miss America pageants ever," said Guccione, "and all of our contestants are to be congratulated." Speaking for all contestants, Guccione also said he has more than three thousand nude color photographs of the fifty young women and will run them in the upcoming January edition of his *Penthouse* magazine, which has sponsored the Miss America pageant since 1985.

12

You've Got to Bend Over
To Pick Grit

FOLLOWING JIMMY AND Billy Carter's rise to
national prominence in the late 1970's, the term redneck became very popular with the American public. It was
a term of derision in the mouths of some uneducated people, but to those of us born and bred in the South, it was
most often used to refer to just good ol' down-to-earth
folks. Those of true grit.

Let's say it is your lot in life to have to pick butterbeans.
Picking butterbeans is a thankless job that requires long
hours of bending over and getting hot and dirty, but somebody has to do it. After a couple of weeks under such
conditions, the back of your neck will be redder than the
home crowd at a Georgia football game.

Rednecks, or butterbean pickers and others who work
the land, have always had trouble with those who see
themselves as being more sophisticated just because they

happen to live where the bus stops, even if nobody is getting on or off. These people are referred to by rednecks as city slickers. In the mouth of a redneck, city slicker can be a term of derision.

"Hey, redneck," city slickers used to say to a farm boy who ventured into town, "what brings you to civilization?"

"Paw's truck," the redneck inevitably would answer, and the city slickers would have a good bellylaugh. That is, until the redneck plowed on their heads with his fists, which is how rednecks got the reputation of being overly hostile.

Ed Koch, the mayor of New York, is one of those city slickers who doesn't care much for rednecks and the rural way of life. In fact, he once was quoted in a *Playboy* interview as saying that country living was a "joke." My friend Billy Bob Bailey, who was one of the original rednecks and a great American, took offense at Koch's remarks and wrote to tell him so. Billy Bob has given me permission to share his letter, which is now enshrined in cellophane wrapping on the bulletin board at Bogator Green's mechanic and body shop:

> Mayor Ed Koch
> New York City
>
> Dear Mr. Mayor,
>
> My name is Billy Bob Bailey and I live in Fort Deposit, Alabama, which is so far back in the country that the sun goes down somewhere between here and Montgomery, the state capital.
> I was over to the store the other evening and they had the television on and I heard what you said about living out in the country. You said

driving around in a pickup truck and driving twenty miles to buy a Sears-Roebuck suit was a waste of time. You said living in the country was a "joke." What kind of fumes have you been inhaling, your honor?

I drive a pickup truck, and one advantage to living out here in the country is the only time I ever get stuck in traffic is when there's a funeral and the hearse breaks down. Those of us in line have to wait until Junior (he's the funeral director's son) goes back to the plant and gets the jumper cables. You got that wrong about Sears-Roebuck suits, too. I don't wear no suits, period. No need to. They don't care what you wear to the Moose Club, long as you ain't barefooted.

They started requiring shoes because of Hoot Dingler, who used to come in regularly to drink beer and shoot pool and was always barefooted. Hoot didn't even own any shoes. Didn't believe in 'em. "Might slow me down if I needed to get somewhere in a hurry," Hoot explained. Problem was that Hoot's a pig farmer and he's always walking around where the pigs live. We might be country, but we don't like to drink beer, shoot pool and smell hog at the same time, so they changed the rule about coming in barefooted. Hoot started drinking with the Elks after that.

They showed a picture of you on television, Mr. Mayor, and you look right slack-eyed and loop-legged to me. Been a little bilious and goofy-headed lately? Sometime when folks don't feel good, they say things they don't mean. I hope you didn't mean what you said about living in the country being a joke, 'cause my dog Rooster heard about it, too (he reads the Montgomery newspaper), and Rooster don't like nobody from New York City throwing off on the way we live. "I wouldn't shoot a rat trying to crawl out of New York City," is what Rooster always says.

If I were you, Mr. Mayor, I wouldn't come around Fort Deposit or Rooster for awhile, because I'm afraid that dog would take a plug out of your leg and I couldn't stop him with a stick.

Rooster and me ain't never been to New York City, but it ain't exactly Hog Heaven either, is what we hear. Vonda Kay Potts from right here in Fort Deposit was state dairy queen one year and won a trip to New York City. She said she liked it fine except that when you went outside, the streets and air were so dirty that the whole place smelled like Hoot Dingler's feet.

We hear that you want to further your political career after you're through being mayor. Maybe be governor or president or something. But I wouldn't count on a lot of support from the rural parts of the nation, Mr. Mayor. It's like Rooster always says: Country people all have one thing in common. They know a rat trying to crawl out of New York City when they see one.

Thanks, all,
Billy Bob Bailey

***

Billy Bob's right when he says that life in the country can be awfully good. I was reminded of that fact recently when I ran into an old friend I hadn't seen since college. He now owns a small drugstore in a small South Georgia town. He has the same wife he started out with and two babies and a dog, a cat and a number of hogs.

"My hog farm is my hobby," he says. "When I'm out there with them, I can really relax."

Maybe Mayor Koch and everyone else who struggles to survive in our cities should take note. Give everybody a small hog farm and maybe there would be less crime and fewer heart attacks.

My old friend also is a member of the city council in his town. "I get $75 a month, and it's rare I get cussed out more than twice a week." He is involved in local charities and organizes an annual tennis tournament which raises money for the county retardation center. My friend donates the hogs for the barbecue which is held in conjunction with the tournament, and the ladies in town bake pies and cookies and make potato salad and cole slaw, and somebody slices a mile of tomatoes. The only thing wrong with any of this lifestyle, my friend says, is the gnats. "We call 'em the South Georgia Air Force."

Comparing my life in the city with his in the country makes me stop and think. He lives the solid rural life and helps sick folks and tries to make his community a better place to live. And in between all that, he raises hogs and children and breaks his butt trying to help those who have trouble helping themselves. Me, I rattle around with a couple million hurrying souls and we fight traffic and each other. Sometimes all I get from the effort is the blues.

They might not believe it on the flat, piney plains of South Georgia, but there are worse things in life than gnats.

***

Of course, life in rural America can be filled with excitement, too. There are more characters in most small towns than gnats in South Georgia. Just the other day a friend was telling me a story about a fellow named Paul in his hometown.

"Paul was having some trouble with the IRS, something about an unauthorized deduction. So when these two IRS men wanted to meet with him, he told them to come down to where he lives — in a trailer way back in the woods with the snakes and armadillos and albino possums — to have lunch.

"Paul, you know, eats about a quart of mayonnaise every day, so he reached into his mayonnaise jar, pulled out a handful, and started spreading it on bread. That's all he wanted on his sandwich, but he put a slice or two of meat on those other fellows'. He sat down at the table, pulled out his gun from one pocket and his brass knuckles from another and laid them on the table. Then he asked the two IRS men to join him in prayer.

"'Lord,' he started, 'please keep these two fellows safe while they're here with me, because you know how much I want to shoot 'em. But, Lord, don't let me do that, much as I want to....' When Paul looked up from praying, the two IRS men were gone. He ain't heard a word from them since."

***

Rural Americans, especially those in the South, have long been misunderstood by other segments of the population. Some folks think just because a fellow has a gun rack in the back window of his pickup that he's on his way to shoot a bunch of liberals. They think grits grow on trees and poke salad is a weed. And possibly their biggest misconception of all is that the pink plastic flamingos positioned in many front yards are "tacky."

Nothing could be further from the truth. Tasteful, well-bred individuals normally paint the trunks of the trees in their yards white; line their driveways with old tires, also painted white; plant flowers between the tires; and place at least three pink flamingos strategically about the lawn.

Common riffraff, meanwhile, decorate their yards by taking the tires off a '52 Studebaker and putting the automobile on cement blocks beside the house.

I remember the day my family moved into a new home. How I swelled with pride when my parents allowed me to stick the legs of our new plastic pink flamingos in our front yard.

"Does this mean we are a tasteful, well-bred family and no longer common riffraff?" I asked.

"It does, indeed, son," answered my mother.

How could anyone, even an unenlightened yankee person, refer to plastic pink flamingos as "tacky"? They lend a tropical flair to any yard. They are graceful in their posture, and their pink color blends most pleasingly with the green hue of the grass, just as a red shirt accentuates a black polyester suit.

My boyhood friend and idol, Weyman C. Wannamaker, Jr., a great American, had a dozen plastic pink flamingos in his yard. Weyman's mother was president of the local garden club, and her yard was the annual winner of the "House Beautiful" award in our community.

Mrs. Wannamaker, being a woman of exceeding taste and breeding, complemented her flamingos with a ceramic hen being followed by her baby chicks, and various other lawn statuary including ducks and deer and one marvelous piece in the form of a fat Sumo wrestler, which she got for free when she purchased four chenille bedspreads.

Mrs. Wannamaker's yard was also quite impressive at Christmas. Her annual decoration included Santa's sleigh being pulled by — you guessed it — eight pink flamingos.

When asked about his mother's Christmas decorations, Weyman said, "My mother is a very sick person."

I would like to add in closing that I have just purchased a new home and have ordered two pair of pink flamingos from the Sears catalog. I haven't decided for sure, but I think I'm going to put them next to the little birdhouse that says, "See Rock City" on the roof.

My neighbors will be pink with envy.

***

So country ain't so bad after all. And if you don't believe it, try calling Ed Koch the next time you have a craving for a big pot of butterbeans.

13

The Bigger They Are, The More They Weigh

NOT EVERYBODY GETS out of life what they put into it. Some folks work hard all their days and never free themselves from the bog of poverty. Others just bounce through life like a pinball, taking the easiest path but lighting up things and racking up points all the way. Yet from one end of the tax scale to the other, from Who's Who to the welfare rolls, real character looks the same.

A GENTLE BEAR OF A MAN

I spent an afternoon drinking with Paul "Bear" Bryant once. I had been to Athens, Georgia, with him for an autographing session for the book he wrote with John Underwood of *Sports Illustrated*. When we returned to the Atlanta airport, there were still a couple of hours before his flight to Tuscaloosa, Alabama.

"Let's get a drink," he said.

The weather was awful. Rain. High winds. Lightning and thunder. Bad flying weather. Good drinking weather. He took me into the Eastern Ionosphere Lounge, where he ordered double Black Jack and Coke. Two at a time.

I probably got the best interview of my life that afternoon, but I don't remember much of it. However, I do remember walking him back to the departure gate two hours later. At the gate, the Bear ran into a doctor from Tuscaloosa who was booked on the same flight. The doctor was also an amateur pilot.

"Coach," said the doctor, "I don't like this weather."

"You a drinking man, son?" Bryant asked him.

"Yes, sir," said the doctor.

"Well, good. Let's get us a couple of motel rooms and have a drink and fly home tomorrow."

There were fifty or sixty would-be passengers awaiting the same flight to Tuscaloosa. When they saw Bear Bryant turning in his ticket, all but a handful did the same thing.

"If Bear Bryant is afraid to fly in this weather," one man said, "I sure as hell ain't about to."

That was the last time I was with the Bear. On January 26, 1983, he died of a heart attack. As soon as I heard the news, I knew I had to get in touch with a friend of mine.

She had met Bear Bryant through her profession, public relations, several years earlier, but their relationship had grown far beyond that. I'm not talking hanky-panky here; grandfather and granddaughter comes closest to describing it.

They were an unlikely pair. He, the gruff, growling old coot of a football coach. She, a bright, young, attractive woman with both a husband and a career and a degree from the University of Texas, of all places.

He would call her even in the middle of football season and they would talk, and he would do her any favor. Once a friend of hers, a newspaper columnist, was having heart surgery. She called the Bear and had him send the fellow a scowling picture with the autograph, "I hope you get well soon. Bear Bryant." The picture still hangs in my home.

I called her the minute I heard that he had died. I didn't want her to get it on the radio. She cried.

"I loved him," she said, "and he loved my baby."

My friend had had a baby a few years earlier. Had it been a boy, she would have named him for the Bear, David Bryant. But it was a girl, and so she named her Marissa.

"I had no problems with naming my son David Bryant, but I wasn't about to name a little girl Beara," said my friend.

Of course, a busy, big-time college football coach like Bear Bryant didn't give it a second thought that somebody else's little girl wasn't named for him. He still sent her gifts. Gifts like a child's Alabama cheerleader uniform, and then an adult-size uniform for use later. He sent her footballs, dolls and probably a dozen or so letters that her mama read to her.

It's funny, though. When he sent his packages and letters, he always addressed them not to Marissa but "To Paula."

LAUGHTER IN THE SKY

Great big ol' Jerry Clower was signing an autograph when I spotted him in a busy airport. Great entertainers need neither stage nor special occasion as opportunity to perform. An airport or an airplane, for instance, is just as good as any.

For the uninformed, Jerry Clower of Yazoo, Mississippi, used to go around telling funny stories and selling fertilizer. Then somebody from Nashville discovered him and signed him to a recording contract. Now all Jerry does is go around telling funny stories, although some insist that he's still spreading verbal fertilizer.

On the plane, Jerry took a seat in front of me, turned around and began to spout forth his philosophy on any number of subjects in a voice loud enough to be heard throughout the plane. With Jerry Clower around, E.F. Hutton would never get a word in edgewise.

I asked him about a mutual friend, a writer.

"We agree on lots of things," he said of the fellow, "but we're a lot different, too. Like, I've been married to the same woman (Homerline) for thirty-seven years. He's been livin' with one about two years and says he don't know if they're going to get married or not because he ain't through trying her out yet."

I mentioned something about college football and his eyes lit up. Jerry used to play a little offensive line at Mississippi State.

"What I like most about college football," he said, "are the rivalries. I was down at the University of Texas the other day. They don't like Texas A&M one bit, you know. Fellow down at Texas told me the Texas A&M men are so lazy that they marry pregnant women."

The passengers, all of them, were his by now, so he kept rolling.

"These network news fellows always amaze me. Big reservoir down in Mississippi has been flooding for years, but up until last year it was just the poor blacks and poor whites who were being flooded out. Then some of them $200,000 houses started gettin' a little mud inside 'em, and it all of a sudden is a big story.

"This network news fellow went down there to one of them big houses and asked this proper woman what she thought caused the flood. She said it was the bass fishermen. She said they hadn't lowered the reservoir enough just so them bass fishermen could still catch fish. Then he interviewed this real intelligent man. He blamed the whole thing on the Corps of Engineers, said they hadn't planned the watershed right.

"Course, them network fellows try not to interview no good ol' boys when they come to Mississippi, 'cause they think they don't know nothing. But one of 'em slipped up and interviewed this ol' boy he figured was highfaluting 'cause he happened to be wearing a coat and tie. He asked him what he thought caused the flood. 'Sixteen inches of rain caused it, and if we get that much rain next year, we'll have another flood.' "

Jerry also told his boots story. He was on a Hollywood talk show one time and a lady producer noticed his boots.

"She jumped up out of her chair like a wasp had done stung her," he said, "and she commenced to hollering about my boots. She said, 'What kind of boots are those, Mr. Clower?' And I said, 'These here are lizard boots.'

"She said, 'I can't believe you would wear such boots. To think that somebody killed an innocent little animal just so you could wear those boots.' I said, 'No, ma'am. This particular lizard was run over by a Greyhound bus. I even stood out there in the road and helped fight the buzzards off him.' "

There was a pause and then Jerry Clower added, "You know, I sometimes get the feeling some people are educated far beyond their intelligence."

And anyone who has spent much time with Jerry Clower

has been blessed far beyond his due.

HE'S THE ONE IN OVERALLS

They buried Junior Samples in his favorite pair of overalls on a cold Georgia day, dark and damp, in November 1983. Junior's bronze, flower-laden casket was closed during the services, but a man standing outside the church confirmed that Junior's family wasn't about to send him across the river wearing anything else.

"All Junior ever wore was overalls, anyway," said the man.

"One thing's for sure," said another, "he's a lot more comfortable than he would have been in a pair of britches."

Junior Samples, Forsyth County's claim to fame, died of a heart attack at age fifty-six. Slow talking, slow moving Junior turned a fish story somebody recorded back in the sixties into a career as a bungling bumpkin on television's "Hee Haw."

Junior's funeral was inside the little white-frame Roanoke Baptist Church out on the Buford Dam Road. An Atlanta television cameraman remarked what a pretty picture the little church made, perched atop a hill, its steeple and cross reaching toward the gray sky.

"These folks up here had a lot of respect for Junior," said a local reporter. "What they liked about him, he didn't change after he got on TV. He still got out amongst folks. He was one of them right until the end."

It was generally agreed that Junior's was one of the biggest funerals in the county's history. Early arrivals got seats inside the church, but by the time the Jenkins Family, local gospel singers, opened the services with "One Day at a Time, Sweet Jesus" and "Just a Rose," there were more

444

gathered on the porch of the church and in the muddy driveway than were inside.

A man from the funeral home told me about Junior's flowers.

"We loaded up a truck plumb full," he said, "and we still got just as many back at the funeral home."

I asked if he had known Junior personally.

"Knowed him all my life," he answered proudly. "People thought he was trying to be funny on television, but he was just being Junior."

Another group of Junior's friends gathered under a barren tree outside the church. The blue hearse pulled up first. Junior's tearful family followed. Next came a Tennessee sheriff's car with some of "Hee Haw"'s other stars.

"There's LuLu," said one of the men. "She looks as fat in person as she does on television, don't she?" She did.

Nobody knew her real name, but the toothless woman who's always beating her husband over the head on the program came, too.

"I thought they made her up to look that ugly," said another onlooker. "Lord, she's just natural ugly."

A tall, blonde woman they identified as Misty Roe, one of the "Hee Haw" girls, got the most attention. She wore high heels and a black miniskirt, and her hair had been teased into a frazzled, frenzied mane.

"Looks like she'd knowed not to have dressed thataway," somebody said.

The boys outside said Junior hadn't been drinking as much the last few months since he had been so sick. The preacher told mourners inside the church that Junior hadn't been doing as much fishing lately, either.

"He knew the final hour was upon him," the preacher said. "And he spent his last days praying. I can tell you

Junior Samples was saved. His name was recorded on the Lamb's Roll of Life."

The Jenkins Family ended the service with "Shall We Gather at the River," and everybody went home, content that Junior was with the angels.

In case you don't watch much television, Lord, he's the one in overalls.

A STORY OF COURAGE AND DIGNITY

She said she remembered the first time she ever saw him. "I was in a seventh-grade music class in my hometown of Provo, Utah," she began. "The teacher introduced us to a new boy who had just moved into town from New York. He was wearing knickers. He had on a pullover sweater and a little cap. He wore them every day. I found out later he was so poor that's all his mother could afford."

They became friends. They moved on to high school together, and they attended dances together.

"He told me there were two reasons he took me to dances," she recalled. "He said he liked me, of course, but I also had paid for my activities card, so he didn't have to pay a nickel to get me in."

Una Clark is a bright, pert lady with an easy smile. She lives in Seattle, Washington. Does her name sound familiar? That's right, Mrs. Barney Clark, widow of the first human recipient of an artificial heart. Dr. Barney Clark, the little boy in knickers, grew up to be a dentist. He developed heart problems, and when there was no alternative, he agreed to try the artificial heart. It kept him alive 112 days.

"We did hope there would be personal gain if we agreed to the artificial heart," said Mrs. Clark, "but Barney also felt this was something he could do for his fellow man. Somebody had to be first."

I wanted to know more about Una and Barney Clark's life together. After Dr. Clark died, his doctor said one of the reasons he was able to live as long as he did was because of the strong support he had from his family, because he had a wife who loved him dearly. I wanted to know how such a relationship came about.

"Barney never had much confidence," Mrs. Clark said. "He never told me how he felt about me. His father had died when he was very young, and he had been so insecure, so poor. I think that's what caused his lack of confidence. Maybe if he had said he cared about me, something would have happened when we were younger, but I never had any idea he wanted anything serious between us. I married his best friend."

That was just before the outbreak of World War II. Una Clark's husband was a flier. He died in action.

"Barney called me when he heard what had happened," she said. "It wasn't long after that when we found out we loved each other."

Dr. Barney Clark was a bombardier during the war. It was his service record, said his wife, that gave him the confidence he had never had before. He went to dental school after the war and established a successful practice.

"Everything he did, he went after it hard," said Una Clark. "If there was anything about him I could criticize, it would be that he was selfish with his time. He was a workaholic. If I could have changed him, I would have made him spend more time with me."

The man showed awesome courage in agreeing to become the first artificial heart recipient. His last days were spent in the discomfort of tubes and tests. But as his wife said, somebody had to be first. As one who has benefited directly from heart research, Una and Barney Clark are heroes to me.

One more thing I had to ask. "Do you miss him?"

"Yes," she answered softly. "I miss him very much."

We all do.

FORGIVE HIM AND TOAST HIS MEMORY

Marvin Griffin was governor of the State of Georgia from 1955-59. When he died in 1982, most of his eulogies included an apology for the fact that he once stood tall for segregation.

Running for political office has a lot in common with show business. You give the people what they want. When Marvin Griffin ran for governor, what the people of Georgia wanted — at least those who could vote — was a segregationist. If you felt differently in those days, about the only thing you could run for was the state line.

I'm not launching a defense of Marvin Griffin's politics; I'm just pointing out that he wasn't singing a solo.

As a person, I liked him very much. I first met him a dozen years ago in a bar. I introduced myself and told him my grandfather had been one of his most ardent admirers.

"What is yo' granddaddy's name, son?" he asked me.

I told him.

"Yes, indeed," said the former governor. "A fine man. I know him well. And how is his health?"

"Been dead ten years," I answered.

"Sorry to hear that, son," said Uncle Marvin. "Let's toast his memory."

Some are born to politick, and I've never drunk with a better practitioner of the art. He had a million great lines, and he growled them in a classic Southernese. He was a big man, robust and full of life. When he talked, he played with each word, milking it for all it was worth.

He was asked once, after his term as governor was over, if he had any advice for young politicians. "Tell 'em to remember just two things," he said. "Keep yo' mouth shut and yo' bowels open."

The last time I saw him was at a banquet before a big Georgia football game. He was the opening speaker and forgot at least the first part of his advice to young politicians. The thousands assembled nearly missed the kickoff of the football game, but I loved every minute of it. There'll be other games, but only one Marvin Griffin.

"Man came up to me one time when I was campaigning in Fayette County," he reminisced, "and said, 'Governor, let's me and you go have a little drink.' I said, 'My friend, soon as I see to it that everybody in Fayette County knows my name, I'll go drink a mule's earful with you.' "

Forgive him his opportunistic bellowings for segregation. Forgive him the improprieties of his administration. He added color to our lives and made us some memories, he did. A mule's earful.

— 14 —

Please Adjust
Your Set

EVERY TIME I HEAR about the modern communica-tions explosion, I keep hoping that somebody has finally blown up most of the television and radio stations and about half of the newspapers in this country.

We are, in fact, besieged with words, spoken and writ-ten. There probably are more satellite dishes in rural Amer-ica today than there are tractors. In the words of a sixties rock hit, "Signs, signs, everywhere signs, funking up the scenery, breaking my mind. Do this. Don't do that. Can't you read the signs?"

Being able to decipher all these communications, to cull the good from the bad, the useful from the useless, the helpful from the harmful, is one of the traits of those who possess true grit. The rest of us merely dog paddle through this alphabet soup. Me, I've progressed to the back stroke.

Just driving to work and reading the signs along the way

can overload your circuits. "Watch for Falling Rocks," says a frequent one. But how, I ask myself, can I watch for falling rocks and at the same time keep from running my car off the accompanying cliff?

"Low Flying Aircraft" is another of my favorite highway signs. Why are they telling me that? It's not flying that low, is it? And what am I supposed to do if I see a low-flying aircraft? Blow my horn and wave? My policy regarding low-flying aircraft is I won't bother them if they won't bother me.

There are signs on many entrances to interstate highways which read, "Take Gap, Give Gap." In public? Sounds like something that ought to wait until you get to a motel room.

I was in a radio station in Austin, Texas, recently. In the vending and coffee area was a sign that read, "Your mother doesn't work here, so clean up after yourself."

Here are some other favorites I've encountered along the way:

● In a Hilton Head, South Carolina, health food store: "Anyone having the audacity to smoke in here will be flogged unmercifully with an organic banana."

● Above a pool table in a roadhouse in Oklahoma: "No gambling. Anybody caught gambling will be prosuted." It's bad enough when they prosute in a doctor's office, much less in a pool hall.

● Handwritten on the front window of a South Alabama service station: "This here is a service station. It ain't no bank. Don't come in here and ask me to cash no checks. And that includes kinfolks."

● In front of a large Baptist church in Atlanta: "Caution: Blind People Crossing."

● In front of a used car lot in Spartanburg, South Carolina, which had closed for the night: "This lot is guarded by armed security three nights a week. Guess which three."

Of course, the most common signs of all are not printed but scrawled — graffiti. And New York, where everyone is handed a paint brush as they cross the East River, is the graffiti capital of the world. Writing on the sides of subway cars is as much a tradition in New York as a $14.95 breakfast in a hotel restaurant.

What I've never understood is how somebody can run alongside a speeding subway train with a can of spray paint and still be able to write "BJ Is One Bad Hombre" legibly. The trains don't stop long enough in the stations to get a shot at them standing still, so I assume BJ is also one fast hombre.

If it weren't for the damage done to public and private property, I would be in favor of graffiti. Not everyone in America can write a column for a newspaper or be a television or radio commentator. There are even a couple of people left in the country who have never spoken to a Rotary Club. For those Americans, graffiti can be an invaluable source of expression. Let me give you an example:

There is a freeway overpass near Atlanta's Hartsfield Airport, by some counts the world's busiest. A message has been painted on it. In black paint and in a scraggly handwriting, it says, "Betty. You Are Missed."

Betty. You are missed. I can't stop my imagination when it comes to that message. The guy is almost dying. He's tried everything. He's called all her friends. Her mother. She didn't even leave a note. Just up and went east. He came home from work — he drives a cab nights — and she was gone. Took her clothes, the albums, the pictures of the bullfighter, and left him with an empty bed and that awful pain that crawls down in your belly and does a dance that won't let you eat, sleep or put two sane thoughts back to back.

Regrets. First he goes through all his regrets. He never took her out. Maybe twice a month they would go get a pizza. Even then she would want anchovies, and he hated anchovies, so they wouldn't order them, and she would get that disappointed look on her face and pooch out her lips. God, she was cute when she pooched out her lips that way. If he could just find her, he'd buy her a truckload of anchovies.

He forgot her last birthday. He should have been more tender. He should have kissed her on her nose occasionally and said mushy things to her. He'd wanted to, but it's tough for some men to do things like that, and he thought she knew that he felt it but just didn't know how to get it out.

He goes for a few beers one night. Alone. Somebody punches B-6 on the jukebox. Willie Nelson. "You Were Always on My Mind." He drinks half a case, remembers the can of spray paint in his cab, drives to the overpass and, with a shaking hand, does the last desperate thing he knows to do. "Betty. You Are Missed."

Maybe one day, I always think, she will see the message and recognize his handwriting and come back home and be up to her ears in anchovies and kisses on the nose. Or maybe she won't. But I have to believe that man felt a little better that night after he sprayed his message on the freeway overpass. As long as the message is there, as long as some yo-yo from the highway department doesn't come along and remove it, he has hope, some slight shade of hope.

I haven't yet succumbed to writing my messages on freeway overpasses, but I've cried out in a similar way. I have a lingering case of Black Cord Fever. This ailment is easily diagnosed. All you have to do is check your monthly long-distance telephone bill. Is the total $11.16? Then relax, you don't have it. Is it $133.28? Does it include calls to places like Anchorage and Hershey? If so, you've got it bad.

Black Cord Fever is a condition that causes people to get an irresistible urge to make long distance calls in the middle of the night. Let's say it's two o'clock in the morning, you've had a couple of toots and start missing your old girl friend Gloria, who stole the mattress from your apartment and moved to Toledo.

"That you Gloria?" you ask when the ringing finally stops.

"Izme," she answers.

"Are you asleep?" you ask. Another symptom of BCF is that you ask stupid questions. Of course, she's asleep. Everyone in Toledo is asleep at two in the morning.

Turns out Gloria is now living with Freddy, who has the phone by this time, and he threatens to reach out and touch your head with a large stick if he ever gets the chance.

Realizing the love of your life and that creep Freddy are probably sleeping on the very mattress she stole from your apartment, you become very sad and call your ex-wife in Omaha. The only thing she didn't take when she left was the mattress that Gloria got. A man suffering from BCF can run up a huge long-distance bill in one night of tracking down ex-girlfriends, ex-wives and ex-mattresses.

I'm convinced that the telephone companies are directly responsible for BCF in this country. Those conductors of words are the ones who're always trying to embarrass us into calling somebody. That's really your mother they picture in their commercials, looking sad that she hasn't heard from her darling in months. "He's forgotten all about me.

He doesn't love me anymore. I know because he never calls," is what your mother says in those commercials.

So you give in and call. Turns out your mother is at the wrestling match and you get Uncle Willie, who just had his gallbladder removed. And it costs you twenty-six bucks to hear him describe his operation. In detail. You'd just as soon talk to that creep Freddy.

Next time Black Cord Fever strikes, I may just reach for a can of spray paint. Another couple of words won't matter at this point.

Another way phones contribute to media pollution is telephone solicitation. I answer and a woman's voice asks, "Are you the man of the house?" I know I don't sound like Broderick Crawford, but I sure don't sound like Aunt Sally come to visit from Shreveport, either.

Usually they're selling portraits. If you can answer a question — "Who was the only American president to resign from office? His initials are R.N." — you win a free family portrait worth $17.95. The idea, of course, is to sucker you into taking the entire family down to the studio for one free portrait, but by the time they've finished taking individual shots of all the young'uns, they're into you for big bucks.

The other day, however, I got a different scam. A woman who sounded about fifteen years old asked, "As you prepared to invest $29.95 for a selection of coupons worth thousands of dollars if you went out and bought each item for yourself?"

Before I could answer, she was off and running.

"I'm certain you are, so allow me to describe what you will be receiving by purchasing these valuable coupons from Earl's Midnight Merchandising Company. First, you

will get a free lube job, wheel balancing, front end align-
ment, wash and wax, two tanks of gas, an oil change including a new filter, one set of spark plugs and three quarts of
transmission fluid.

"You also will receive a free membership to the Reverend
Leon Goforth's Spiritual Health Spa, including one free
consultation with Reverend Goforth hisself, who will tell
you how you can find salvation through deep knee-bends.
This offer also includes free Putt-Putt golf, four trips down
Willie's Wild 'n' Wet Water Slide, a case of ping-pong balls
and a year's free bowling at Lucky's Pin-o-Matic Lanes,
including shoe rental.

"Don't think this is all you will receive from this once-in-
a-lifetime opportunity, however, 'cause there's much, much
more. You will also get one honey-baked ham, a case of Diet
Pepsi Free, three packages of luncheon meat, a free sub-
scription to People Magazine and nine baby chicks, guaranteed live on arrival. Then you'll get a night's free stay at
Purdy's Bide-a-Wee Motel in the fabulous Rock City resort
area, a pet goat, a nine-by-twelve color photograph, suitable for framing, of the Wilburn brothers and volumes A
through M of the Encyclopedia Britannica."

The girl had not breathed in five minutes, but I was afraid
to stop her.

"And that's not all. You will be receiving a man's and a
woman's Timex watch, a Tennessee Ernie Ford album collection of inspirational hymns, two bamboo steamers, a
pocket fisherman, a tea strainer and three live Maine lob-
sters.

"For one payment and one payment only of $29.95, you
will be entitled to all that and more, including a free esti-
mate from the Mug-a-Bug man, a Hertz once-a-month flea
and tick collar for your dog or cat, a year's supply of Prepa-

ration H, a package of Velveeta cheese, a road map of Idaho, the complete works of Zane Grey, a dozen personalized No. 2 lead pencils, seven pairs of ladies' underpants with each day of the week printed on the backs and a Shetland pony named Arnold.

"Now, will someone from your family be at home for the next hour so that one of our sales representatives can drop by and allow you to take advantage of this fabulous offer?"

I asked her if she would mind reading the list to me one more time, that I thought I had missed a couple of important things. When she got to the part about transmission fluid, I softly depressed the button and hung up.

***

Television obviously is the biggest culprit when it comes to communications pollution, and nowhere is the pollution more evident than in TV weather reports. You can actually see it. Those high-priced meteorologists (a week before, they were slapping hoods in used car commercials) don't call it pollution, of course; they refer to it as "ground clutter."

"Looking on the hundred mile scan of our Super-Duper Weather Scooper, you'll see that it's completely clear. All those patches of color that look like torrential rain are really just ground clutter that the radar is picking up."

I'm still not sure what "ground clutter" is. Will it stick to the soles of my shoes? Will it cause ring worm? If there's nothing on the radar, why do they spend so much time showing it anyway?

Ludlow Porch, who included a weather report in his popular radio talk show, had a better way of dealing with the weather. He'd send his dog outside. "If Rover came back wet, I knew right away that it was raining. If he came back with ice on him, I knew it was cold. That's really all anybody needs to know about the weather. The rest is just pollution."

The best weatherperson I ever knew was my grandmother, Mama Willie. She watched the weather like a hawk.

"Looks like it's about to come up a cloud," she would say. "Come up a cloud" is Deep South for, "It's about to rain."

Mama Willie always knew when it was about to rain because the corns on her little toe would ache. When the corns on her big toe ached, it meant fair to partly cloudy. Mama Willie also had a unique way of forecasting cold.

"Going to turn cold soon," she would say.

"How can you tell?" I would ask.

"Saw a hog frowning today," she would answer. "He knows what's coming."

I've never seen a hog frown or smile, but by the time they get to the stage I like them — sausage, bacon and barbecue — facial expressions are pretty much a thing of the past. Then again, maybe they smile only in the summer; if that's so, I also never would have seen one, because nobody in his right mind goes near a hog dwelling when it's hot.

Late one spring we had a frost which Mama Willie failed to predict. "It's them satellites," she said. "Fouls up the weather. Shame none of them astronauts don't have any chickens to worry about. Maybe then they'd think about staying on the ground."

Then again, maybe chickens are responsible for ground clutter.

***

Television soap operas are another form of television pollution. Does that stuff really go on in the suburbs? And if so, what kinds of vitamins are those guys taking?

I haven't spent much time watching them, but it seems to me that all the soaps I've seen follow the same formula. So I

459

figured if other folks are getting rich from packaging the same sleaze over and over, I might as well give it a try myself. Thus, Grizzard Entertainment proudly presents "General Popsicle" — love, lust and other steamy stuff you used to have to go to the movies to see, set in a Baskin-Robbins ice cream parlor in a shopping center on the outskirts of Bismarck, North Dakota.

The cast:

• NORENE — Sexy eighteen-year-old vaporhead who works the counter during the early shift. Still has trouble telling the difference between chocolate and vanilla. "I know one is dark and one isn't," she says, which at least indicates a step in the right direction. Wears tight-fitting uniforms and brings in customers from miles around who have no interest in ice cream but enjoy watching Norene shake her pistachio.

• DORENE — Sexy eighteen-year-old vaporhead who works the counter during the late shift. Gets confused when a customer asks for more than one scoop of any flavor. The mop has a higher IQ. Also wears tight-fitting uniforms and is so well endowed that she once reached deep into a bucket of almond toffee and was stuck there for nearly an hour until the Roto-Rooter man could be summoned to free her. There was no charge for his services.

• ARNOLD — Assistant manager who flunked out of the Bismarck School of Bartending. Twenty-ish, handsome, smiles out of the corner of his mouth and steals out of the cash register to support his Clearasil addiction.

• MR. PALMER — The manager. Forty-ish, balding, former wrestler and veterinarian. Friendly and fatherlike to his employees, especially Norene and Dorene. Likes Arnold, too, but is suspicious of him. "I wouldn't trust him as far as I could throw the mop," says Mr. Palmer.

● THE MOP — Has more acting ability than anyone else in the cast.

The show opens as Norene and Dorene vie for Arnold's attention. They get into a huge, hair-pulling, name-calling fight behind the counter over near the chocolate mint, and Mr. Palmer has to break it up. During the confusion of the fight, the refrigeration system is accidentally shut off and six thousand gallons of ice cream melt and begin to run all over the floor and out into the parking lot of the shopping center.

As the melting ice cream shorts out the center's lighting system, Arnold goes from store to store cleaning out the cash registers and then splits for Fargo in Mr. Palmer's black 1958 Buick.

Norene and Dorene, their uniforms torn in revealing fashion during the fight, both tell Mr. Palmer they are pregnant and that Arnold is the father of their babies. Mr. Palmer marries both Norene and Dorene because that's the only honorable thing to do, and the Roto-Rooter man reappears to demand payment for freeing Dorene from the almond toffee.

Millions of dollars in lawsuits result from the ice cream meltdown, and Mr. Palmer is now completely broke. He decides to commit suicide by sticking his head in a bucket of chocolate syrup. Before he can do so, however, Arnold, who has used the money he stole from the shopping center to stage a successful campaign and become governor of North Dakota, returns to the scene and pays off all of Mr. Palmer's debts.

Norene and Dorene find out they weren't really pregnant after all, and they run away with the Roto-Rooter man. The mop falls off the wall in disgust.

Next on "General Popsicle": Mr. Palmer hires a new counter girl. Or is she? Guest appearance by Renee Richards.

***

Actually the soap operas are no more offensive than the television commercials which run with them. Take those feminine hygiene products, for example. One manufacturer touts the fact that its products are disposable. Now, I ask you: Who would want to keep such a thing?

Deodorant commercials are the same way. "Oh, Marge," says one Junior Leaguer to another, "how do you manage to stay so dry?" I'll tell you how Marge manages to stay so dry. She lies around in bed all day eating bon-bons and not hitting a lick at a snake, that's how.

I saw a commercial the other day for medicine to remove canker sores. What on earth are canker sores and where do they come from? Do you get them on your canker, and if so, where is mine?

Recently attorneys have gotten into the act. They show pictures of rear-end collisions where everybody ends up with whiplash. Then they follow with a cute little jingle, like,

Wilson, Jones, Morris and Pate, The ones to call when you lit-ah-gate.

May they get sores on their cankers, and may their wives dispose of their feminine hygiene products by storing them in their husbands' golf bags.

And then there's the commercial for burial plots which begins, "We started not to make this commercial...." So why did you, casket face? It was that commercial which convinced me to give my body to science when I die. I want them to figure out how a man in my condition could live so long.

***

But to paraphrase an old adage, there's some good in the

worst of everything, even television. Amid all that harmless (or is it mindless?) clutter, there occasionally is a program that can make you think. And squirm.

The best squirmmaker of them all, I suspect, is "60 Minutes." Sunday after Sunday, Mike Wallace always gets his man.

"And so, Mr. Ferndorf, you say you know nothing whatsoever about the falsified expense reports," Mike Wallace says, and his victim, that lying cheat Ferndorf, thinks he's about to get off the hook.

"I know nothing about it, Mike," says Ferndorf, who is sadly mistaken.

"Then what about these?" asks Wallace, suddenly producing from some unknown place the falsified expense reports. And guess whose signature is all over them.

Ferndorf, dead duck, begins to squirm.

"We're waiting, Mr. Ferndorf," says Wallace, twisting the knife.

"Well...I, huh," explains Ferndorf, who by now is perspiring and turning blue while all of America watches.

"Look at this, Martha," says the average "60 Minutes" viewer in Des Moines. "Ol' Mike just got another one!"

As a squirmmaker, Perry Mason was small time compared to Mike Wallace.

I have this recurring dream, part of the Mike Wallace Syndrome, where "60 Minutes" gets in touch with me and says they would like to get some footage for a possible future profile. This is my big break, I think, and soon all the cameras are there and I'm sitting across from Mike Wallace and we're having a lovely chat.

"Well," I say, "after knocking out my column each day, I enjoy a few sets of tennis or maybe I relax at home with a good book and . . ."

Then Mike Wallace interrupts me and says, "That's enough beating around the bush, Mr. Grizzard. Why don't you come clean?"

Startled, I begin to stutter. "Wwwwwwhat on earth are you talking about, Mmmmmmmike?"

"This," says Wallace, holding a copy of an essay I did in high school on the Clayton-Bulwer Treaty, an essay which won first place in the county literary meet. "Did you actually write this essay without notes, as the rules of the literary meet specified, or did you, in fact, smuggle in your history book and write your essay by copying word for word from the book?"

I'm squirming from side to side in my chair.

"Look at this, Martha," says the guy in Des Moines.

I did, in fact, smuggle in my history book. How else could anybody write five pages on the Clayton-Bulwer Treaty? But how did Mike Wallace? . . .

"You're probably wondering how we found out about this fraud," says Wallace. "We were first contacted by Arthur Norbest, who finished second in that contest and who just happens to be Harry Reasoner's nephew."

I usually awaken before breaking down in front of the cameras, disgracing not only myself but all my family. Not to mention everybody who signed the Clayton-Bulwer Treaty.

Wouldn't it be ironic, I often catch myself thinking, if one day somebody got something on Mike Wallace, like maybe he wet his bed at camp, and then made him squirm before the entire country? That's a better dream than the one I've been having.

***

I have spent more than half my life working for newspapers. Like many other things in this world, our relationship has been one of love and hate. I love newspapers, but I hate it when they misplay their hands.

I have my own ideas about what should and shouldn't be in a newspaper and about how a newspaper should look. I've never found anyone who was particularly interested in my ideas, but I have them nonetheless. You never know when some wealthy eccentric might leave me a major metropolitan daily.

First of all, if I owned a newspaper, I wouldn't run any color. There is something to be said for good ol' black and white. "It's right here in black and white, Gladys," a man says to his wife when he wants to assure her that something is true beyond a doubt. He would never say, "It's right here in orange and green, Gladys."

I would never run stories in my newspaper about how many fatalities the highway patrol is predicting during the holiday weekend. Too gruesome. If you're going to run that kind of story, why not run one where local cardiologists predict how many people are going to croak from heart attack over the same period?

I wouldn't run scoring summaries from hockey games in my newspaper. They don't make any sense.

I wouldn't allow lengthy interviews with twenty-year-old defensive linemen who, given the choice, probably would rather eat a newspaper than attempt to read one.

I would run follow-ups to society marriage announcements in my newspaper: "Mr. and Mrs. Arnold Crampton announce the divorce of their daughter, Heide Mildred Crampton Millingham III, son of Dr. and Mrs. William Harvey Millingham, Jr. Grounds for the divorce were that Mr. Millingham III whomped his former wife on the head with his polo mallet whenever she complained about his riding his pony in the house."

I would tell my movie critics to cool it on all that imagery and symbolism be-bop and just tell the readers whether or not the movie is worth seeing and how the popcorn is where it's playing and what time the darn things starts.

I would allow precious few interviews with artists. They're more boring than twenty-year-old defensive linemen.

I wouldn't give Ted Kennedy any more publicity. Let him take out an ad.

I'd run fewer stories about abortion, dieting, sex after seventy and before seventeen, how to dress if you're a career woman and have decided being married and having kids is not for you, sperm banks and what to do about liver spots. We have Phil Donahue to cover those things.

I would run more stories about little boys who lost their dogs and then found them, and I'd run eighty percent of all political stories next to the comics page.

Finally, I would watch my columnists very closely. They can be real troublemakers.

— 15 —

Are We Missing
A Few Cards?

I HAVE ALWAYS SUSPECTED that some of my friends
are not sane. Of course, I would never come right out and
say that to them, but in the polite South we have several
euphemisms for getting the point across. For instance, we
might say of such a person that he's not playing with a full
deck. Or, she doesn't have both oars in the water. Or, his
lights are on, but there's nobody home. Or, his elevator
doesn't stop at all floors. Such phrases seem to be more civil
than saying, "He's crazier than a billy goat at mating time."

Although I seldom invite such people to my house for
fear they might not leave, I keep them on my Christmas
card list to demonstrate to the world how open-minded I
am. Besides, in the eternal quest for the origins of true grit
and two socks that match, you never know when there
might be a gem hiding inside a rock. So, with hammer in
hand, allow me to present a few of my rock-headed friends.

***

Not long ago, I decided it was time to invest some of my very small fortune in the stock market (it's the only form of legalized gambling in Georgia). I called my broker friend, Willard "The Bull" Saperstein of Saperstein, Silverman and Simpson, Inc., the brokerage house with the famous slogan, "Yes, yes, yes, buy from SSS."

"Cat food," Willard said the minute he answered the phone.

"Cat food?" I asked.

"Cat food is hot," he said. "More and more people are owning cats these days, and a cat has got to eat."

So I invested heavily in companies that manufacture cat food. A week later, a rumor circulated that Morris the cat had a severe case of indigestion. Nine Lives cat food plummeted two and a half down to just six and a half lives, and the bottom fell out of Puss 'n' Boots as well.

"Just an unlucky break," said Willard, who then suggested that he buy IBM stock for me. IBM has always been a sound company, so I gave him the go-ahead. Sure enough, a week later IBM announced a major breakthrough that sent the stock soaring.

I called Willard and told him to sell, expecting to make a handsome profit on my investment.

"You don't have that IBM," said Willard.

"What other IBM is there?" I asked.

"I bought you International Banjo Makers. It's down eight points and falling fast."

I should have learned my lesson but didn't. Willard soon called with another hot tip.

"American Chinchilla," he said.

"Chinchillas?"

"You should buy every share of American Chinchilla you can get your hands on," said Willard. "It's going to be a cold winter, and there's going to be a heavy demand for chinchilla coats."

It wasn't long before that investment went sour, too, when American Chinchilla discovered that seventy-five percent of the male chinchillas it had bought for its large breeding farm in Oklahoma were gay.

"Don't buy me any more risky stocks," I told Willard.

"Well, why didn't you say so?" He immediately placed an order in my name for one hundred shares of Asbestos Toys. I lost another bundle.

"Get away from me," I said to Willard the next time he called.

"You've just had a few bad breaks," he said. "Give me one more chance and I'll make it all up to you."

Fool that I am, I trusted him once more. Willard came back to me with a new portfolio of can't-miss stocks. He had International Cranberry; a blight killed most of the crop.

He had a new company that had perfected a way to breed worms for fish bait in half the time and at half the cost; one night the worms all crawled out of their boxes and disappeared into the ground.

He had stock in a company that manufactures salt. Salt took a bad health rap. When it rains, it pours.

He had me invest in a company that had developed a chemical that would cure runny nose, itchy throat, stuffy head and that ache-all-over feeling. Unfortunately, it also would inflame your hemorrhoids.

He had Royal Lippizan Stallions, Inc. Several mares came down with herpes and the stallions all had nervous breakdowns.

He had Chrysler. I panicked after all my other stocks fell through the floor and sold two days before it started to soar.

Willard, meanwhile, got out of the stockbroker business.

469

He's now my bookie.

***

Contrary to what some people have said about me, I don't hate all liberals. I have a very good friend named Blanton who is one of the country's leading liberals.

Blanton is, of course, anti-nuke, except for the one bomb he would like to drop on Ronald Reagan's Civil Rights Commission. He supported George McGovern in '72 but has dropped George like a bad habit in '85. The ticket he would like to see the Democrats offer would feature Jesse Jackson and Jane Fonda. Blanton is against prayer in school, tax write-offs for the rich, capital punishment, boxing, designer clothes and Senator Jesse Helms. He is for passage of the Equal Rights Amendment, the legalization of marijuana, the impeachment of Nancy Reagan, a national holiday honoring John Lennon and giving the Russians the benefit of the doubt.

"You don't agree with President Reagan that Russia is the 'Evil Empire'?" I asked him.

"Conservative claptrap," he answered.

"But what about the Russian invasion and occupation of Afghanistan?"

"Nothing worse than what we did to the American Indians," he said.

I had forgotten about Blanton's interest in the plight of the American Indians. For starters, he wants to give back the land we got in the Gadsden Purchase and make Marlon Brando the new Secretary of the Interior.

What stirs Blanton's liberal blood more than anything, however, is environmental issues. He fought tirelessly to save the snail darter. He has protested vigorously against the slaughter of baby seals. He tried to get chicken put on the endangered species list when a Mrs. Winner's went up next door to a Popeye's in his neighborhood.

Last time I saw Blanton, he was loudly spewing forth his usual tirade against The Right when I asked him what was new.

"Pelicans," he answered.

"Pelicans?"

"Somebody has got to do something for the pelicans in this country."

I had no idea pelicans were in any sort of trouble, but Blanton set me straight.

"Do you know what causes pelicans to die?"

"I don't even know what causes them to get sick," I said. Blanton did not laugh.

"It's the most horrible thing I've ever heard," he explained. What happens is that pelicans have to keep their eyes open when they're diving for fish, and after diving into salt water day after day with their eyes open, they become blind and can't see the fish. Consequently, they eventually die of starvation.

I asked him what we were supposed to do.

"I'm going to Washington to demand that the government provide a pair of goggles for every pelican in America," he said.

Can Blanton save the pelicans? The hell he can. But at least he has a cause, and I know enough about his kind to know this: A liberal without a cause is like, well, a pelican without goggles. What good is a big mouth if you can't find anything to aim it at?

***

Scientists have been trying for years to talk to porpoises, supposedly the most intelligent members of the underwater crowd. Me, I've never understood why there's so much interest. If you could talk to a porpoise, what would you ask him? How's the water?

I once tried to talk to a girl in a singles bar who bore an amazing resemblance to a porpoise. She had a large nose and wore lots of blue eyeshadow.

"What's your sign, sweetheart?" I asked. That one was hot for awhile.

"Pisces," she said.

"I thought so."

"Why is that?"

"Easy," I said. "You look a lot like something that lives underwater." When the swelling went down in about a week, I could see as well as ever.

I really don't find it so incredible that animals might be able to communicate with people. That's because I grew up with the legendary Claude "Goat" Rainwater, who not only smelled like an animal but could also talk to them. Dogs were his specialty. He would talk to any dog in town, except poodles.

"Don't talk to no poodles," said Claude.

"Why not?" I asked.

"Had one once," he explained. "Dog wouldn't talk but one time a year. First year, he said the food I was giving him was bad. After another year, he said he didn't like sleeping outside with the beagles. Third year, he said he wanted to leave and find a new place to live."

"What did you tell him?" I inquired.

"I told him, 'Go ahead. All you've done since you've been here is gripe.' "

Goat also once had a bird dog he bought from a fellow in Texas.

"Dog's a big football fan," said Goat. "Every time he sees a game on television, he raises his paw and says, 'Hook 'em, Horns!' "

"Hook 'em, Horns," incidentally, is the battle cry for University of Texas football fans, a rather rowdy bunch.

I tried to get Goat to make his bird dog do that trick for me, but Goat said it wouldn't be right since it wasn't football season. He said I'd have to wait until the fall. When fall came, however, the dog was gone. Word was he'd been dognapped by a bunch of Oklahoma fans.

I probably didn't miss much anyway. If a drunk Texan can fall off a bar stool in Austin and bellow "Hook 'em, Horns!" twice before he hits the floor, I don't know what's so special about a perfectly sober bird dog being able to do the same thing.

Goat also talked to cows, horses, pigs, chickens and mules. And he also smelled like cows, horses, pigs, chickens and mules.

"Hate trying to talk to a mule," he once said.

"Too stubborn?" I asked.

"Like trying to talk a tomcat into staying home on a Saturday night."

I remember asking Goat what was the most unusual animal he had ever talked to.

"Girl skunk," he said.

"What did she say to you?"

"'What's your sign, big boy?'"

***

My friend Fred was complaining about his children.

"All they do is beg for things and then bellyache if they don't get them," he said.

"What are they begging for?" I asked.

"My son wants a sports car and my daughter wants a trip to Europe."

"How old are your children, anyway?"

"The boys is six," he said, "and the girl is nine."

I used to employ the same strategy with my parents. I'd ask for things like an air rifle, or a Flexy racer or a motor scooter — things I knew they'd never give me. But the idea was to inflate the request so that what I ended up getting was still pretty good.

Actually, I didn't figure out that strategy alone. An older playmate explained it to me one day. I was six at the time and wanted a dog, but my parents weren't ready to take care of one, so they refused. I ran off crying and bumped into the older kid.

"What's wrong?" he asked.

"My parents won't let me have a dog," I sobbed.

"Did you ask them for a dog?" he asked.

"Of course I asked them for a dog."

"Dummy," said my wiley playmate. "That was your mistake. You should have asked them for a little brother. Then they would have given you a dog."

I tried to explain the old ruse to Fred, but he wasn't listening. He seemed preoccupied and generally irritated.

"Come on," I said, "what's really bothering you?"

"Well, it's my fortieth birthday today," he confessed.

"Hey, congratulations! Are you going out tonight to celebrate?" I asked.

"Why should I celebrate?"

"Because it's a milestone in your life, that's why."

"Not to me," said my friend. "It's just another year I didn't get a pony."

***

Rigsby is one of those people who will try anything once. And if he likes it, he'll try it several more times.

He was having dinner at a Mexican restaurant recently when someone suggested a round of straight tequila shooters.

"I'll try anything once," said Rigsby.

He tried one straight tequila shooter, liked it, and proceeded to drink a dozen more. Before finally passing out in his cheese enchilada, he did a Mexican hat dance on the table, sang three verses of "La Cucaracha" and tried to ride a fat lady with shaggy hair because he was convinced she was a burro.

Rigsby has tried sky diving, mountain climbing, square dancing, snake charming, body painting, goat roping and escargot, so I shouldn't have been surprised when he told me he also had tried cocaine. "You know me," he said. "I'll try anything once."

I've never tried cocaine myself, but I'm fascinated by the number of people who apparently think it's worth going to jail for. I asked Rigsby how he came to try it.

"I was at a party," he said, "and somebody introduced me to this fellow from Southern California. He had buttoned up just enough of his shirt so you couldn't see his navel, and he had enough chains around his neck to open a hardware store. We started talking and all of a sudden he looked around the room to see if anybody was watching us. Then he leaned over and asked me if I wanted some coke.

"I told him I'd just stick to the beer, but that there was plenty of Coke and Tab and even some 7-Up in the refrigerator. He thought I was pulling his leg, so he insisted that I come out to his car for a toot. I wasn't sure what a 'toot' was, but you know me — I'll try anything once," continued Rigsby.

"We got to his car and he pulled out one of those bags you wrap sandwiches in. I asked, 'What's in your bag?' He said, 'It's cocaine, man. You want some?' And I said, 'Sure, I'll try anything once.'

"He poured some of it out on this little piece of glass and

then handed me a straw and told me to sniff it up my nose. About two sniffs and I had this powerful urge to sneeze. My sinuses are always giving me trouble, you know. I let out this big one and that cocaine went all over this fellow's car and in his hair. He started cussing me hard and told me I had just blown away $300 worth of cocaine. I said, 'Well, that's show business, Hoss,' and went on back to the party for another beer."

I asked Rigsby if he thought he would ever try cocaine again.

"Once was enough," he said. "But if that fellow paid $300 a sniff for that stuff, I sure would like to meet the man who sold it to him, because, brother, there goes a salesman."

***

My friend Worthington was scared to death when he got the call last week that the boss wanted to see him immediately. He was still shaking when he told me about it.

"Worthington," the boss said, "how are things out in Shipping and Receiving?"

"Fine sir," he said. "We could use an extra forklift, but . . ."

"I'll check into it next week, Worthington. Frankly, I didn't call you in to discuss forklifts. I understand you are the chairman for this year's company Christmas party."

"I am, sir. I'm replacing Van der Meer from Personnel."

"What happened to Van der Meer?"

"He got run over by a forklift."

"What's the damage?"

"Darn thing will probably be out of service for another month, sir. That's why I was saying that we need another forklift."

"I'm not talking about the forklift, Worthington. I'm talking about Van der Meer."

"Oh. He'll be back in a couple of weeks but not in time to

coordinate the Christmas party."

"Well, I know this thing has been practically dumped in your lap, Worthington, but what are your plans?"

"Well, sir, I thought we'd get drunk and chase the secretaries around."

"I'd expect that from somebody in Personnel, Worthington, but you're from Shipping and Receiving. Can't we do something a little more original?"

"Like what, sir?"

"Like drawing names and exchanging gifts."

"Don't you remember, sir? We tried that three years ago, but Whipple from Accounting drew Beulah Riddick from Quality Control and gave her a pair of underpants from Frederick's of Hollywood."

"So?"

"So, Beulah Riddick's husband who worked in Building Maintenance was at the party, and when he saw what Whipple had given his wife, he tried to pull off one of Whipple's ears with a pair of pliers."

"Whatever came of all that?"

"Nothing, really. Beulah and her husband got back together, and if you speak up, Whipple can hear you just fine."

"OK, so forget the gifts. What about we have some coffee and cake and sing Christmas carols?"

"We tried that two years ago, sir, but a couple of the stock boys slipped in some beer and cheap wine, and everybody started throwing cake and a fight broke out and the cops came and the whole thing made the newspapers the next day."

"I seem to remember the headline, now that you mention it, Worthington: 'Workers Deck Each Other in Halls of Local Factory.'"

"You fired Himmerman in Public Relations over that one, sir."

"Himmerman schimmerman. There must be something decent we can do for the annual company Christmas party. What about a dance? We can rent a hall and get a band and have a Christmas dance."

"Tried that last year, sir."

"And?"

"I'm surprised you don't remember, sir. Beulah Riddick got stewed and did a strip number, and when she got down to her unmentionables, her husband started looking for the creep who had given them to her."

"And who was the guilty party? My memory is so bad these days, Worthington. I'm getting on up there, you know."

"Well, sir, Beulah spilled the whole story. You gave them to her."

"Did her husband come at me with those pliers?"

"No, sir. You promoted him to manager of the Houston plant before he had a chance to go out to his truck for his toolbox."

"Worthington?"

"Sir?"

"Let's go with the getting drunk and chasing secretaries. And if I happen to catch one, please remind me what I'm supposed to do next."

***

The majority of my life has been spent either learning to be or being a newspaperman. In the course of that pursuit, I have encountered a plethora of unbelievable and unbelievably talented people.

One such person was John E. Drewry, dean of the Henry Grady School of Journalism at the University of Georgia when I arrived there in the mid-1960's. Founder of broad-casting's revered Peabody Awards, Dean Drewry was a master of the language with a wit that one sees today only in such distinguished gentlemen as Sir John Gielgud and John (Smith-Barney) Houseman.

The Dean wore round glasses that gave him the appear-ance of an owl, and he wore three-piece suits with a long watch fob hanging from the vest. His accent was aristocrat-ically Southern, making it a joy to hear him pronounce polysyllabic words such as, "im-proh-pri-uh-tee."

As he lectured one day to our class of approximately three hundred students, he walked back and forth across the room that had an exit door to either side of the podium. Each time he reached one of the doors, he would peer out. This routine went on for about forty-five minutes before he offered an explanation.

"Class, I know there are those among you who are won-dering why I have made regular visits to each of these doors today, peeking out each time in search of, you are no doubt saying, God knows what. My purpose for this effort is quite simple, my young friends.

"I, as I am sure you have, have become quite interested in our country's missions into outer space. I have said to myself, 'Is it not pompous on the part of all earthlings to consider that we are the only intelligent beings in this universe?' The answer can be only one: of course, it is, and there must be other civilizations out there who, as we are they, are trying to contact us at this very moment.

"Let us consider what might happen if these beings from another planet landed on earth for the first time here on the campus of the University of Georgia. It is certainly not unthinkable that these beings would want first to see the environs of our nation's oldest state chartered institution of higher learning.

"It is further apparent to me," he continued, "that once they removed themselves from whatever contraption it might have been that brought them here, they would first want to visit the School of Journalism where we specialize in the art of communication.

"That being the case, I have been walking to each door today assuming that this might be the day for our first encounter with the extra-terrestrials. Were they to arrive here in our building, I would not want them to have to wander the halls with no one to greet them. As dean, I think that certainly would be my duty."

A couple of years later, when I had taken my college journalism education and put it into practice at the Athens Daily News, I encountered an equally fascinating and talented character in my editor, Glenn Vaughn.

One afternoon when I reported for work, Glenn asked me to step into his office. "What," he asked, "would be the biggest story we could have in this newspaper?"

I thought for a moment before answering. "Coed dorms at the university."

"Bigger than that," said Glenn.

"A four-lane highway to Atlanta."

"Even bigger," he prompted.

"Georgia signs a quarterback who can pass."

"Close," said Glenn, "but that's still not it. The biggest story we could have would be the Second Coming."

I did not argue with him.

"So just in case it breaks while we're here, I've gone ahead and designed page one."

He had the page neatly drawn in green ink on a layout pad. There would be a large file photograph of Jesus on the front, although Glenn was hopeful that the wire services would provide a photo of the actual moment of touchdown. He also had written the headline as well. In bold, 124-point type, it would say, "HE'S BACK!" Underneath that headline would be a smaller one reading, "Details on Page 2."

To this day, I don't know whether Glenn was joking or not.

Billy Bob Robinson was another character spawned by newspapers. He was a member of the Atlanta Journal sports staff when I went to work there in 1968. Robinson's beat was auto racing and outdoors, and he was one of the finest writers in the business . . . even when he didn't make it to an event. "Never let the facts stand in the way of a good story," was one of Robinson's favorite lines.

Once he wrote a piece about fishing for bass with his good pal, ol' so-and-so down in South Georgia. "Fish are bitin' so good down here," he quoted his friend as saying, "we have to hide the bait to keep 'em from jumpin' in the boat."

Several days after that article appeared, I fielded a phone call in the department.

"Let me speak to that Robinson fella," said the voice on the other end.

"I'm sorry," I said, "but he's out of the office right now."

"Well," said the caller, "just give him a message. Tell 'im that there fella he was supposed to have been fishin' with down here in South Georgia the other day's been dead for six months."

Another Robinson quirk was that he never showed up for work on time. He carried a flat tire around in his trunk to use as an excuse anytime he couldn't think of something more exotic.

Finally the boss told him that if he was late one more time, he would be fired. Sure enough, the next morning Robinson appeared two hours late.

"OK, you know what I told you," said the boss. "You're fired and I don't want to argue about it. But just for the record and for one last time, why were you late?"

"Well," began Billy Bob, "you know that Maria and I have been married for almost nine years and that we have eight children."

The boss nodded in agreement, waiting for the rest of the story.

"Well, this morning was the first time since we've been married that Maria has had a period, and she was too sick to take the kids to school, so I had to do it."

Instead of firing Robinson, the boss took a week off to regain his composure.

***

I had this roommate named Charlie once. We lived in what was basically a dive, but it was our first home away from home, our first taste of independence, so it was special.

We did what all anxious young men do when they first leave the nest — we played our music loud, stayed up late and sought the company of women. I got lucky and met a dazzling young thing. The fact that she had another year of high school left and I was headed off to college seemed to impress her considerably.

I cleaned all the trash out of my car, bought a bottle of English Leather cologne, and even bought a new pair of yellow Gold Cup socks to go with the yellow shirt I planned to wear on our big date. Gold Cup socks were a fashion must in those days. They came in a variety of colors and cost $1.50 a pair, an obscene price even now.

As the time drew near for my date, I showered, shaved

and splashed English Leather all over my body. Then I started putting on the clothes I had meticulously laid out on my bed. But my new yellow Gold Cup socks were missing.

"Have you seen my new yellow Gold Cups?" I yelled to Charlie, who was watching "Bonanza" in the living room.

"Haven't seen 'em," he answered, never taking his eyes off the screen as Hoss Cartwright thrashed a man to within an inch of his life.

I never found those new socks, and my date turned out to be a total bust. I don't know if one was the result of the other, but I spent a good deal of the evening pulling up a stretched-out pair of white socks.

More than twenty years later, I was speaking at a public gathering when a woman came up and asked me if I remembered Charlie, my old roommate.

Of course, I told her.

"Well," she said, "he's a friend of mine, and when I told him I was going to see you here tonight, he asked me to bring you something."

She reached into her pocketbook and pulled out a pair of yellow Gold Cup socks.

"Charlie said he stole a pair of these from you once, and it's been worrying him ever since. He said to give you these and ask you to please forgive him."

I don't wear yellow socks anymore, but there's a pair in my sock drawer anyway.

— 16 —

Grit Is In the Eye
Of the Beholder

A Little Old-Fashioned Justice

IT WAS ALAN'S BIRTHDAY. He met his girlfriend for
lunch and they had a few drinks, and then a few more,
and then she gave him his presents, one of which was a
bouquet of flowers. They had one more for the road before
she went back to work and Alan headed home.

On the way, a policeman pulled him over. "Have you
been drinking?" he asked.

Alan admitted to having a couple at lunch with his
girlfriend. "It's my birthday," he added.

The policeman apologized for ruining Alan's birthday,
but he told him he obviously was too drunk to drive, so he
loaded Alan into the back of the patrol car.

"I don't know why I did it," Alan explained later, "but I
decided to take my flowers with me."

At the police station, they booked Alan for drunken
driving and put him in a cell with several others. Again, he

took his flowers.

"As they were opening the cell door for me," Alan said, "I realized I shouldn't have brought the flowers with me. One fellow yelled right away, 'Hey, Flower Boy, did you bring those for me?'

"There was a group of black guys sitting in one corner of the cell. When I looked at them and smiled, they smiled back, so I went and sat down with them and tried to make friends," said Alan.

"I told them it was my birthday and that my girlfriend had given me the flowers. They sang, 'Happy birthday, dear Flower boy.' I've never been so embarrassed and so scared in my life. I tried again to make friends.

"I asked one guy what he was in for. He said he was hungry and didn't have any money, so he went into a convenience store and put a can of Spam in his pocket and walked out. He said he didn't even get a chance to eat it before the police stopped him and brought him in with the Spam still in his pocket."

Alan spent the night in jail. At his hearing the next morning — both he and his flowers were somewhat wilted from the experience — the judge was hard on him despite his first-offender status. He received a hefty fine and was placed on probation.

"I learned my lesson," he said. "The quickest way to get people to stop drinking and driving is to make them spend a night in a jail cell holding on to a bouquet of flowers. It's a frightening experience."

Alan was released along with the man who had stolen the can of Spam. "I thought it was a nice gesture," he said. "They gave him the can back."

A citizen learns his lesson about drinking and driving and the Spam bandit, hungry enough to steal for his supper, is allowed to eat the evidence. Just a little old-fashioned justice goin' round.

LOYALTY EVEN UNDER DURESS

Tom first met blue-eyed Mary nearly forty years ago when they both were students at Auburn University. They eventually married and had three daughters and a son.

The family settled in a small Alabama town where Tom began a successful business. Mary took care of the kids and dreamed of finishing her degree, which had been cut short by the kids. Maybe when they were grown . . .

Three of their children ended up with degrees from Auburn, and the family became loyal supporters of the school and especially of the football program. Mary was the biggest War Eagle fan in the entire family. She often clipped headlines about her beloved team and taped them to the refrigerator door.

When the kids had finished their educations, Mary decided it was time to fulfill her dream of returning to school. "School's so hard when you get as old as I am," she told friends, but she wanted that degree. Her grades were high and her family and friends were proud of her.

It all came on suddenly. One day Mary was bounding with energy and enthusiasm; the next day she was in the hospital after suffering a heart attack. A week later, she died at age fifty-seven.

As a friend of the family, I attended the funeral. The preacher talked about how much Mary loved that family but about how she also was her own person: "Completing her education was so important to her," he said. He also talked about her love for Auburn University: "She was fanatical," the preacher said lovingly, and the family even broke into smiles as they remembered the woman's loyalty.

As they rolled Mary's casket from the church, the family followed it down the aisle. Tom held to one of his weeping daughters, trying to comfort her. As he passed, I couldn't help noticing the tie he had chosen to wear to his wife's funeral. On the front, in blue script, were the words, "War Eagle."

"At first," one of the children told me later, "we couldn't believe Daddy was wearing that tie to Mama's funeral. But then, it just sort of made sense somehow."

Yes, it did. It certainly did.

ONE VOTE FOR A POKE

Jason, who is eleven, was walking home from school with a friend. They were doing what all kids that age do — walking through vacant lots, throwing rocks and dirt bombs, "anything to get dirty," his mother said.

Behind a convenience store, Jason accidentally stepped on a board with a rusty nail protruding through it. The nail penetrated his shoe and lodged in his foot. In such excruciating pain, Jason could not get the nail out of his foot, so his friend had to pull it loose.

Bleeding badly and still in pain, Jason limped into the store, showed the clerk his wound and asked for a Band-Aid or some sort of bandage.

"Yeah, I got plenty of Band-Aids," said the clerk. "But have you got a dollar?"

Jason said he didn't have any money, and neither did his friend.

"Sorry," said the clerk. "No money, no Band-Aids."

There was no money for the telephone either, so Jason, still bleeding but aided by his friend, limped the half-mile home.

His mother rushed him to the doctor's office, where he received a tetanus shot. He spent the rest of the weekend hot-soaking his foot. Jason will be fine, but his mother may never be the same again.

"I know now how wars start," she said, "how people get murdered, how hate grows from a tiny little thing into a monster. Ever since this happened, I have wanted to walk into that store and poke that man's eyeballs out. I have wanted to stay home from work and march in front of that store with signs saying, 'Do not buy anything from this store; you might bleed to death.'

"So far I haven't poked anyone's eyeballs out, and to my husband's relief I haven't picketed the store, either. I haven't even called the company to complain; they'd probably just tell me the man was doing his job. I did pray for the man, but I worry about this rage I can't shake.

"You've seen those containers near cash registers that say, 'Take a penny, leave a penny.' Well, I've given enough pennies in this same neighborhood store to buy a large box of Band-Aids. And I would have gladly paid for anything Jason used. I would have appreciated it if the clerk had even allowed him in the bathroom to pack his shoe with toilet paper. And I certainly would have appreciated it if he had called me so I could have picked up my injured child.

"I'm just a mother whose child has been done wrong, and I just don't know about people sometimes.... I just don't understand, and I don't know that I ever will."

Me either. And, Lord, forgive me for wishing she had gone for the guy's eyeballs just once.

A DEAL IS A DEAL, SOMETIMES

A man was walking along the river that flows behind a

expensive neighborhood when three guys told him he was trespassing. He argued briefly, but when one of them pulled a gun, he left and went for the police.

He returned later with a police cruiser following him. Behind the police car just happened to be eighteen-year-old Nuno de Almeida, a native of Portugal who had recently come to live with his American-born stepfather.

The man in the lead car stopped when he reached the scene of his trouble and spotted two of the guys who had pulled the gun on him. The police car then stopped, and so did Nuno de Almeida. Suddenly, the police cruiser backed up and crashed into the front of Nuno's car. The cop jumped out of his car, rushed to Nuno's window and accused him of following too closely.

The cop called his sergeant, who arrived on the scene a few minutes later. They conferred and then told Nuno that if he would forget the whole thing, there would be no ticket for following too closely and no chance of losing his license.

Nuno wouldn't make the deal. His car was damaged, and there was still his stepfather to answer to. The two fellows who had pulled the gun had witnessed the whole event. The cop walked over to them, mentioned they could be in big trouble, and asked if they had seen the accident.

"The inference was there," said one of the fellows named Kenny, "that if we backed him, he wouldn't do anything about the gun."

So Kenny and his buddy said they hadn't seen anything. No charges were filed against them for the incident with the gun. The fellow in the lead car also said, truthfully, that he hadn't seen anything.

Nuno de Almeida was given a court date. His stepfather, despite the advice of three lawyers to forget the matter and take the fine, urged his son to fight. "Nuno doesn't lie," he said.

Nuno pleaded not guilty. The policeman gave his side of the story, then Nuno told his version.

"Are you saying the officer is lying?" asked the judge.

"He hit my car when he backed up," said Nuno.

The courtroom laughed. Kenny was then called to the witness stand to testify against Nuno. A deal is a deal. Nuno looked to be in big trouble. It was his word against the cop's and the cop had a witness.

But Kenny and his friend had talked things over. "We just couldn't live with our consciences if we didn't tell the truth," he said. "Why should this kid look like a liar when he wasn't?"

Kenny told the judge the truth about what had happened, that Nuno was not lying. The courtroom broke into applause. The judge dismissed the charges. The officer was left to his superiors.

Only in America.

A LESSON IN SAVING

Brad, age eight, and his sister Linda, age eleven, recently received gifts of fifty dollars each from their grandparents. Brad wanted to spend his money on candy; fifty smackers will buy a lot of Reese's Cups. Linda wanted to spend hers on rock tapes; fifty dollars worth should keep her gyrating till she's sixteen.

Brad and Linda's mother, however, didn't want her children blowing their first serious amounts of money on frivolity. "I wanted them to use their money to learn a lesson," Karen said. "I convinced them that the way to accomplish the American dream was to put their money in a savings account. I explained that the bank would pay them for using their money."

The kids agreed, and so the next morning they all headed down to the bank to open an account. At the bank, however, the kids were told they couldn't have their very own savings accounts because the minimum amount needed was one hundred dollars. Bank policy, it was explained to Karen.

She tried to talk them into pooling their money and opening a single account, but sibling rivalry won out and the kids wouldn't go for that.

A few days later, the grandparents heard of the ordeal, were impressed and decided to give each child another fifty dollars so they could have their own savings accounts. Back to the bank.

This time they were told that Brad and Linda couldn't open their own accounts because they didn't have social security numbers. "The government is afraid somebody will make some interest and they won't get any of it," explained a bank official. Frustrated for a second time, the kids burst into tears.

"I didn't know what to tell them after that," said Karen. I thought teaching the children to save now would make them more likely to do the same when they were older."

To try to make amends to the kids, Karen took them on a shopping spree for candy and rock tapes. It was the only thing left to do. Besides, the children will learn another valuable lesson about money: Easy come, easy go.

— 17 —

From Sea To
Shining Sea

A S I'VE TRIED TO demonstrate, true grit is not indige-
nous to any group or any place. Some of the best
examples of the developing and the finished product I've
seen, for instance, appeared in Italy.

I was there for three weeks of R&R (Note to IRS agents:
That stands for Research and Reflection. I worked night and
day, as this chapter proves, and that's why I was forced to
list the trip as a deduction). Like most tourists, the first
challenge I had to face was the language. To better prepare
myself, I bought one of those Berlitz guides of "two thousand helpful phrases."

They were right. The guide would have been very helpful . . . if I had been having a convulsion. The way to say, "I
am having a convulsion," in Italian is, roughly, "Io ho le
convulsioni." But who's got time to look it up if they're
having a convulsion face down in the pasta? If they really

wanted to be helpful in those books, they would tell you how to say, "Last night I went out and got drunker than a four-eyed Italian dog, and I desperately need something for this hangover." I couldn't find that phrase anywhere. And I needed it. Bad.

The book did provide me with a useful phrase for the train. The way to say, "I think you are in my seat," is, "Penso che questo sia il mio posto." What it didn't do, however, was tell me what to say when the fellow in my seat was the toughest hombre in Genoa, and he replied with an Italian phrase which I interpreted to mean, "One more word out of you, salami-face, and I'll slice you up like so much prosciutto."

What I finally did was what most Americans do when they can't speak the language. I started using American-Italian, which means putting a vowel on the end of each English word and waving your arms a lot. For instance, if you want to say, "You are standing on my foot," in Italian, you say, "Youo areo standingo ona mya foota." If you look down and point at your foot, it will helpo.

Italians, to their credit, will attempt to speak English with you, thus making it easier for visitors in their country. There is a problem here, too, however: Italians, especially taxi drivers and waiters, know only certain English phrases, and they use them for a multitude of responses.

"If you don't slow down," you might say to the taxi driver, "you are going to kill us all!"

To which he will reply, "Dank you berry much."

Or, to your waiter you say, "This soup is rancid."

"Meddy Chreestmas," he replies.

All the communications problems I had in Italy reminded me of a similar qroblem Bogator Green, the world famous mechanic from my hometown, once had. An Italian couple was driving through in a rental car when it developed engine trouble. A local deputy sheriff came to their rescue and had the car towed to Bogator's "garage," a large shade tree behind his trailer.

The couple spoke no English, and Bogator was only slightly better versed in Italian. After checking their car, Bogator said, "Your manifold's busted."

The man shook his head in bewilderment.

"He's Italian, Bogator," said the deputy sheriff. "He doesn't understand you."

"Oh," said Bogator. He then cupped his hands around his mouth and screamed in the man's ear, "YOUR MAN-IFOLD'S BUSTED!"

***

Once you've mastered the language, another way Americans build character in Italy is by walking the streets.

"You go out for a walk?" asked the bellman at my hotel in Rome.

"Yes," I replied.

"Be careful," he suggested. "The drivers are very aggressive here." And the Pope is Catholic, he might have added.

In a matter of minutes, I had figured it out — it was a game of demolitionio derbyo. The buses try to run over the cars. The cars try to run over what seems to be everybody and his Italian brother on a motor scooter. And all three try to run down the helpless pedestrians, who are nothing more than human bowling pins. The taxi driver who drove me from the train station to my hotel narrowly missed picking up a 7-10 split on the Via Condetti, and he left an easy spare on the Via Veneto when a shopper dived away from his speeding taxi just in time.

"An Italian taxi driver," said another man at the hotel,

"would try to run over his grandmother if she got in his way." I guess that explains the shortage of Italian grandmothers I noted in Rome. I finally figured out that red lights are merely for decoration in Italy, brakes routinely last 100,000 miles since they're seldom used and the quickest way to become rich is to open a body and paint shop.

"Why do people drive this way in Rome?" I asked the bellman.

"Because," he laughed, "ninety-five percent of the Italian people think they are Beppe Gabbiani."

"Beppe Gabbiani?" I asked.

"Richard Petty, to you."

That cleared it up nicely.

***

In Florence, my traditional American values were challenged on every corner. You see, there are a million statues in Florence, and every one of them is naked.

There's "David" by Michelangelo, a masterpiece completed in 1504 when the artist was only twenty-five years old. David makes Bo Derek look overdressed.

There's "The Rape of the Sabine Women" by Giambologna. Children under seventeen must be accompanied by a parent or legal guardian to get a gander at this one.

"Hercules and Diomedes" by Vincenzo de Rossi apparently is a tribute to the sport of wrestling. If you liked watching Argentina Rocca throw Lou Thesz out of the ring, you'll adore "Hercules and Diomedes."

"Perseus" by Cellini is another example of a woman losing her head over a man, and "Bacchus's Fountain" is a sculpture of a fat man riding a turtle. Must be some sort of tribute to Italian turtle racing.

We are not accustomed to such rampant nudity in the United States, and any time it appears, there is always some group stepping forward to protect us. I remember when Marvin Knowles, a fellow from my hometown, made it big in professional wrestling. Using the name "The Masked Pork Chop," Marvin wrestled in National Guard armories and high school gymnasiums as far away as Tupelo, Mississippi.

Because of the acclaim he brought to our town, the local ladies club arranged for "Marvin Knowles Day," which would feature the unveiling of a statue of Marvin in his ring crouch, to be placed on the elementary school ballfield where Marvin got his start wrestling Cordie Mae Poovey, the ugliest and meanest girl in town. The day before the unveiling, however, some of the ladies dropped by to inspect the statue and were shocked to find Marvin wearing nothing but his wrestling tights. They had the sculptor back the next morning before dawn, carving Marvin a pair of loose-fitting underdrawers that reached all the way down to his wrestling boots.

I think maybe they were right. Try as I may, I just can't picture Stonewall Jackson on his horse in the town square wearing nothing but his sword. It ain't fittin'.

***

By the time I reached Venice, I was delighted to hear Americans talking at a table beside me during dinner. It was an elderly couple grappling with noodles and salmon and drinking white wine from a pitcher. I asked where they were from.

"Massachusetts," said the lady, obviously someone's grandmother.

"Originally from Arizona, though," her husband added. He had the look of an ex-soldier.

Apparently they also were glad to hear a voice from home, and we swapped stories over dinner that night. They were both widowed, the lady said, but had been friends back in Arizona before their mates had died. Living alone had not appealed to either of them, so they had married recently. Their eyes met and stayed together as she talked about their marriage.

"So this is a honeymoon?" I asked.

"Just a nice, long trip," the man said. I think I noticed a blush as he spoke. He had started slowly in the conversation, but now the wine was beginning to take effect. They were to be in Europe for three months, he said. First they had visited Germany, then it was on to Austria. The old man told me about the archbishop who once ruled over Salzburg.

"He built a large house," he explained. "And why would an archbishop need such a large house? For the woman he kept there who gave him fifteen illegitimate sons!"

The old man roared with laughter. There's at least a spark left there, I thought.

"Newspaperman," I answered when they asked. The old man brightened again. What a coincidence, he said; his brother-in-law used to be a newspaperman, too.

"He was the music critic for the Washington Post, the one Harry Truman threatened to kick where you don't want to be kicked when he questioned Margaret Truman's musical talents. Years later, my brother-in-law was visiting Independence, Missouri, and was going through the Truman library. Somebody recognized him and asked if he would like to say hello to the former President. Well, of course he would, and do you know what Truman said to him?"

No, I couldn't imagine.

"He said my brother-in-law was right all along. He said his daughter Margaret really didn't have much talent as a musician." The man roared again with laughter.

It was getting late. The man started into the story about the archbishop again.

"You've already told that one, dear," his wife said.

I offered my goodbyes and said maybe we would see each other again sometime. Of course, we wouldn't, but Americans always tell each other that sort of thing. As I left, I heard the man ask his wife, "One more half-liter of wine before bed?"

"OK, let's have one more half-liter," she answered, smiling at him.

Oh, to be young — relatively or otherwise — and in love as night falls on Venice. Or even on Cleveland.

***

I can't think of anything, short of gun-totin' federal marshalls, that would make me move out of the United States. But if for any reason I ever had to pick another country to live in, I think it would be Switzerland.

In the first place, it's a naturally beautiful country with mountain peaks and crystal clear lakes. It's also very clean, the banks are discreet, it's a nice place to shop for cheese and watches and the taxi service is wonderful.

Most of the cabs in Switzerland are late model Mercedes or BMWs. I've ridden in taxis in the U.S. that were so old the driver had to pull off the road to reshoe his mule. Also, when a taxi picks you up in Switzerland, the driver gets out and opens the door for you. In the U.S., most taxi drivers are surlier than Mr. T with a bad case of hemorrhoids and wouldn't open the door for their grandmother if she were carrying a steamer trunk.

Here are some other nice things about Switzerland:

● When you cross the street, motorists stop and allow you to pass. In most American cities, it's open season on pedestrians.

• When you swim in a Swiss pool, you must wear a bathing cap. I asked the pool attendant why. "You shouldn't have to swim with other people's hair floating in the water," she said. Darn straight.

• There are very few billboards along the Swiss roadways. You can actually see the countryside.

• While I was in Switzerland, I didn't see a single snake or mosquito.

• The air in Switzerland doesn't burn your nose, and when the temperature reaches eighty, they think they're having a heat wave.

• I don't think they have much of a crime problem in Switzerland, either. I base this assumption on an experience I had in Lugano. I noticed a man down on his hands and knees drawing a beautiful picture of the Virgin Mary on the sidewalk with colored chalk. Around the man were several shoe boxes in which those who appreciated his artwork had dropped coins. The following evening I happened to pass by the same spot. The artist was gone, but the shoe boxes were still there along with the day's collection. "You mean to say," I asked a native, "that he can leave his coins out there all night and nobody will steal them?" The man looked shocked. "Steal from a poor artist?" he asked. "Who would steal from the poor?"

That's another thing I like about Switzerland: It still has a ways to go to catch up with the rest of civilization.

***

Of course, if Italy or even Switzerland isn't your cup of wine, there are many other options for interesting vacations closer to home which can also teach you about the world and the wonderful characters who populate it. Here are just a few American vacation packages I could recommend:

• GALA ARKANSAS — Four days and five nights in the

"Land of the Razorback." Learn to stand on a table in a restaurant and scream, "Soooooooooie Piiiig!" like the happy University of Arkansas football fans do when they go out of town. Learn to jump-start a pickup truck like the University of Arkansas football fans do when they try to get back home. Visit the lovely Ozarks and stay in a real mountain shack near Dogpatch, USA. See firsthand what outdoor plumbing is all about! The kids will love it! (Soap, towels, heat, lights, snakebite kits and ammunition NOT included.)

• THE OTHER FLORIDA — Tired of crowded beaches and fancy hotels? Then this might be just right for you. A trip off Florida's beaten paths to lovely, exciting Bugspray Swamp Resort, located in the mysterious Everglades. Explore the hidden world of reptiles and insects with guide, cook and medicine man. Take a hike in Quicksand Alley. (Who got left behind?) See mosquitoes the size of eagles and gnats as big as bats. Four days, five nights and six chances out of ten that at least one member of your family gets eaten by an alligator.

• OLD SOUTH TOUR — Get a real feel for the Old South with a tour of Fort Deposit, Alabama, and meet Fort Deposit's leading citizen, Billy Bob Bailey, and his dog, Rooster. See the local diner where Governor George Wallace once had lunch during a campaign trip. See the local hospital where the governor recuperated. Visitors from New Jersey and other places Up North will want to ask Billy Bob about his special deals on souvenirs, like water actually carried by soldiers during the Civil War, dirt from historic Civil War battlefields and trained boll weevils. And, if you're lucky, Rooster might even do some tricks for his northern friends, like removing their distributor caps. Don't worry. Billy Bob's Service Station, located next to the souvenir shop, is open twenty-four hours a day.

- NUDE BEACH — Just think of it! Nude swimming, nude tennis, nude golf and nude volleyball. And we know just the rock you can hide behind to see it all. Film extra.

- DINOSAUR WORLD — Located off Highway 78 near beautiful downtown Snellville, Georgia. Huge replicas of dinosaurs and other prehistoric animals. Great fun for the kids and educational, too. Would you like to own Dinosaur World yourself? Ask for Harvey and make him an offer. Any offer.

- DUDE RANCH — Here's a dude ranch with a new twist. Instead of riding a bunch of smelly horses, ride dinosaurs and other prehistoric animals. Located off Highway 78 near beautiful downtown Snellville, Georgia. Tell Harvey, the dude who got stuck with this joint, to "saddle 'em up!"

***

If your tastes run more to the great outdoors, I could recommend a rafting trip down the raging Colorado River. But before you sign up for such an arduous undertaking, you may want to ask a few questions — to which I already have the answers.

1. How do I get to the Colorado River? Fly from Las Vegas out into the middle of the Arizona desert in a small airplane (envision a '53 Ford with wings) and land in a wide place between two cacti. Then ride a mule down the treacherous ledges of the canyon to the river and pray the mule doesn't make one false step, because mules, unfortunately, don't have wings.

2. How can the Arizona desert best be described? Ten zillion acres of dust.

3. Is there ever a change of scenery? Occasionally you see a cow pie.

4. Once on the river, are the rapids exciting? Lie down on a water bed and get a small child to jump up and down on it. Same thing, except you don't get as wet.

5. How hot is it on the river? During the day, about 120 degrees, but at night it cools down nicely to maybe 102.

6. Where do you camp? On sandy river banks.

7. What is it like camping when the wind starts blowing at night? Think of a blast furnace.

8. What do you eat on the trip? Mostly sand.

9. How did the brochure describe camping at night along the river? "...Drift slowly off to sleep under the starry western skies as you are caressed by a cool breeze, the restful sound of rushing water and the pleasant blend of guitars and mellow voices."

10. Has the person who wrote the brochure ever actually taken the trip? No.

11. Was there anybody interesting along with you? Yes. A newlywed couple on their honeymoon.

12. What do you call people who take a rafting trip down the raging Colorado for their honeymoon? Weird.

13. Did you encounter any scorpions? Yes, but the red ants were worse. Scorpions sting only in self-defense; red ants bite because they enjoy it.

14. What about rattlesnakes? Don't worry. We never found more than one at a time in a sleeping bag.

15. What are the restroom facilities like in camp? A little green tent.

16. What is the most important thing to know about camping on the Colorado River? Never spread your bedroll near the little green tent.

17. Will you ever take such a trip again? Sure, as soon as mules sprout wings and fly.

***

I used to recommend Hilton Head, South Carolina, as a wonderful getaway spot, but not long ago a friend sent me a clipping from the island's newspaper which warned of trouble. For the sake of an informed public, following is a reprint of that article:

Members of an elite corps of South Carolina state militia stormed the beach here Saturday and reclaimed the plush resort from thousands of Northern vacationers who took over the island several years ago after surrendering Miami Beach.

"Hilton Head is a part of the sovereign state of South Carolina," declared Governor Willis Peabody, "and nobody else has any right to any part of the soil our forefathers grabbed off the Indians. Any attempt to retake the island will result in the gravest of consequences."

The governor would not elaborate on what he meant by "gravest of consequences," but the South Carolina militiamen have put the island under what some of the Northern vacationers are referring to as "the next thing to martial law." One new order disallows the sale of piña colada mix to anyone who cannot prove he or she was born south of Richmond, Virginia.

Hilton Head Island, with miles of beach, numerous golf courses and tennis courts and Ralph Lauren's coastal headquarters, is just off the South Carolina mainland near the Georgia port city of Savannah.

The pre-brunch raid which reclaimed the island was believed to have been launched from Williams' Seafood Restaurant in Savannah in bass boats rented from the Thunderbolt Marina, Bait and Tackle. "We even brought our own beer," said Captain Charlie "Swamp Fox" Ravenel, head of the Carolina militia.

It is believed that the militia also included volunteers from the neighboring state of Georgia, which has had a recent problem with a growing number of Northerners moving into its Golden Isles resorts of Jekyll Island, St. Simons Island and Sea Island. This belief was stimulated by reports that some of the militiamen, upon storming across the beach and reaching the lobby of the Hilton Head Holiday Inn, cried out, "How 'bout them Dawgs!" — a familiar Georgia exclamation for any occasion, including selected funerals.

The Northern-bred occupants of the island, including visitors from the Canadian province of Ontario who were on the island looking for reptile farms and glass-bottom boats, were caught completely off guard by the attack. There apparently was only one casualty, however; a lady from Akron, Ohio, on the beach to catch some early rays, was stepped on by an attacking militiaman and suffered a pair of broken sunglasses.

"You can spot yankee men on the beach from a mile out in the ocean," Captain Ravenel said. "They all wear Bermuda shorts, sandals and black socks pulled up to their armpits. But yankee women, they put on those white bathing suits and they haven't been in the sun in so long, then blend right into the sand. My man said he thought that lady was some kind of jellyfish that had washed up on the beach. If he'd have looked a little closer, he'd have seen her mustache and probably would have missed her."

Reaction came swiftly from the North. One possible retaliatory move, said Governor Fitzhugh Stratsworth III of Ohio, was to move the Ohio National Guard south to Hilton Head to meet the Carolina militia head-on. "If we don't have to stop every time somebody has to go to the bathroom, we could be in the Hilton Head area in three to four days," Governor Stratsworth said.

Meanwhile, Secretary of State George Schultz has already landed in Hilton Head and announced that he is prepared to "stay as long as necessary" to help mediate the dispute. Told at a ninth-hole briefing that rumors were flying that the Carolina militiamen were feeding some of the yankee inhabitants to the many alligators that live on the island, Schultz quipped, "I thought they only ate grits."

***

Not long ago I was strolling down New York's Fifth Avenue with a native. He pointed out things I'd never thought to observe before.

"Watch the Japanese tourists," he said. "They'll take pictures of anything, even the sky."

That made sense to me. I explained to the New Yorker that in most other parts of the world the sky is blue, and that the visitors from the East probably were intrigued by the fact that the sky in New York has a brownish or yellowish tint to it.

Then my guide told me how to distinguish a native New Yorker from a tourist. "Watch their eyes," he said. "New Yorkers never look up. They either look down or straight ahead. Only visitors to the city look up."

In addition to being bored with tall buildings, I suspected that most natives had suffered some misfortunes with pigeons and therefore did not look up.

My friend further explained that if I watched closely, I would observe that three out of every five New Yorkers would be wearing headsets. "It's our way of dealing with noise pollution," he said.

But if their ears are plugged with loud music, how are they going to hear the two-second blast of the horn which taxi drivers politely give before driving over pedestrians?

Further down Fifth Avenue, my guide showed me yet another point of interest. Along the sidewalk, a crowd gathered to watch large amounts of money changing hands in a little card game being played on top of cardboard boxes. It was like the old shell game: three cards face down, two black and one red. The dealer switches the cards around; the object is to find the red one. I saw people betting as much as a hundred dollars.

"Don't get involved," said my friend. "The people you see winning are shills for the dealer. The tourists see them win and so they give it a try, but they almost always lose."

"Isn't that illegal?" I asked.

"Of course, it is," said the native, "but they have lookouts for the police. If a cop heads their way, they simply grab their box and go to another street."

"You said tourists almost always lose. Does that mean some occasionally win?"

"Yes and no," he answered. "If they do happen to win, one of the shills follows them down the street, mugs them and gets the money back."

About that time we passed a group of Japanese tourists. I nodded and said hello to them. They all took my picture as if I were unusual.

***

They told me about Old Faithful, the world-famous geyser that's the main attraction at Yellowstone National Park in Wyoming, when I was a kid in school. I wasn't much impressed. So every hour on the hour this hole in the ground spews out a lot of steam and hot water. That's a big deal?

Rock City and Disneyland certainly were on my list of things to see when I could afford it, but Old Faithful wasn't in the running. My traveling companion through the wilds of Wyoming, however, had a different idea.

"People come from all over the world to see it," he explained. "We're crazy to come this far and not get a look at it."

I checked the map. We were 120 miles roundtrip from Yellowstone. "You want to drive that far just to see hot water and steam?" I asked. "Why don't you just turn on the shower and close the bathroom door tonight?"

He responded by questioning my patriotism, so the next thing I knew we were on our way to Yellowstone, where bears eat people, to see Old Faithful. We arrived just after eight o'clock.

My friend explained that since a major earthquake in the area in 1983, Old Faithful — which previously had been spewing forth on the hour for more than a hundred years — was running as much as eighty-two minutes between eruptions.

"You mean we've come this far and the thing might not even go off?" I complained.

"It'll go off," he said. "That's why they call it Old Faithful."

There must have been three thousand people sitting on

benches patiently waiting for the show. Me, I went for an ice cream cone.

"You might miss it," warned my friend.

"So I'll see the highlight film," I quipped.

When I came back with my cone, Old Faithful was smoking a little steam but nothing more. The crowd still waited quietly. Then, at about half past eight, it happened. There was steam, and more steam, and then there was a roar and I think the ground trembled. Old Faithful belched forth with a boiling, steamy column of water that reached over a hundred feet into the sky.

The crowd gasped in awe. The explosion seemed to go higher and higher, and when it ended a few minutes later, the crowd fell silent for a moment before bursting into spontaneous applause.

Later, as we were driving in the darkness of the park, my friend asked me how I felt when I saw Old Faithful come through for her audience.

"Proud to be an American," I answered.

I can't explain why. You just had to be there.

***

From New York to Dallas, from Florence to Yosemite, there are men, women and children walking around with hearts full of true grit. It may be hidden beneath the surface of poverty or tattoos or behind the face of wrinkles, but it's there just the same, pure and clear.

So what if they might be riding Shetland ponies instead of gallant steeds? They all could have ridden alongside Marshall Rooster Cogburn, hallowed be his name and theirs.